Entrepreneurial Process and Social Networks

Entrepreneurial Process and Social Networks

A Dynamic Perspective

Edited by

Alain Fayolle

Professor of Entrepreneurship and Director, Entrepreneurship Research Centre, EMLYON Business School, France

Sarah L. Jack

Lancaster University, UK

Wadid Lamine

Toulouse Business School, France

Didier Chabaud

University of Avignon, France

EE Edward Elgar PUBLISHING

Cheltenham, UK • Northampton, MA, USA

Published by
Edward Elgar Publishing Limited
The Lypiatts
15 Lansdown Road
Cheltenham
Glos GL50 2JA
UK

Edward Elgar Publishing, Inc.
William Pratt House
9 Dewey Court
Northampton
Massachusetts 01060
USA

A catalogue record for this book
is available from the British Library

Library of Congress Control Number: 2016931520

This book is available electronically in the **Elgar**online
Business subject collection
DOI 10.4337/9781785364884

FSC
www.fsc.org
MIX
Paper from responsible sources
FSC® C013056

ISBN 978 1 78536 487 7 (cased)
ISBN 978 1 78536 488 4 (eBook)

Typeset by Servis Filmsetting Ltd, Stockport, Cheshire
Printed and bound in Great Britain by TJ International Ltd, Padstow

Contents

List of contributors vii

Introduction 1
Alain Fayolle, Sarah L. Jack, Wadid Lamine and Didier Chabaud

PART I THE EVOLUTION OF NETWORKS ACROSS ENTREPRENEURIAL STAGES

1 Entrepreneurial network composition and the venture creation process: an empirical investigation 29
Tammi C. Redd, Michael A. Abebe and Sibin Wu

2 Dynamic social networks of entrepreneurs: five years of change in the networks of Dutch entrepreneurs 49
Marianne de Beer, Gerald Mollenhorst and Veronique A.J.M. Schutjens

3 Entrepreneurs' social networks and formation of business opportunities: an exploratory study 79
Didier Chabaud and Joseph Ngijol

4 Start-ups repositioning in business networks 113
Lise Aaboen and Frida Lind

PART II FORMAL NETWORKS: A NEW RESEARCH AGENDA?

5 Business and professional networks: scope and outcomes in Oxfordshire, UK 129
Helen Lawton Smith and Saverio Romeo

6 Women entrepreneurs and the process of networking as social exchange 157
Claire M. Leitch, Richard T. Harrison and Frances M. Hill

7 Cooperation versus coordination relations in SME networks: a new view of collective strategy dynamics 189
Christophe Leyronas and Stéphanie Loup

PART III CONTEXT: A BENIGN NEGLECT?

8 The competitiveness of entrepreneurial firms from a network perspective 217
Christian Lechner

9 The role of family members in entrepreneurial networks: beyond the boundaries of the family firm 236
Alistair R. Anderson, Sarah L. Jack and Sarah Drakopoulou Dodd

10 Social network structures of nascent entrepreneurs: an exploratory study of advisor networks in MENA countries 263
Sarfraz A. Mian and Shahid Qureshi

11 *Ubuntu* in family businesses: a case in the Democratic Republic of the Congo 279
Albert B.R. Lwango

PART IV DEBATES AND PERSPECTIVES: THEORETICAL CHALLENGES

12 Entrepreneurial mingling secrets: investigating the performance impact of network structure for control-based entrepreneurship using agent-based simulation 303
Willem Jansen, René Mauer and Malte Brettel

13 Actor-network theory and the entrepreneurial process 335
Wadid Lamine, Alain Fayolle and Hela Chebbi

Index 361

Contributors

Lise Aaboen, Norwegian University of Science and Technology, Norway

Michael A. Abebe, The University of Texas Rio Grande Valley, USA

Alistair R. Anderson, Robert Gordon University, UK

Marianne de Beer, Utrecht University, the Netherlands

Malte Brettel, RWTH Aachen University, Aachen, Germany

Didier Chabaud, University of Avignon, France

Hela Chebbi, EDC Paris Business School, France

Sarah Drakopoulou Dodd, University of Strathclyde, UK

Alain Fayolle, EMLYON Business School, France

Richard T. Harrison, University of Edinburgh Business School, UK

Frances M. Hill, independent researcher, UK

Sarah L. Jack, Lancaster University, UK

Willem Jansen, RWTH Aachen University, Aachen, Germany

Wadid Lamine, Toulouse Business School, France

Helen Lawton Smith, Birkbeck, University of London, UK

Christian Lechner, Free University of Bozen-Bolzano, Italy

Claire M. Leitch, Lancaster University, UK

Christophe Leyronas, Toulouse Business School, France

Frida Lind, Chalmers University of Technology, Sweden

Stéphanie Loup, Toulouse University, France

Albert B.R. Lwango, Groupe ESC Troyes, France

René Mauer, ESCP Europe, Berlin, Germany

Sarfraz A. Mian, State University of New York, Oswego, USA

Gerald Mollenhorst, Utrecht University, the Netherlands and Stockholm University, Sweden

Joseph Ngijol, Université Paris 3 Sorbonne Nouvelle, France

Shahid Qureshi, Centre for Entrepreneurial Development, IBA Karachi, Pakistan

Tammi C. Redd, Ramapo College of New Jersey, USA

Saverio Romeo, Birkbeck, University of London, UK

Veronique A.J.M. Schutjens, Utrecht University, the Netherlands

Sibin Wu, The University of Texas Rio Grande Valley, USA

Introduction

Alain Fayolle, Sarah L. Jack, Wadid Lamine and Didier Chabaud

1. INTRODUCTION

By its very nature, entrepreneurship is processual and social (Aldrich and Zimmer, 1986). Even if these two observations are now largely consensual (Gedajlovic et al., 2013; Hoang and Antoncic, 2003; Slotte-Kock and Coviello, 2010), we observe a paradox. This observation about entrepreneurship was explicitly made very early on in the field in the seminal work of Aldrich and Zimmer (1986: 3), who emphasized 'two essential issues that research on entrepreneurship must address: (1) entrepreneurship is a process and must be viewed in dynamic terms rather than in cross-sectional snapshots; and (2) entrepreneurship requires *linkages or relations* between key components of the process'. However, recent work by Slotte-Kock and Coviello (2010: 48) considered that 'the entrepreneurship literature has only just begun to investigate how network relationships are developed and transformed'.

The chapters in this book consider two essential issues relating to entrepreneurship: process and the social dimension. In dealing with these issues, this book aims to go 'one step beyond' (Lamine et al., 2015)[1] with the aim of enhancing knowledge and understanding about these issues and so contribute to a better appreciation of the connection between the entrepreneurial process and social networks.

This introduction sets out some of the foundations we feel are relevant for a more social dynamic perspective of entrepreneurship. Thereafter, we show how each chapter contributes to this subject and helps shed light on our understanding. Four overarching themes emerge from these chapters. These have been used to organize this book into its various sections. The first focuses on the classic analysis of the evolution of social networks across the diverse phases of the entrepreneurial project. The second addresses the issue of formal networks and shows how, while these (1) appear to be important to sustaining an entrepreneurial project and (2) constitute an important issue for public policy, they have been under-explored. The third theme deals with the issue of context. While for some time context was neglected, recent years have shown a growing interest in this topic because it enables us to arrive at a better understanding of the success of entrepreneurial projects, whether in developed or less-developed countries. In the final section, we separate those works that seem to focus on the theoretical challenges of the analysis of social networks.

2. ENTREPRENEURSHIP PROCESS AND SOCIAL NETWORKS: SOME MILESTONES

Since the work of Aldrich and Zimmer (1986), numerous studies have aimed to shed light on the dynamic interplay of social networks and the entrepreneurial process. Considering that, as researchers, we are all standing 'on the shoulders of Giants', it nevertheless seems interesting to track some specific steps that have been crucial to the development of our research questions and empirical understanding. As some surveys exist that are particularly stimulating and well arranged (Hoang and Antoncic, 2003; Jack, 2010; Slotte-Cock and Coviello, 2010; Martinez and Aldrich, 2011; Gedajlovic et al., 2013), our aim here is not to provide another one, but rather to point to some milestones in the development of the topic, before proposing a tentative integrative view.

Some Steps in the Literature

If Aldrich and Zimmer (1986) were among the first to insist on the need to consider the relationship between both process and social networks in entrepreneurship, the attention that followed showed a real enthusiasm by others to learn more about this connection.[2] Following Granovetter (1973), their paper provides an insightful discussion of social networks that resonates with the works of Burt (1982, 1992), characterizing entrepreneurs as being 'between structural holes', even if Burt depicts an individual as having a rational view of the management of networks. We observe that these works have been followed mainly by papers that try to track the respective impact of strong versus weak ties on diverse dimensions of entrepreneurship (discovery of opportunity, exploitation of opportunity etc.). For instance, several studies emphasize the importance of social networking or of social resources for entrepreneurs (Hansen, 1995; Johannisson, 1998). Others emphasize the importance of social networks on the performance of the venture (Brüderl and Preisendörfer, 1998), on the number of business opportunities (Hills et al., 1997), or the respective impact of weak and/or strong ties on the discovery of opportunities (Singh et al., 1999).

A further step is made in the papers of Butler and Hansen (1991) and Larson and Starr (1993), this last one proposing 'a network model of organization formation'. Larson and Starr's (1993) work is mainly conceptual, but points to the possibility of 'network crystallization', which can be seen as a way to create teams from social networks (Chabaud and Condor, 2009). Hite and Hesterly (2001) also provide a stimulating treatment of the evolution of social networks of entrepreneurs, emphasizing the possible differentiation of phases that are led by strong ties and others driven by weak ties. What is especially stimulating about both these papers is that they insist on different uses of ties (and social networks) across the diverse phases of an entrepreneurial project, but also they point to the possibility of the changing nature of ties: if at the beginning of the relationship ties are weak, a persistent relationship can lead to the development of a strong tie. Conversely, initial strong ties mobilized to obtain financial resources can become weak ties. This is especially the case when an entrepreneur is faced with new challenges and does not have the time needed to maintain the former strong ties. In both cases, it seems that we depict the entrepreneur as someone influenced by the nature of the needs of his/her project. However, an entrepreneur who has 'so many ties, so less time' (Hansen et al., 2001) has not enough time to maintain all those ties that exist within his/her social network.

But if these papers are stimulating, they share the nature of conceptual papers (with the exception of Butler and Hansen, 1991). So, do they fit with reality? Are their hypotheses verified by the observations of real entrepreneurs? It seems to us that some empirical work has also been interesting because it shows that it is difficult to build conceptual papers without empirical content. And also, as Slotte-Cock and Coviello (2010) emphasize, there is a lack of papers that directly address the issue of entrepreneurial process. This is one of the interests of this book. By providing multiple empirical analyses through a variety of approaches,[3] the chapters help us to arrive at a better understanding of the dynamic connection between social networks and entrepreneurial processes.

An Integrative Proposal

In other work, Lamine et al. (2015) propose four dimensions that coevolve over time (see Figure I.1). This model emphasizes the necessity to consider four building blocks. The classical view emphasizes the need to take into account the entrepreneur–opportunity nexus (Shane, 2003) or the dialogue between the entrepreneur and his/her project (Bruyat and Julien, 2001)

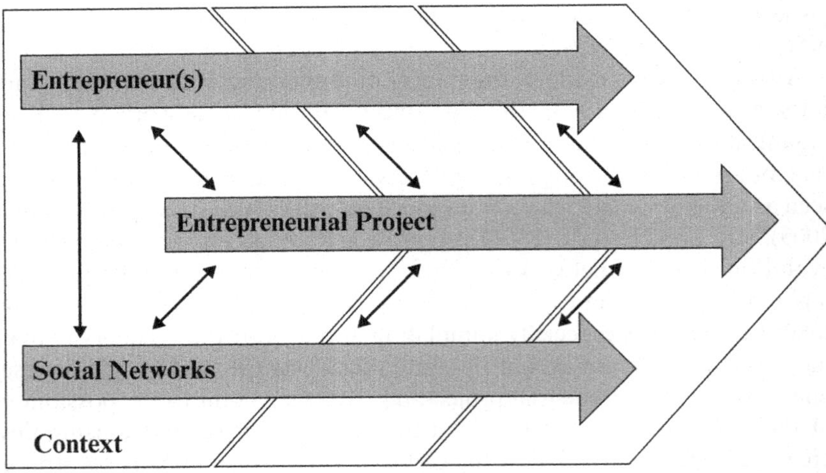

Figure I.1 The coevolution of entrepreneur(s)/project/networks

and the need to follow it over time. However, Lamine et al. (2015) show the need to (1) have a more inclusive view of the entrepreneurial project, one that takes into account artefacts; (2) specify the social networks and their connections with each dimension over time; and (3) take into account the cultural and institutional context, as this can drastically affect each element of the process, and offers some infrastructures and/or governance mechanisms that will influence the entrepreneurial journey.

This integrative model is heuristic, guided by the dimensions we suggest should be taken into account. Choosing to focus on partial elements will produce only partial results and no 'general theories' or 'general conclusions'. In this way, a research programme arises that promotes the development of studies that will articulate the diverse dimensions and their coevolution across time and will test what variables, mechanisms or processes will be important to understanding the entrepreneurship phenomenon. Also, this will lead us to understand much more the 'nuts and bolts' required for entrepreneurship (see Elster, 1989) and so be more effective than providing a general theory (Shane, 2003).

3. PART I: THE EVOLUTION OF NETWORKS ACROSS ENTREPRENEURIAL STAGES

This topic is a 'classical' one. Very early on, scholars considered the evolution of social networks during the entrepreneurial project (Butler and

Hansen, 1991; Larson and Starr, 1993; Hite and Hesterly, 2001). Four chapters address this issue, either looking at the possible diversity of social networking across time or studying the reorganization of networks before (or after) a critical event. They question if (and how) social networks evolve across the entrepreneurial stages, the nature of these networks (weak or strong ties, family or professional) and how they can change in the process. They even notice that sometimes professional and personal networks overlap. Moreover, they enable us to think about the respective role networks play in changing a project and the impact of the change of relationships on this journey.

Tammi Redd, Michael Abebe and Sibin Wu's chapter (Chapter 1) questions if an 'entrepreneurs' social network composition differs significantly across different stages of the entrepreneurial process', differentiating between opportunity identification, organizing, stability and growth stages. To do so, they elaborate hypotheses by using social network and resource dependence theories, and realize a (cross-sectional) survey of over 2151 participants (obtaining 592 responses). Variables were measured using a 7-point Likert Scale and PSED Scale measurements.

They expected that there would be a difference in the number of strong ties (Hypothesis 1.1) and the number of weak ties (Hypothesis 1.2) between different stages of the venture creation process. But, if Hypothesis 1.2 is supported, finding 'a significant difference . . . between the three stages of the venture creation process in the number of weak ties possessed in the social network', Hypothesis 1.1 is rejected: 'there is no significant difference in the number of strong ties possessed across the three venture creation stages'.

Redd et al. also test for significant differences across the three stages for weak ties and find that 'The post hoc analysis shows that, for the significant hypothesis, the only two stages which do not differ at $\alpha = 0.05$ in the LSD analysis are the Organizing Stage and the Growth and Stability Stage. However, through further analysis of the means plots for the total of weak ties for the sample, it is evident that with each stage of the venture creation process the total of weak ties has an upward trend.'

Redd et al. 'found that no differences exist across the stages of venture creation in terms of strong ties as these relationships may be easier to maintain over the long term. We also found that the number of weak ties in an entrepreneur's social network tends to increase as the entrepreneur passes through the stages of entrepreneurial development. This perhaps suggests that there are resources offered by weak ties that cannot be obtained through maintenance of strong network ties.' Also, the authors observe that, whereas Larson and Starr (1993) as well as Hite and Hesterly

(2001) lead us to think that networks can rapidly change and experience a great deal of evolution, in their study reported here it is shown that (1) strong ties are probably more stable than we think, and (2) logically (?) they are easier to create, less costly to maintain and easily moved, but weak ties move and change faster.

This leads to analysis of both (1) the networking behaviour of entrepreneurs, as well as their relational competence (Baron and Markman, 2000), and (2) the *modus operandi* of networks. If we generally think that an entrepreneur can extend ties in order to obtain information and resources, and if we also think that ties are costly to maintain or manage, we also have to think that ties can lead to other ties, that is, that an entrepreneur can leverage some ties, using some to create new ones. On these questions, Chapter 2 (de Beer et al.) and Chapter 3 (Chabaud and Ngijol) probably provide complementary views.

In Chapter 2, Marianne de Beer, Gerald Mollenhorst and Veronique Schutjens analyse the dynamics of social networks of Dutch entrepreneurs in residential neighbourhoods.[4] Observing the lack of longitudinal studies of social networks of entrepreneurs, they decided to use data from two waves (2008 and 2013) of a Dutch panel of 214 entrepreneurs (197 usable answers) from the Survey on the Social Networks of Entrepreneurs (SSNE1 and SSNE2), located in 161 residential neighbourhoods of 40 Dutch municipalities.

De Beer et al. specifically use the name-generating method to collect data to explore 'both network size change and network composition change. Network composition is analyzed on three dimensions: (1) family versus non-family network contacts; (2) local versus non-local network contacts; and (3) overlap between business-related and private-related network contacts'. All these themes are important in generating a better understanding of the networking behaviours of entrepreneurs across time. Also, this stimulating initiative enables De Beer et al. to shed light on the global evolution of networks and on the network composition of entrepreneurs, but also to test the impact of several dimensions, internal (age of the firm and of the entrepreneur, market orientation – whether local or not) as well as external (location change) ones.[5]

The authors make a number of empirical observations, including:

- Network average size did not change significantly between 2008 (3.79) and 2013 (4.05).
- Regarding network composition: (1) 'the average number of contacts that may provide practical help has grown significantly from 1.90 in 2008 to 2.18 in 2013. This growth is especially apparent in the category of practical help for business purposes in particular, as this

number increased significantly from 0.61 to 0.83 on average'; (2) 'the average number of local network contacts has increased as well: while in 2008 the entrepreneurs reported 0.91 local network contacts on average, this number increased substantially to 1.20 in 2013'. This led the authors to determine that, 'over time, the neighbourhood became a more important arena for network contacts of the entrepreneurs'. Note also that this observation is valid even if the firm is not commercially orientated locally.

- Role overlap, that is, the fact that the entrepreneur uses the same contact for business as well as private purposes, is important: (1) 'role overlap is present within entrepreneurial networks as on average 1.1 network contact[6] gives support for both private and business purposes. Role overlap is found to be more important for entrepreneurs with a small network than for entrepreneurs with larger network, which is to be expected as the former group had to compensate for their limited network size by getting support of the same people for different purposes. At the entrepreneurial level, we found that the role overlap between 2008 and 2013 decreased for older entrepreneurs and for entrepreneurs who already had a great deal of overlap in their networks'; (2) 'the proportion of network contacts with "role overlap" is smaller among entrepreneurs with larger networks'. This suggests that those with relatively small networks to a certain extent compensate for a potential lower amount of available support with an increase in role overlap. Next to network size, the other factors included in the analysis show only that older entrepreneurs reported a relatively small number of network contacts for business purposes and relatively many network contacts for private purposes.

Didier Chabaud and Joseph Ngijol's chapter (Chapter 3) considers the impact of entrepreneurs' social networks at the beginning of the entrepreneurial journey – that is, during the formation of business opportunities. Their point of departure is the relative under-analysis of this topic; they note that, 'although social network theory (SNT) has been repeatedly applied to entrepreneurship, it is symptomatic that the review undertaken by Slotte-Kock and Coviello (2010) on social networks shares only one common reference with the review undertaken by Short et al. (2010) on opportunities'. After reviewing the literature on the diverse phases of the formation of opportunities (i.e. discovery of business ideas, evaluation, obtaining resources, social network management mode), they provide an empirical study that considers six cases of innovative venture creation in the service sector. This study enables them to show:

- the central role of strong ties in the formation process of opportunities, weak ties being activated by relying on strong ties ('leverage'), confirming for these innovative projects the leverage effect emphasized by Jack (2005);
- that management of a social network is observed and the relational competence of the entrepreneur (Baron and Markman, 2000) plays a role in the formation process. Moreover, a learning process is observed that shows that relational competence varies across the stages of the formation process.

Moreover, the necessity to take into account the fact that the formation process of opportunities is not linear, but much more complex, is also emphasized. Chabaud and Ngijol argue that this relationship is not a linear process (Shane, 2003); their study demonstrates the need to take into account the coevolution of social networks and business opportunities (Lamine et al., 2015; Jack et al., 2008), rather than thinking of a linear process (Shane, 2003).

Lise Aaboen and Frida Lind, in Chapter 4, wonder 'how start-ups can overcome the loss of all their customer relationships through repositioning'. This question matters because start-ups can be frequently confronted with the difficulty of the end of a business relationship, sometimes with their few (or first) customers. Faced with this, how can they react? Their question is also important because Slotte-Kock and Coviello (2010) show interest in connecting the social network and business network literatures, but the business network literature generally emphasizes the persistence of ties.

To deal with this question, Aaboen and Lind use a longitudinal case-study approach that arises from a former study realized with 22 start-ups in order to understand 'their development and how they developed their first customer relationships' (see Aaboen et al., 2012).

Investigating the repositioning by three firms showed the breakdown of commercial relationships; Aaboen and Lind find that 'Even though they did not necessarily return to the exact same actors or (potential) customers, all three firms repositioned through returning to the history in the sense that they again sought a context they was part of in earlier phases for initiating new relationships. For two of the start-ups this context was a development context, while it was more of again selling to a certain market segment for the third start-up.' In this way, Aaboen and Lind emphasize that history really matters, as 'network structures that have been previously useful may be remembered and used again later. Furthermore, Greve and Salaff (2003) argued that the successful transition between development phases for an entrepreneurial firm depends on the ability to develop their network and on the initial network position.'

This first set of chapters (Part I) provides interesting views on the evolution of social networks across time. They enhance our view of the way social networks evolve over time, by providing some new observations regarding the role of overlap between networks (De Beer et al.), recourse to history in the face of critical events (Aaboen and Lind) and also confirming the role of strong ties, including their leverage effect (Chabaud and Ngijol) and relational competences (Redd et al., Chabaud and Ngijol).

At the same time, the necessity to look deeper into the tie content and to appreciate the 'costs' of maintaining and developing networks also appears to be important, opening new perspectives and avenues of thought.

If all scholars agree that entrepreneurs are embedded in social networks, they have – on this topic – mainly studied the networks of the entrepreneur from an individual perspective by looking at the (entrepreneur's) ego-centred network. Even if it has been possible to differentiate between the nature of the relationship (weak or strong ties, business or family ties and so on), it would be interesting to look at formal networks and their impact.

4. PART II: FORMAL NETWORKS – A NEW RESEARCH AGENDA?

As early as 1985, Birley took into account the role of formal networks, including 'all the local, state and Federal agencies, such as banks, accountants, lawyers, realtors, Chamber of Commerce, or the Small Business Administration (SBA)' (p. 109), even if her observation was that entrepreneurs did not really know them, and that they were not very efficient. In 1991, Dubini and Aldrich insisted on the necessity to distinguish between the personal (ego) network and the extended networks of the entrepreneur, that is, those connected to collectives and referred to as 'within firms (intrafirm relations) or between firms (interfirm relations)' (p. 305), opening the way to extend the research agenda. More recently, Parker (2008) provided an economic analysis of 'formal business networks comprising voluntary groupings of entrepreneurs who share knowledge and experiences between themselves' (p. 627) and considered that this topic is under-analysed. Lefebvre et al. (2015) and some of the authors of the chapters collected in this part of the book seem to agree. Before emphasizing the content of these chapters, it is important to shed some light on the apparent paradox of a topic that is both important and under-analysed.

Several causes probably explain this. First, there has been a great deal of work on business networks and inter-organizational networks, specifically in the field of strategic management (Gulati et al., 2000; Breschi and

Malerba, 2005; Gulati, 2007), and this can lead scholars to think that the issue is more connected to strategy than to entrepreneurship. Also, entrepreneurship scholars want to understand the entrepreneurial journey of the entrepreneur, and somewhat naturally tend to focus on their ego-network. In this situation, scholars frequently introduce some questions regarding participation of a club, business association or business incubator structure. But these formal networks are only one kind of network (see, e.g., Chapters 2 and 3). In this way, the objective is to depict the global view rather than to look closely at the formal one. Some results on formal networks are sometimes mentioned. Elfring and Hulsink (2007) emphasize that business incubation can be a contingency or mediating variable. The objective is to understand the way entrepreneurs manage their network and/or networking behaviour (Burt, 1992), even if the analysis of the structure (and properties) of the whole network is also important (Burt, 2005). In this way it can probably be stated that entrepreneurship scholars overemphasize the influence of the ego-network on the analysis of the structural or complete network. Also, it is not easy to depict the complete network of a set of entrepreneurs in order to analyse – and compare – their properties and network strategies; this needs a collective research programme. Last, but not least, definitions and characterizations of formal entrepreneurial networks are diverse, probably not leading to a unified core of knowledge. Quoting Birley (1985), Dubini and Aldrich (1991) or Parker (2008), we can also refer to 'business associations' (Bennett, 1998), 'formal business and occupationally-based professional (OBP) networks' (Lawton Smith and Romeo, Chapter 5 in this volume; 2011), 'learning networks' (Bessant and Francis, 1999), and even more global forms such as clusters (Porter, 1990) or industrial districts (Marshall, 1890)!

The topic seems nevertheless very important. First, some studies argue that structures like business incubators can have a networking effect, and so need to be deeply scrutinized (Hansen et al., 2000; Chabaud et al., 2004; Bøllingtoft and Ulhøi, 2005), even if their effect can sometimes be negative. Also, formal networks are increasingly perceived to be like a public-policy tool. This has led some scholars to adopt a more restrictive view than Parker (2008), and consider that by their very nature formal entrepreneurial networks are 'policy-led organisations aimed at sustaining entrepreneurship development at a regional or national level by providing participants with a practical means to increase the variety and number of their social contacts within the entrepreneurial community (hence their social capital)' (Lefebvre et al., 2015, p. 500), or that '"learning networks" [are] primarily set up by a third party' (Bessant and Francis, 1999: 377). As Lefebvre et al. (2015, p. 500) remind us, 'evidence exists that SMEs entrepreneurs value formal peer networks more than any other policy-led formal business networks dedicated to business support (Sexton et al. 1997; Chell and Baines 2000)'. Davidsson and Honig (2003, p. 322), on the other hand, emphasize the important role of these networks: 'The weaker tie (bridging) social capital variable "member of a business network" was consistently important and significant in predicting gestation activity at the start of our screening, and the pace during the following 18-month period. It was also a very strong predictor of having a first sale or in being profitable, where most other variables failed to show an influence.'[7]

So, in editing this book, we considered that it was important to collect chapters on the topic of formal networks. One main view seems particularly important: understanding the 'what' (characterizing the formal networks), the 'why' (their reasons and impact) and the 'how' (their *modus operandi* and their properties). Each of the chapters provides stimulating views on these. The first two chapters in Part II address these formal networks. The chapter by Helen Lawton Smith and Saverio Romeo (Chapter 5) provides an interesting global view, explaining both the 'what' and the 'why'. Claire M. Leitch, Richard T. Harrison and Frances M. Hill (Chapter 6) also shed light on the 'why' regarding formal women entrepreneurs' networks created by governments. Chapter 7, by Christophe Leyronas and Stéphanie Loup, provides a kind of 'bifocal view' by investigating closely 'how' a formal network would operate. Their view focuses on an organized business network that emphasizes the role of governance of the network.

Helen Lawton Smith and Saverio Romeo (Chapter 5) aim to contribute to 'a better understanding of the formation and utilization of various types of formal networks in different places'. To do so, they emphasize 'three different logics relating to their formation, utilization and outcomes':

1. network logics: why individuals/firms engage in particular kinds of networks;
2. networks as a service: what individuals/firms seek to procure from these networks; and
3. networks as a resource: what value do they provide?

But, beyond the theoretical identification of these logics, Lawton Smith and Romeo's empirical study used 221 formal networks in the Oxfordshire to Cambridge arc in the UK. They provide information on the number and types of networks in Oxfordshire and gather data on the use of networks, using an online survey. Participating in formal networks is an important way to access new clients and boost business collaboration, and, even if their results are somewhat different from what members initially anticipated, they suggest that 'investment decisions on participation based on "calculative trust" (Bennett, 1998) and "network capital" (Huggins 2010) paid off'. Also, the authors emphasize 'a three-stage process in the development of network density: (1) a rise in the number of networks; (2) institutionalization of networks; and (3) rationalization and consolidation', and discuss the importance of formal networks to local dynamics.

In Chapter 6, Claire Leitch, Richard Harrison and Frances Hill present their study on women entrepreneurs and networking as social exchange. Whereas many studies focus on informal networking, Leitch et al. address 'three questions: what are women's motivations for participating in formal business networks and what are their expectations of such participation? What networking behaviours do they engage in, especially regarding the initiation, development and maintenance of contacts and relationships? What are the potential and actual benefits which they perceive to accrue from networking?' These questions are important, as female entrepreneurship requires increasing attention, and studies of public institutions promote formal networks dedicated to female entrepreneurs in order to develop women entrepreneurship. Thus this chapter enhances understanding of the topic, and the effectiveness of public policy in relation to this topic.

For their study, Leitch et al. conduct in-depth interviews with 18 female entrepreneurs involved in formal networks. Eight are inexperienced, early-stage entrepreneurs whose businesses are less than three years old, whereas ten have businesses older than three years. Also, the entrepreneurs can be part of women-only networks, mixed-gender networks, or both. This enabled Leitch et al. to contrast observations according to these elements, and consider if there are differences among populations. Also, a specific choice is made by these authors: they focus only on women, in order to take into account the diversity of women entrepreneurs' practices, instead of focusing on the differences between men and women. This seems particularly suitable, as specifically addressing diversity among women is most important (Aldrich, 1989; Foss, 2010).

Their observations are interesting. Leitch et al. emphasize that 'social exchange is key to entrepreneurial networking and entrepreneurs' networks involve not only dyadic but also collective relationships, which are reflected in direct, productive and generalized exchange'. They show that, 'even within the context of formal networks, women identify these as structures of mutual dependence within which reciprocal rather than negotiated exchanges take place. While some participants engage in network membership with a clear view of the expected benefits that might accrue, for most this is overlain by a belief that network participation confers membership of a community, which enhances social solidarity, trust and cooperation.'

Also, their observation 'suggests that for early-stage entrepreneurs, intangible benefits tend to relate to personal development, while for more established entrepreneurs these are to do with both personal and business development, indicating some change in focus over time (Leitch et al., 2009; 2013)'. Here again, entrepreneurs' networking seems to evolve with time and the development of the firm.

Last, these observations enable Leitch et al. to conclude that establishing formal 'women-only' networks will have only an indirect and long-term effect on efficiency, as women seem to valorize the collective dimension and discuss common problems specific to them.

In their chapter (Chapter 7), Christophe Leyronas and Stéphanie Loup's objective is to provide a better understanding of the collectives, or collective strategies, in which there is 'joint mobilization of resources and the formulation of joint actions within communities of organizations'. But, if 'the question of "why?" has been dealt with at some length, the question of "how?" and therefore of its operation remains open'. So they propose to look 'inside the black box of relations', in order to:

- distinguish between coordination and cooperation: 'cooperation involves an exchange of resources whose objective is to increase access to both resources and expertise; coordination means pooling or exchanging resources at a given time without any increase in the stock of resources or expertise of the companies in the relationship. Unlike cooperation, coordination does not generate new resources/skills in the companies themselves';
- examine a single case study of a collective, that of the association '*Les Artisans Réunis*', in the French city Revel, which involves 17 companies in the (artistic) furniture sector, including cabinet-makers (creators and restorers), ironworkers, upholsterers and stained-glass specialists. In their case study they follow a three-step approach, with a first set of interviews focused on the context and the global history of the association, a second set to collect data exploitable by sociometrics techniques, and a last set that enables them to qualify the ties between actors. Data were dealt with using UCINET software, which enables them to elaborate graphs of relations, and to complete the picture through in-depth analysis of the content of the relationships established between the members of the Association.

Comparing the graph of relations and a matrix of the content of all the dyadic relations (with 45 dyadic projects) between firms of the Association enables Leyronas and Loup to state that, 'while structural analysis is a promising approach for analysing how the strategies and positioning of companies (centrality) in the collective enable them to derive certain benefits (access to information, power etc.), it does not really help us to grasp the nature of the collective as such, and especially the link between the individual and the collective'. In fact, having an in-depth view of the content of relations between members is necessary in order to understand the potential, the content and the dynamics of the collective. In the Revel case, for instance, even if relationships seem important, it appears that they are mainly of a technical kind and constitute a way to coordinate by sharing resources, rather than of a cooperative kind. Most of the members are not really involved in the collective project; nor do they try to develop collective resources and projects.

So, in this chapter, Leyronas and Loup offer an interesting depiction of a collective action and lead us to think about the interests and limits of methods used to analyse it. They also point to the difficulty of creating a real cooperative strategy that would create new resources for members and provide a kind of collective strategy.

Moreover, they develop a new way of thinking about the evolution and the analysis of networks of entrepreneurs. On the one hand, they insist on the need to look at the real content and motives of ties between individuals and/or organizations, and, on the other hand, they emphasize the interest (and difficulty) of creating collective strategies between SMEs. If the coordination of actors is (relatively) easy to observe, it is much more difficult to create a cooperative strategy.

These complementary chapters offer, in our opinion, ways to extend the research agenda on entrepreneurial processes and social networks of entrepreneurs. By providing richer analysis of the interplay of an entrepreneurial project and social networks across time, they open the way to new questions and even methodological choices. Questions such as the origin (auto-organization of third-party creation), *modus operandi* and governance mechanisms of formal networks must be studied in order to understand their impact on the entrepreneurial project, but so too must the collective (government, local authority, business association, groups of entrepreneurs) involved in the formal network, as well as methodological choices, because analysing formal networks can be done at different levels, from the formal network (see Leyronas and Loup, who analyse the whole network) to a region, as in Lawton Smith and Virahsawmy's analysis of the Oxfordshire to Cambridge arc, and, between these, analysis of the use of formal networks made by some populations of entrepreneurs (Leitch et al.). Also, the methods used can be diverse, from the classical analysis of ego-networks to the analysis of complete networks.

5. PART III: CONTEXT – A BENIGN NEGLECT?

There is probably also (one more!) paradox in the literature on our topic. We should recall that Granovetter (1985) argued against undersocialized analyses of the economy, as well against oversocialized views. Social network theory appeared to be a solution to this problem, with an analysis that enables us to take into account individual and social forces. And, looking at the literature on entrepreneurs and social networking, we probably suffer the same kind of bias, with little insistence on the context and/or cultural and institutional forces that can affect the observations made about the behaviours of entrepreneurs. Appreciating context is of crucial importance if we are to have a deeper understanding of entrepreneurship (Zahra, 2007; Welter, 2011).

One of us (Sarah Jack) recently emphasized in a paper the need to look at community in order to understand entrepreneurial processes and social networks (McKeever et al., 2015). The various chapters of Part III enable us to shed light on the impact of context in order to understand social networking and entrepreneurial processes, with a specific insistence on cultural and institutional context (Bruton et al., 2008, 2010).

In Chapter 8, Christian Lechner puts into perspective various levels of action that can affect the entrepreneurial firm and provides a framework for analysis. Following chapters shed light on two important issues. The first element that has to be taken into account is family, and Anderson et al.'s chapter (Chapter 9) illustrates this well. The second element is the diversity of the cultural and institutional contexts. Mian and Qureshi (Chapter 10) look at social networking in the Middle East and North Africa, whereas Albert Lwango (Chapter 11) emphasizes specifics relating to social structures in Congo. Thus this part closes with an in-depth scrutiny of social networks in the African context.

In Chapter 8, Christian Lechner addresses the questions 'Why do some firms perform better than others?' and 'Why do some firms survive and others not?' To do so, he emphasizes the role of networks in the competitiveness of the firms and differentiates between three levels of effects on firm performance:

1. firm-level effects
2. firm-constellation effects
3. regional or national level effects.

At each of these levels the relational dimension has to be taken into account in order to understand the competitiveness of the firm. Lechner provides insights into each of these dimensions. This is particularly relevant if we want to depart from a 'firm-as-an-island perspective', that is a view that considers the firm as an autonomous and isolated entity.

For Chapter 9 we decided to reprint the paper by Alistair Anderson, Sarah Jack and Sarah Drakopoulou Dodd. This chapter, originally published in *Family Business Review* in 2010, seemed to us particularly relevant in introducing the topic of context.

As Aldrich and Cliff (2003) put it, family has a 'pervasive effect on entrepreneurship'. Here, Anderson et al. extend this 'family embeddedness perspective' by providing a two-step study to investigate 'if, to what extent, and how entrepreneurs capitalized on resources embedded in the family, but beyond the formal traditionally defined boundaries of the family firm'.

A quantitative study carried out with a sample of 68 entrepreneurs enables them to show that around 'a quarter of the most important network contacts in our survey were kin, and the majority of them worked outside the family's company'. More importantly, a qualitative study conducted on a sample of 12 entrepreneurs emphasized that 'most entrepreneurs made extensive use of family members in the running of the business', whether there is or not a formal connection between the firm and the family member. Two aspects should be noted. First, these ties are characterized by the 'high quality of the help provided, the heterogeneity of resources and viewpoints made available, and the rapidity of the service provided and its low or non-existent cost'. Second, there seem to be diverse configurations of the connection between the entrepreneur and his/her family. Family business seems a special situation and it is interesting that that some entrepreneurs want to preserve a complete distinction between them and the family.

So, from our point of view it is important to note that family must be taken into account when analysing the dynamics of the entrepreneurial project, whether studying family business, teams, or other arrangements. Also, family is an important context for entrepreneurs. Nevertheless, is this situation European (or even Scottish) centred, as Phan and Butler (2008) would say?

Two chapters will help us to provide a more complete picture. Mian and Qureshi (Chapter 10) provide an empirical study that enables us to observe if networking activities are the same among countries, whereas Lwango (Chapter 11) deepens the analysis by looking at the specific role of family in Congo.

In Chapter 10, Sarfraz Mian and Shahid Qureshi provide an exploratory study of social network structures of nascent entrepreneurs in MENA (Middle East and North Africa) countries. Their chapter is a contribution to an important debate: are social networks the same, and used in the same way, whatever the country? Or is there a cultural or institutional dimension that influences the way entrepreneurs use their networks? Here, Mian and Qureshi propose to investigate this point by using data from the Global Entrepreneurship Monitor (GEM) project (2009–2011). Following Schott (2014), who distinguishes between private, work, professional, market and international advisory networks, they observe the way entrepreneurs' networks differ among 15 countries, at the beginning of the project (start-ups or nascent entrepreneurs) and for established firms. Thanks to a hierarchical cluster analysis of network characteristics, they can distinguish three sets of countries that tend to have 'similar structures of adviser networks'. Specifically, they show that nascent entrepreneurs 'from factor-economy-driven countries tend to rely on family advisers more than other countries. Entrepreneurs from innovation-economy-driven countries, while still consulting with family advisers, are far more likely than start-ups from other countries to use advisers from the workplace, professional, market, and even international environments. Finally, start-up entrepreneurs from efficiency-economy-driven countries tend to use fewer advisers, of all types, than those from other countries.' The observation made for operating entrepreneurs tends to be much more differentiated, leading them to observe that there is some country effect not necessarily mitigated by the development of the firm. So Mian and Qureshi's chapter challenges non-institutional or a-cultural views of social networks.

With a different methodological setting, Albert Lwango, in Chapter 11, also contributes to this question. Gupta et al. (2010, p. 148) emphasize that 'Ubuntu is the popular principle of indigenous African business which means "humanity to others"', and Lwango provides an empirical study organized around a set of five interviews with three owner-managers of a family business, one founder, another engaged in succession, and the last who achieved succession ten years ago. This enables Lwango to shed light on the tension between the extended family and business development. If the creation of the firm is facilitated by the involvement of the extended family, and specifically by the role of the brothers of the founder, it seems that – with the transmission – the obligation changes, and the family business is influenced by the necessity to support the family. The author points out that, 'although clan solidarity is an important factor for both creation of family businesses and of survival through periods of crisis, such solidarity is less and maybe a hindrance to business growth'. In this way, Lwango's empirical study of family businesses in an urban area of Congo emphasizes the importance of looking at the connection between family and business in other institutional environments than those of developed countries. His *ubuntu* view seems to provide a *modus operandi* explaining some of the observations made by Mian and Qureshi: family matters!

These chapters emphasize the relevance and importance of context.

But they also show why context matters. In doing so, they engage with the current debate about the need for entrepreneurship and social networks to be studied in the contexts in which they occur (Batjargal, 2010; Fayolle, 2014; Stam et al., 2014; McKeever et al., 2015). What is also interesting about two of these chapters is that they look at entrepreneurial processes and social networks in parts of the world about which we have too little understanding – MENA and Congo. Thus they help expand our knowledge and understanding of different situations in different contexts too.

6. PART IV: DEBATES AND PERSPECTIVES – THEORETICAL CHALLENGES

In the last part of this book, we present two chapters that relate to radically different methodologies, but have a common objective: to interrogate the theories and conceptions of social networks and, in particular, of the entrepreneurial journey or project. The chapter by Jansen, Mauer and Brettel offers a stimulating analysis of social networks in the context of effectual entrepreneurs and reasoning (Sarasvathy, 2001, 2008), asking if we have to change our vision of social networks. The other, by Lamine, Fayolle and Chebbi, proposes to go back to a strong (French) sociological tradition – that of actor-network theory (Callon, 1986; Akrich et al., 1988a, 1988b) to shed light on the role of artefacts in the dynamics of networks.

Chapter 12, by Willem Jansen, René Mauer and Malte Brettel, is ambitious, emphasizing the need to reconstruct the analysis of social networks in the context of control-based entrepreneurship, that is, entrepreneurs who follow an effectual reasoning.

The authors put the literature in perspective and consider that 'key theoretical contributions (Burt, 1992; Granovetter, 1973) assume an entrepreneurial behaviour that uses predictive planning, causal logic and the classical exploration–exploitation scheme (Holland, 1975). Despite the widespread assumption of the universality of this prediction-based approach, a growing body of studies reveals that expert serial entrepreneurs prefer an alternative control-based entrepreneurship approach. In this study, we use effectuation (Sarasvathy, 2001) as an exemplary prototype. In light of these discoveries, in this study we re-evaluate findings regarding entrepreneurial network structure and deepen the understanding of the interaction dynamics of entrepreneurs using control-based logic and their networks as well as their impact on venture performance.'

Jansen et al. make two key points. First, they emphasize that social networks are an important part of Sarasvathy's framework, as effectual entrepreneurs focus on available means; they 'take a set of means as given and focus on selecting between possible effects that can be created with that set of means' (Sarasvathy, 2001: 245). In this situation, available means are central, asking: 'who I am', 'what I know' and 'whom I know' (Sarasvathy, 2001; Sarasvathy and Dew, 2005a). 'Consequently, social networks ("whom I know") are essential in acquiring "new means" and "new goals" (Sarasvathy and Dew, 2005a). Although interaction with other market participants is regarded as "the very essence of the effectual process" (Dew et al., 2008: 50), research on intersubjective interaction remains sparse (Sarasvathy and Venkataraman, 2011).' Second, Jansen et al. insist that, by its very essence, networking refers classically to *tertius gaudens* (Burt, 1992), that is, the fact that entrepreneurs take advantage of structural holes – of non-redundant networks. With effectuation, the authors argue that the nature – and essence – of networking is different. Instead of taking advantage of non-connected networks, the entrepreneur will close 'the gap between disconnected others by bringing them together', what Obstfeld (2005: 103) refers to as *tertius iungens* (the third who joins). So we obtain a very different picture of networking, with an entrepreneur who will use artefacts to discuss and connect with others, in order to create opportunities (Sarasvathy, 2008).

While Jansen et al. contrast these two views of networking, they go further by constructing a simulation model of effectual entrepreneurs. This enables them to show 'how control-based entrepreneurship reorganizes social networks towards a dense web with few structural holes, high personal centrality and highly constrained stakeholders'. Their simulation experiments 'regarding network position reveal a significant performance impact of the network position in general and the initial position in particular. Moreover, the analysis of development over time reveals that control-based entrepreneurship actively improves the network position over time. However, these developments are captured to varying degrees by established centrality measures. Although degree centrality is positively correlated with demand satisfaction, betweenness centrality is negatively correlated with performance.'

So, this chapter is stimulating and opens up a debate: does the literature miss the point regarding networking strategies? Does classical literature overemphasize *tertius gaudens* over *tertius iungens*? Do we need to reconstruct our views about the social networking of entrepreneurs?

Clearly, Jansen et al. provide an interesting chapter that will lead to further studies. If one can insist on the possible bias of the simulation model that is constructed, it seems to us that this model is nevertheless interesting: (1) it enables us to consider possible futures and consequences of effectual hypotheses by examining equilibrium trajectories connected to theses hypotheses; (2) it provides an interesting way to put in perspective the classical views of literature (Aldrich, Burt, Granovetter) with Obstfeld's (2005) view of social networking, leading to a more subtle analysis of social networking. Here, we think of diverse strategies of networking, of diverse *modus operandi* – with a *tertius iungens* orientation that leads to connect with others, and involving them in the project – and this can explain why we observe crystallization of social networks, with the creation of entrepreneurial teams (Larson and Starr, 1993; Chabaud and Condor, 2009).

Nevertheless, it seems to us that we need to refine the analysis. With the observation of the diversity of entrepreneurial reasoning, some scholars also point out that social competence is a specific matter to study (Baron and Markman, 2003), whereas others insist on the important networking differences between necessity and opportunity entrepreneurs (Tessier-Dargent, 2015). So we probably have to complete the simulation model with many more empirical studies in order to examine the diverse networking strategies of entrepreneurs.

Interestingly, Wadid Lamine, Alain Fayolle and Hela Chebbi convey a view that is probably reconcible with that of Jansen et al., even if it comes from a different intellectual tradition. In Chapter 13 they propose to connect 'actor-network theory and the entrepreneurial process'. Their main point is to emphasize the interest of actor-network theory to entrepreneurship, following the sociological point of view of Callon and Latour. Specifically, use of Akrich et al. (1988a, 1988b) is made in order to examine the crucial elements that explain the dynamics of the entrepreneurial project. In Akrich et al.'s view, it is necessary to take into account the micro-processes in force in the project in order to understand the success or failure of innovation, and particularly what they call 'the art of interessement' (1988a) and 'the art of choosing good spokespersons' (1988b). Innovation is never taken for granted and planified:

> To understand success or failure, i.e., diffusion and its adventures, the idea that an object is only taken up if it manages to interest more and more actors must be accepted. To consider that the socio-economic context was known once and for all, as if it were possible to define the product outside of all interaction with it, is contrary to all that we know about innovation. Innovation is perpetually in search of allies. It must integrate itself into a network of actors who take it up, support it, diffuse it. (Akrich et al., 1988a: 203–4)[8]

In this chapter, Lamine et al. transpose this actor-network theory of innovation – but also Bruyat's theory – to the analysis of the entrepreneurial project, and they show how these can be useful and lead to new perspectives on the understanding of entrepreneurial dynamics. To do so, they present a theoretical argument, and they develop an in-depth longitudinal case study of an innovative firm that has been followed for two years in order to emphasize the interest of this theoretical approach.

Their analysis enables them to explain 'the dynamics of building a nascent entrepreneur's socio-technical network', insisting both on the necessity to put the social network at the centre of the analysis and to emphasize the role of technical artefacts in order to explain the dynamics. Doing so, they open the way for new research agendas and demonstrate the interest of deeper understanding of the entrepreneurial journey.

In both chapters, we observe that social networks are central to the entrepreneurial journey. But this centrality comes from the necessity to understand all the dimensions of this journey. It is not possible to focus on only one dimension – the entrepreneur, the project, social network or context – it is necessary to understand the interactions or co-construction of the whole project. In this way, it seems to us that integrative views become increasingly necessary to enhance our understanding of entrepreneurship.

Such an understanding will necessitate a mix of research methods, and deepen appreciation of the trajectories of the entrepreneurial project. It is also probably necessary to change our points of view, and if it will be difficult to use or elaborate 'a general theory of entrepreneurship', it will be necessary both to use theories, in the context of rigorous methods, and to lead to actionable knowledge.

In this way, we hope that readers will appreciate these diverse studies, and that these will demonstrate the interest of insisting on this 'dynamic perspective' of the entrepreneurial process and social networks. Moreover, we hope that these studies will give readers new ideas, stimulate debates, and help to develop this research programme.

7. CONCLUSION

Each chapter conveys its own view of the subject of entrepreneurial processes and social networks. But, as readers will see, an integrated picture emerges from these diverse chapters, with many nuances. So, in this book we offer an impressionistic view. As for these 'paintings', the reader can choose various strategies: reading the whole from beginning to end; or reading each part separately, as each provides a special view of the topic; or even each chapter (or detail) independently. The various parts of the book propose only one way (our way) of discovering much more about entrepreneurial processes and social networks. We hope that this book – and these chapters – will provide ideas and ways to understand, and to go beyond paradoxes and omissions.

NOTES

1. Notice that this book originated from the strong interest of colleagues who wanted to contribute to the special issue of *Entrepreneurship and Regional Development* (2015) devoted to the specific question of the connection between entrepreneurial process and social networks. Because it was impossible to publish all the papers, we decided to coordinate this book. We see it as a way to contribute to a further extension of knowledge and understanding. We are grateful to the authors for their valuable contributions and to the reviewers for their help and support; without them, it would have been impossible to produce this book.
2. Aldrich (2011: xiii) also points out that this paper 'on entrepreneurship through social networks led to other invitations to present my work and I began to meet others in the entrepreneurship research community'.
3. See Howard Aldrich's recent blog at http://blogs.lse.ac.uk/impactofsocialsciences/2014/11/28/stand-up-and-be-counted-social-science-qualitative-quantitative-dichotomy/.
4. 'The firm was included in the sample only if the entrepreneur lived at the same address as, or within ten minutes walking distance from, his or her firm' (Sleutjes and Schutjens 2012).
5. Note that the authors distinguish 25 types of relationships between the entrepreneur and others, which enables them to provide a fine-grained analysis.
6. Compare with the average 4.0 network contacts in 2013, of which 3.1 were for private purposes and 2.2 for business purposes.
7. Whatever the variables, regarding characteristics of the entrepreneur, of his/her social capital or 'contact with an assistance agency'.
8. We quote from the English translation (published in 2002), rather than the French one.

REFERENCES

Aaboen, L., Dubois, A. and Lind, F. (2012), 'Capturing processes in longitudinal multiple case studies', *Industrial Marketing Management*, **41**(2), 235–46.

Akrich, M., Callon, M. and Latour, B. (1988a), 'A quoi tient le succès des innovations? Premier épisode: l'art de l'intéressement', *Gérer et comprendre*, **11**, 4–17; translated in *International Journal of Innovation Management*, **6**(2), 187–206.

Akrich, M., Callon, M. and Latour, B. (1988b), 'A quoi tient le succès des innovations? 2: Le choix des porte-parole', *Gérer et comprendre*, **11**, 15–29; translated in *International Journal of Innovation Management*, **6**(2), 207–25.

Aldrich, H.E. (1989), 'Networking among women entrepreneurs', in O. Hagan, C. Rivchun and D. Sexton (eds), *Women-Owned Businesses*, New York: Praeger, pp. 103–32.

Aldrich, H. and Cliff, J. (2003), 'The pervasive effects of family on entrepreneurship: toward a family embeddedness perspective', *Journal of Business Venturing*, September, 573–96.

Aldrich, H. and Zimmer, C. (1986), 'Entrepreneurship through social networks', in D. Sexton and R. Smilor (eds), *The Art and Science of Entrepreneurship*, Cambridge, MA: Ballinger, pp. 1–23.

Baron, R.A. and Markman, G.D. (2000), 'Beyond social capital: how social skills can enhance entrepreneurs' success', *Academy of Management Executive*, **14**, 106–16.

Baron, R.A. and Markman, G.D. (2003), 'Beyond social capital: the role of

entrepreneurs' social competence in their financial success', *Journal of Business Venturing*, **18**, 41–60.
Batjargal, B. (2010), 'The effects of network's structural holes: polycentric institutions, product portfolio, and new venture growth in China and Russia', *Strategic Entrepreneurship Journal*, **4**(2), 146–63.
Bennett, R.J. (1998), 'Business associations and their potential contributions to competitiveness of SMEs', *Entrepreneurship and Regional Development*, **10**, 243–60.
Bessant, J. and Francis, D. (1999), 'Developing strategic continuous improvement capability', *International Journal of Operations & Production Management*, **19**(11), 1106–19.
Birley, S. (1985), 'The role of networks in the entrepreneurial process', *Journal of Business Venturing*, **1**, 107–17.
Bøllingtoft, Anne and Ulhøi, John P. (2005), 'The networked business incubator – leveraging entrepreneurial agency?', *Journal of Business Venturing*, **20**, 265–90.
Breschi, S. and Malerba, F. (2005), *Clusters, Networks and Innovation*, Oxford: Oxford Univerity Press.
Brüderl, J. and Preisendörfer, P. (1998), 'Network support and the success of newly founded businesses', *Small Business Economics*, **10**, 213–25.
Bruton, G.D., Ahlstrom, D. and Oblój, K. (2008), 'Entrepreneurship in emerging economies: where are we today and where should the research go in the future?', *Entrepreneurship Theory and Practice*, **32**(1), 1–14.
Bruton, G.D., Ahlstrom, D. and Li, H.-L. (2010), 'Institutional theory and entrepreneurship: where are we now and where do we need to move in the future?', *Entrepreneurship Theory and Practice*, **34**(6), 421–40.
Bruyat, C. and Julien, P.-A. (2001), 'Defining the field of research in entrepreneurship', *Journal of Business Venturing*, **16**(2), 165–80.
Burt, R.S. (1982), *Toward a Structural Theory of Action: Network Models of Social Structure, Perception and Action*, New York: Academic Press.
Burt, R.S. (1992), *Structural Holes: The Social Structure of Competition*, Cambridge, MA: Harvard University Press.
Burt, R.S. (2005), *Brokerage and Closure: An Introduction to Social Capital*, Oxford and New York: Oxford University Press.
Butler, J.E. and Hansen, G.S. (1991), 'Network evolution, entrepreneurial success, and regional development', *Entrepreneurship and Regional Development*, **3**, 1–16.
Callon, M. (1986), 'The sociology of an actor-network: the case of the electric vehicle', in M. Callon, J. Law and A. Rip (eds), *Mapping the Dynamics of Science and Technology: Sociology of Science in the Real World*, London: Macmillan, pp. 19–34.
Chabaud, D. and Condor, R. (2009), 'La formation des équipes entrepreneuriales: une étude exploratoire', *Revue Internationale PME*, **22**(1), 81–102.
Chabaud, D., Ehlinger, S. and Perret, V. (2004), 'Les pépinières et incubateurs dans l'accompagnement de la création d'entreprises', in C. Voisin, S. Ben Mahmoud-Jouini and S. Edouard (eds), *Les Réseaux: dimensions stratégiques et organisationnelles*, Paris: Economica, pp. 215–27.
Davidsson, P. and Honig, B. (2003), 'The role of social and human capital among nascent entrepreneurs', *Journal of Business Venturing*, **18**(3), 301–31.
Dubini, Paola and Aldrich, Howard (1991), 'Personal and extended networks are central to the entrepreneurial process', *Journal of Business Venturing*, **6**, 305–13.

Elfring, T. and Hulsink, W. (2007), 'Networking by entrepreneurs: patterns of tie formation in emerging organizations', *Organization Studies*, **28**(12), 1849–72.
Elster, J. (1989), *Nuts and Bolts for the Social Sciences*, Cambridge: Cambridge University Press.
Fayolle, A. (2014), *Handbook of Research on Entrepreneurship: What We Know and What We Need to Know*, Cheltenham, UK and Northampton, MA, USA: Edward Elgar.
Foss, L. (2010), Research on entrepreneur networks: the case for a constructionist feminist theory perspective', *International Journal of Gender and Entrepreneurship*, **2**(1), 83–102.
Gedajlovic, E., Honig, B., Moore, C.B., Payne, G.T. and Wright, M. (2013), 'Social capital and entrepreneurship: a schema and research agenda', *Entrepreneurship Theory & Practice*, **37**(3), 455–78.
Granovetter, M.S. (1973), 'The strength of weak ties', *American Journal of Sociology*, **78**(6), 1360–80.
Granovetter, M. (1985), 'Economic action and social structure: the problem of embeddedness', *American Journal of Sociology*, **91**(3), 481–510.
Gulati, R. (2007), *Managing Network Resources: Alliances, Affiliations, and Other Relational Assets*, Oxford: Oxford University Press.
Gulati, R., Nohria, N. and Zaheer, A. (2000), 'Strategic networks', *Strategic Management Journal*, **21** (Special Issue), 203–15.
Gupta, V., Levenburg, N., Moore, L., Motwani, J. and Schwarz, T.V. (2010), 'Family business in sub-Saharan Africa versus the Middle East', *Journal of African Business*, **11**, 146–62.
Hansen, E.L. (1995), 'Entrepreneurial networks and new organisation growth', *Entrepreneurship Theory & Practice*, **19**(4), 7–19.
Hansen, M.T., Chesbrough, H.W., Nohria, N. and Sull, D.N. (2000), 'Networked incubators. Hothouses of the new economy', *Harvard Business Review*, **78**(5), 74–84, 199.
Hansen, M.T., Podolny, J.M. and Pfeffer, J. (2001), 'So many ties, so little time: a task contingency perspective on corporate social capital', in S.M. Gabbay and R.T.A.J. Leenders (eds), *Research in the Sociology of Organizations*, Vol. 18, Amsterdam: Elsevier Science, pp. 21–57.
Hills, G.E., Lumpkin, T.G. and Singh, R.P. (1997), 'Opportunity recognition: perceptions and behaviors of entrepreneurs', *Frontiers of Entrepreneurship Research*, Babson College, Wellesley, MA, pp. 168–82.
Hite, J. and Hesterly, W. (2001), 'The evolution of firm networks: from emergence to early growth of the firm', *Strategic Management Journal*, **22**, 275–86.
Hoang, H. and Antoncic, B. (2003), 'Network-based research in entrepreneurship: a critical review', *Journal of Business Venturing*, **18**, 165–87.
Holland, J.H. (1975), *Adaptation in Natural and Artificial Systems: An Introductory Analysis with Applications to Biology, Control, and Artificial Intelligence*, Ann Arbor, MI: The University of Michigan Press.
Huggins, R. (2010), 'Forms of network resource: knowledge access and the role of inter-firm networks', *International Journal of Management Reviews*, **12**(3), 335–52.
Huggins, R. and Johnston, A. (2009), 'Knowledge networks in an uncompetitive region: SME innovation and growth', *Growth and Change*, **40**(2), 227–59.
Jack, S. (2005), 'The role, use and activation of strong and weak network ties: a qualitative analysis', *Journal of Management Studies*, **42**(6), 1233–60.

Jack, S. (2010), 'Approaches to studying networks: implications and outcomes', *Journal of Business Venturing*, **25**(1), 120–37.
Jack, S., Dodd, S.D. and Anderson, A.R. (2008), 'Change and the development of entrepreneurial networks over time: a processual perspective', *Entrepreneurship & Regional Development*, **20**(2), 125–59.
Johannisson, Bengt (1998), 'Personal networks in emerging knowledge-based firms: spatial and functional patterns', *Entrepreneurship and Regional Development*, **10**, 297–312.
Lamine, W., Chabaud, D., Fayolle, A. and Jack, S. (2015), 'One step beyond? Towards a process view of social networks in entrepreneurship', *Entrepreneurship & Regional Development*, **27**(7–8), 413–29.
Larson, A. and Starr, J. (1993), 'A network model of organization formation', *Entrepreneurship Theory and Practice*, **17**(2), 5–15.
Lawton Smith, H. and Waters, R. (2011), 'Scientific labour markets, networks and regional innovation systems', *Regional Studies*, special issue on Regional Innovation Systems, **45**(7), 961–78.
Lefebvre, V., Radu Lefebvre, M. and Simon, E. (2015), 'Formal entrepreneurial networks as communities of practice: a longitudinal case study', *Entrepreneurship & Regional Development*, **27**(7–8), 500–525.
Leitch, C.M., McMullan, C. and Harrison, R.T. (2009), 'Leadership development in SMEs: an action learning approach', *Action Learning: Research and Practice* (Special Issue on Action Learning and SMEs), **6**(3), 243–64.
Leitch, C.M., McMullan, C. and Harrison, R.T. (2013), 'The development of entrepreneurial leadership: the role of human, social and institutional capital', *British Journal of Management*, **24**(3), 347–66.
Marshall, A. (1890), *Principles of Economics*, London: Macmillan.
McKeever E., Jack, S. and Anderson, A. (2015), 'Embedded entrepreneurship in the creative re-construction of place', *Journal of Business Venturing*, **30**(1), 50–65.
Martinez, M. and Aldrich, H. (2011), 'Networking strategies for entrepreneurs: balancing cohesion and diversity', *International Journal of Entrepreneurial Behaviour & Research*, **17**, 7–38.
Obstfeld, D. (2005), 'Social networks, the tertius iungens orientation, and involvement in innovation', *Administrative Science Quarterly*, **50**(March), 100–130.
Parker, Simon C. (2008), 'The economics of formal business networks', *Journal of Business Venturing*, **23**(6), 627–40.
Phan, Phillip H. and Butler, John E. (eds) (2008), *Theoretical Developments and Future Research in Family Business*, Charlotte, NC: Information Age Publishing.
Porter, M.E. (1990), *The Competitive Advantage of Nations*, New York: Free Press, Macmillan.
Sarasvathy, S.D. (2001), 'Causation and effectuation: toward a theoretical shift from economic inevitability to entrepreneurial contingency', *Academy of Management Review*, **26**(2), 243–63.
Sarasvathy, S.D. (2008), *Effectuation: Elements of Entrepreneurial Expertise*, Cheltenham, UK and Northampton, MA, USA: Edward Elgar.
Shane, S. (2003), *A General Theory of Entrepreneurship. The Individual–Opportunity Nexus*, Cheltenham, UK and Northampton, MA, USA: Edward Elgar.
Singh, R.P., Hills, G.E., Hybels, R.C. and Lumpkin, G.T. (1999), 'Opportunity recognition through social network characteristics of entrepreneurs', *Frontiers of Entrepreneurship Research*, Babson College, Wellesley, MA, pp. 228–41.

Sleutjes, B. and Schutjens, V. (2012), 'The added value of firm networks: an empirical study of local firm success determinants', *Entrepreneurship Research Journal*, **2**(2), 1–29.
Schott, T. (2014), 'Components of a network around an actor', *Encyclopedia of Social Network Analysis and Mining*, Heidelberg: Springer Verlag, pp. 241–50.
Short, J.C., Ketchen, D.J., Shook, C.L. and Ireland, R.D. (2010), 'The concept of "opportunity" in entrepreneurship research: past accomplishments and future challenges', *Journal of Management*, **36**(1), 40–65.
Slotte-Kock, S. and Coviello, N. (2010), 'Entrepreneurship research on network processes: a review and ways forward', *Entrepreneurship: Theory & Practice*, **34**(1), 31–57.
Stam, W., Arzlanian, S. and Elfring, T. (2014), 'Social capital of entrepreneurs and small firm performance: a meta-analysis of contextual and methodological moderators', *Journal of Business Venturing*, **29**, 152–73.
Tessier-Dargent, C. (2015), 'Les entrepreneurs par nécessité: d'une dichotomie simplificatrice à un continuum complexe', thèse de doctorat en sciences de gestion, Université de Grenoble–Alpes.
Zahra, S. (2007), 'Contextualizing theory building in entrepreneurship research', *Journal of Business Venturing*, **22**(3), 443–52.

PART I

The Evolution of Networks across Entrepreneurial Stages

1. Entrepreneurial network composition and the venture creation process: an empirical investigation

Tammi C. Redd, Michael A. Abebe and Sibin Wu

INTRODUCTION

Numerous entrepreneurship scholars have explored the role of social networks in the entrepreneurship process (Katz and Gartner, 1988; Reynolds and Miller, 1992; Liao and Welsch, 2005). Still others have maintained focus on the acquisition of resources through social network contacts (Shane and Venkataraman, 2000; Aldrich and Zimmer, 1986). However, in the social networking literature pertaining to entrepreneurship, a disproportionate number of studies has presented a rather static view of social networks. Such a static view seems to overlook the fact that social networks are dynamic in nature, changing in structure and composition over time (Jack et al., 2008; Doreian and Stokman, 1997; Liao et al., 2005; Maurer and Ebers, 2006). In addition, the networking perspective of entrepreneurship has either focused on network characteristics such as strength of ties (Shane and Cable, 2002), embeddedness among the ties (Hite, 2005) and structure of the network (Human and Provan, 1997), or placed emphasis on developing networks such as networking ability (Semrau and Sigmund, 2010) and network practices (Anderson et al., 2010). While there is general understanding of entrepreneurship as a dynamic process at the nexus of individuals and opportunities (Shane and Venkataraman, 2000; Shane, 2003), how entrepreneurs maintain social networks at different stages of their venturing becomes crucial to business performance (Slotte-Kock and Coviello, 2010). To our knowledge, whether and why entrepreneurs' social network composition systematically varies across stages of the new venture formation has not been empirically examined. Our research intends to fill this research gap. Specifically, this study empirically investigates whether the number of entrepreneurs' strong and weak ties significantly differs across the opportunity identification, organizing and stability/growth stages of new venture formation. We draw from the social network (Adler and Kwon, 2002; De Carolis and Saparito, 2006) and resource dependence (Pfeffer and Salancik, 1978) theories to present a social network typology model that encompasses the network configuration that will cause fit between network contacts created and resources needed in creating a viable business. Further, based on the model, we derive and test hypotheses on the relationship between social network ties and stages of entrepreneurial process. Specifically, this research will address the following question: 'Do entrepreneurs' social network compositions differ significantly across different stages of the entrepreneurial process?'

The remainder of this chapter is organized as follows. A review of the literature detailing social network dynamics as well as the stages of entrepreneurship is presented, with related hypotheses on the relationships between social networking and the entrepreneurship process. We then summarize the literature on social network characteristics and the stages of the entrepreneurial process. Next, we propose and test hypotheses and discuss our results. The chapter concludes with limitations and suggestions for future research opportunities.

LITERATURE REVIEW

Social Network Theory and Entrepreneurship

Social networks, which often provide information leading to profitable opportunities, crucial resources and other supports, play an important role in entrepreneurial performance (Slotte-Kock and Coviello, 2010). The entrepreneurial endeavor is also a dynamic process full of uncertainty and hardships (Liao et al., 2005). Hence a stage model of venturing is deemed appropriate for such research (Shane and Venkataraman, 2000). Therefore we review literature related to social networking, resource acquisition and characteristics of different venturing stages.

Resource acquisition through social networking has been examined at many levels, both in the social networking literature in general and in entrepreneurship literature. In earlier studies, the basic structural features and theory of social networking were linked to entrepreneurship in terms of resources offered: knowledge and information transfer (Shan et al., 1994; Powell et al., 1996); capabilities and learning (McEvily and Zaheer, 1999); and explicit knowledge transfer (Uzzi and Lancaster, 2003). These studies confirm the value of examining relationships within a social network for a better understanding of resource acquisition and business outcomes (Semrau and Sigmund, 2010).

In the entrepreneurship literature on social networking we see a focus on the use of social ties in transitioning from conceptual stage of the venture to the actual launch of the business (Katz and Gartner, 1988; Reynolds and Miller, 1992). A summary of studies conducted in the past is given in Table 1.1.

As we can see in the literature overview, social networks are dynamic, changing structurally over time (e.g. Hite, 2005; Liao et al., 2005), but also must be diverse. Each network node or contact offers specific resources needed at different times (Doreian and Stokman, 1997). This suggests that entrepreneurs create and sever ties within the social network as necessary in order to acquire resources at any specific time (Granovetter, 1985; Kossinets and Watts, 2006). Those resources can be physical, financial, human and organizational, and may help a company gain sustainable competitive advantages (Barney, 1991). Contacts are called on when the sources they provide are appropriate (Doreian and Stokman, 1997). Social networks evolve over time; adaptation is key to obtaining necessary resources that are critical to successful new ventures.

Research has also found that those with heterogeneous networks, consisting of both strong and weak ties, are more likely to succeed with business start-up than those with homogeneous social networks (Renzulli et al., 2000). Furthermore, networks spanning multiple domains of social life apparently provide nascent entrepreneurs with greater access to multiple sources of information than do more homogeneous networks (ibid.).

Resource Dependence Role of Social Networks

The resource dependence theory (RDT) provides an important theoretical lens in the study of the role that network relationships play in the successful management of entrepreneurial ventures. This theory, first introduced by Pfeffer and Salancik (1978), has been widely used in the areas of organization theory, strategy and entrepreneurship research (Scherer and Lee, 2002; Casciaro and Piskorski, 2005; Hillman et al., 2009; Arthurs et al., 2009). RDT basically argues that organizations actively engage in responding to and shaping their immediate environment for the purpose of acquiring critical resources needed for achieving their objectives. As such, this theory assumes that (1) organizations are part of a broader environment that controls critical resources needed to achieve their objectives, and (2) organizations are capable of manipulating and changing the external environment in order to acquire resources. RDT is particularly relevant in the study of social networks and entrepreneurship for at least two major reasons. First,

Table 1.1 Summary of major studies on social networks and entrepreneurship

Source/year	Social network dimension examined	Research type	Findings
Aldrich and Martinez (2001)	Theoretical perspectives for the study of entrepreneurship	Conceptual	Future research in entrepreneurship will require a new focus on entrepreneurial actions as opposed to characteristics
Greve and Salaff (2003)	Network creation on migrating to another country; child care issues for dual-career couples	Cross-sectional	The biggest obstacle for female migrants is the loss of social capital on arrival in the host country
Renzulli et al. (2000)	Differences of strong ties based on gender and entrepreneurial outcome	Longitudinal	Network homogeneity poses a critical disadvantage for potential small business owners
Greve and Salaff (2003)	Proportion of kin in female social networks; multiple countries	Archival cross-sectional	Social networking patterns for nascent entrepreneurs are similar across countries, but between males and females the size of the networks and time spent networking differ
Skinner (2001)	Female entrepreneurship; barriers to venture creation	Cross-sectional	Female entrepreneurs are more in need of financial and emotional support than male
De Carolis and Saparito (2006)	Social capital; bonding and bridging relationships; strong ties and weak ties	Conceptual	Nascent behavior of entrepreneurs is created by a combination of social variables and cognitive biases
Verheul et al. (2006)	Female responsibilities as barrier to networking	Cross-sectional	Unemployment and life satisfaction influence the difference in entrepreneurial success based on gender

Katz and Gartner (1988)	Use of social networking in transition from conception to gestation phase	Conceptual	Nascent venture can be identified based on four dimensions: intention, resources, boundary, and exchange
Menzies et al. (2004)	Female entrepreneurs: family as barrier to creation of social networks	Cross-sectional	Unattractiveness of business choice as barrier to entry and attractiveness element for venture capitalism
Gargiulo and Benassi (2000)	Network cohesiveness, structural holes and strong ties	Cross-sectional	Resistance to network change can jeopardize the function of the social network
Granovetter (1985)	Creation and severing of ties; network dynamics	Longitudinal	Discovery that trust and malfeasance play a role in the selection and maintenance of social network players
Kossinets and Watts (2006)	The activities and affiliations that cause social networks to evolve over time	Longitudinal	Social networks evolve immensely and differently for each individual
Sequeira et al. (2007)	Influence of social ties and self-efficacy on intention	Cross-sectional	Weak ties have a strong influence on nascent entrepreneurial intention

RDT emphasizes the importance of interdependence in inter-organizational relationships. As a number of studies have shown (e.g. Pfeffer, 1972; Hillman et al., 2000; Park et al., 2005), firms often operate in an interdependent external environment and as a result employ various tactics such as mergers and acquisitions, and board of director alliances in order to minimize their dependence on external actors. Second, RDT also emphasizes the importance of obtaining critical resources from external actors in the environment. These external actors may include venture capitalists, banks, investors and governmental agencies (Hillman et al., 2000; Hillman et al., 2009). In the entrepreneurship context, the emphasis on resource acquisition is particularly important in order to realize entrepreneurs' dreams of building successful and viable ventures (De Carolis and Saparito, 2006).

In this study, we combine the insights from RDT with those in social network theory to propose that social ties are important conduits in securing critical resources needed at the various stages of the entrepreneurial process (Adler and Kwon, 2002). In the following section, we briefly review the major stages of the entrepreneurial process.

Stages of the Entrepreneurial Process

There seems to be a fairly well-defined path of development for entrepreneurship, referred to as the entrepreneurship life cycle (Aldrich and Martinez, 2001). The beginning of an entrepreneurship venture is marked by opportunity identification, followed by an organizing stage in which resource acquisition is the key activity, and finally the stage of stability and growth once the venture has been launched (Greve and Salaff, 2003; Shane and Venkataraman, 2000). During this entrepreneurial process the creation of social capital is crucial to the successful launch and sustainability of a business venture.

Opportunity identification stage

The first stage in the venture creation process is opportunity identification. This stage is marked by the recognition of an idea in response to a perceived need for a product, service or innovative solution. Opportunities may arise as they are identified through search activities, just as often as they are discovered by those who searching for them; however; entrepreneurs must be alert to opportunities when they arise (Baron, 2006; Kaish and Gilad, 1991). Research has found that the opportunity identification stage is greatly influenced by potential social network relationships (Ozgen and Baron, 2007; Singh et al., 1999). It is during this stage that the entrepreneur discovers products or services that can be exploited (Casson, 1982; Shane and Venkataraman, 2000).

Organizing stage

The second stage of the venture creation process is the organizing stage. Here the entrepreneur begins to assemble the resources required to begin the business venture. These may be tangible, in the form of property and financial capital (Katz and Gartner, 1988), or they can be intangible, in the form of credit, information or tacit knowledge (De Carolis and Saparito, 2006). The entrepreneur's goal during this stage is to identify the appropriate method to acquire all resources needed for the business start-up.

Stability and growth stage

The final stage of the venture creation process is the stage of stability and growth. It is hoped that by this point the entrepreneur has assembled resources so that not only have they been able to become business-active, but that this status is sustainable. For successful ventures, this stage is categorized by efficiency, growth and generation of revenue (Murphy et al., 1996). During this phase the entrepreneur focuses on long-term economic stability (Renski, 2009). It is also during this phase that entrepreneurs face the most risk, and those who are unable to attain stability and growth experience failed ventures. As a result, it is of utmost importance that relationships to actors within the social network are maintained so that access to crucial resources can be sustained over time.

THEORY AND HYPOTHESIS DEVELOPMENT

Social Network Composition and Entrepreneurial Ventures

Social network composition is often determined by examining the strength of ties, specifically the type of ties that are used in transitioning from the conceptual stage of the venture to the actual launch of the business (Katz and Gartner, 1988; Reynolds and Miller, 1992). It has also been suggested in the literature that social networks leading to successful business outcomes are those that maintain a balanced level of strong ties and weak ties (Greve and Salaff, 2003). The strength of these ties is determined by relationship characteristics such as intensity, time and reciprocity, according to De Carolis and Saparito (2006). In the entrepreneurship literature, strong ties have maintained the sociological definition developed in the early literature as family members, kin or those with whom there is a very strong relationship (Aldrich et al., 1995; Greve and Salaff, 2003). Scott (1998) defined kin to include parents, in-laws and spouses, while weak ties consist of friends, co-workers and any acquaintances outside of the family. Although most weak ties are casual acquaintances, Levin and

Cross (2004) found that weak ties are still very important to the entrepreneur's social network because they often give the nascent entrepreneur access to different resources that may not be supplied by the strong ties of family members (Granovetter, 1973; Gargiulo and Benassi, 2000). The strength and mix of ties often determine whether the entrepreneur is being exposed to the information redundancy that is apparent in more homogeneous social networks that lack numerous information sources (Lin et al., 2001).

The relationships used within the social network change over time according to the need for appropriate resources to support each stage of the venture creation process. Relationships are created and severed as needed as entrepreneurs attempt to align the resources supplied by social network connections with resources needed by the entrepreneur at a particular time. This implies that different types of network ties supply varying types of resources.

As stated above, at the opportunity identification stage entrepreneurs face a large number of uncertainties, which need structural adjustments in order to cope successfully with change or varying requirements (Donaldson, 1996). Due to the dynamic nature at this stage, entrepreneurs need to find trustworthy advisors to guide them in exploring the right opportunities. In addition, uncertainties often raise business owners' stress levels, at which point their families' and close friends' emotional support becomes crucial. Thus strong ties are important when entrepreneurs probe for new ideas and seek psychological support.

At the organizing stage, however, entrepreneurs begin to exploit the chosen opportunity, registering the business, building a prototype, testing the markets and trying to achieve profitability (Gartner and Carter, 2004). These activities require entrepreneurs' skill and knowledge about internal operations and external markets so as to know where to gain the needed financial resources. To engage with so many activities, entrepreneurs' networks expand to include partners, government agencies, bankers, employees, customers and suppliers, among other stakeholders (Donaldson, 1996). Hence entrepreneurs have to manage many weak ties at this stage.

Lastly, when entrepreneurs have achieved the growth or stability stage, we expect that they will have developed strong ties with their stakeholders. Because strong ties require more trust, effort and intimacy (Granovetter, 1985), after years of operations of their businesses they will have chosen the right vendors, for example, and will have built a long, trustful relationship. Semrau and Sigmund (2010), for example, found that, compared with older firms, younger companies often lack organizational legitimacy. Therefore they have to compensate for the deficit by building larger networks. Established firms, however, have built strong ties with and gained the trust of their stakeholders. Based on the above argument, we examine following hypotheses:

Hypothesis 1.1: There is a significant difference in the number of entrepreneurs' strong ties among the three venture creation (opportunity identification, organizing and growth) stages.

Hypothesis 1.2: There is a significant difference in the number of entrepreneurs' weak ties among the three venture creation (opportunity identification, organizing and growth) stages.

METHODOLOGY

Sample and Data Collection

Data were collected from three groups of entrepreneurs in order to capture data at each of the three stages of the venture creation process (Greve and Salaff, 2003). A survey research design has been chosen for two reasons. First, even though some of the relationships tested in this study have never been tested before, the measurement items to be used in testing the hypotheses already exist. Second, a survey can easily reach a wide-ranging sample throughout the USA, making a large variety of entrepreneurs from different environmental contexts more accessible.

The target population for this study includes entrepreneurs throughout the USA who own or plan to own business ventures that can be classified as small businesses. The business owners included in the sample were identified both through Small Business Development Centers (SBDC) and also through an online panel. A detailed description of the respondents used in this study is presented in Table 1.2.

The survey design procedure used was based on the electronic survey design methods suggested by Dillman (2007). The response rate for electronic surveys is typically 28 percent, according to Dillman (2007), and a long survey can contribute to a lower response rate. However, the length of the survey used for this study should allow for the response rates to remain high as the entire questionnaire contains fewer than 40 questions.

In order to determine the correct sample size and effect size for the main study, a power analysis was performed with the pilot study data. The effect size 0.02 will be used in order to be conservative, as suggested by Cohen and Cohen (1983), since large effect sizes rarely occur in the

Table 1.2 Sampling method across stages of entrepreneurship

Entrepreneurship stage	Sampling source	Sample size	Description of participants
Opportunity identification	Small Business Development Centers and online panel	153	Prospective business owners chosen for participation due to a strong interest in starting a business such as that displayed by participation in development activities offered by a local Small Business Development Center
Organizing	Online panel	149	New business owners chosen for participation based on being within the first to fourth year of business ownership
Stability and growth	Online panel	207	Established business owners chosen for participation based on being in business for 5+ years

behavioral sciences. Cohen's sample and power tables were used in order to obtain the target sample size as suggested by Cohen (1988). With a target effect size of 0.02 and alpha (α) = 0.05, in order to obtain a power of approximately 0.80 a sample size of 392 is needed. In total, 2151 invitations to participate were extended. A total of 681 surveys were completed, 89 of which were unusable. The unusable surveys were classified as such because of instances in which respondents logged into the online survey but did not answer any questions or did not meet the age qualification to participate. Of the final of 592 responses, less than 1 percent were obtained by distributing face-to-face surveys; 6 percent were obtained from the state-level SBDCs; and 93 percent of the respondents were collected from Survey Monkey Audience. This procedure resulted in a 26.4 percent response rate.

Survey Instrument

A comprehensive measurement instrument was developed in order to measure strength of ties and stage in the venture creation process. Many of the items are borrowed from the Panel Study of Entrepreneurial Dynamics (PSED). The borrowed scales used in this study have typically measured using a 5-point Likert Scale. A 7-point Likert Scale was used here because 5-point Likert Scales are used less frequently in current research and because increasing the number of positions available on the Likert Scale increases the reliability and validity of the resulting data (Warner, 2008; Kaynak, 1997).

Strength of ties

Information on the strength of ties within the social network was gathered using an existing scale. The measurement items used are based on the work of Granovetter (1985). Since Granovetter's work, a measurement scale for strength of ties has been adapted by Marsden and Campbell (1984). Specifically, the respondents were asked not only to report the size of their social network used for business purposes, but also to supply information on the frequency and method of using this business contact either for resources or to discuss business matters in addition to the type of relationship (i.e. brother, work colleague etc.). A similar scale of questions was used in the PSED II; however, the PSED II scale measured strength of ties based on relationship status (Marsden and Campbell, 2004). The Marsden and Campbell scale was used in this study since it captures all the necessary dimensions of tie strength, including relationship type and frequency of contact.

Venture creation stages

The stage in the venture creation process is measured using adapted questions from the PSED II questionnaire (Gartner and Carter, 2004). This questionnaire, developed by Gartner et al. (2004), helps to gather information that will indicate activities in which the entrepreneur participates and the stage at which they function in the venture creation process. These questions remain unchanged from those used in the PSED I. Together these measurements are among the most used measurement items for capturing venture creation stage data (Frid et al., 2011). Gartner et al. (2004) categorized business outcomes of entrepreneurs by length of activity, specifically by asking in what month and year the business came into existence. Similar categorizations were used in this study in order to classify respondents into one of four groups based on the literature presented in the literature review. The respondents will be classified into the following categories: (1) have not started business yet; (2) have been in business 1 to 5 years; (3) have been in business 5 to 10 years; and (4) have been in business 10 or more years. These categories will allow identification of the opportunity identification, organizing and growth/stability stages.

DATA ANALYSIS AND RESULTS

Non-response Bias

Typically, self-report surveys are distributed by mail; however, for this study the survey responses were collected using intercept and electronic surveys. In survey research it is always a concern that a non-response bias exists in the data, resulting in the exclusion of one or more groups (Singleton and Straits, 2005). For this study, non-response bias was tested using Hotelling's T. Early and late responders were sorted by date and used as a proxy for responder and non-responder respectively. The Hotelling's-T^2 statistic indicated that there was no significant difference between early and late responders (Oppenheim, 1992).

Strength of Ties

According to Hypotheses 1 and 2, it was expected that there would be a difference in the number of strong ties and the number of weak ties between different stages of the venture creation process. The ANOVA test results are presented in Table 1.3. The ANOVA test for Hypothesis 1 rendered a non-significant result, lending no support for Hypothesis 1. Thus there is no significant difference in the number of strong ties possessed across the three venture creation stages. On the other hand, in testing Hypothesis 2, a significant difference was found between the three stages of the venture creation process in the number of weak ties possessed in the social network. Thus Hypothesis 2 is supported.

Supplemental Analysis of Network Composition across Venture Stages

Given the significant differences in the number of entrepreneurial weak ties across the three entrepreneurial stages, we conducted a follow-up analysis to understand the specific differences among the three stages. A least significant difference (LSD) *post hoc* analysis was conducted in order to test for random differences among the three stages of entrepreneurship. The results of the analysis are shown in Table 1.4. The *post hoc* analysis shows that, for the significant hypothesis, the only two stages that do not differ at $\alpha = 0.05$ in the LSD analysis are the organizing stage and the growth and stability stage. However, through further analysis of the means plots for the total of weak ties for the sample, it is evident that, with each stage of the venture creation process, the total of weak ties has an upward trend.

Table 1.3 Analysis of variance (ANOVA) of entrepreneurs social network composition by stages of entrepreneurship

Type of network ties	Opportunity identification stage (Stage 1)	Organizing stage (Stage 2)	Stability and growth stage (Stage 3)	df	F-value
No. of weak ties	M = 14.268 SD = 6.384 N = 41	M = 18.264 SD = 4.142 N = 261	M = 18.947 SD = 3.029 N = 207	2 506	23.779**
No. of strong ties	M = 2.969 SD = 5.271 N = 33	M = 4.586 SD = 15.267 N = 220	M = 3.889 SD = 8.919 N = 181	2 431	0.313

Note: * p-value < 0.05; ** p-value < 0.01.

Table 1.4 A Tukey HSD post hoc analysis of the mean differences in social network composition across stages of entrepreneurship

Type of social network composition	Venture creation stages		Mean differences	Standard error
No. of strong ties	Stage 1 vs	Stage 2	−1.617	2.356
		Stage 3	−0.919	2.389
	Stage 2 vs	Stage 3	0.697	1.266
No. of weak ties	Stage 1 vs	Stage 2	−3.966**	0.667
		Stage 3	−4.679**	0.679
	Stage 2 vs	Stage 3	0.682	0.369

Notes:
Stage 1 = opportunity identification; Stage 2 = organizing; Stage 3 = stability and growth.
* p-value < 0.05; ** p-value < 0.01.

DISCUSSION

Social network theory suggests that relationships, either personal or interfirm, may facilitate acquisition of information and resources. Hite (2005) and Jack (2010) concluded that network relationships provide enterprises with channels, bridges and ways to access opportunities and resources, two critical factors for entrepreneurial success. Johannisson (1988) proposed that the entrepreneur is a networker where he/she utilizes interfirm relationships to access resources so as to gain competitive advantages. However, due to time and budget constraints, entrepreneurs have to manage those relationships. Specifically, when to build strong ties and when to maintain weak ties become crucial to business owners.

The current research aims to find an answer to the above question. We employed social network theory to compare the composition of weak ties and strong ties during the entrepreneurial process, from opportunity identification stage, to organization stage, to growth/stability stage.

Our first hypothesis states that, during the three stages of entrepreneurial venturing, a variation in strong ties should be expected. However, the results do not support what we predicted. Our finding indicates that strong ties seem to be stable over the three phases, from an average of 3.0 strong ties at opportunity identification, to 4.6 at organizing, to 3.9 at growth/stability. We argue that the non-finding may be due to the following. First, entrepreneurs may view only family and close friends as strong ties, and, therefore, their family members whom they can trust and seek advice from remain stable over years. Second, entrepreneurs build ties and also sever ties at the same time. Strong ties may be more likely to be retained rather than severed throughout the venture creation process. Third, strong ties often lend emotional support to entrepreneurs and require time and intimacy. Therefore it is difficult for entrepreneurs to sustain too many critical friendships (Gladwell, 2010).

We also predicted that weak ties would vary across different stages of the entrepreneurial process. The analysis lends support to our hypothesis. We found that entrepreneurs build and maintain more and more weak ties along with their venturing effort. This particular finding is of value to social network research for the following reasons. First, the measures for social network ties were developed before the introduction of the Internet and Internet-ready devices (Boase et al., 2006). The proliferation of Internet access through the use of even mobile devices has made access to new network connection and the creation of weak ties easier than it has ever been before (Washington, 2011). The second reason has to do with the classic definition of weak ties, categorizing these online ties as distant and as contacted less frequently. The availability of the Internet in most areas has now made it possible for someone who has never been met face to face to be a strong tie, when in the past they would have been classified as a weak tie because of simple acquaintance. Third, when entrepreneurs progress with their business venturing, their networking ability is enhanced, which leads to more and bigger networks (Semrau and Sigmund, 2010).

Pfeffer and Salancik (1974) examined resource dependency theory (RDT) at the organizational subunit level. If we examine the nodes or connections within the social network as subunits, we can see how network relationships arise and how that subunit's resources are used once acquired. Perrow (1970) argued that all subunits are not equally influential, and Thompson (1967) suggested that the subunit that is best able to cope with contingency will be dominant. Perhaps this means, in terms of social network connections, that the influence of each relationship will vary, and some connections will become dominant because of the resources they offer. Relationships that contribute the most scarce and critical resources for the organization will be the most significant subunit, with a relationship tie that will be maintained throughout the growth and stability stage. Pfeffer and Salancik (1974) also found that these more powerful subunits had more outside support, giving them more influence over internal allocation of resources. For an entrepreneur, this may mean that network ties that remain dominant may increase the number of relational ties within a social network.

Perhaps a larger effort must be made to become more active in the local business community, in addition to attending local chamber of commerce events, small business development centers, networking events and local charity events held by local business owners. These types of activity allow entrepreneurs to maintain valuable relationships as well as develop new ones.

The linkage of social network theory to the field of entrepreneurship certainly suggests implications for future research that will expand knowledge of the field about resource acquisition and the importance of network ties in the entrepreneurial process. Although the scope of this chapter does not allow a more detailed exploration of network dynamics, the study does, however, give a better understanding of the resource acquisition process and the ability to overcome the already established social networking barriers to venture creation. Many entrepreneurial business decisions are shaped by social relationships, and creating a sustainable business venture depends heavily on the resources and contacts gained through these relationships (Greve and Salaff, 2003).

Future research should address this phenomenon from a longitudinal standpoint, or perhaps through case studies to enable description of the network orientation typologies with more precision. We must also consider that each entrepreneur, based on personal differences and strategic approaches, along with variation in environmental constraints and different levels of networking ability, faces different challenges that have not yet been captured in the entrepreneurial social networking literature. Future research could also address specific network orientations that cause ventures to fail.

CONCLUSION

This research investigates the dynamics of the structural composition of social networks during different stages of the venture creation process. Specifically, we have examined the possession of strong and weak ties during these different stages. This study was conducted in hopes of furthering the study of entrepreneurs' dynamic social networks. We found that no differences exist across the stages of venture creation in terms of strong ties, as these relationships may be easier to maintain over the long term. We also found that the number of weak ties in an entrepreneur's social network tends to increase as the entrepreneur passes through the stages of entrepreneurial development. This perhaps suggests that weak ties offer resources that cannot be obtained through maintenance of strong network ties. We hope our findings will enhance the understanding of the role social network composition plays in various stages of new venture formation.

REFERENCES

Adler, P.S. and S.W. Kwon (2002), 'Social capital: prospects for a new concept', *Academy of Management Review*, **27**(1), 17–40.

Aldrich, Howard, Amanda Elam and Pat Ray Reese (1995), 'Strong ties, weak ties, and strangers: do women business owners differ from men in their use of networking to obtain assistance?', in Sue Birley and Ian MacMillan (eds), *Entrepreneurship in a Global Context*, London: Macmillan, pp. 1–25.

Aldrich, Howard and Martha Martinez (2001), 'Many are called, but few are chosen: an evolutionary perspective for the study of entrepreneurship', *Entrepreneurship Theory and Practice*, Summer: 41–56.

Aldrich, Howard and Catherine Zimmer (1986), 'Entrepreneurship through social networks', in Donald Sexton and Raymond Smilor (eds), *The Art and Science of Entrepreneurship*, Cambridge, MA: Ballinger, pp. 1–23.

Anderson, Alistair, Sarah Dodd and Sarah Jack (2010), 'Network practices and entrepreneurial growth', *Scandinavian Journal of Management*, **26**: 121–33.

Arthurs, Jonathan, Lowell Busenitz, Robert Hoskisson and Richard Johnson (2009), 'Firm-specific human capital and governance in IPO firms: addressing agency and resource dependence concerns', *Entrepreneurship Theory and Practice*, **33**(4): 845–65.

Barney, Jay (1991), 'Firm resources and sustained competitive advantage', *Journal of Management*, **17**: 99–120.

Baron, Robert (2006), 'Opportunity recognition as pattern recognition: how entrepreneurs "connect the dots" to identify new business opportunities', *Academy of Management Perspectives*, **20**:104–19.

Boase, Jeffrey, John Horrigan, Barry Wellman and Lee Rainie (2006), 'The strength of Internet ties', *Pew Internet and American Life Project*. Accessed May 20, 2009. http://www.pewInternet.org/pdfs/PIP_Internet ties.pdf.

Casciaro, Tiziana and Mikolaj Piskorski (2005), 'Power imbalance, mutual dependence, and constraint absorption: a closer look at resource dependence theory', *Administrative Science Quarterly*, **50**(2): 167–99.

Casson, Mark (1982), *The Entrepreneur*, Totowa, NJ: Barnes & Noble.

Cohen, Jacob (1988), *Statistical Power Analysis for the Behavioral Sciences*, 2nd edn, Hillsdale, NJ: Lawrence Erlbaum Associates.

Cohen, Jacob and Patricia Cohen (1983), *Applied Multiple Regression/Correlation Analysis for the Behavioral Sciences*, 2nd edn, Hillsdale, NJ: Lawrence Erlbaum Associates.

De Carolis, Donna and Patrick Saparito (2006), 'Social capital, cognition, and entrepreneurial opportunities: a theoretical framework', *Entrepreneurship Theory and Practice*, **30**(1): 41–56.

Dillman, Donald (2007), *Mail and Internet Surveys: The Tailored Design Method 2007 Update with New Internet, Visual, and Mixed-mode Guide*, Hoboken, NJ: John Wiley & and Sons.

Donaldson, L. (1996), 'The normal science of structural contingency theory', in Stewart Clegg, Cynthia Hardy and Walter Nord (eds), *Handbook of Organizational Studies*, London: Sage Publications, pp. 57–76.

Doreian, Patrick and Franz Stokman (1997), 'The dynamics and evolution of social networks', in Sue Birley and Ian MacMillan (eds), *Social Network Evolution*, London: Macmillan, pp. 17–18.

Frid, Casey, S. Gordon and Per Davidsson (2011), 'Publications based on the Panel Study of Entrepreneurial Dynamics', St Louis, MO: The Kauffman Foundation.
Gargiulo, Martin and Mario Benassi (2000), 'Trapped in your own net? Network cohesion, structural holes, and the adaptation of social capital', *Organization Science*, **11**(2): 183–96.
Gartner, William and Nancy Carter (2004), 'Overview: the startup process', in William B. Gartner, Kelley G. Shaver, Nancy M. Carter and Paul D. Reynolds (eds), *Handbook of Entrepreneurial Dynamics*, Thousand Oaks, CA: Sage Publications, pp. 237–43.
Gladwell, Malcolm (2010), 'At 42', *The New Yorker*, October 4. http://www.newyorker.com/2010/10/04/101004fa_fact_gladwell.
Granovetter, Mark (1973), 'The strength of weak ties', *American Journal of Sociology*, **78**: 1360–80.
Granovetter, Mark (1985), 'Economic action and social structure: a theory of embeddedness', *American Journal of Sociology*, **91**(3): 481–510.
Greve, Arent and Janet Salaff (2003), 'Social networks and entrepreneurship', *Entrepreneurship Theory and Practice*, Fall: 1–22.
Hillman, Amy, Albert Cannella and Ramona Paetzold (2000), 'The resource dependence role of corporate directors: strategic adaptation of board composition in response to environmental change', *Journal of Management Studies*, **37**(2): 235–55.
Hillman, Amy, Michael Withers and Brian Collins (2009), 'Resource dependence theory: a review', *Journal of Management*, **35**(6): 1404–27.
Hite, Julie (2005), 'Evolutionary processes and paths of relationally embedded network ties in emerging entrepreneurial firms', *Entrepreneurship Theory and Practice*, **29**(1): 113–44.
Human, Sherrie and Keith Provan (1997), 'An emergent theory of structure and outcomes in small-firm strategic manufacturing networks', *Academy of Management* Journal, **40**(2): 368–403.
Jack, Sarah (2010), 'Approaches to studying networks: implications and outcomes', *Journal of Business Venturing*, **25**(1): 120–37.
Jack, Sarah, Sarah Drakopolou Dodd and Alistair Anderson (2008), 'Change and the development of entrepreneurial networks over time: a processual perspective', *Entrepreneurship and Regional Development*, **20**(2): 125–59.
Johannisson, Bengt (1988), 'Business formation: a network approach', *Scandinavian Journal of Management*, **4**(3–4): 83–99.
Kaish, Stanley and Benjamin Gilad (1991), 'Characteristics of opportunities search of entrepreneurs versus executives: sources, interests, general alertness', *Journal of Business Venturing*, **6**: 45–61.
Katz, Jerome and William Gartner (1988), 'Properties of emerging organizations', *Academy of Management Review*, **13**: 429–41.
Kaynak, Hale (1997), *Total Quality Management and Just-in-time Purchasing: Their Effects on Performance of Firms Operating in the U.S.*, New York: Garland Publishing.
Kossinets, Gueorgi and Duncan Watts (2006), 'Empirical analysis of an evolving social network', *Science*, **311**(5757): 88–90.
Levin, D.Z. and R. Cross (2004), 'The strength of weak ties you can trust: the mediating role of trust in effective knowledge transfer', *Management Science*, **50**: 1477–90.
Liao, Jianwen and Harold Welsch (2005), 'Roles of social capital in venture

creation: key dimensions and research implications', *Journal of Small Business Management*, **43**: 345–62.
Liao, Jianwen, Harold Welsch and Wee-Liang (2005), 'Venture gestation paths of nascent entrepreneurs: exploring the temporal patterns', *Journal of High Technology Management Research*, **16**: 1–22.
Lin, Nan (2001), 'Building a network theory of social capital', in Nan Lin, Karen Cook and Ronald Burt (eds), *Social Capital*, New York: Gruyter, pp. 3–31.
Marsden, Peter and Karen Campbell (1984), 'Measuring tie strength', *Social Forces*, **63**: 482–501.
Maurer, Indre and Mark Ebers (2006), 'Dynamics of social capital and their performance implications: lessons from biotechnology start-ups', *Administrative Science Quarterly*, **51**: 262–92.
McEvily, Bill and Akbar Zaheer (1999), 'Bridging ties: a source of firm heterogeneity in competitive capabilities', *Strategic Management Journal*, **20**(12): 1133–56.
Menzies, T.V., M. Diochon and Y. Gasse (2004), 'Examining venture-related myths concerning women entrepreneurs', *Journal of Developmental Entrepreneurship*, **9**: 89–107.
Murphy, Gregory, Jeff Trailer and Robert Hill (1996), 'Measuring performance in entrepreneurship literature', *Journal of Business Research*, **36**: 15–23.
Oppenheim, A.N. (1992), *Questionnaire Design, Interviewing and Attitude Measurement*, London: Pinter.
Ozgen, Eren and Robert Baron (2007), 'Social sources of information in opportunity recognition: effects of mentors, industry networks, and professional forums', *Journal of Business Venturing*, **22**: 174–92.
Park, Namgayoo, John Mezias and Jaeyong Song (2005), 'Before and after the technology sector crash: the effect of environmental munificence on stock market response to alliances of e-commerce firms', *Strategic Management Journal*, **26**(11): 987–1007.
Perrow, C. (1970), *Organizational Analysis: A Sociological View*, London: Tavistock Publications.
Pfeffer, J. (1972), 'Merger as a response to organizational interdependence', *Administrative Science Quarterly*, 382–94.
Pfeffer, Jeffrey and Gerald Salancik (1974), 'The bases and use of power in organizational decision-making: the case of a university', *Administrative Science Quarterly*, **19**(4): 453–73.
Pfeffer, Jeffrey and Gerald Salancik (1978), *The External Control of Organizations: A Resource Dependence Perspective*, Stanford, CA: Stanford Business Press.
Powell, Walter, Kennthus Koput and Laurel Smith-Doerr (1996), 'Interorganizational collaboration and the locus of innovation: networks of learning in biotechnology', *Administrative Science Quarterly*, **41**(1): 116–45.
Renski, Henry (2009), 'New firm entry, survival, and growth in the United States: a comparison of urban, suburban and rural areas', *Journal of the American Planning Association*, Winter: 60–77.
Renzulli, Linda, Howard Alrdrich and James Moody (2000), 'Family matters: gender, networks, and entrepreneurial outcomes', *Social Forces*, **79**(2): 523–46.
Reynolds, Paul and Brenda Miller (1992), 'New firm gestation: conception, birth, and implications for research', *Journal of Business Venturing*, **7**: 405–17.
Scherer, P.D. and K. Lee (2002), 'Institutional change in large law firms: a resource dependency and institutional perspective', *Academy of Management Journal*, **45**(1): 102–19.

Scott, John (1988), 'Social network analysis', *Sociology*, **22**: 109–27.
Semrau, Thorsten and Stefan Sigmund (2010), 'The impact of networking ability on new venture performance', presented at *Academy of Management Best Paper Proceedings 2010*, August 1–6.
Sequeira, J., S. Mueller and J. McGee (2007), 'The influence of social ties and self efficacy in forming entrepreneurial intentions and motivating nascent behavior', *Journal of Developmental Entrepreneurship*, **12**: 275–93.
Shan, Weijian, Gregory Walker and Bruce Kogut (1994), 'Interfirm cooperation and startup innovation in the biotechnology industry', *Strategic Management Journal*, **15**(5): 387–94.
Shane, S.A. (2003), *A General Theory of Entrepreneurship: The Individual–Opportunity Nexus*, Cheltenham, UK and Northampton, MA. USA: Edward Elgar Publishing.
Shane, Scott and Daniel Cable (2002), 'Network ties, reputation and the financing of new ventures', *Management Science*, **48**: 364–381.
Shane, Scott and Sankaran Venkataraman (2000), 'The promise of entrepreneurship as a field of research', *Academy of Management Review*, **25**: 217–26.
Singh, R.P., G.E. Hills, G.T. Lumpkin and R.C. Hybels (1999), 'The entrepreneurial opportunity recognition process: examining the role of self-perceived alertness and social networks', in Academy of Management (ed.), *Academy of Management Proceedings*, pp. G1–G6.
Singleton, Royce and Bruce Straits (2005), *Approaches to Social Research*, 4th edn, New York: Oxford University Press.
Skinner, S. (2001), 'Female entrepreneurs in the retail trade: a study of personal and professional traits as they impact on business environments', *Journal of Small Business Management*: 183–95.
Slotte-Kock, Susanna and Nicole Coviello (2010), 'Entrepreneurship research on network processes: a review and ways forward', *Entrepreneurship Theory and Practice*, **35**: 31–56.
Thompson, James (1967), *Organizations in Action: Social Science Bases of Administrative Theory*, New York: McGraw-Hill.
Uzzi, Brian and Ryon Lancaster (2003), 'Relational embeddedness and learning: the case of bank loan managers and their clients', *Management Science*, **49**: 383–99.
Verheul, I., A. Van Stel and R. Thurik (2006), 'Explaining female and male entrepreneurship at the country level', *Entrepreneurship & Regional Development*, March: 151–83.
Warner, Rebecca (2008), *Applied Statistics: From Bivariate through Multivariate Techniques*, Los Angeles, CA: Sage Publications.
Washington, Jesse (2011), 'For minorities, new digital divide seen', *USA Today*, January 1. http://www.usatoday.com.

2. Dynamic social networks of entrepreneurs: five years of change in the networks of Dutch entrepreneurs*

Marianne de Beer, Gerald Mollenhorst and Veronique A.J.M. Schutjens

INTRODUCTION

Within the field of entrepreneurial studies it has been widely accepted that the network of the entrepreneur matters greatly to firm development, for both private and business purposes (Johannisson, 2011; Gedajlovic et al., 2013). These network contacts provide the entrepreneurs with relevant information, resources and meaning (Anderson et al., 2010). This so-called 'social capital' is understood to be important for both the formation and the survival of small-scale businesses. Through their network contacts, entrepreneurs can gain access to resources they themselves lack, especially when their firms are young or small. And it is exactly these new and small-scale businesses that are upcoming in residential neighborhoods (see Folmer and Risselada, 2013). Increasingly, the residential neighborhood is becoming a place for both living and working, as the shift from the industrial era to the post-industrial service economy, together with advancements in telecommunications, has created possibilities for neighborhood-based working (Folmer, 2014; Mason et al., 2011; Sleutjes et al., 2012). Furthermore, a growing number of entrepreneurs decides to start their business from or nearby their own home. This is what Johannisson (2011) calls 'the everydayness of entrepreneuring', the ways in which entrepreneurs can combine their living with their working spaces and, by doing so, centralize their daily activities in a neighborhood. For these entrepreneurs, this means that parts of their family, social and business networks can overlap, as the boundaries between their working and their private lives become blurred. Overlap in these two components of entrepreneurial networks, private and business, has to our knowledge not yet received much research attention.

In addition, the local context can also play an important role in the supply of external resources. Mason et al. (2011) discuss three types of resources, the first being supporting services, such as printing, postal services and technical support. The second type has to do with the availability of spaces to socialize and network. Nowadays places like coffee bars and cafés are increasingly being used as informal meeting places where entrepreneurs can network with other self-employed workers (Mason et al., 2011). Lastly, entrepreneurs sometimes feel the need to use formal meeting places, for example when meeting a client, giving a presentation or using specialized facilities for business support. Often entrepreneurs can fulfill their needs for each of these three types of resources within their own neighborhood, which reinforces their ties with the local environment (Mason et al., 2011).

However, entrepreneurial networks (i.e. the networks of entrepreneurs) are not stable: in today's turbulent economic landscape it is important that entrepreneurs react and adapt quickly to opportunities and threats. As a response, social capital, and therefore networks of entrepreneurs, will change over time (Jack et al., 2010). To a limited degree scholars are adopting a dynamic perspective on entrepreneurial networks – but mostly still in a rather static comparison of network structures at two points in time. Stam et al. (2014) concluded from a meta-analysis of 59 studies focusing on the relation between small-firm performance and entrepreneurial networks that only five studies adopted a true longitudinal analysis whereby the same set of firms is followed over time. However, these five panel studies vary considerably in the time span used and the number of firms under research. The meta-analysis by Stam et al. (2014) showed that the majority of the studies analyzed used a cross-sectional research design instead. As Martinez and Aldrich (2011) state, static cross-sectional studies can offer insights into the structure of networks, but lack detailed information on the stability and change of ties over time.

It is therefore interesting to gain more insight into the ways entrepreneurial networks change over time. Do entrepreneurs rely on different types of network contacts as time progresses? Does the number of strong ties, for example family members or friends, change over time? Or do entrepreneurs rely more on weak ties, contacts with whom they do not have an ongoing and deep social relation (Davidsson and Honig, 2003; Martinez and Aldrich, 2011)? Is the 'everydayness' of entrepreneurship still prevalent over a longer period of time or does the importance of the local or neighborhood level change (Johannisson, 2011)?

In this chapter we want to explore these questions by focusing on the social networks of entrepreneurs in 161 neighborhoods in the Netherlands. We add to the existing literature by employing a genuine panel study looking at entrepreneurial network changes over a period of five years. This chapter deals with the following research question: to what extent have the social networks of entrepreneurs in Dutch residential neighborhoods changed between 2008 and 2013 with respect to network size and composition? We explore the change of network composition on three dimensions: (1) family/non-family network contacts; (2) local/non-local network contacts; and (3) overlap between personal/private and entrepreneurial network contacts. In a repeated measurement design, entrepreneurial panel data enable us to observe and examine the changes that have taken place in the entrepreneurs' professional and personal networks over a five-year period. An important addition to earlier studies is that we are also able to look at overlap in the parts of the entrepreneurial networks used for private and business purposes. A family member, for instance, can offer both emotional support on a personal level and give assistance with business-related activities, thus having role overlap within the network of the entrepreneur. The findings of our explorative study can provide us with new insights into the dynamics of entrepreneurial networks of small-scale businesses in a world that is becoming increasingly interconnected and relational.

THEORETICAL PERSPECTIVE

This chapter focuses on the changing networks of entrepreneurs running firms in residential neighborhoods. Research on entrepreneurial networks is far from new. However, large-scale empirical studies on entrepreneurial network change are still in a pioneering stage. The extensive review of entrepreneurial network studies by Hoang and Antoncic (2003) demonstrated that, over time, academics have viewed networks from at least two different angles: from an instrumental and a dynamic perspective.

The Instrumental View on Networks

The first perspective focuses on the effect of social networks on the entrepreneurial process or the success of firms. There is abundant theoretical (e.g. Martinez and Aldrich, 2011; Nahapiet and Ghoshal, 1998; Welter, 2011; Westlund and Adam, 2010) and empirical work on the importance of social networks for entrepreneurs and the performance of their firms measured in terms of revenue growth (Arregle et al., 2015), turnover, profitability and employment (Cooke, 2007), time to break even and sales (Lechner et al., 2006), firm survival, profit and return on equity (Watson, 2007). Network contacts are extremely valuable to an entrepreneur as they constitute the conduits through which complementary resources and useful information for the firm can be accessed. This resource-based view of relationships is commonly referred to as social capital (Burt, 1992). The social capital resulting from networking is seen to have a positive relation with firm performance (Watson, 2007; Westlund and Adam, 2010). Cooke (2007) found that for small and medium-sized enterprises social capital is 'a key ingredient' for the firm's successful performance measured by turnover, profitability, employment and indicators of innovation. Other authors agree that this relation exists, but they question the real contribution networks have on firm performance. Sleutjes and Schutjens (2012) found that the support networks of neighborhood-based firms could only marginally explain the growth of these firms in terms of sales, profit and employment. The link is there, but other factors, such as characteristics of the firm and the entrepreneur himself, are found to play a more important role (Sleutjes and Schutjens, 2012).

From the literature on entrepreneurial networks it is understood that entrepreneurs can obtain different types of resources from their networks. Renzulli and Aldrich (2005) discern the following three types of resources: instrumental support, emotional support and unique information. Arregle et al. (2013) follow this distinction in their study on the family embeddedness of entrepreneurial networks. They discern three ways in which networks can provide benefits for entrepreneurs and their firms. First, entrepreneurs use their networks to access resources, such as financial capital and supplies. This form of support helps entrepreneurs to obtain tangible resources. Second, the networks of entrepreneurs can provide emotional support, advice and encouragement during different phases of the entrepreneurial process. Family and friends play an important role in this emotional support for the entrepreneur (Arregle et al., 2013; Welter, 2011). Last, the network of an entrepreneur can serve as a source of information, allowing them to deal with uncertainty issues and to explore and exploit opportunities.

Much of the research on the networks of entrepreneurs is focused only on the benefits of social capital for business purposes. This is remarkable, as the ideas on entrepreneurial social capital stem from the wider field of social network research. Social capital is seen to have an influence on many different aspects of a person's life. For instance, research has shown that someone can use his or her personal network to gain access to a certain job (Lin and Dumin, 1986), to improve performance at work (Burt, 2000) and to find a house (Röper et al., 2009). Therefore, as stated by Arregle et al. (2013) and Welter (2011), the network of an entrepreneur can be beneficial both for support at the level of the firm (business support) and for private support. This holds in particular for the group of entrepreneurs under research in this chapter. They represent the growing number of firms in Western countries like the UK and the Netherlands that is home-based or is located in close proximity to the home of the entrepreneur. These entrepreneurs are likely to have interaction with their local environment, both for business purposes and for private matters (Mason et al., 2011; Schutjens and Völker, 2010). The importance of local ties is also argued by Schutjens and Völker (2010), who found that firms located in a particular neighborhood benefit from the local social capital. Consequently, entrepreneurs located in residential neighborhoods experience a blending of their business life with their private life within the local context (Johannisson, 2011). Network contacts can fulfill different roles within the network of an entrepreneur, as a contact can be used for both business purposes and private purposes. Not much research has been done on the overlapping roles of a network contact. Mollenhorst et al. (2014) pay some attention to overlapping roles in their research on personal networks of Dutch neighborhood residents, but research on overlap within entrepreneurial networks is scarce.

The network of an entrepreneur can consist of different types of network contacts, ranging from family and friends to business contacts. All these ties can be seen as sources of social capital. In the sociological and entrepreneurship literature a common distinction is made between strong and weak ties (Granovetter, 1973; Lechner and Dowling, 2003; Jack, 2005). Strong ties refer to people with whom the entrepreneur has a close personal relationship, such as family members and friends (Davidsson and Honig, 2003; Greve and Salaff, 2003; Jack, 2005). This close relationship enables easy exchange of resources, especially that of in-depth knowledge. This can be very beneficial for both parties, but it has been argued that these relationships can also form a risk due to the lack of new information resulting from the close-knit relationship. To gain access to new information and new resources, weak ties, those that are not based on a close personal relationship but, for example, are more market-based, are vital (Arregle et al., 2013; Granovetter, 1973; Lechner and Dowling, 2003).

The Dynamic View on Networks

As the first perspective proposed by Hoang and Antoncic (2003) views entrepreneurial networks as a source of social capital from which entrepreneurs can tap ideas, resources and knowledge, the second perspective focuses on the network itself and, more explicitly, network development over time. In most studies on network change a rather static research design is used to study network change (see the extensive meta-analysis by Stam et al., 2014). A smaller but increasing number of academic studies points to the dynamic nature of the network itself (Hoang and Antoncic, 2003; Schutjens and Stam, 2003; Jack et al., 2010; Slotte-Kock and Coviello, 2010; Stam et al., 2014). This perspective on entrepreneurial networks emphasizes its dynamic character in acknowledging that social networks are constantly changing because entrepreneurs themselves, their network contacts and their preferences can change over time. Research by Mollenhorst et al. (2014) on the personal networks of Dutch neighborhood residents showed high turbulence in these networks over time. The researchers focused on confidants and people who act as practical helpers as the two main roles that network contacts could have. They found that between the two waves (1999/2000 and 2007) only 30 percent of the network contacts kept their role within the networks of the respondents. A large part of the 1999/2000 network disappeared and was replaced by new network contacts (Mollenhorst et al., 2014). A similar pattern could occur for the network change of entrepreneurs in residential neighborhoods. These entrepreneurs in particular combine their professional activities closely with their private life within the local environment, in line with Johannisson's idea on the 'everydayness of entrepreneuring' (Johannisson, 2011). With respect to entrepreneurial networks, both the network contacts and their importance to the entrepreneur or the firm can change over time, due to firm-internal forces and firm-external events.

Internal forces within the firm often result in a changing need for resources of the firm or the entrepreneur over the (firm) life course, which calls for other network contacts (Garnsey, 1998; Stam et al., 2014). In their model of network evolution Butler and Hansen (1991) discern three phases, from pre-start-up to start-up towards an ongoing business phase. The resources needed by the entrepreneur differ by phase, so that, for example, opportunity identification is important in the pre-start-up phase and a more focused network in terms of information is important in later phases of the model. To keep up with these changing needs the network of the entrepreneur must change over time (Butler and Hansen, 1991). Also, when a firm grows in size, an entrepreneur needs more information on hiring/firing regulations, for which other network contacts are sought and found. In the same vein, entrepreneurs learning from earlier experiences or those who have followed courses may no longer depend on resources provided by their initial network contacts. In other words, parts of their social capital are exchanged for (new) human capital (Elfring and Hulsink, 2007; Lavie, 2006; Martinez and Aldrich, 2011).

Entrepreneurial networks can also change as a consequence of firm-external events. For instance, network partners may move to other neighborhoods or areas, thereby potentially losing their significant role in the entrepreneurial network in favor of other network contacts (Knoben,

2011). In this sense, relocation of network partners can be a disruptive force in relational links. The private circumstances of the entrepreneur and changes therein, such as personal well-being or career ambitions, can also bring about alterations in entrepreneurial networks. This also goes for the personal household of the entrepreneur and changes in the household life course, for example with respect to income or childcare responsibilities (Jayawarna et al., 2011). Finally, market developments could impel entrepreneurs to change their networks and networking strategies in order to stay in business or to increase firm performance.

In sharp contrast to the abundant literature on entrepreneurial network effects (the first perspective by Hoang and Antoncic (2003)), only a limited number of studies have focused on network dynamics (the second perspective), leaving the time-dimension of networks highly unexplored (Stam et al., 2014). Jack (2010) made a plea for both more qualitative and quantitative empirical studies to extend knowledge on entrepreneurial relations. The lack of empirical studies on network change is strongly related to the longitudinal and detailed network information necessary for measuring such changes, and to the difficulty in avoiding reversed-causality issues (Sleutjes and Schutjens, 2012). However, over the last decade attempts have been made to address this lack of (empirical) research (Davidsson and Honig, 2003; Schutjens and Stam, 2003; Jack et al., 2008; Jack et al., 2010, Anderson et al., 2010; Batjargal, 2010). These, mainly small-scale, longitudinal empirical studies have shown that both network tie strength, network size and network contact type change over time. A well-known example is the panel study by Davidsson and Honig (2003). They show that over the firm life course, the role of weak ties with business associations or team members takes over the role of strong ties (family, relatives, close friends) for business purposes due to the specific needs of entrepreneurs to become profitable. Schutjens and Stam (2003) found that over a period of five years entrepreneurs annotated their contacts differently, often changing from commercial to social. The final example is the study by Batjargal (2010) on the effect of network skills and strategies of Internet entrepreneurs in the Chinese city of Beijing on the changes in their network over time. Batjargal followed a panel of entrepreneurs over a period of two years and found that networking skills are important to obtain an advantageous position in the network over time (Batjargal, 2010).

Notwithstanding recent empirical studies, network dynamics is still an under-researched field of study (Jack, 2010). Research with a more theoretical focus does exist. However, these – mostly conceptual – studies often use models to discuss ideal types of network change. Birley and Cromie's model (1988) of network development, for example, consists of two stages, the start-up stage and the stage of firm growth. During the start-up stage

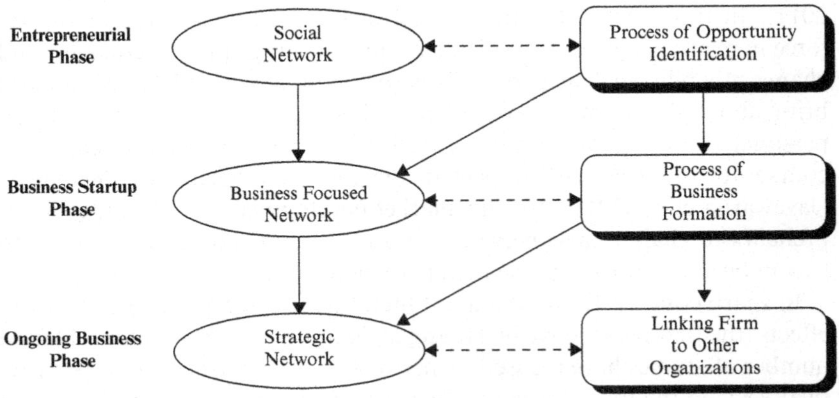

Source: Butler and Hansen (1991).

Figure 2.1 The model of entrepreneurial network evolution

mainly social or private-related network contacts dominate the network of the entrepreneur. As the firm moves into the next stage, parts of the social network will be replaced by business contacts in order to keep up with the changing needs of the entrepreneur (Birley and Cromie, 1988). Another straightforward and therefore well-cited example is the model by Butler and Hansen (1991) addressed earlier, describing networks developing from a pre-start-up phase to an ongoing business phase, roughly chronologically (Figure 2.1).

In the first phase the social network (i.e. family and friends) of the entrepreneur is important, as the network contacts provide the entrepreneur with diverse information on business opportunities. But for a business start-up to succeed, the entrepreneurial network needs to be a mix of both old private-related contacts and new business-related contacts. These business-related contacts are important for the entrepreneur in providing information needed to face new challenges in the start-up process. To reach the final phase of firm growth and profit, the entrepreneur needs to shield his/her own firm from competitors by forming ties with competing firms. This strategic network with a mutually dependent relationship is important for the continued survival of the firm (Butler and Hansen, 1991).

The model of Butler and Hansen (1991) implies that every entrepreneur has to go through the same steps to get to the final, ongoing business phase, and that their networks change accordingly (Butler and Hansen, 1991; Schutjens and Stam, 2003). The question is whether this is really the case. Do entrepreneurial networks evolve in the same, orderly way, or do different, more chaotic forms exist? By empirically measuring network change over a period of five years, we hope to give a more realistic view of network dynamics. As we approach existing entrepreneurs (and in this sense necessarily skip the pre-start-up phase of Butler and Hansen's model), we explore only the network changes of businesses that were either in the start-up phase or the ongoing business phase in 2008 (in the first wave). In contrast to Butler and Hansen (1991), we study different dimensions in the evolution of entrepreneurial networks, also paying attention to the meaning of local and non-local ties and the potential overlap in private-related and business-related network contacts.

DATA AND METHODS

The Survey on the Social Networks of Entrepreneurs

In this study we use data from two waves of The Survey on the Social Networks of Entrepreneurs, collected in 2008 and 2013 (referred to as SSNE1 and SSNE2 respectively). This panel study primarily focuses on networks, performance and local involvement of small and medium-sized entrepreneurs in Dutch residential neighborhoods. The data collection follows the design of a larger academic survey on the networks of inhabitants of Dutch neighborhoods in 2000 (Survey on the Social Networks of the Dutch, SSND). In this 2000 survey, a sample of 40 out of the approximately 500 municipalities in the Netherlands was drawn, in both urban and rural areas (see Figure 2.2). For each municipality, four neighborhoods were randomly selected (in one case five neighborhoods were selected). The sampled neighborhoods can be defined as residential, as the number of inhabitants and building density were taken into account when drawing the sample. Five-digit postal code districts are used to define the neighborhoods. This demarcation resembles the routes of postal workers and mostly involves areas without physical barriers (Mollenhorst et al., 2009; Sleutjes and Schutjens, 2012). On average, a five-digit postal code area contains 230 addresses (Mollenhorst et al., 2009; Sleutjes and Schutjens, 2012).

In 2008, in each of the 161 sampled neighborhoods, up to 12 private firms (if present) were contacted by telephone to determine whether the owner or entrepreneur also lived in or near the neighborhood, in order to explore the interdependency of entrepreneurs, firms and local social and physical interaction at the neighborhood level (as this was the aim of the original study). As a result, a firm was included in the sample only if the entrepreneur lived at the same address as or within ten minutes' walking distance from his or her firm (Sleutjes and Schutjens, 2012). The first wave

Source: Survey on Social Networks of the Dutch (SSND); see Mollenhorst et al. (2009).

Figure 2.2 The 40 municipalities included in the Survey on the Social Networks of Entrepreneurs (SSNE)

of this panel study (SSNE1) contains information on 385 firms and their entrepreneurs, collected in 2008 in 145 Dutch residential neighborhoods. In 2013, five years after the first wave, all 385 respondents were contacted to participate in a second wave (SSNE2), of whom 214 responded positively. This resulted in panel data (2008 and 2013) of the networks of 214 entrepreneurs in over 140 Dutch residential neighborhoods.

Network Delineation

In both waves of the SSNE, all entrepreneurs were interviewed about various kinds of personal and professional relationships, using name-generating questions. By using this method, the egocentric networks of the entrepreneurs can be constructed, giving insights into the composition and density of the network (Burt, 1992; Arregle et al., 2013).

A large part of existing research on the networks of entrepreneurs focuses on the core business discussion network (Renzulli and Aldrich, 2005; Arregle et al., 2013). Here, we focus on both the business and the private networks of the entrepreneurs. With the use of four name-generating questions, we have acquired the network contacts that are used for private purposes and those that serve business purposes. In the questionnaire, entrepreneurs were allowed to give the initials of persons they had already mentioned in response to previous name-generating questions, and could add a maximum of five new persons at each of the following four name-generating questions.

The first name-generating question regarding private purposes addressed the so-called 'core discussion network'. The question reads: 'With whom did you discuss important personal matters during the last six months?' (cf. Burt, 1984; Marsden, 1987; Bailey and Marsden, 1999). Next to these emotional support contacts, we also look at more practical means of help. For that reason, we asked, 'If you are doing an odd job at home and you need someone to give a hand, e.g., to carry furniture or to hold a ladder, whom do you ask for help?' Alters who were mentioned at one or both of these questions are seen as part of the respondent's network used for private purposes.

Regarding business purposes, similar questions related to the business part of the entrepreneurial network were asked. The business-related core discussion network was constituted by the answer to the question: 'With whom did you discuss important matters regarding your firm and its development during the last six months?' (cf. Burt, 1984; Marsden, 1987; Bailey and Marsden, 1999). Practical help was addressed by the question: 'If you are doing odd jobs regarding the firm and you need someone to give a hand, e.g., to carry furniture or to hold a ladder, whom do you ask for help?' Again, a network tie that was mentioned at one or both of the business-related questions is understood to belong to the business network of the entrepreneur.

Indeed, network contacts can fulfill roles within both the private and the business networks. As mentioned before, we are particularly interested in this type of role overlap in entrepreneurial networks and therefore discuss this below. For reasons of simplicity, in the following sections we use (a) the term 'private contacts' to refer to network contacts with whom important personal matters are discussed and/or who can be asked for practical support in or around the house, (b) the term 'business contacts' to refer to network contacts with whom business-related matters are discussed and/or who can be asked for business-related practical support, (c) the term 'contacts for emotional support' to refer to network contacts with whom personal and/or business-related matters are discussed, and (d) the term 'contacts for practical support' to refer to network contacts who can be asked for private-related and/or business-related practical support.

Measurements

Dependent variables

The network size and three dimensions of the network composition are used as dependent variables in our research. The first dependent variable is the change in entrepreneurial network size between the two waves (i.e. 2008 and 2013). Both the network size in 2008 and 2013, and the network change over time, are measured as the total number of network contacts for each respondent (every alter is counted once, irrespective of their different roles within the network).

After having collected the names or initials of all these network contacts, various name-interpreting questions were asked with regard to each of these alters. Among other things, we asked for the type of relationship between the respondent and the alter, and where the alter resides. In the empirical analyses, the following three dimensions of the entrepreneurial network composition are taken into account (see Arregle et al., 2013; Johannisson, 2011; Schutjens and Völker, 2010; Welter, 2011, among others).

First, we look at family versus non-family network contacts. In the survey, 25 types of relationships between the entrepreneur and their alters are discerned. This list ranges from romantic partner to colleague and neighbor.[1] An alter is considered 'a family contact' when he/she is mentioned as romantic partner, parent, child, parent-in-law, sibling or other family member (irrespective of whether he or she is living in the same house). The number of family contacts in a network is often seen as an indicator of the strength of ties, but a family member is not necessarily a strong tie. Therefore we prefer to use the family versus non-family distinction when giving an insight into the composition of the social networks of the entrepreneurs.

Second, local and non-local network contacts are discerned. As discussed in the previous section, the neighborhood level may be the appropriate scale for social capital entrepreneurs to tap into, in particular for small and medium-sized entrepreneurs whose firms are located in – and who themselves are living in or close to – these residential neighborhoods. Network contacts are considered 'local' if they (or their firm) are located within a 1 km range from the respondent, with household members excluded (cf. Sleutjes and Schutjens, 2012).

Third, role overlap within the entrepreneurial networks is addressed. If the private and professional lives of local entrepreneurs are to some extent intertwined, it is likely that there will be some overlap between the network parts used for private purposes and the parts of the entrepreneurial networks used for business purposes. In this study, we consider overlapping network contacts as those network contacts who are used for both private and business purposes. This means that this network contact is mentioned in response to at least one question concerning the private purposes and at least one question concerning the business purposes of the social network of an entrepreneur.

Independent variables

Our multivariate analyses on the size and composition of entrepreneurial networks, as well as changes in both size and composition, include several independent variables. In every model the age of the respondent, the firm's age and the economic sector (serving local or non-local markets) are included. From the literature on social networks it is understood that the age of the entrepreneur is related to network size and change over time, as it is an indicator of the time available to form a network. The age of the firm is used to gain insight into the differences between firms at different stages of the life cycle, which is also an important criterion in Butler and Hansen's original model (1991). Both the age of the firm and of the entrepreneur are divided by ten years, after which we center these variables around the mean. At the level of the firm's business activities, we distinguish between firms that are locally oriented and non-locally oriented. Firms active within, for example, retail, the catering industry, personal services and private education serve the local market, whereas sectors such as business services and manufacturing are seen as non-locally oriented. This distinction is important as the networks of firms that have to rely on the local environment for customers may be different from firms that have a broader market orientation (Sleutjes and Schutjens, 2012).

Information on relocation to outside the neighborhood since 2008 is also included in the model, whereby we distinguish between firm relocation and/or residential relocation of the entrepreneurs themselves. This dummy variable uses the category 'no firm relocation' as the reference category. Both firm and personal relocation can cause changes in the network of an entrepreneur. Firm relocation is seen as a firm-internal force and residential relocation can be thought of as a force external to the firm.

Finally, when estimating changes in network size and composition between 2008 and 2013, we take network size in 2008 into account.

Analytical strategy

In the empirical analysis we used OLS regression models to explore network change in the period between 2008 and 2013. A significance level of 95 percent ($p < 0.05$) is applied to all models, but we decided to include the parameter effects significant at a 90 percent significance level also in order to give an exhaustive overview of the findings. In Tables 2.1, 2.2 and 2.3, network change was measured in total number of network contacts. Additional analyses measuring the proportional network change can be found in Appendix Tables 2A.1 and 2A.2.

RESULTS

Table 2.1 and Figure 2.3 present descriptive results on the size and composition of the networks of all entrepreneurs who participated in both waves of our survey, who answered the complete network module in our questionnaire, and who were still entrepreneurs in 2013. Of all 214 respondents who participated in both waves, 14 respondents were no longer entrepreneurs in 2013, while another 3 respondents did not (correctly) answer all four network questions. This implies that the results presented in this section are based on a set of 197 entrepreneurs.

Table 2.1 shows that in 2013, the entrepreneurs on average mention 4.05 network contacts with whom they discuss important matters (regarding personal and/or business matters) and/or whom they could ask for practical support (for private and/or business purposes). An average of 3.08 of these network contacts are private-related contacts (providing emotional and/or practical support), while 2.03 of them are business-related contacts. Indeed, this implies that 1.06 network contacts on average are mentioned in response to at least one private-related name-generating question and at least one business-related name-generating question. We also see that an average number of 1.66 family contacts are mentioned in 2013. Furthermore, 1.20 network contacts live within a range of 1 km from the respondent (household members excluded).

As shown in Table 2.1, there is no significant change in the average size of the networks of the respondents between 2008 and 2013. But regarding network composition change, two findings stand out. First, the average number of contacts that may provide practical help has grown significantly, from 1.90 in 2008 to 2.18 in 2013. This growth is apparent in the category practical help for business purposes in particular, as this number increased significantly from 0.61 to 0.83 on average. Second, the average number of local network contacts has increased as well. While in 2008 the entrepreneurs reported 0.91 local network contacts on average, this

Table 2.1 Network changes between 2008 and 2013 (average, standard deviation in parentheses)

	2008	2013	Change
Network size	3.79 (2.07)	4.05 (2.08)	+0.26
Number of private-related contacts[1]	2.94 (1.76)	3.08 (1.70)	+0.13
Percentage of private-related contacts	0.78 (0.23)	0.77 (0.24)	−0.01
Number of business-related contacts[2]	1.83 (1.23)	2.03 (1.33)	+0.20†
Percentage of business-related contacts	0.50 (0.29)	0.53 (0.29)	+0.02
Number of family contacts in network[3]	1.70 (1.16)	1.66 (1.07)	−0.04
Percentage of family contacts in network	0.49 (0.31)	0.45 (0.29)	−0.03†
Number of local network ties in network[4]	0.91 (1.09)	1.20 (1.27)	+0.28**
Percentage of local network ties in network	0.21 (0.24)	0.28 (0.25)	+0.06**
Number of contacts for emotional support[5]	2.59 (1.60)	2.76 (1.55)	+0.16
Percentage of contacts for emotional support	0.69 (0.25)	0.69 (0.23)	+0.00
Number of contacts for practical support[6]	1.90 (1.33)	2.18 (1.43)	+0.27*
Percentage of contacts for practical support	0.50 (0.29)	0.56 (0.26)	+0.05*
Number of private emotional support contacts	1.82 (1.37)	1.99 (1.32)	+0.16
Number of business emotional support contacts	1.49 (1.03)	1.62 (1.03)	+0.13
Number of private practical support contacts	1.58 (1.19)	1.68 (1.12)	+0.11
Number of business practical support contacts	0.61 (0.80)	0.83 (1.09)	+0.22**

Table 2.1 (continued)

	2008	2013	Change
Number of overlap business–private-related contacts[7]	0.98 (0.94)	1.06 (0.87)	+0.07
Percentage of overlap business–private-related contacts	0.30 (0.32)	0.31 (0.28)	+0.00

Notes:

1 Private-related contacts were mentioned in response to at least one of the questions concerning either private emotional support or private practical support.

2 Business-related contacts were mentioned in response to at least one of the questions concerning either business emotional support or business practical support.

3 Family contacts = including partner living in the same house and in-laws. Missing values = no family members.

4 Local = person is located within a 1 km range of the respondent, excluding housemates.

5 Contacts for emotional support were mentioned in response to at least one of the questions concerning either private emotional support or business emotional support.

6 Contacts for practical support were mentioned in response to at least one or both questions concerning either private practical support or business practical support.

7 Overlap = network contact is mentioned in response to at least one question concerning the private purposes and at least one question concerning the business purposes of the entrepreneurial network.

† $p < 0.10$, * $p < 0.05$, ** $p < 0.01$, *** $p < 0.001$.

Source: SSNE 2008 and 2013.

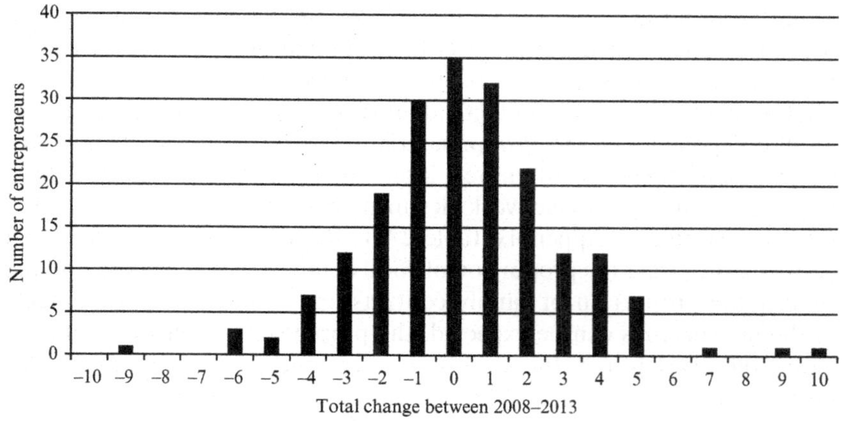

Source: SSNE 2008 and 2013.

Figure 2.3 Changes in the total number of network contacts between 2008 and 2013

number increased substantially to 1.20 in 2013. This outcome, together with the significant rise in the proportion of local network ties (see Appendix Table 2A.2), indicates that over time the neighborhood became a more important arena for network contacts of the entrepreneurs.

Although Table 2.1 indicates that the average network size of the entrepreneurs did not change significantly between 2008 and 2013, neither the size nor the composition of the networks of individual entrepreneurs remained stable over time. The histogram as presented in Figure 2.3 shows that, while 35 entrepreneurs reported the same number of network contacts during both interviews, most entrepreneurs added or removed one or more contacts to or from their network. On top of that, initial network contacts may have been replaced by other contacts, which means that also among those whose network size remained stable in terms of the total number of ties reported, network contact changes occurred.[2]

Altogether, the aforementioned results provide sufficient reason to zoom in on the changes that have taken place between 2008 and 2013 in the size and composition of the networks of entrepreneurs, and to explore the factors related to these changes. Table 2.3 presents results of a number of regression models on network changes, controlling for both the initial number of network contacts (i.e. mentioned in 2008) and the initial number of specific types of network contacts. However, before analyzing network changes, it is crucial to understand the network structure in 2008. We analyze the factors related to the initial size and composition of entrepreneurial networks in Table 2.2. We find no evidence that age of the entrepreneur, firm age or local firm orientation relate to the overall network size in 2008 (Table 2.2). In 2008, however, network size (i.e. the total number of network contacts) does relate significantly and positively to all components of the entrepreneurial networks analyzed. This makes sense, as entrepreneurs who have a larger network are more likely to have more different types of network ties in their network. Additional analyses, as presented in Appendix Table 2A.1, show that the larger the total network, the larger the proportion of local contacts in the network and the smaller the proportion of family contacts and business-related contacts in the network. As can be expected, the proportion of network contacts with 'role overlap' (i.e. those who are mentioned for private as well as business purposes) is smaller among entrepreneurs with larger networks (see Appendix Table 2A.1). This suggests that those with relatively small networks to a certain extent compensate for a potential lower amount of available support with an increase in role overlap. Next to network size, the other factors included in the analysis only show that older entrepreneurs reported a relatively small number of network contacts for business purposes and relatively many network contacts for private purposes.

Table 2.3 shows that the initial total network size significantly and negatively relates to the change in network size between 2008 and 2013. In other words, small initial networks are more likely to expand than larger initial networks, while entrepreneurs who had a relatively large network in 2008 are most likely to have experienced a downsizing of their network. Network size is also significantly associated with firm age, as older firms experienced a slightly stronger decrease in the total number of network contacts between 2008 and 2013 than younger firms.

Regarding changes in network composition, each model in Table 2.3 shows that the initial number of a particular type of contact is significantly and negatively associated with a change in the number of that particular type. Only with regard to family contacts we see an additional effect of the overall number of network contacts, which means that over a five-year period, a decrease in the number of family contacts in the network is more likely, not only for entrepreneurs who had relatively many family contacts in their network, but even more so for those who had a larger network in 2008. Additional analyses on proportions of networks instead of number of network contacts yield the same results (Appendix Table 2A.2).

Furthermore, Table 2.3 shows that the effects of the independent variables differ per model. Entrepreneurs who both relocated their firm and moved house privately reported an increase in the number of contacts for practical support compared to entrepreneurs who did not relocate privately nor relocate the firm. This result seems to make sense as a relocation

Table 2.2 Network size and network composition in 2008

		Network composition						
	Network size	Number of contacts for emotional support	Number of contacts for practical support	Number of business-related contacts	Number of private-related contacts	Number of local network contacts	Number of family contacts	Number of overlapping contacts[a]
Total number of network contacts		0.65***	0.47***	0.39***	0.75***	0.30***	0.28***	0.14***
Age of the entrepreneur (per 10 years)[b]	−0.10	−0.07	0.00	−0.23***	0.12*	0.00	−0.13†	−0.10
Age of the firm (per 10 years)[b]	−0.03	−0.05†	0.00	0.04	−0.04	0.03	0.06†	0.00
Locally orientated firm[c]	−0.31	0.05	0.22	0.07	0.09	−0.11	0.15	0.16
Constant	3.89***	0.07	0.03	0.32***	0.04	−0.20	0.55***	0.36*
Adj. R^2	−0.00	0.73	0.52	0.45	0.78	0.33	0.27	0.10
N	197	197	197	197	197	197	197	197

Notes:

[a] Overlapping contacts are ties that are both business-related and private-related contacts.
[b] Variable centered around the mean.
[c] Locally orientated firms: firms active in retail and catering industry, personal services and private education.
† $p < 0.10$, * $p < 0.05$, ** $p < 0.01$, *** $p < 0.001$.

Source: SSNE 2008 and 2013.

Table 2.3 Change in network size and network composition between 2008 and 2013

		Network composition						
	Change in network size	Change in number of contacts for emotional support	Change in number of contacts for practical support	Change in number of business-related contacts	Change in number of private-related contacts	Change in number of local network contacts	Change in number of family contacts	Change in number of overlapping contacts[a]
Number of network contacts (2008)	−0.82***						−0.09*	
Number of contacts for emotional support (2008)		−0.81***						
Number of contacts for practical support (2008)			−0.89***					
Number of business-related contacts (2008)				−0.71***				
Number of private-related contacts (2008)					−0.87***			
Number of local network contacts (2008)						−0.72***		
Number of family contacts (2008)							−0.62***	

Number of overlapping contacts (2008)								−0.83***
Age of the entrepreneur (per 10 years)[b]	−0.05	−0.08	−0.00	−0.22*	−0.00	0.05	0.01	−0.19**
Age of the firm (per 10 years)[b]	−0.15*	−0.10†	−0.03	−0.02	−0.10†	−0.04	−0.00	0.02
Move since 2008:								
No move nor relocation	ref.	ref.	ref.	ref.	ref.	ref.	ref.	ref.
Only residential move	−0.36	0.01	−0.86	−0.45	−0.11	−0.68	0.35	−0.20
Only firm relocation	−0.22	0.57	−0.31	−0.39	0.12	−0.37	−0.07	−0.05
Both residential move and firm relocation	0.80	0.06	1.03*	0.45	0.50	0.13	0.47	0.17
Locally orientated firm[c]	−0.59†	−0.14	−0.45*	0.02	−0.61*	−0.26	−0.27†	0.00
Constant	3.59***	2.30***	2.11***	1.50***	2.90***	1.06*	1.46**	0.89***
Adj. R^2	0.41	0.40	0.43	0.30	0.46	0.28	0.41	0.45
N	197	197	197	197	197	197	197	197

Notes:
[a] Overlapping contacts are ties that are both business-related and private-related.
[b] Variable centered around the mean.
[c] Locally orientated firms: firms active in retail and catering industry, personal services and private education.
† $p < 0.10$, * $p < 0.05$, ** $p < 0.01$, *** $p < 0.001$.

Source: SSNE 2008 and 2013.

usually involves a great deal of work and therefore practical help is often needed and asked for.

Next, we find a significant negative association between the age of the entrepreneur and a change in the number of business-related contacts. This implies that, while Table 2.2 already showed that older entrepreneurs relied less on business-related contacts in 2008, they also reported a relatively large decrease in business-related contacts between 2008 and 2013. Older entrepreneurs might have gathered enough information over the course of their life to be less dependent on help for business purposes.

Compared to firms serving non-local markets, firms active in locally orientated sectors are more likely to have reported decreasing numbers of both network contacts for practical support and private-related network contacts. In line with this, the additional analyses (see Appendix Table 2A.2) show that for these locally orientated firms, the proportion of contacts for emotional support and/or for business-related purposes significantly increased between 2008 and 2013.

Furthermore, we find a significant negative association between the age of the entrepreneur and the change in role overlap in the network. Older entrepreneurs are thus more likely to report a decrease in role overlap than younger entrepreneurs. Finally, additional analyses (Appendix Table 2A.2) show that the increase in the proportion of network overlap is smaller when entrepreneurs already had many overlapping network contacts in 2008, and, beyond that, is especially substantial for entrepreneurs who had a large initial network with a great deal of overlap.

CONCLUSION AND DISCUSSION

The main contribution of this chapter to the existing literature is the dynamic perspective adopted in studying social networks. Although promising efforts have recently been made, research on entrepreneurial networks still suffers from a lack of longitudinal panel studies. This is closely related to existing conceptual models of network development in which network change is often viewed as a straightforward and fixed development consisting of consecutive stages. To explore whether entrepreneurial networks in reality develop in such an orderly way, we have measured changes in the networks of individual Dutch entrepreneurs between 2008 and 2013.

First, we studied changes within the entrepreneurial networks as a whole. By looking at changes in the network size, we were able to measure the stability of the entrepreneurial networks over time. The panel of entrepreneurs did not show a significant change in average network size between 2008 and 2013 (3.79 and 4.05 respectively). But a detailed analysis at the entrepreneurial level showed significant network size change over time, as entrepreneurs with relatively large networks in 2008 experienced a downsizing of their networks, whereas small initial networks were more likely to expand over time. Older firms experienced a stronger decrease in terms of network size over time than younger firms, which indicates an overall convergence in network size.

Although, at first sight, network size seemed to stay quite stable, we found clear changes in network composition over the period studied. We explored three dimensions of network composition. The relevance of including a local dimension stems from our specific panel structure, as entrepreneurs of firms located in residential neighborhoods are likely to experience a blending of their private and business lives (cf. Johannisson's claim of 'the everydayness of entrepreneuring'). Regarding this local network dimension, we found that, on average, local network ties have become more important over time than non-local networks. This suggests that the local tissue is strengthening over time, as entrepreneurs increasingly find network contacts within their own neighborhood. Interestingly, we found that the local networks of entrepreneurs with firms targeting local markets changed in the same way as entrepreneurial networks with non-local firms: it seems that locally orientated firms did not rely more on local contacts than non-locally orientated firms.

The number of family contacts within the entrepreneurial networks is also taken into account as a specific dimension, as family members tend to be important network contacts and can be seen as an indication for the use of strong ties within a network (Arregle et al., 2015). We could not discern significant changes in the number of family contacts within the entrepreneurial networks. As such, there did not seem to be a shift from strong to weak ties over time, which is in line with the findings of Schutjens and Stam (2003).

The third dimension concerns role overlap within the network, as an entrepreneur can use his social capital to obtain valuable resources such as emotional support, information and tangible resources for business purposes, private purposes, or both. The entrepreneurs mentioned on average 4.0 network contacts in 2013, of which 3.1 were for private purposes and 2.2 for business purposes. This indicates that role overlap is present within entrepreneurial networks as 1.1 network contact on average gives support for both private and business purposes. Role overlap is found to be more important for entrepreneurs with a small network than for entrepreneurs who have a larger network, which is to be expected as the former group had to compensate for their limited network size by getting support from the same people for different purposes. At the entrepreneurial level, we found that the role overlap between 2008 and 2013 decreased for older entrepreneurs and for entrepreneurs who already had a great deal of overlap in their networks.

Limitations

The study presented in this chapter has some limitations. First, the focus of our study is on the networks of entrepreneurs whose firms are located in residential neighborhoods in the Netherlands. Our findings are therefore valid within residential districts in the Dutch context, which makes generalization of the outcomes difficult. This explicitly goes for our results on the local dimension of networks, as we analyzed only entrepreneurs who are themselves also located in these residential neighborhoods. It can be assumed that entrepreneurs located in or in close proximity to their homes have a relatively strong relationship with the local environment, which may be different for entrepreneurs who live further from their firm location.

Second, our data collection took place between 2007 and 2013, a period characterized by economic recession in the Western world. This economic situation could also have influenced the outcomes of our study, as, in difficult times, entrepreneurs may have to rely on more or different network members. Only from a third wave of the panel study, hopefully after this economic dip, can we learn whether, and, if so, to what extent, this recession has influenced the entrepreneurial networks and therefore our results.

Finally, although the explorative character of this chapter has yielded interesting initial descriptions of the changes in network size and network composition and a first exploration of the factors involved in these changes, there is a need for additional analyses resulting in a thorough insight in the mechanisms behind network change.

Options for Future Research

Of course, the limitations described above are the exciting windows of opportunity in our future research. Our extensive panel dataset contains rich information on 214 entrepreneurs in 2008 and 2014, but also on their respective network contacts (alters), the quality of every relationship between the entrepreneur and alter, and even on the relationships between the main alters in the network. As such, this explorative chapter has only touched upon the mere surface of the huge amount of network information available. Furthermore, the great variety in the change of network size depicted in the bar diagram (Figure 2.3) already suggests quite turbulent networks at the entrepreneurial level. Although still untapped, detailed information is available on new, changing and exiting network contacts and their respective importance in the network of entrepreneurs. This information can help to answer remaining questions, such as: Which ties remain in the network? And which ones are cut – and why? Jack et al. (2008), for instance, found that firms are reluctant to cut their older ties over time and that they often complement older ties with new ones, with whom they have already had some contact in the past (pre-tested ties). Finally, there is still more data available from the SSNE on a variety of topics, such as the relationships of the entrepreneurs with business associates, private neighbors and business neighbors. Exploring these data in future work and thereby unraveling the changing networks of entrepreneurs will shed more and brighter light on the dynamics of social capital – a person's and an entrepreneur's crucial asset in our increasingly interconnected and relational world.

NOTES

* This chapter is part of the research project 'Entrepreneurs in Residential Neighborhoods: A Study on Networks, Firm Success and Strategies', which is funded by a Netherlands Organization for Scientific Research (NWO) Research Talent Grant.

1. Answer categories are 'romantic partner, living in', 'romantic partner, not living in', 'former romantic partner', 'parent, living in', 'parent, not living in', 'child, living in', 'child, not living in', 'parent in-law, living in', 'parent in-law, not living in', 'sibling, living in', 'sibling, not living in', 'other relative, living in', 'other relative, not living in', 'friend', 'boss', 'direct colleague', 'other colleague', 'former colleague', 'someone who works for you', 'someone from the neighborhood', 'next-door neighbor', 'former neighbor', 'co-member of a club or association', 'acquaintance' or 'other'.
2. An analysis and interpretation of such changes on the relationship level, however, is beyond the scope of this chapter.

REFERENCES

Anderson, A.R., S. Drakopoulou Dodd and S.L. Jack (2010), 'Network practices and entrepreneurial growth', *Scandinavian Journal of Management*, **26** (2), 121–33.

Arregle, J.-L., B. Batjargal, M.A. Hitt, J.W. Webb, T. Miller and S.A. Tsui (2015), 'Family ties in entrepreneurs' social networks and new venture growth', *Entrepreneurship Theory and Practice*, **39** (2), 313–44.

Bailey, S. and P.V. Marsden (1999), 'Interpretation and interview context: examining the general social survey name generator using cognitive methods', *Social Networks*, **21**, 287–309.

Batjargal, B. (2010), 'Network dynamics and new ventures in China: a longitudinal study', *Entrepreneurship & Regional Development*, **22** (2), 139–53.

Birley, S. and S. Cromie (1988), 'Entrepreneurial networks in Northern Ireland', Ulster Business School, Belfast.

Burt, R.S. (1984), 'Network items and the general social survey', *Social Networks*, **6**, 293–339.

Burt, R.S. (1992), 'Structural holes and good ideas', *American Journal of Sociology*, **110**, 349–99.
Burt, R.S. (2000), 'The network structure of social capital', *Research in Organizational Behavior*, **22**, 345–423.
Butler, J.E. and G.S. Hansen (1991), 'Network evolution, entrepreneurial success, and regional development', *Entrepreneurship and Regional Development*, **3**, 1–16.
Cooke, P. (2007), 'Social capital, embeddedness, and market interactions: an analysis of firm performance in UK regions', *Review of Social Economy*, **65** (1), 79–106.
Davidsson, P. and B. Honig (2003), 'The role of social and human capital among nascent entrepreneurs', *Journal of Business Venturing*, **18** (3), 301–31.
Elfring, T. and W. Hulsink (2007), 'Networking by entrepreneurs: patterns of tie formation in emerging organizations', *Organization Studies*, **28** (12), 1849–72.
Folmer, E. (2014), 'Entrepreneurship in the neighborhood: shifting patterns of economic activities in residential neighborhoods in five Dutch cities', *Journal of Urban Affairs*, **36** (4), 742–59.
Folmer, E. and A. Risselada (2013), 'Planning the neighbourhood economy: land-use plans and the economic potential of urban residential neighbourhoods in the Netherlands', *European Planning Studies*, **21** (12), 1873–94.
Garnsey, E. (1998), 'A theory of the early growth of the firm', *Industrial and Corporate Change*, **7** (3), 523–56.
Gedajlovic, E., B. Honig, C.B. Moore, G.T. Payne and M. Wright (2013), 'Social capital and entrepreneurship: a schema and research agenda', *Entrepreneurship Theory and Practice*, **37** (3), 455–78.
Greve, A. and J. Salaff (2003), 'Social networks and entrepreneurship', *Entrepreneurship Theory and Practice*, **28** (1), 1–22.
Granovetter, M. (1973), 'The strength of weak ties', *American Journal of Sociology*, **78**, 1360–80.
Hoang, H. and B. Antoncic (2003), 'Network-based research in entrepreneurship: a critical review', *Journal of Business Venturing*, **18** (2), 165–87.
Jack, S.L. (2005), 'The role, use and activation of strong and weak network ties: a qualitative analysis', *Journal of Management Studies*, **42** (6), 1233–59.
Jack, S.L. (2010), 'Approaches to studying networks: implications and outcomes', *Journal of Business Venturing*, **25** (1), 120–37.
Jack, S.L, A.R. Anderson, S. Moult and S. Dodd (2010), 'An entrepreneurial network evolving: patterns of change', *International Small Business Journal*, **28** (4), 315–37.
Jack, S.L., S. Drakopolou Dodd and A.R. Anderson (2008), 'Change and the development of entrepreneurial networks over time: a processual perspective', *Entrepreneurship and Regional Development*, **20** (2), 125–59.
Jayawarna, D., J. Rouse and J. Kitching (2011), 'Entrepreneur motivations and life course', *International Small Business Journal*, **31** (1), 34–56.
Johannisson, B. (2011), 'Towards a practice theory of entrepreneuring', *Small Business Economics*, **36** (2), 135–50.
Knoben, J. (2011), 'The geographic distance of relocation search: an extended resource-based perspective', *Economic Geography*, **87** (4), 371–92.
Lavie, D. (2006), 'The competitive advantage of interconnected firms: an extension of the resource-based view', *The Academy of Management Review*, **31** (3), 638–58.
Lechner, C. and M. Dowling (2003), 'Firm networks: external relationships as sources

for the growth and competitiveness of entrepreneurial firms', *Entrepreneurship & Regional Development*, **15** (1), 1–26.
Lechner, C., M. Dowling and I. Welpe (2006), 'Firm networks and firm development: the role of the relational mix', *Journal of Business Venturing*, **21** (4), 514–40.
Lin, N. and M. Dumin (1986), 'Access to occupations through social ties', *Social Networks*, **8**, 365–85.
Marsden, P.V. (1987), 'Core discussion networks of Americans', *American Sociological Review*, **52**, 122–31.
Martinez, M.A. and H.E. Aldrich (2011), 'Networking strategies for entrepreneurs: balancing cohesion and diversity', *International Journal of Entrepreneurial Behaviour & Research*, **17**, 7–38.
Mason, C., S. Carter and S. Tagg (2011), 'Invisible businesses: the characteristics of home-based businesses in the United Kingdom', *Regional Studies*, **45** (5), 625–39.
Mollenhorst, G., B. Volker and H. Flap (2014), 'Changes in personal relationships: how social contexts affect the emergence and discontinuation of relationships', *Social Networks*, **37**, 65–80.
Nahapiet, J. and S. Goshal (1998), 'Social capital, intellectual capital, and the organisational advantage', *Academy of Management Review*, **23** (2), 242–66.
Renzulli, L.A. and H. Aldrich (2005), 'Who can you turn to? Tie activation within core business discussion networks', *Social Forces*, **84** (1), 323–41.
Röper, A., B. Völker and H. Flap (2009), 'Social networks and getting a home: do contacts matter?', *Social Networks*, **31** (1), 40–51.
Schutjens, V. and B. Völker (2010), 'Space and social capital: the degree of locality in entrepreneurs' contacts and its consequences for firm success', *European Planning Studies*, **18** (6), 941–63.
Schutjens, V. and E. Stam (2003), 'The evolution and nature of young firm networks: a longitudinal perspective', *Small Business Economics*, **21**, 115–34.
Sleutjes, B. and V. Schutjens (2012), 'The added value of firm networks: an empirical study of local firm success determinants', *Entrepreneurship Research Journal*, **2** (2), 1–29.
Sleutjes, B., F. Van Oort and V. Schutjens (2012), 'A place for area-based policy? The survival and growth of local firms in Dutch residential neighborhoods', *Journal of Urban Affairs*, **34** (5), 533–58.
Slotte-Kock, S. and N. Coviello (2010), 'Entrepreneurship research on network processes: a review and ways forward', *Entrepreneurship: Theory & Practice*, **34** (1), 31–57.
Stam, W., S. Arzlanian and T. Elfring (2014), 'Social capital of entrepreneurs and small firm performance: a meta-analysis of contextual and methodological moderators', *Journal of Business Venturing*, **29** (1), 152–73.
Watson, J. (2007), 'Modeling the relationship between networking and firm performance', *Journal of Business Venturing*, **22** (6), 852–74.
Welter, F. (2011), 'Contextualizing entrepreneurship – conceptual challenges and ways forward', *Entrepreneurship Theory and Practice*, **35** (1), 165–84.
Westlund, H. and F. Adam (2010), 'Social capital and economic performance: a meta-analysis of 65 studies', *European Planning Studies*, **18** (6), 893–919.

APPENDIX

Table 2A.1 Network size and network composition in 2008 (proportions)

		Network composition						
	Network size	Proportion of contacts for emotional support	Proportion of contacts for practical support	Proportion of business related contacts	Proportion of private related contacts	Proportion of local network contacts	Proportion of family contacts	Proportion of overlapping contacts[a]
Total number of network contacts (2008)		−0.00	−0.00	−0.02*	−0.00	0.02***	−0.04***	−0.04***
Age of the entrepreneur (per 10 years)[b]	−0.10	−0.02	0.01	−0.04*	0.03†	0.00	−0.01	−0.02
Age of the firm (per 10 years)[b]	−0.03	−0.00	0.00	0.01	−0.00	0.01	0.01†	0.00
Locally orientated firm[c]	−0.31	−0.00	0.03	0.01	−0.00	0.00	−0.00	0.02
Constant	3.89***	0.73***	0.51***	0.57***	0.82***	0.11	0.66***	0.46***
Adj. R^2	−0.00	−0.00	−0.01	0.02	0.00	0.04	0.07	0.06
N	197	197	197	197	197	197	197	197

Notes:

[a] Overlapping contacts are ties that are both business-related and private-related.

[b] Variable centered around the mean.

[c] Locally orientated firms: firms active in retail and catering industry, personal services and private education.

† $p < 0.10$, * $p < 0.05$, ** $p < 0.01$, *** $p < 0.001$.

Source: SSNE 2008 and 2013.

Table 2A.2 Change in network size and network composition between 2008 and 2013 (proportion)

		Network composition						
	Change in network size	Change in proportion of contacts for emotional support	Change in proportion of contacts for practical support	Change in proportion of business related contacts	Change in proportion of private related contacts	Change in proportion of local network contacts	Change in proportion of family contacts	Change in proportion of overlapping contacts[a]
Number of network contacts (2008)	−0.82***	0.00	−0.01†	0.00	−0.01	0.00	0.00	0.02†
Proportion of contacts for emotional support (2008)		−0.79***						
Proportion of contacts for practical support (2008)			−0.81***					
Proportion of business related contacts (2008)				−0.80***				
Proportion of private related contacts (2008)					−0.91***			
Proportion of local network contacts (2008)						−0.75***		
Proportion of family contacts (2008)							−0.58***	
Proportion of overlapping contacts (2008)								−0.51***

Table 2A.2 (continued)

	Change in network size	Network composition						
		Change in proportion of contacts for emotional support	Change in proportion of contacts for practical support	Change in proportion of business related contacts	Change in proportion of private related contacts	Change in proportion of local network contacts	Change in proportion of family contacts	Change in proportion of overlapping contacts[a]
Age of the entrepreneur (per 10 years)[b]								−0.10**
Age of the firm (per 10 years)[b]	−0.05	−0.02	0.02	−0.06**	0.01	0.03	0.00	−0.04*
Move since 2008:	−0.15*	−0.00	0.01	0.01	0.00	0.00	0.0*	0.01†
No move								
Only residential move	ref.	ref.	ref.	ref.	ref.	ref.	ref.	ref.
Only firm move	−0.36	0.03	−0.19†	−0.07	0.04	−0.16	0.11	−0.01
Both residential and firm move	−0.22	0.16	−0.07	−0.04	0.02	−0.11	0.01	−0.04
Locally orientated firm[c]	0.80	−0.10	0.06	−0.03	−0.00	−0.00	0.02	−0.04
	−0.59†	0.08*	−0.06	0.11**	−0.06†	−0.03	−0.00	0.07†
Constant	3.59***	0.52***	0.55***	0.38***	0.76***	0.23***	0.24	0.15***
Adj. R^2	0.41	0.44	0.47	0.42	0.42	0.34	0.30	0.46
N	197	197	197	197	197	197	197	197

Notes:
[a] Overlapping contacts are ties that are both business-related and private-related contacts.
[b] Variable centered around the mean.
[c] Locally orientated firms: firms active in retail and catering industry, personal services and private education.
† $p < 0.10$, * $p < 0.05$, ** $p < 0.01$, *** $p < 0.001$.

Source: SSNE 2008 and 2013.

3. Entrepreneurs' social networks and formation of business opportunities: an exploratory study*

Didier Chabaud and Joseph Ngijol

Relying on social networks is fundamental to the entrepreneurial approach (Aldrich and Zimmer, 1986; Burt, 1992), and promotes both the survival and growth of young companies (Brüderl and Preisendörfer, 1998; Hite and Hesterly, 2001). While this general theme has given rise to numerous studies – Hoang and Antoncic (2003) have identified over 70 – few studies have focused on the role of social networks in business opportunities (Chabaud and Ngijol, 2005; Slotte-Kock and Coviello, 2010; Gedajlovic et al., 2013). Moreover, studies undertaken have generally favored the exploitation phase, which, chronologically, is situated downstream of the process of formation of business opportunities (Shane, 2003).[1] To go beneath what may appear as the visible part of the 'entrepreneurial iceberg', we believe it is essential to focus the discussion on what happens upstream. Understanding how entrepreneurs activate their networks and identifying the relational strategies they implement during the formation of business opportunities will enhance our knowledge. This information will also provide us with levers to support nascent entrepreneurs more effectively.

Our objective is to understand how entrepreneurs, in the context of innovation, use their social networks to validate the existence of business opportunities: to certify the existence of potential economic gain. The first section of the chapter highlights studies that associate social networks and business opportunities. We will focus on an empirical study undertaken among six innovative entrepreneurs in the service sector. The second section presents the cases studied as well as the method used. In the third section we present the results, before discussing them in the fourth section.

1. SOCIAL NETWORKS AND BUSINESS OPPORTUNITIES: TOWARDS A PROCESS-BASED APPROACH

Although social network theory (SNT) has been repeatedly applied to entrepreneurship, it is symptomatic that the review undertaken by Slotte-Kock and Coviello (2010) on social networks shares only one common reference with the review undertaken by Short et al. (2010) on opportunities.[2] The explanation probably lies in the particularity of the evidence provided by the survey undertaken by Slotte-Kock and Coviello (2010): these authors focused their study on the analysis of processes, but did not pay attention to the analyses that only highlighted, generically, the impact of social networks (SN).[3] Indeed, bringing the role of SN to the fore in the formation of opportunities severely limits literature that has often focused, generically speaking, on underscoring the role of SN and their positive or negative impact. Few studies have focused on the role of SN in the formation of business opportunities. Clarifying the concept of opportunity will enable us to better specify the role of SN in the formation of these business opportunities.

1.1 The Formation of Business Opportunities

An opportunity is 'an idea or a dream that is discovered or created by an entrepreneurial entity and that is revealed through analysis over time to be potentially lucrative' (Short et al., 2010, p. 55). Speaking of a business opportunity thus requires one to be rooted in current trends and take into account the dynamics of evolution.

This begins with formulating a business idea: linking a product and/or service with a commercial target, knowing that linking the two may be largely incomplete and uncertain. Both Ardichvili et al. (2003) and Short et al. (2010) underscore the extent to which opportunities are rooted in entrepreneurs' ideas and dreams. By analyzing creative business processes such as preparation and incubation,[4] it is therefore possible to focus on the origin of these aspects. However, a business idea only becomes an opportunity when, over time and after analysis, the idea is proven to be potentially lucrative (Short et al., 2010). This is the phase we seek to better understand.

The end of the process is, however, harder to define. Scholars share the view that the end of the process of formation of an opportunity cannot be identified in absolute terms. Indeed, while, from a logical perspective, the formation phase of an opportunity is followed by the exploitation phase (see Shane, 2003), these two phases overlap – or get mixed up – much more than they follow each other in a linear manner (Bhave, 1994; Davidsson,

2004; Vohora et al., 2004). For example, the formation of a business opportunity can lead to the initiation of a commercial activity involving the entrepreneur in a process of exploitation that, in turn, can have a retroactive effect on the initial business idea, thus changing it.

This characterization of the end of the process leads us to introduce an additional dimension in the definition of business opportunities: the demonstration by the entrepreneur of potential economic gain (Dutton and Jackson, 1987; Venkataraman, 1997). In this perspective, we consider that the process ends when an entrepreneur succeeds in demonstrating the existence of potential economic gain, thus obtaining some form of validation of the business opportunity. In the absence of such an element, one can speak only of a simple business idea or dream, and not a business opportunity in the full sense of the term.

The formation of a business opportunity can thus be considered to be a process that leads an entrepreneur to link a product (and/or a service) with a commercial target, resulting in the identification of the existence of an opportunity for economic gain. This vision underscores the significance of the activities carried out by the entrepreneur. These activities are connected by flows of interaction, information and interpretation that combine to provide a well-defined product and/or service to a clearly identified commercial target. What, then, is the role of SN?

1.2 Social Networks and the Formation of Business Opportunities

To understand the extent of the role of SN, the path followed by an entrepreneur to transform a business idea into a valid business opportunity must be identified. If one follows Aldrich and Zimmer (1986), two different solutions are possible:

- The entrepreneur can rely on his or her strong ties. According to Granovetter (1973, p. 1361), 'the strength of a tie is a (probably linear) combination of the amount of time, the emotional intensity, the intimacy (mutual confiding), and the reciprocal services which characterize the tie'. Strong ties are somewhat similar to 'ongoing' relationships and are thus trusted. This trust placed in family members and relatives, for instance, makes it possible to discuss with them while limiting opportunism issues (see Jack, 2005, p. 1244). We can thus understand the ease of dialogue between the entrepreneur and his or her interlocutor, and the limitations that arise due to the cognitive proximity that can exist within a dense network – leading to the redundancy of information – as well as the limited skills of the actors of this network.

- The entrepreneur can rely on weak ties (including distant relationships) to uncover business ideas or mobilize the relationships acquired notably in his or her past experience (professional or otherwise) in order to allow his or her project to be critically assessed by interlocutors who possess complementary knowledge or positions. Weak ties are often perceived as promoting access to differentiated networks, a source of greater informational added value (see Granovetter, 1973).[5]

The issue therefore revolves around the role of SN. These networks can have a direct impact on the process of formation of opportunities and on performance. However, it is also possible to underscore the extent to which the approach used to manage SN by the entrepreneur can differ throughout this process of formation (Chabaud and Ngijol, 2005; Kreiser et al., 2013). It must be stated that few studies have specifically addressed these aspects. Moreover, existing studies are consistent neither on the meaning of the proposals (and the results), nor on analyzed dimensions. We can identify different proposals in literature that address how social networks are activated: Table 3.1 allows such a prospect, around the main themes that constitute the discovery and evaluation of business ideas, access to resources and the issue of network management.[6] One of the few points of convergence among authors revolves around the role of strong ties in resource acquisition: these ties are thought to be the first to be mobilized by entrepreneurs to acquire resources. With regard to other points such as the source of business ideas or the evaluation of these ideas of the management of SN by entrepreneurs, the proposals put forward by existing studies frequently diverge. It is clear that these proposals from literature should be compared against empirical materials.

As soon as we turn to how entrepreneurs manage social networks, it seems necessary to reflect on the possible differences in modes of management, and on the fact that individuals – entrepreneurs – possibly possess different social competencies. As Kreiser et al. (2013, p. 545) have underscored: 'Social competence relates to the ability of an individual to effectively utilize his or her social skills (Baron and Markman, 2003)'. Social competence undoubtedly has an impact on the ability of a project initiator (nascent entrepreneur) to activate and/or develop his or her social networks in order to make them effective in the formation of opportunities. Diversity, efficiency and networking strategies should thus be incorporated into the analysis (Martinez and Aldrich, 2011).

Table 3.1 The SN–formation of opportunities connection: elements from literature

Entrepreneurial process	Generic proposals	The context
Discovery of business ideas	Weak ties are fundamental in providing access to non-redundant networks.	Following Granovetter's (1973) studies, we can mention the following authors: Hills et al. (1997): questionnaire survey among 190 entrepreneurs. Entrepreneurs who claimed to have found their business idea through their network tended to find more business ideas than those who declared to favor a purely individualistic approach. The distinction between weak and strong ties that gives primacy to weak ties was merely suggested but was not demonstrated empirically. Singh et al. (1999): questionnaire survey among 256 entrepreneurs in the IT sector. The entrepreneurs who had a network with the highest number of weak ties identified more business ideas than the others.
	Strong ties make it possible to access contextual information that is useful in recognizing opportunities.	Jack and Anderson (2002): ethnographic study of 7 rural entrepreneurs showed that the embedding of entrepreneurs in their rural context enabled them to recognize opportunities.
	Strong ties have a negative effect given the cognitive and informational proximity among network members.	Hills et al. (1997): the negative role of strong ties was assumed but not demonstrated empirically. Singh et al. (1999): entrepreneurs who possessed networks with a high number of strong ties identified fewer business ideas than the others.

Table 3.1 (continued)

Entrepreneurial process	Generic proposals	The context
	Moderating role of the degree of innovation.	Elfring and Hulsink (2003): based on 3 case studies, they showed that, in: • incremental innovation, weak ties were more important (advantage of access to non-redundant networks); • radical innovation, strong ties were more important as they made it possible to maintain confidence in the exchanges and access tacit knowledge. Interest of mixing strong–weak ties to discover opportunities in the event of radical innovations.
	Moderating role of the context of formation of the opportunity (freelance, incubated or spin-off).	Elfring and Hulsink (2007): 32 case studies conducted in the IT sector showed that freelancers favored weak ties and entrepreneurs in incubators and spin-offs favored strong ties rooted in their local context.
Evaluation of business ideas	Relying on weak ties.	De Koning (2003): a qualitative study based on interviews among entrepreneurs who successfully created several businesses. The entrepreneurs relied on weak ties when seeking and analyzing information. The manner in which the entrepreneur and these weak ties formed a relationship was, however, not explicitly addressed.

	Relying on strong ties.	De Koning (2003): entrepreneurs relied on strong ties during recurrent conversational activities in order to refine their idea and validate the relevance of their business model. Elfring and Hulsink (2003) emphasized the importance of strong ties during discussions on the potential of a business idea.
Obtaining resources	Strong ties are mobilized to gain access to resources.	Hite and Hesterly (2001); Jack and Anderson (2002); De Koning (2003); Elfring and Hulsink (2003, 2007); Jack (2005); Lechner et al. (2006).
SN management modes	'Opportunistic' management, i.e. the network structure is modified depending on the needs of the business project.	Larson and Starr (1993); Hite and Hesterly (2001); Chabaud and Ngijol (2005); Elfring and Hulsink (2007); Saleilles (2007).
	Weak ties are activated by relying on strong tics ('leverage').	Jack (2005) pointed out that strong ties have an essential mediation role that makes it possible to activate weak ties.
	Social skills play on the entrepreneur's ability to activate and develop the social network.	Baron and Markman (2000, 2003); Baron and Tang (2009); Lans et al. (2015).

2. CASE STUDIES AND RESEARCH METHODOLOGY

To analyze how entrepreneurs mobilize their SN when they develop a business opportunity and, in particular, to see whether they rely on strong and/or weak ties – and to eventually understand their motivations – we have focused on six case studies. For each of these case studies, we have reconstructed the individual networks that enabled the entrepreneurs to validate their business opportunity. The presentation of the case studies and the data collection method clearly reveal the significance of this approach.

2.1 Presentation of the Case Studies

This exploratory case study is based on a longitudinal study of six cases of the development of innovative services from the formulation of the business idea to the moment the business achieved a level of significant commercial activity. These projects of creation are innovative, as defined by authors such as Becker and Whisler (1967) and Drucker (1985): they all bring something new, a change from what is done in the sector targeted by the entrepreneur (see Table 3.2). The entrepreneurs in our study differed in three ways: (1) their profile: while three were trained engineers, the other three had a rather literary background; (2) their level of mastery of the business project: only three entrepreneurs – owing to their past experiences – had prior knowledge of their sector, whether in terms of knowledge of the target market (KT) or mastery of the technical skills needed to develop the proposed offer (Scientific Adventure and Synthesio); (3) getting help from a supporting structure: three entrepreneurs got support from an incubator, in this case the ESSEC academic incubator.

2.2 Research Methodology

Data collection was primarily based on interviews supplemented by secondary data such as archival materials and business documents. These documents enabled us to reconstruct entrepreneurs' social networks. The interviews took place between September 2004 and December 2006. To strengthen the internal validity of the research, all the interviews were conducted on the same principle, and reformulations were often used to reiterate in other words the subject's thoughts while respecting his or her framework (Merton et al., 1990). This made it possible to ensure the first step in data collection validation by the source (Baumard et al., 2001). Each case study was based on four interviews. Two semi-structured interviews were conducted: one with the entrepreneur and the other with one of his

Table 3.2 Summary of the case studies

Case study	Date of formation	Founder, training	Opportunity	Past experience of the founder (s)	Incubator
Alternacom	2002	J.-L. Regnier, business and finance	Introduction of new support media in the area of advertising displays: the surface provided by refrigerated vehicles in order to run campaigns on virgin territory in the area (highways), due to legislation prohibiting advertising displays fastened or installed on the ground if they are visible from a highway or a ramp within or outside towns.	No	Yes
Scientific Aventure (SA)	2001	C. Javault, engineer	Holiday offer around a theme, primarily the sciences, to youth aged between 6 and 18 years, with an innovative pedagogical approach (initiation in science and recreational activities are ensured by the same people, holders of dual training) integrating a very strong renewal rate of the catalogue (50% annually), breaking with practices within the sector.	Yes	No

Table 3.2 (continued)

Case study	Date of formation	Founder, training	Opportunity	Past experience of the founder (s)	Incubator
Khawa Technology (KT)	2000	V. Valide and E. Rechaussat, engineers	Offers an application service provider, i.e. the company provides subscription-based applications and IT infrastructure as well as necessary support services.	Yes	No
Synthesio	2006	L. Moisand, commercial; T. Hanin, engineer	Offers professional Internet-based monitoring and news services via a specialized search engine.	Yes	Yes
Visual Friendly (VF)	2000	J. Adam, business	The first company to provide software to increase the readability of Web screen pages by simplifying navigation and retrieval.	No	Yes
New Power Soul (NPS)	1997	O. Daniel, autodidact	Production of artists in the French rap sector at a time when major record labels were practically absent from this niche.	Yes	No

or her associates, in order to understand the business formation process, the actors involved, the reasons for their involvement and the benefits and constraints of the relationships formed. These interviews, which lasted 1 hour 20 minutes on average, were conducted according to the recommendations proposed by Merton et al. (1990), and were recorded and fully transcribed (Baumard et al., 2001). A third interview was conducted with a third party, privileged witness to the project's process, generally as counsel, to test the coherence of the discourse of the first two interlocutors.

Conducting three interviews on the history of formation of each business allowed us to benefit from several points of view, and to offer new ways to cross-check information, thus limiting the risk of rationalization *a posteriori* (Nutt, 1993). The study ended with a final confirmatory interview with the entrepreneur. It was therefore the second interview with the entrepreneur and the fourth interview conducted as part of the case study. This interview at the end of the analysis process sought to submit to the entrepreneur the interpretations formulated by the researcher following data analysis in order to obtain a validation of these interpretations by the actors on the ground (Miles and Huberman, 1994).

To analyze the data, we retained the narrative strategy, which is an analytical strategy that seeks to understand a process based on the construction of an organized and chronological narrative of events from primary sources (Langley, 1999). The first goal of this narrative is therefore descriptive and comprehensive, and corresponds to our desire to give empirical content to the relational dynamics of the entrepreneur during the formation of the business opportunity. To do this, network characteristics are grasped through the strength of ties measured on the basis of emotional closeness (Perry-Smith, 2006). Consequently, for each relationship, we evaluated whether it was an acquaintance, remote colleagues or partners, close colleagues or partners, or good friends. The more or less recent nature of the relationship was also taken into account. If the first time two stakeholders met was on the occasion of the business project, then their relationship was described as weak. While the cases studied differed on several variables, the data-processing stage revealed that three phases or moments appeared to be narrated in a systematically dissociated manner. While the idea originated from the individuals themselves and was relatively idiosyncratic, the entrepreneurs placed strong emphasis on the fact that, in their opinion, it was pertinent to differentiate the manner in which they had used their SN to validate their business ideas, and thus the potential opportunity. Though close to the evaluation taken into account by the literature, this view underscores that the aspect of 'discovery' is present as the idea can change considerably when interacting with respondents. However, the exploitation phase appears to give rise to two key moments:

(1) a moment in which the entrepreneur seeks to validate the development of his or her offer on a small-scale basis, before (2) working on the deployment of the offer on a more substantial scale, which enables him or her to demonstrate that economic gain is possible.

3. RESULTS

Analyzing the case studies made it possible to highlight how entrepreneurs mobilized their SN during the formation of their business opportunities. Given the results on the ground, we present them by distinguishing three key moments of the process: first, with regard to the clarification of the business idea; second, with regard to the elaboration of the offer on a small-scale basis; and, finally, with regard to the rolling-out of the offer leading to the demonstration of potential economic gain.

3.1 Social Networks and Social Skills in the Discovery and Evaluation of Business Ideas

Discovery and evaluation of business ideas have emerged as two intricately linked phases of monitored entrepreneurial projects. The entrepreneur seeks to clarify the business idea and validate its market potential.

The longitudinal approach to the six case studies of business formation enabled us to better understand the relational dynamics of the entrepreneur. The observations made are consistent with the idea that entrepreneurs are not isolated beings, right from the formulation of the business idea. Indeed, five out of the six entrepreneurs studied sought, from the start, to expose their ideas to a third party in an attempt to reassure themselves of the merits of a new idea concerning which there was no existing model to serve as a reference point and a model to build on. Five entrepreneurs considered that the venture progressed as a team, with the quest for one or several associates. It thus seems necessary to underscore the extent to which the choice of those contacted is far from coincidental. To obtain preliminary feedback and constitute their teams, entrepreneurs seek individuals perceived to be both well intentioned and experts in the domain in which the project falls. Clearly, entrepreneurs demonstrate social perception, understood as the ability to accurately gauge the intentions or moods of their interlocutors (Baron and Markman, 2000). The desire to be able to 'read' the personality of those contacted leads project initiators to compare their feelings with those of people relatively close to them. Similarly, this desire leads these initiators to choose their associates from a pool of individuals belonging to their immediate SN.

In the KT case, V. Valide explained his idea to close relations, working like him in the IT sector. These included friends, colleagues, clients and suppliers he had met during the course of his duties: 'Naturally, I explained the idea to those close to me . . . Close friends are the most caring people: they can listen to what one has to say about the project for hours then politely express all their negative opinions.' When he started forming his team, V. Valide sought, still among his acquaintances, competent individuals from a technical viewpoint that he felt might be interested in a business formation project. The ability to anticipate the degree of interest of an acquaintance for a business formation project in the field of IT reflects once again the entrepreneur's social perception. This perception led the entrepreneur to propose a partnership to individuals with whom he saw himself working over the middle term and whose motivations, intentions and key personality traits he had identified *a priori*. Bearing in mind that the development phase could be difficult, V. Valide favored individuals likely to help him overcome the project's technical difficulties. He thus sought E. Réchaussat, one of his old friends, who had a profile similar to his own in that, for three years, she had been a consulting engineer in information systems in a software and computing services company. E. Réchaussat was responsive to V. Valide's enthusiasm: V. Valide was convinced that there was room in the market for a new type of IT service provider, capable of offering large firms, meaning those that spent the most money in IT, an outsourcing service based on a new technology known as 'thin client'.[7] The two engineers thus met in the evenings after work, at the home of one or the other, to reflect on the business formation project.

In the two other case studies, the entrepreneurs adopted a more individualistic position. In the case of Synthesio, we encountered T. Hanin, an entrepreneurial engineer who initially focused on the technical aspects of his offer within an academic incubator. The issue of the feasibility of a specialized search engine prototype initially mobilized the bulk of his energy. It is through the intermediary of the incubator that he met L. Moisand, another project initiator. After four months of informal discussions within the incubator, L. Moisand saw in T. Hanin's reflections an opportunity to get involved in a project he deemed particularly attractive. By joining T. Hanin, he also saw an opportunity to overcome solitude by forming a highly complementary team in terms of skills. Indeed, while T. Hanin was passionate about technology, he felt much less comfortable with regard to business issues:

> I don't know how to sell . . . me, I sell like an engineer, I'll simply say that I developed the best product possible. When it comes to worrying about presenting the product depending on what people want, I don't know how to do that but Loïc

> does; he knows how to listen to what people want and present things according to their expectations.

Thus, aware of the fact that they complemented one another, and after having mutually 'socialized' during their informal discussions within the incubator, the two students decided to join forces to create Synthesio.

Finally, in the NPS case study, O. Daniel embarked on the creation of a record label after observing what might be referred to as the explosion of rap in the USA.[8] Passionate about music, Daniel had an intimate knowledge of the rap environment as a whole. This knowledge was the result of a long and patient impregnation cultivated over a period of almost five years, a period in which he himself was an artist. Confident in his judgment, he did not feel the need to expose it to other possible points of view and thus started his venture alone.

In all these case studies, unlike what has been suggested by much of the available literature, the role of strong ties in the quest for information was crucial. This role was all the more important given that, when the project was deployed outside all support structures (such as incubators), strong ties were used as levers, making it possible to gain access to the contacts likely to provide the information sought. V. Valide (KT) provides an illustration of this approach: 'To identify the concrete modalities for starting a business, we turned to our close relations. In fact we began by speaking to our friends, friends who would tell us "I know a friend who started a business". We then tried to meet the person and so on.' The situation was modulated when entrepreneurs progressed within support structures, as these structures facilitated access to a certain number of information resources. In the case of Synthesio, a firm hosted by the ESSEC incubator, the project initiators compiled a file featuring approximately 200 individuals with responsibilities in businesses in various sectors, and all members of the ESSEC network. They presented themselves to the individuals as two young graduates attempting to start a business and seeking to offer services they would like to receive advice in order to improve them: 'I went to see those people without being too commercially aggressive, but by simply saying, I'm asking for you advice concerning a product and I would like to run it by you in order to improve our offer' (L. Moisand).

When the immediate SN does not provide the information sought, entrepreneurs may be led to change their network by directly contacting individuals likely to support their business formation attempts. This proactive activity that involves transforming the network for informational purposes was notably observed with C. Javault (SA) when he transformed a hitherto associative activity into a business entity. Indeed, unable to believe in the long-term sustainability of his firm, Javault intensified the number of consultations, hoping that these would give him a clearer picture of things. Thus, within a few months (April to May 2000), he met with one of his competitors in the industry, accountants, a director of a bank branch and, in particular, entrepreneurs. Javault set up these meetings himself, mostly with individuals he didn't know, in order to discuss his project.

The three situations mentioned with regard to the systematic quest for information underscore the need for entrepreneurs to display strong skills in matters of social adaptability (Baron and Markman, 2000, 2003) in order to interact effectively with resource persons who often fall within the entrepreneurs' weak ties and are sometimes far from their usual environment. Entrepreneurs should therefore not fear reaching out to people in different professional fields that are sometimes distant from their own. Better still, the quality of exchange and thus of the relevance of information collected is closely linked to the ability of entrepreneurs to be comfortable and to adapt to different types of interlocutors. This is precisely what V. Valide (KT) demonstrated when he spoke to the friends of his friends who had already had a first entrepreneurial experience. L. Moisand (Synthesio) also had to accomplish this step when he found himself in a business development meeting with all types of firms from his 200 contact list. Finally, C. Javault (SA) also had to possess this quality when he solicited professionals left, right and center to reinforce his decision to fully commit to his entrepreneurial project.

3.2 Social Networks and Social Skills in Obtaining the Necessary Resources to Develop an Offer on a Small-scale Level

From the outset, the issue of material and financial resources needed to develop the product offer arose. In all the cases studied, entrepreneurs first drew funding from their own resources and from 'love money': from members of their close circle who, because of friendship, agreed to support their project financially. O. Daniel (NPS) relied on one of his own high-school friends, rap enthusiast like himself, to obtain approximately 10 000 euros as a loan, funds necessary to produce his disc. Similary, C. Javault (AS) managed to obtain a hosting venue for his first holiday through a family relation of his associate who managed a holiday resort in Brittany. This contact allowed him to book holiday places for a week, under special financial conditions, against an advance of 1500 euros: 'At the time, we told ourselves we believed in our project, so we invested.' Finally, J.-L. Regnier and his team integrated the ESSEC incubator. This enabled them to access different means – local, telephone and computer equipment – and facilitated the project's management. It is clear that, as proposed in Table 3.1, strong ties played a fundamental role.

As soon as one quits the particularly benevolent context of 'love money' and plans to raise funds from investors – which corresponds to three case studies (VF, Synthesio and KT) – entrepreneurs need to use strong social skills to convince investors to finance their project. On this occasion, it is not simply about linking the entrepreneur with a given investor via the mobilization of a particular personal contact. Obtaining funding depends on the quality of interactions that the entrepreneur is able to establish with the investor, which brings us to the social skills of the project initiator (Baron and Markman, 2000).

It all begins with the entrepreneur's ability to make a good impression on the investor, as the first contact is the first step towards building a relationship of trust between the two parties. Beyond this first contact, the entrepreneur must also use a great deal of persuasion to convince an informed investor to finance his or her project, knowing that this investor is often much sought and must decide between several investment opportunities. This is why, in the case of VF, a business plan was presented orally by J. Adam in front of the incubator's investment committee in June 2000, after six months working closely with the head of the incubator. The investment committee comprises venture capitalists and experienced entrepreneurs on whom one must make a good impression in order to prove to them the project's growth potential. The VF project was selected by the incubator's investment committee, making it possible to raise 150 000 euros in seed funding. This first distinction gave credibility to the project and made it easier to persuade other financial partners. In December of the same year, the firm also obtained the 'innovative company' label issued by ANVAR (National Agency for the Promotion of Scientific Research) and an innovation grant of 75 000 euros.

Beyond the initial financial and material resources that made it possible to launch the project, entrepreneurs encountered a wide range of challenges that, once again, could be overcome only through the mobilization of relational resources. Two situations were key stumbling blocks in the entrepreneurial process: first, the ability to effectively seek occasional expertise as and when unexpected problems arose; and, second, the ability to associate with partners indispensable to the project's success.

The Alternacom case study provides an eloquent illustration of these difficulties. First, in his quest for complementary skills, J.-L. Regnier felt the need to rely on an individual knowledgeable in the world of advertising when undertaking prospecting among advertisers. He thus called on P. Cohen, a publicist by profession and lecturer at ESSEC, whose courses he had taken. J.-L. Regnier believed that Cohen's knowledge of the publicist world could prove valuable in developing business contacts. This communication professional, who was a member of the incubator's eco-system, did not spontaneously put his talents to the service of the entrepreneurial project. It was only after several weeks of negotiation during which J.-L. Regnier used his social skills in persuasion that P. Cohen agreed to join the entrepreneurial team as an associate. In exchange, he brought his knowledge of the world of advertising to the firm and radically transformed its commercial approach: 'Your brochures are not something one dreams about . . . the concept of advertising on trucks is a rather hard sell. It is better to "package" things by finding a name.' He then said:

> First, you must no longer talk about advertising on trucks, but rather, for instance, on Megamobiles. Advertisers will entrust you with their image and must be reassured on every level. They will not entrust you with their image to put on trucks. But they will accept to entrust you with their image to put on Megamobiles, even if in reality, it is one and the same thing. But the 'packaging' is different and more reassuring in the second case.

We find similar dynamics when the entrepreneur encounters difficulty in finding transporters willing to make available the surfaces of their trucks for use in advertising for a fee. The transporters were thus contacted by telephone on the basis of business directories. The entrepreneurs realized that one of the greatest challenges was to get through the barricades erected by secretaries. When they managed to get over these barricades, their interlocutors quickly dismissed them: 'We couldn't understand why they didn't want to meet us yet we were offering them money.' Actually, the persons contacted realized that at the other end of the line were students who knew nothing about the world of transportation. They therefore doubted the credibility of their interlocutors and the conversation was thus quickly brought to an end. This failure can be explained by the fact that the entrepreneur underestimated the social skills (and the legitimacy) needed to reassure and convince industrial partners. Subsequently, J.-L. Regnier turned to one of his father's friends, a former sales director in a company manufacturing trucks. This friend had kept numerous relationships in the world of transport. Recommended by this contact, the entrepreneur managed to get an appointment with a transporter in November 2001.

These case studies clearly reveal the extent to which strong ties are essential from the very beginning of project implementation. In the case of Alternacom, these ties played a fundamental role from the moment the entrepreneurs decided to investigate the possibility of placing advertising posters on trucks on highways. While strong ties – by their own action – did not make it possible to solve problems, they provided points of support linking the entrepreneur with weak ties that enabled him to overcome the difficulty encountered: similar results are mentioned by Jack (2005). These studies also clearly reveal that entrepreneurs rely on social skills in management, first from the first impression, then from persuasion and social influence, to effectively solicit – initially from close relations, then from distant ones – financial, material and human resources. The same process holds when seeking partners likely to promote the development and commercialization of their services.

3.3 Social Networks and Social Skills in the Rolling-out of the Services Proposal

The rolling-out of the services proposal integrates three critical steps: the systematic introduction to the market; the refining or redefining of the business idea; and the demonstration of potential economic gain.

The phase of systematic introduction is the period when an entrepreneur turns to potential clients and engages commercial actions. In the case of VF, J. Adam relied on his personal relationships and on the contacts provided by the supervisors of the incubator to begin soliciting potential clients. Indeed, J. Adam's passion for football allowed him to meet the chairman of a professional football club who was also one of the leaders of a large international advertising agency in France. The chairman agreed to help J. Adam by offering him his address book, thus making it easier for him to contact large consumer-oriented firms in different sectors such as transport, tourism and supply. The same was true for the public sector, where very favorable contacts were established with the prime minister's office, central authorities, several towns and political parties. Once again, it is worth highlighting the skills used by the entrepreneur in terms of social adaptability in order to interact effectively with such varied interlocutors. In addition, considerable effort was undertaken to raise awareness among the economic stakeholders and administrative authorities with regard to the preparation of the draft bill that was expected to reinforce accessibility to the Internet. Awareness-raising mainly involved the organization of a conference at Paris City Hall in September 2002, which brought together 200 people including numerous elected officials, around the theme of the incorporation of the visually impaired in Internet projects. The organization of such an event was part of the necessary lobbying and 'evangelization' efforts with regard to Internet accessibility for the visually impaired. It therefore appears that entrepreneurs rely on their social adaptability and, if necessary, on their persuasion skills, beginning with their close relations, to drive actions that involve linking their commercial offer with potential clients.

The refining or redefining of the business idea is a phase of strategic reflection where entrepreneurs demonstrate their reflexive capacity based on the idea's introduction to the market. This phase, which was seen as 'crucial' by all entrepreneurs, led to two options: either, as was the case with Alternacom, VF and NPS, the entrepreneurs simply adjusted their offer; or, as with SA, KT and Synthesio, they radically challenged the commercial offer based on their perceptions and understanding of the expectations and aspirations of potential clients. This explains why, in the case of Synthesio, project initiators were driven to change their proposed services several times according to their evolving perception of market needs. L. Moisand's interaction with the market led the two associates to redefine their position and significantly expand their service, which initially revolved around providing a specialized search engine for information that was economic in nature. Taking into account the feedback from prospects led them to reflect on a more comprehensive and complex offer that would add Internet monitoring tools to the search engine.

The entrepreneurs thus relied on their social perception to learn from feedback from the market and thus refine or redefine their commercial offer.

The last phase of the business formation opportunity coincides with demonstrating potential economic gain. This demonstration depends on the verdict of the market, that is, the ability to convince the very first clients. This is never easy for a new player competing with already established firms, or for an actor opening up or creating a 'new market'. It is therefore hardly surprising that all the entrepreneurs analyzed experienced great difficulty achieving their first sale. J.-L. Regnier and his team (Alternacom) undertook intensive business development over several months that led them to become aware of prospects' demands with regard to the size of posters. The new poster dimensions aroused more interest from advertisers during commercial presentations, but the entrepreneur and his team failed to transform this very strong interest into sales: 'We were still not selling and we really wondered why . . . We were starting to really lose motivation. The people we met liked the concept, but we had no answer to the following question: "Who have you worked for?"' J.-L. Regnier and his associate then understood that they were coming up against the problem of references. Despite their interest in the product, no advertiser wanted to risk being the first to experiment with this new mode of communication. The reluctance of prospects to work with a provider with no references was a problem experienced with the same acuteness in the other cases studied.

As in the other phases, it appears that the entrepreneur must develop strong social skills in persuasion in order to transform prospects into first clients. The NPS case perfectly illustrates this: according to O. Daniel, the main difficulty was in convincing the distributor to accept to 'reference' the product. O. Daniel therefore went from door to door and rapidly found that he was up against a brick wall:

> The hardest thing is to get an appointment with an artistic director. To succeed in this . . . you have to know how to present things to your advantage. For example, know how to highlight the big names with whom one has worked, even indirectly. Having worked with someone from the entourage of a known artist can enable one to benefit from some of the aura of that artist. It's references that attract the interest of an artistic director and make it possible to obtain that first appointment. It is a commercial act where one must sell his product.

When entrepreneurs managed to overcome this difficulty, it appeared that their first client was generally not completely unknown to them (this was true for SA, KT and NPS[9]). In the case of NPS, as a result of his persistence, O. Daniel finally managed to reach an agreement with the artistic director of an independent distributor. By signing a distribution contact with the latter, O. Daniel actually signed with a partner with whom he had long-standing ties from the time he himself was an artist.

Ultimately, the personal network of the project initiator plays a fundamental role in the capturing of clients and the validation of the opportunity. Once again, the important role played by strong ties is clear.

In this area, several configurations can be observed: either the first client is a strong tie who, having already established trust with the entrepreneur, is more easily convinced by the latter and disregards the issue of references (NPS); or the first client is influenced by the actions of a strong tie from the project initiator's network. This was the situation in the case of KT, where the first contract was obtained only through the mediation of one of V. Valide's friends who, at the time of negotiation, was working as a computer consultant for V. Valide's prospect. This relationship clearly played an influential role in recommending KT to the management team of the prospect, greatly facilitating the signing of the contract. Finally, and this is the last case in point, entrepreneurs' strong ties are a lever by which they can access other resources and skills that make it possible to unblock commercial situations, as Alternacom has clearly illustrated. In this case, the professional contacts of the professor who became an associate made it possible to enlist the services of a highly experienced salesperson[10] in the sale of advertising space. Alternacom gained credibility and market efficiency, as evidenced by the signing, in January 2004, of a major contract with Renault.[11] The signing of this contract marked the launch of the firm and the change in dimension of its activities.

It appears that entrepreneurs ultimately rely on their persuasion and social influence skills to effectively seek, among their close relations, supports likely to boost the signing of the first contract.

4. DISCUSSION AND CONCLUSION

This study on the role of SN in the formation of business opportunities is consistent with the results observed in the literature and makes it possible to highlight both lessons learnt and avenues for further research. Comparing field results with the literature review conducted allows us to highlight lessons learnt at several levels. First, one must pay attention to the very process of opportunity, as the observations emphasize a non-linear formation process. Second, the interplay of the evolution of SN and the formation process of opportunity has to be completed by taking into account the fact that opportunity can also change in the process. Third, one must explicitly take into account the entrepreneur's role, as his/her mode of management seems to be a distinctive skill with regard to how he/she uses SN during different phases, or how the management of SN seems to be a full-fledged skill in the entrepreneurial process. These points must be made clear before discussing the limitations of the research and its research avenues.

While these elements seem to dispute existing literature, they also naturally lead to a discussion on the limitations of this study and the avenues for future research.

4.1 A Complex and Non-linear Process of the Formation of Business Opportunities

Analyzing the formation of business opportunities initially led us to position the phases typically found in literature: discovery, evaluation and exploitation via the acquisition of resources (Shane, 2003). While each of these phases has been discussed repeatedly in the literature, their partition and distinction seems a matter of a linear vision of the entrepreneurial process (Chabaud and Messeghem, 2010) that, though attractive, remains simplistic or reductionist.

This aspect emerged in particular from the case studies analyzed and led us to structure the presentation of our results around three phases:

- discovery and evaluation of the business idea;
- obtaining the resources necessary for the development of the offer on a small scale;
- expanding the offer on a large scale.

Beyond a partition into divisions that can appear relatively trivial, we believe that questioning the difference between the phases typically found in literature and field observations deserves further attention.

First, the discovery and evaluation of opportunities appeared inseparable among the entrepreneurs analyzed. The initial business idea always gave rise to exchange, discussions and interactions that sought to clarify the business idea or opportunity while reflecting on the relevance of the idea. Did this moment represent an evaluation of the opportunity or simply of the business idea? This question is extremely important as, although the entrepreneurs did not typically engage in market research, they nevertheless sought to clarify the potentiality of the idea to generate a profitable market. This allows us to consider that there was a real evaluation of the opportunity. Consequently, separating discovery from evaluation appears relatively artificial, as evaluation seems to underlie the process of formation of the business opportunity.

Similarly, obtaining resources seems important and deserves further attention, given that this activity is based on a real discussion that revolves around the evaluation of the opportunity. Only here, discussions on the opportunity and its significance are primarily centered on exchange with stakeholders who are capital or opportunity providers. While we have already seen the role of strong ties and social skills relative to these points, it should be noted that entrepreneurs – when they develop their entrepreneurial project – seek at the same time to clarify their business opportunity, evaluate it, and give themselves the means to exploit it on a small scale. Their objective is to find a first client, the first step in exploiting a larger market.

Finally, the phase in which the offer is rolled out 'integrates three crucial steps, namely: discovery and evaluation of the business idea; obtaining the resources necessary for the development of the offer on a small scale; and expanding the offer on a large scale' (see above). Of primary importance here is the fact that the exploitation of the opportunity is based on proposing a real offer on the market and signing the first contracts with clients or with a wider market. This phase appears interesting for two reasons: first, it naturally underscores maintaining an evaluative approach, as well as what Callon (1986) calls a 'translation', that is, a process by which the entrepreneur will create 'interessement' around his project translation/profit-sharing approaches (see Lamine et al., Chapter 13 in this volume). Second, the rolling-out phase of the offer is also based on a reflexive vision of the opportunity or a discussion on its redefinition. It is, without doubt, important to underscore here how – for five or six of the entrepreneurs – this phase seemed to place them in a logic of opportunity formation construction (Chabaud and Ngijol, 2004; Alvarez and Barney, 2007). This leads to a reflection on the very nature of the opportunities that emerge in an effectual logic (Sarasvathy, 2008). More broadly, this aspect underscores the extent to which the entrepreneurial project – and the opportunity – actually draws on the interactions between the entrepreneur and his or her social networks. In terms of process, the dynamics at work are much more complex than linear: the beginning of the operation is accompanied by recursive reasoning on opportunity, which requires the coevolution of different aspects of the opportunity (cf. Anderson et al., 2010; Chabaud et al., 2015; Jack et al., 2008) and not simply the succession of distinct phases (Shane, 2003).

4.2 From Flexible Networks to Entrepreneurial Projects Subject to Change?

If we focus on how SN were used by the entrepreneurs during the development of their entrepreneurial project, we can note significant differences from the majority of studies that confer a strategic advantage on weak ties. We can notably refer to the studies that implemented Granovetter's (1973) argument on the strength of weak ties (Hills et al., 1997) to the formation of business opportunities, or those that tested the generic role of specific ties (weak or strong) in a static manner (Singh et al., 1999; Elfring and Hulsing, 2003, 2007;[12] Lechner et al., 2006). Two findings emerge.

On the one hand, entrepreneurs primarily relied, whenever possible, on strong ties in the interests of pragmatism. These ties appeared to be easier to access and were characterized by trust. Indeed, we noted a predominance of the use of strong ties both in the quest for information and in resource acquisition, which is consistent with the results obtained by Jack and Anderson (2002) and Jack (2005). However, while Jack's approach was in line with a study on non-innovative opportunities (apart from the local context), we have shown that entrepreneurs act in the same way in a highly innovative context. This is all the more surprising given that innovation is generally perceived as an element prompted by the logic of weak ties and/or structural holes (Burt, 1992, 2005).

On the other hand, introducing a more processual vision – as Larson and Starr (1993) or Hite and Hesterly (2001) did in their studies on the ormation (or development) of organizations – emphasizes the leverage effect of strong ties and the (possible) change of team composition and of the whole entrepreneurial project. Empirical study underscores the connection between the different ties mobilized during the rolling-out phase. This coincides in particular with De Koning's (2003) observations that underscored the coexistence of strong and weak ties at every moment of the business opportunity formation. However, if these two sets of ties coexist, the role of strong ties is more important than expected: entrepreneurs use their strong ties to access new connections, and to access new weak ties. In doing so, they use the leverage effect of strong ties emphasized by Jack (2005).

Also, the possible evolution of the entrepreneurial team appears here: while, generically, we tend to place emphasis on the entrepreneur – or the fact that the entrepreneur can be defined in multiple ways (Reich, 1987) – this empirical study underscores that the original entrepreneur, in many cases, expands his or her original entrepreneurial team. In this respect, we observe almost a crystallization of the SN (Larson and Starr, 1993; Chabaud and Condor, 2009), with strong ties – or recurrent relationships (weak ties initially) – that become stronger and lead to the creation of an entrepreneurial team. It seems that we even observe what Obstfeld (2005) qualifies as a *tertius iungens* orientation, where an entrepreneur is ready to associate with partners (ties) rather than to play on the disconnection between networks (*tertius gaudens*; cf. Burt, 1992).

4.3 Social Skills, a Specific Marker of the Process of Opportunity Formation?

The study undertaken subsequently led to highlighting the importance of the management of social networks. If strong ties occupy a central position in the formation of business opportunities, it is also because they provide the entrepreneur with a lever to act and contact other actors (Jack, 2005). When strong ties are insufficient, entrepreneurs use them as a lever to contact useful weak ties. Should this fail, they can – as a last resort – reshape their network in an attempt to reach appropriate contacts directly. This observation, which refers to the idea of pro-active behavior in network management (Burt, 1992; Chabaud and Ngijol, 2005), is highly significant in a logic of support: business incubators can stimulate entrepreneurs' ability to access new social networks by offering them the possibility of privileged access to differentiated networks (Hansen et al., 2000, Chabaud et al., 2004, Bøllingtoft and Ulhøi, 2005). In addition, they can also attract the attention of entrepreneurs with regard to how to access certain networks, and advise them on how to mobilize their personal and professional networks (Akrich et al., 1988a, 1988b). In so doing, we were thus able to see – in each of the phases – the extent to which the social skills of the entrepreneur were crucial when we attempted to understand how the entrepreneur activated his or her network to obtain information and/or resources (see Table 3.3).

Our analysis of the role of SN in the formation of entrepreneurial opportunities thus leads us to reflect on the significance of an entrepreneur's social skill: this skill is crucial during the whole process, and the case study illustrates that all have to use it in order to go beyond the difficulties they encounter. A side effect is that we observe that the entrepreneurs in an incubator context can benefit from help in order to develop the

Table 3.3 The role of the entrepreneur's social skills in mobilizing social networks

Entrepreneurial process	Generic proposals	Empirical illustrations
Clarification of the business idea		
Discussing initial feelings with a third party	Entrepreneurs use their social perception to identify, among their close relations, people likely to give them initial well-informed feedback on the merits of their business idea.	In the case of KT, the entrepreneur explained his idea to close relations, working like him in the IT sector. These included friends, colleagues, clients and suppliers he had met during the course of his duties: 'Naturally, I explained the idea to those close to me . . . Close friends are the most caring people: they can listen to what one has to say about the project for hours then politely express all their negative opinions.'
Forming the entrepreneurial team	Entrepreneurs use social perception and, if necessary, persuasion skills to identify and persuade their close relations likely to join their business project.	In the case of KT, the entrepreneur sought out one of his old friends, a consulting engineer in information systems. His friend was responsive to Valide's enthusiasm: Valide was literally convinced that there was room in the market for a new type of IT service provider, capable of offering large firms an outsourcing service based on a new technology known as 'thin client'. The two engineers thus met in the evenings after work, at the home of one or the other, to reflect on the business formation project.
In-depth evaluation of the business idea	Entrepreneurs use their social adaptability to effectively solicit strong or weak ties in order to systematically examine the feasibility and profitability of their business project.	In the case of AS, the entrepreneur was led to restructure his network for informational purposes when he transformed a hitherto associative activity into a business entity. Indeed, unable to believe in the long-term sustainability of his firm, the entrepreneur intensified the number of consultations with different professionals unknown to him (bankers, accountants, competitors, entrepreneurs etc.), thus highlighting the need for significant capacities in social adaptation.

Table 3.3 (continued)

Entrepreneurial process	Generic proposals	Empirical illustrations
Development of the offer on a small-scale level		
Acquisition of financial and material resources		In the case of VF, a business plan was presented orally by Adam in front of the incubator's investment committee in June 2000, after six months working closely with the head of the incubator. The investment committee comprises venture capitalists and experienced entrepreneurs in front of whom one must make a good impression (management of first impressions) in order to prove to them the project's growth potential. The VF project was selected by the incubator's investment committee, making it possible to raise 150 000 euros in seed funding.
Acquisition of complementary skills	Entrepreneurs use their skills in the management of first impressions as well as their persuasion and social influence skills to effectively solicit, first from their close relations, then from their distant relations, financial, material and human resources, and partners likely to boost the development and commercialization of the proposed services.	In the Alternacom case, in order to better solicit advertisers, Regnier decided to rely on the skills of one of his lecturers whose courses he had keenly followed. This lecturer was P. Cohen, a publicist by profession and lecturer at ESSEC. This communication professional, who was a member of the incubator's eco-system, did not spontaneously put his talents to the service of the entrepreneurial project. It is only after several weeks of negotiation during which Regnier used his social skills in persuasion that Cohen agreed to join the entrepreneurial team as an associate.

Mobilization of commercial and industrial partners		In the Alternacom case, Regnier and his team encountered great difficulty getting through the barricades erected by secretaries. When they managed to get over these barricades, they were rapidly dismissed by their interlocutors who had no faith in their professional credibility in the transport sector. This failure can be explained by the fact that the entrepreneur underestimated the social skills needed to reassure and convince industrial partners.
Rolling out the offer		
Systematic confrontation to the market	Entrepreneurs use their social adaptability and, if necessary, their persuasion skills to drive, using their close relations, actions that link the commercial offer with potential clients.	In the case of VF, Adam relied on his personal relationships and on the contacts provided by the supervisors of the incubator to begin soliciting potential clients in different sectors. Moreover, intense lobbying and 'evangelization were undertaken by members of the firm with regard to accessibility of the Internet to the visually impaired.
Refining or redefining the business idea	Entrepreneurs use their social perception to learn from the feedback from the market and thus refine or redefine their commercial offer.	In the case of Synthesio, project initiators radically changed their services on several occasions based on their changing perception of market needs. This explains why the firm changed from a service that initially revolved around providing a specialized search engine to a more comprehensive and complex offer that included Internet monitoring tools.

Table 3.3 (continued)

Entrepreneurial process	Generic proposals	Empirical illustrations
Acquiring the first client reference	Entrepreneurs use their persuasion and social influence skills to effectively solicit, among their close relations, assistance likely to favor the signing of the first contract.	The NPS case illustrates the difficulty a creator of an independent music label encounters in finding an established firm likely to ensure the distribution of his or her products. As a result of his persistence, Daniel finally managed to reach an agreement with the artistic director of an independent distributor. By signing a distribution contact with the latter, Daniel actually signed with a partner with whom he had long-standing ties from the time he himself was an artist. The two men were bound by some form of trust, facilitating the persuasion activity Daniel undertook with respect to his distributor.

relational skill. The analysis presented here doubtless illustrates the studies that have built on those undertaken by Baron and Markman (2000) and reinforce their perspective. More generally, our study makes it possible to identify the social skills that an entrepreneur needs during different phases of actual projects; these go beyond pedagogical situations experienced when one was a student, as addressed by Lans et al. (2015). Additional studies that carefully take into account the role of social skills are certainly necessary to refine the perspective. Beyond the generic emphasis on social skills – or on some of their dimensions, as we have seen here – it would be useful to carry out a comprehensive diachronic study on the role of these dimensions of social skills. Are some skills more useful at certain project development phases? Are all individuals equal with regard to this issue? Is learning in this field easy? The empirical elements we have highlighted make it possible to underscore strong similarities in the social skills mobilized during certain phases. They also enable us to highlight that, in this regard, the entrepreneurs studied appear to be more efficient than other entrepreneurs. There is therefore a clear need for: (1) more precise qualitative studies that make it possible to link the types of social skills mobilized during each phase, or to clarify the variables to consider in order to operationalize the concept; but also for (2) quantitative studies with larger samples – or control samples – to establish the impact (and important dimensions) of social skills.

4.4 Limitations and Avenues for Future Research

Naturally, this exploratory study has limitations with regard to the generalization of the results obtained. First, the personal characteristics of the entrepreneur can influence him or her to rely on a particular network. The entrepreneurs in our sample are highly qualified (except for the NPS case), and are from elite higher education institutions. In such a context, calling on a qualified classmate or relying on a relation of the latter is easy. The approach that consists in using strong ties as a lever is therefore much easier. There is need for further studies among entrepreneurs with a less elitist schooling (even if Jack, 2005, shares this observation in a different context). These studies should explore whether the network effect of a university degree plays a key role in determining the type of relations mobilized. More broadly, such studies would determine whether taking into account the cultural dimension is necessary in these types of studies. Finally, all the cases studied fell within the services sector, in which it is possible to start projects on a small scale, with limited means that are therefore relatively easy to acquire. What would happen in sectors with significant financial barriers to entry? Similarly, what would become of the management of social networks that, initially introduced as an element among others in project management, emerged as an essential element that should be linked to the social skills of the entrepreneur? While our study has shown the importance of social skills, it has not sought to identify the extent to which individuals possess different degrees and forms of social skills, an element we believe requires further investigation.

Beyond these reflections, the avenue seems open for more comprehensive studies on the role of SN in the process of formation of opportunities. However, while our study has underscored the importance of taking into account the different phases of the entrepreneurial project, it also seems necessary to reflect on including additional elements – beyond the unique individual–opportunity dyad.

NOTES

* This chapter is a modified version of Chabaud and Ngijol (2010). We thank the reviewers for their useful comments.

1. We use the term 'formation' rather than the conventional terms 'recognition' and 'discovery' to underscore that formation is not only a part of a process that can take time and mobilize resources; it also cannot continually be reduced to sudden illumination (Casson, 1982).
2. Moreover, this reference does not feature in the study used by de Short et al. (2010).
3. However, Short et al. (2010) overlooked some references, such as Elfring and Hulsing (2007).
4. One can refer to Getz and Lubart (2001) for a summary of the various stages of the creative process identified as preparation, incubation, illumination and verification, and to Carrier et al. (2010) for a discussion on the relative merits of the different techniques for stimulating creativity.
5. One can refer to Burt (1992, pp. 24–30) for a discussion on the criticism leveled against this idea that tends to connect weak ties and structural holes. Though questionable, several studies have alleged a connection between weak ties and the number of structural holes.
6. It should be noted that many studies have highlighted the role of social networks in the construction of legitimacy (Jack and Anderson, 2002; Elfring and Hulsink, 2003; Jack, 2005). This will need additional exploration.
7. In the 'thin client' architecture, all the computing power (data and applications) is concentrated in the remote center that acts as a server. The firm can thus limit its IT investments to dumb terminals that are cheaper and have less costly maintenance demands.
8. Marginal in terms of sales in the early 1980s, rap music caught up with country music from the mid-1990s and is today second in terms of musical styles in the USA (with close to 14 percent market share; data from the Recording Industry Association of America, the trade organization that represents the American recording industry).
9. It should be noted that Alternacom was the only case in which the first client was completely unknown to the entrepreneur. At the time of the study, Synthesio had not yet stabilized its services and VF had not yet succeeded in marketing its software.
10. The professor had been doing this job for almost 20 years. This allowed him to be particularly well placed in the advertising and media industries.
11. The contract concerned the launch of Modus in September 2004. From June 28 to September 5, Renault's small minivan was displayed on the sides of 150 refrigerated

vehicles. Renault sought to take advantage of an original event support solution measuring 43 m^2 and spanning 3.7 million kilometres. The 70-day campaign was expected to generate over 200 million contacts and reach at least 56 percent of the French population aged 15 and above.

12. Elfring and Hulsink propose a longitudinal study of the process of creation and development of a start-up company but they only address business opportunities in terms of discovery. This makes their approach static and prevents it from rendering an in-depth account of the formation of business opportunities.

REFERENCES

Akrich, M., Callon, M. and Latour, B. (1988a), 'A quoi tient le succès des innovations? Premier épisode: l'art de l'intéressement', *Gérer et comprendre*, **11**: 4–17; translated in *International Journal of Innovation Management*, **6**(2) (June 2002): 187–206.

Akrich, M., Callon, M. and Latour, B. (1988b), 'A quoi tient le succès des innovations? 2: Le choix des porte-parole', *Gérer et comprendre*, **11**: 15–29, translated in *International Journal of Innovation Management*, **6**(2) (June 2002): 207–25.

Aldrich, H. and Zimmer, C. (1986), 'Entrepreneurship through social networks', in D.L. Sexton and R.W. Smilor (eds), *The Art and Science of Entrepreneurship*, Cambridge, MA: Ballinger, pp. 3–23.

Alvarez, S.A. and Barney, J.B. (2007), 'Discovery and creation: alternative theories of entrepreneurial action', *Strategic Entrepreneurship Journal*, **1**(1): 11–26.

Anderson, A.R., Dodd, S.D. and Jack, S. (2010), 'Network practices and entrepreneurial growth', *Scandinavian Journal of Management*, **26**(2): 121–33.

Ardichvili, A., Cardozo, R. and Ray, S. (2003), 'A theory of entrepreneurial opportunity identification and development', *Journal of Business Venturing*, **18**(1): 105–23.

Baron, R.A. and Markman, G.D. (2000), 'Beyond social capital: the role of social skills in entrepreneurs' success', *Academy of Management Executive*, **14**: 106–16.

Baron, R.A. and Markman, G.D. (2003), 'Beyond social capital: the role of entrepreneurs' social competence in their financial success', *Journal of Business Venturing*, **18**: 41–60.

Baron, R.A. and Tang, J. (2007), 'Entrepreneurs' social skills and new venture performance: mediating mechanisms and cultural generality', *Journal of Management*, **35**(2): 282–306.

Baumard, P., Donada, C., Ibert, J. and Xuereb, J.-M. (2001), 'Data collection and managing the data source', in R.-A. Thiétart (ed.), *Doing Management Research*, London: Sage Publications, pp. 172–95.

Becker, S.W. and Whisler, T.L. (1967), 'The innovative organization: a selective view of current theory and research', *Journal of Business*, **40**(4): 462–69.

Bhave, M.P. (1994), 'A process model of entrepreneurial venture creation', *Journal of Business Venturing*, **9**(3): 223–42.

Bøllingtoft, A. and Ulhøi, J.P. (2005), 'The networked business incubator – leveraging entrepreneurial agency?', *Journal of Business Venturing*, **20**: 265–90.

Brüderl, J. and Preisendörfer, P. (1998), 'Network support and the success of newly founded business', *Small Business Economics*, **10**(3): 213–25.

Burt, R.S. (1992), *Structural Holes: The Social Structure of Competition*, Cambridge, MA: Harvard Business Press.
Burt, R.S. (2005), *Brokerage and Closure. An Introduction to Social Capital*, New York: Oxford University Press.
Callon, M. (1986), 'Some elements of a sociology of translation: domestication of the scallops and the fishermen of St Brieuc Bay', in J. Law (ed.), *Power, Action and Belief: A New Sociology of Knowledge?* London: Routledge, pp. 196–223.
Carrier, C., Cadieux, L. and Tremblay, M. (2010), 'Créativité et génération collective d'opportunités: quelles techniques pour supporter l'idéation?', *Revue française de gestion*, **7**(206): 113–27.
Casson, M. (1982), *The Entrepreneur*, Totowa, NJ: Barnes & Noble.
Chabaud, D. and Condor, R. (2009), 'La formation des équipes entrepreneuriales: une étude exploratoire', *Revue internationale P.M.E.*, **22**(1): 81–102.
Chabaud, D. and Messeghem, K. (2010), 'Le paradigme de l'opportunité. Des fondements à la refondation', *Revue française de gestion*, **7**(206): 93–112.
Chabaud, D. and Ngijol, J. (2004), 'The recognition of market opportunities by entrepreneurs: towards a constructivist perspective', 17th Annual Research Symposium on Marketing and Entrepreneurship, UIC.
Chabaud, D. and Ngijol, J. (2005), 'La contribution de la théorie des réseaux sociaux à la reconnaissance des opportunités de marché', *Revue internationale P.M.E.*, **18**(1): 29–46.
Chabaud, D. and Ngijol, J. (2010), 'Quels réseaux sociaux dans la formation de l'opportunité d'affaires?', *Revue française de gestion*, **7**(206): 129–47.
Chabaud, D., Ehlinger, S. and Perret, V. (2004), 'Les pépinières et incubateurs dans l'accompagnement de la création d'entreprises', in C. Voisin, S. Ben Mahmoud-Louini and S. Edouard (eds), *Les réseaux: dimensions stratégiques et organisationnelles*, Paris: Economica, pp. 215–27.
Davidsson, P. (2004), *Researching Entrepreneurship*, New York: Springer.
De Koning, A. (2003), 'Opportunity development: a socio-cognitive perspective', in J.A. Katz and D.A. Shepherd (eds), *Advances in Entrepreneurship, Firm Emergence and Growth*, vol. 6, Oxford: JAI Press, pp. 265–314.
Drucker, P.F. (1985), *Innovation and Entrepreneurship*, New York: Harper & Row.
Dutton, J. and Jackson, S. (1987), 'Categorizing strategic issues: links to organizational action', *Academy of Management Review*, **12**(1): 76–90.
Elfring, T. and Hulsink, W. (2003), 'Networks in entrepreneurship: the case of high-technology firms', *Small Business Economics*, **21**(4): 409–22.
Elfring, T. and Hulsink, W. (2007), 'Networking by entrepreneurs: patterns of tie formation in emerging organizations', *Organization Studies*, **28**(12): 1849–72.
Gedajlovic, E., Honig, B., Moore, B., Curt, C.B., Payne, T.G. and Wright, M. (2013), 'Social capital and entrepreneurship: a schema and a research agenda', *Entrepreneurship Theory and Practice*, **37**(3): 455–78.
Getz, I. and Lubart, T. (2001), 'Psychologie, économie et créativité: exploration de leurs liens', *Psychologie Française*, **46**(4): 365–78.
Granovetter, M. (1973), 'The strength of weak ties', *American Journal of Sociology*, **78**(6): 1360–80.
Hansen, M.T., Chesbrough, H.W., Nohria, N. and Sull, D.N. (2000), 'Networked incubators. Hothouses of the new economy', *Harvard Business Review*, **78**(5): 74–84, 199.
Hills, G.E., Lumpkin, T.G. and Singh, R.P. (1997), 'Opportunity recognition:

perceptions and behaviors of entrepreneurs', *Frontiers of Entrepreneurship Research*, Babson College, Wellesley, MA, pp. 168–82.
Hite, J. and Hesterly, W. (2001), 'The evolution of firm networks: from emergence to early growth of the firm', *Strategic Management Journal*, **22**: 275–86.
Hoang, H. and Antoncic, B. (2003), 'Network-based research in entrepreneurship. A critical review', *Journal of Business Venturing*, **18**(2): 165–87.
Jack, S.L. (2005), 'The role, use and activation of strong and weak network ties: a qualitative analysis', *Journal of Management Studies*, **42**(6): 1233–59.
Jack, S.L. and Anderson, A.R. (2002), 'The effects of embeddedness on the entrepreneurial process', *Journal of Business Venturing*, **17**(2): 467–87.
Jack, S.L., Dodd, S.D. and Anderson, A.R. (2008), 'Change and the development of entrepreneurial networks over time: a processual perspective', *Entrepreneurship & Regional Development*, **20**(2): 125–59.
Kreiser, P.M., Patel, P.C. and Fiet, J.O. (2013), 'The influence of changes in social capital on firm founding activities', *Entrepreneurship Theory and Practice*, **37**(3): 539–67.
Lamine, W., Chabaud, D., Fayolle, A. and Jack, S. (2015), 'One step beyond? Towards a process view of social networks in entrepreneurship', *Entrepreneurhip & Regional Development*, **27**(7–8): 413–29.
Lans, T., Blok, V. and Gulikers, J. (2015), 'Show me your network and I'll tell you who you are: social competence and social capital of early-stage entrepreneurs', *Entrepreneurship & Regional Development*, **27**(7–8): 458–73.
Langley, A. (1999), 'Strategies for theorizing from process data', *Academy of Management Review*, **4**: 691–710.
Larson, A. and Starr, J. (1993), 'A network model of organization formation', *Entrepreneurship: Theory & Practice*, **17**(2): 5–15.
Lechner, C., Dowling, M. and Welpe, I. (2006), 'Firm networks and firm development: the role of the relational mix', *Journal of Business Venturing*, **21**(4): 514–40.
Martinez, M.A. and Aldrich, H.E. (2011), 'Networking strategies for entrepreneurs: balancing cohesion and diversity', *International Journal of Entrepreneurial Behaviour & Research*, **17**(1): 7–38.
Merton, R.K., Fiske, M. and Kendall, P.L. (1990), *The Focused Interviews: A Manual of Problems and Procedures*, New York: Free Press.
Messeghem, K. and Sammut, S. (2007), 'Poursuite d'opportunité au sein d'une structure d'accompagnement: entre légitimité et isolement', *Gestion 2000*, **24**(3): 65–81.
Miles, M.B. and Huberman, M.A. (1994), *Qualitative Data Analysis: An Expanded Sourcebook*, Beverly Hills, CA: Sage.
Nutt, P.C. (1993), 'The formulation processes and tactics used in organizational decision making', *Organization Science*, **4**(2): 226–51.
Obstfeld, D. (2005), 'Social networks, the tertius iungens orientation, and involvement in innovation', *Administrative Science Quarterly*, **50**(March): 100–130.
Perry-Smith, J.E. (2006), 'Social yet creative: the role of social relationships in facilitating individual creativity', *Academy of Management Journal*, **49**(1): 85–101.
Reich, R.B. (1987), 'Entrepreneurship reconsidered: the team as hero', *Harvard Business Review*, **65**(3): 77–83.
Saleilles, S. (2007), 'Le "réseautage" chez les entrepreneurs néo-ruraux', *Revue de l'entrepreneuriat*, **6**(1): 73–91.
Sarasvathy, S.D. (2008), *Effectuation: Elements of Entrepreneurial Expertise*, Cheltenham, UK and Northampton, MA, USA: Edward Elgar.

Shane, S. (2003), *A General Theory of Entrepreneurship. The Individual–Opportunity Nexus*, Cheltenham, UK and Northampton, MA, USA: Edward Elgar.
Short, J.C., Ketchen, D.J., Shook, C.L. and Ireland, R.D. (2010), 'The concept of "opportunity" in entrepreneurship research: past accomplishments and future challenges', *Journal of Management*, **36**(1): 40–65.
Singh, R.P., Hills, G.E., Hybels, R.C. and Lumpkin, G.T. (1999), 'Opportunity recognition through social network characteristics of entrepreneurs', *Frontiers of Entrepreneurship Research*, Babson College, Wellesley, MA, pp. 228–41.
Slotte-Kock, S. and Coviello, N. (2010), 'Entrepreneurship research on network processes: a review and ways forward', *Entrepreneurship Theory & Practice*, **34**(1): 31–57.
Venkataraman, S. (1997), 'The distinctive domain of entrepreneurship research', in J.A. Katz and R.H. Brockhaus (eds), *Advances in Entrepreneurship, Firm Emergence and Growth*, Greenwich, CT: JAI Press, vol. 3, pp. 119–38.
Vohora, A., Wright, M. and Lockett, A. (2004), 'Critical junctures in the development of university high-tech spinout companies', *Research Policy*, **33**(1): 147–75.

4. Start-ups repositioning in business networks

Lise Aaboen and Frida Lind

INTRODUCTION

Entrepreneurship is about connectedness, since what entrepreneurs do is to connect things like technologies, ideas, places and products (Anderson et al., 2012). Networks are about more than resource acquisition (Jack et al., 2010). However, according to the overview by Semrau and Werner (2014), there have been ambiguous results in previous research regarding the connections between network characteristics and entrepreneurial success. There is a need for more research on the process aspect of entrepreneurial networks (Slotte-Kock and Coviello, 2010).

Building on the literature review of Hoang and Antoncic (2003), Slotte-Kock and Coviello (2010) identify contributions that focus on process and argue that the social network approach and business network approach offer opposing views. Furthermore, it is argued that the two approaches can offer a useful bifocal lens for studies of entrepreneurial network processes if they are considered integratively. In this respect the important contributions of the business network perspective are analyses of interactions and changes within ties, management in a network, and that future and past are taken into account as well as dormant relationships (Slotte-Kock and Coviello, 2010). In this chapter, we rely on the business network perspective (Håkansson et al., 2009). The business network approach emphasizes business as interactive by pinpointing activities and resources as interdependent and actors as interacting across firm boundaries. For this reason, the business network approach is useful for analyzing how start-ups change positions in business networks. In business networks, actors are collectively the driving force in resource combination, and these resource combinations are conceived in interaction in business relationships (Cantú et al., 2012). Since the value of resources depends on how they are combined with other resources in business relationships (Håkansson and Waluszewski, 2002a), losing all customer relationships will make it more difficult to combine resources and thereby potentially destroy some of the value of the start-up resources. Similarly, given that it is the relationships that define the position (Johanson and Mattsson, 1992), repositioning refers to the process by which actors build relationships and how they develop those relationships. Losing all customer relationships will destroy an important part of the foundation of the current position as well as the opportunity to reposition.

In order to contribute to research on the process aspect of entrepreneurial networks, the present chapter address the topic of how start-ups can overcome the loss of all their customer relationships through repositioning. One of the start-ups in this chapter witnessed that their first major customer filed for bankruptcy. Simultaneously, all the other customer relationships had come to a halt. The other two start-ups in this chapter had to face the situation that all their potential customers had experienced financial constraints and suddenly decided to choose a more widely used technology, a cheaper technology or just discontinued the project while waiting for the financial downturn to pass.

From a business networks point of view these should be almost impossible situations to overcome, which highlights the need for the suggested bifocal view between the social network approach and the business network approach. From a practitioner's point of view it is not uncommon for start-ups to lose customers. Kim et al. (2006) argue that if an organization has managed to overcome the obstacles of a network transformation, it should achieve superior performance, and Mu (2013) links new venture survival and success with networking capability. Similarly, Andries and Debackere (2007) demonstrated that start-ups that have made at least one major adaptation in their initial business model have a significantly higher probability of survival compared to start-ups that have not made any changes.

The structure of the chapter is the following. After this introduction, the theoretical frame of reference primarily taking a business network perspective is presented. Thereafter the research method is accounted for, which is followed by the case descriptions and analysis. Then a pattern of repositioning for start-ups is identified and conclusions and implications are offered.

THEORETICAL FRAME OF REFERENCE

In order to analyze start-ups repositioning in business networks, the theoretical frame of reference is based on two parts. The first focuses on how to change position within and across the opportunities and limitations built into business networks (cf. Håkansson and Waluszewski, 2002b), and the second focuses on conditions built in through historical patterns in the surrounding network.

Start-ups in Business Networks

A position in a business network is defined by a firm's business relationships (Johanson and Mattsson, 1992). A business relationship develops before, during, and after a product and/or service is sold, when interactions start to take place between the firms involved – the seller and the buyer. The interaction can regard technical issues, administrative questions or cost aspects. Over time the interaction among involved people institutionalizes into what is referred to as a business relationship (Håkansson and Snehota, 1995). What happens between two firms in a business relationship influences and is influenced by other business relationships, and this is the base for conceptualizing them as business networks (Håkansson et al., 2009).

When start-ups are becoming established in business networks, finding and developing a position in the network is crucial (Aaboen et al., 2011). In this process, initiating business relationships is an important ability (La Rocca et al., 2013). Finding a position in a business network is about embedding the start-up. Among the important ingredients in this embedding are social relationships. According to Jack and Anderson (2002, p. 484), 'The process of embedding is about establishing those social relationships which enable the entrepreneur to become part of the local structure. Embedding is about joining the structure.'

Hence business relationships and their connections are important parts of the context of firms in business networks. Another central part of business networks is time as a context (Håkansson et al., 2009; Jahre et al., 2006), which contains the history, in terms of the actors' memories and learning from previous episodes, and the plans for the future in terms of expectations of future interaction. A particular interaction episode connects past and future episodes. However, each interaction episode is also part of a continuous interaction process, meaning that the time context around an interaction episode is extended. The parties will take into account the history, and both parties will have expectations about their future interaction that will impact on the current interaction. Even though the past sets conditions for the future, it should be noted that interaction is not predetermined (Jack and Anderson, 2002) by what has happened before in the history. 'Interaction will also be affected by the concerns or problems of the actors as they arise and by influences on them from their parallel interaction or those from elsewhere in the network' (Håkansson et al., 2009, p. 37).

Network Imprinting

The pattern of interaction and networking tends to be the same over time in a structure; this is referred to as network imprinting. The pattern may be adjusted to the conditions at the time of the network foundation, even if the members of the network change (Johnson, 2007). After a review of the literature, Marquis (2003) argued that the two most important mechanisms behind network imprinting are social institutions as connecting mechanisms and locally legitimate templates of action. Furthermore, local culture and locally legitimate action are particularly important to consider for start-up firms trying to establish themselves in the network (Marquis, 2003).

Milanov and Fernhaber (2009) addressed the phenomenon of network imprinting for start-ups and more specifically how the size and centrality of the initial alliance partners influence the size of the start-up companies' networks. Ferriani et al. (2012) used the term 'reimprinting' in relation to spin-offs to describe what happens when the initial imprinting from the organization of origin is changed as a response to customers and market conditions. They introduced the term 'because [reimprinting] has lasting impact and reconstitutes past experience to enable both continuity and change' (Ferriani et al., 2012, p. 1013).

Contrasting clock time with other perceptions of time is a popular theme, along with analyses of how the future and past experience interact with the present (Halinen et al., 2012; Hernes et al., 2013). More specifically, these studies of past, present and future focus on how 'heritage of the past, and the (everchanging) shared projections of the future, are both linked and enacted by actions in the present' (Dodd et al., 2013, p. 35). It is important to note that it is not the past and future as such that are of importance, but the perceptions of the past and the projections of the future. As argued by Hernes et al. (2013, p. 2), 'the ascription of meaning upon past events . . . gives rise to a projection of future events. It is the temporal experience of actors that forces them to reconstruct past and future on an ongoing basis.' Furthermore, the events in focus when constructing the perception of past events will change over time, creating a rolling past (Aaboen et al., 2012).

Hence the current position of a firm is defined by the relationships it has. A firm repositions itself in a manner that gradually brings it closer to its projected future position based on its present position, its past position and expectations of future position. However, it is important to remember that the projected future position may change as a consequence of the repositioning.

RESEARCH METHOD

More qualitative and longitudinal work is needed to increase understanding of how networks transform and change (Jack et al., 2010). Initially, about 20 start-ups were interviewed regarding their development and how they developed their first customer relationships. All the start-ups in the study were selected based on the criteria that they were technology-based, had quite recently formed their initial customer relationships and had at least one paying customer. The start-ups in Sweden and Norway were selected with help from representatives from incubators in connection with the technical universities. The ten start-ups in Sweden were interviewed in 2009 and 2012. The 12 start-ups in Norway were interviewed in 2012 and at the beginning of 2013. From those start-ups, three have been selected based on the criterion that they had lost all their customer relationships and needed to reposition in order to see a viable future, which seemed intriguing given that no business is an island (Håkansson and Snehota, 1989). This was the main criterion for selection. The three start-ups included were interviewed again in 2014 in order to follow up particularly on the problematic situation described in the earlier interviews. In other words, the study of the three start-ups that reposition due to that they lost their customers is a sub-case of the case (Yin, 2003; Easton, 2010) of initiation of start-ups. Being sub-cases also made the selection of those start-ups as cases of repositioning an informed selection. We knew what these cases were cases of (Ragin, 1992).

The interviews were conducted, recorded and transcribed by the authors. The interviews regarded the present situation of the start-up, looked back and reflected on the development up to this point, and finally asked how the interviewed managers foresaw the future in two years' time. Similar to the studies of Jack et al. (2008) and Greve and Salaff (2003), we tried to capture the ego-centered networks of three entrepreneurs over time. In other words, we focused on the relationships that the interviewees were involved in rather than attempting to make a holistic picture of a larger part of the network. However, in the present study we focused only on the customer relationships. By having start-ups as the focal study objects, the identified repositioning pattern can contribute to entrepreneurship literature by providing details of the interactive nature of entrepreneurship (Mu, 2013; Anderson et al., 2010; Lechner and Dowling, 2003).

The analysis started during the data collection that also included secondary data about the start-ups. After the data collection, the transcripts and the literature were important starting points. A draft of the chapter was also discussed with colleagues, raising new lines of thought for how to present and analyze the cases. Hence analyzing how start-ups reposition in the network is a topic that has emerged from the case stories in interplay with the theoretical framework and the case-based method (Dubois and Gibbert, 2010).

The three start-ups are made anonymous, using the names Firm A, B and C. The limited number of cases as well as the limited number of employees in each start-up hinders us from making a multifaceted analysis of various perspectives. However, the start-ups are small and the selected interviewees had often been in the firm since foundation; the interviewee in all cases knew about the activities and events that took place in the firm at the time when the customers were lost and in the time following this. Hence, for the purpose of this study, the start-up-centered collection is argued to be appropriate.

CASE DESCRIPTION – OUR BUSINESS IS AN ISLAND

Table 4.1 summarizes the history and the problem, as well as actions and interactions of the three start-ups. Here we present how three start-ups

Table 4.1 Summary of the three start-ups

Firm	History	Problem	Actions and interactions
A	Had sold the product to several customers and initiated collaborations.	All customers 'paused' and disappeared.	EU research project had a good impact on product development, followed by development projects together with other actors. Spin-offs started.
B	Tried to initiate customer relationships within several industries. Had found their first major customer.	First main customer went bankrupt and all other customer projects failed.	Participated in research projects together with other actors. A number of development projects together with potential customers, found through the research projects.
C	Many potential industrial customers tried the product and consumers bought a private market version of the product.	All industrial customers 'paused' and the consumer market disappeared.	Interacted with a consultant and considered selling the firm; in the end returned to the initial business concept.

repositioned in order to solve the problem of having lost all customer relationships.

History – Before Losing the Customers

Firm A had sold its product to cruise ships and different official buildings such as one of the largest hospitals in Norway. Firm A had also explored business opportunities in the USA and started to collaborate with three companies within acoustics and design. The product of Firm A is a thin flat sound absorber in plastic, developed at the local university, which can be installed primarily in offices. Firm A had received funding from Innovation Norway, but the main investor was a Norwegian who had made a fortune in the oil industry.

Firm B had already started over once after a failed attempt to sell its product, a lightweight but hard metal, to the defense industry. After a shift in focus towards the aircraft industry, Firm B soon formed a relationship with an Italian manufacturer of cabin food trolleys for airplanes. A contract was signed for 5000 units of a component for the trolleys, and indications had been given of an additional order of 10 000 units. Simultaneously, Firm B had started to develop a relationship with a German firm that wanted to use the material for boat kitchens since it was lightweight and hygienic. The product of Firm B had been included in the product catalog of its global collaboration partner. In addition, Firm B had initiated a collaborative project together with a research institute and three potential customers within the aircraft industry to develop seats for aircraft. An application for funding had been made to a funding agency.

Before all trials came to a halt for Firm C, a battery manufacturer had been trying out the device for measuring the content level in batteries. A medicine manufacturer and a food manufacturer had started to try the measurement device on large stainless-steel tanks. In South Africa the device had been tested for monitoring the contents of transformers in order to detect theft, and there had also been indications of interest from Japanese companies. Furthermore, Firm C had also started to initiate relationships with actors within freight boats and ferries. When the private-boat market was in better shape, Firm C had no trouble finding distributors all over Europe.

Problem – Losing Customers

The manager of Firm A explained its situation: 'as soon as the financial crisis came, there was just a pause', and added, 'this was the problem with the financial crisis that nobody dared to do anything, nobody dared to buy, nobody dared to, everybody just sat there and waited'. The three American firms put all projects on ice. Firm A was almost certain that it would get a large project at a bank since it had passed all the tests for fire and so on, but it was cancelled the week before the signing of the contract with the excuse: 'sorry, we do not dare to do this'. This meant that Firm A had five employees and no sales.

When the first major customer, an Italian manufacturer of flight trolleys, filed for bankruptcy, the manager of Firm B even used the expression 'It went completely to pipsvängen!' to describe the situation. This is a Swedish euphemism for the more offensive expression of going to hell. Firm B had also lost its German potential customer since its product never passed the tests, the relationship with a collaboration partner did not work out and the research project related to aircraft seats had not received any funding.

Firm C, which had developed a device for measuring the content of tanks from the outside, experienced a similar situation to Firm A in that large corporations were afraid to take chances during the financial downturn and therefore did not proceed with their trials. Simultaneously the market for private boats, where Firm C had originally sold the device to measure the level of content in septic tanks, did not benefit from customers having less money in their wallets, and this market was therefore not enough for Firm C to rely on.

Actions and Interactions – How the Situation was Resolved

Firm A needed to find new customers and reconsider its product, but now consisted of only one person. A relationship was initiated with a research institute in Oslo that does research on packaging material for the food industry. The research institute and Firm A organized a research project to develop a cheaper version of Firm A's product. Together with four other firms and a couple of British and Irish universities, it applied to the EU for funding and was granted 1 100 000 euros. In order to continue to sell the original product of Firm A to new customers, relationships were initiated with distributors in Norway and Germany. Firm A had to spend a long time teaching the two firms about acoustics and how the sound absorbers should be placed in a room in order for the distributors to be able to handle customers independently. Simultaneously, Firm A has been involved in projects exploring the possibility of using the material off shore and in ventilation. A spin-off company has also been started from Firm A that makes loudspeakers using the same material.

In 2014 the EU project had resulted in a product that was 80 percent finished. As planned, the product was a cheaper version of the main product of Firm A. The project consortium had received an offer from a large corporation that was willing to buy the rights to the 80 percent finished product. The project consortium discussed whether to sell the rights to the corporation or to continue to develop the product itself. The projects exploring the possibility of using the material offshore had by this time resulted in about three projects together with a large Norwegian offshore corporation. Working in these large projects demanded a great deal of reporting, which was resource-demanding considering that Firm A had only one employee. However, the documentation in connection with the EU project and the offshore projects was far more straightforward compared to that required by the large South Korean heavy industry corporation that Firm A had also had a couple of projects with during recent years. The distributors in Norway and Germany were selling to customers and paying Firm A. One of the American companies that Firm A had a relationship with before the problems started had now won a large contract in the Middle East using Firm A's product. However, the American company still had not paid Firm A. Firm A was therefore worried that the American company would resume in the same way now, so that it would not get any money from the large contract and lacked the financial resources to fight the American company in court for the rights. The attempts to develop the product into screen walls was currently on ice since the Danish firm that Firm A collaborated with was waiting for projects to use it on. Firm A then collaborated with a Norwegian firm with German owners regarding developing the product for use in ventilation. The tests were originally scheduled to take place in 2013 but had still not taken place in 2014. The spin-off company that makes loudspeakers using the same material had in 2014 become two spin-off companies: one was developing the loudspeakers, albeit a bit slower now due to discussions with the patent owner regarding exploration versus exploitation; and the other was developing microphones. Firm A had had a couple of good years in terms of turnover after having initiated new customer relationships. However, Firm A had still not been able to experience growth that was stable enough to allow it to hire more employees.

In September 2011, Firm B made its first delivery to its new 'first' customer. The relationship was initiated by coincidence. The customer manufactures trolleys to be used in hospitals for carrying medicines and other equipment. However, when the relationship was initiated, Firm B was not able to meet the quality requirements for the boxes for the trolleys. The new customers had faith in Firm B and allowed it to deliver the boxes in solid material during the year it took until the quality issues with its own material had been solved. This customer relationship is still in place, and it has proven to be important for learning reasons. Firm B managed to learn more about the material regarding how to tune it. This has been important in relation to another potential customer with which Firm B currently (in 2014) is developing prototypes.

In 2012, Firm B had 27 active development projects running in interaction with potential customers within construction, electronics and vehicles. Two years later, Firm B had changed strategy to focus on some selected customer projects. In 2014, five ongoing customer projects are running. Two are with potential customers in the automotive industry, one is a project together with a supplier to be able to deliver a ventilation application in the construction industry and two are electronics applications. One of the projects in the electronics area comes from personal contacts of the CEO in one of his former positions.

Within the automotive industry Firm B has benefited from participation in two ongoing national research projects that include many important actors within the industry. These projects were funded by Sweden's Agency for Innovation and involved approximately 30 actors. Both of the abovementioned customer projects within the automotive sector came as a result of one of the national research projects.

If any of the five ongoing customer projects were to materialize, they would save the company. However, until a new production facility is built, Firm B will not be able to deliver. Firm B is actively seeking additional capital in order to fund the production facility. In addition to this, Firm B has focused on internal product development to be able to perform well in development projects.

Firm C also needed to find new customers and reconsider its product, given its very small organization. However, Firm C was not able to see any other applications of its product except for the options already tried. In 2012, Firm C therefore initiated a relationship with a German consultant tasked with exploring the possibility of transforming Firm C into a sellable concept in terms of what parts of the firm should be included in such a package and what type of potential buyers should be approached. Firm C has received a couple of offers but no acceptable ones so far.

In 2014, the leisure-boat market started to develop again after the financial crisis. In Sweden, but also in other European countries, there has been legislation that prevents leisure boats from emptying their septic tanks into the ocean. This and a general environmental trend have been facilitators of the leisure-boat market. Working with distributors in different geographical markets was still an important way of reaching its customers, and using its web page and phone for sharing information and support guidelines was considered important. The leisure-boat market accounted for approximately 100 percent of its sales, and Firm C is optimistic about the future. The CEO says it is a relief to be leaving those financially difficult years behind.

ANALYSIS

Firms A, B and C utilized their history by moving backwards in time in order to initiate new relationships. Firm A went back to research projects that helped get the product ready and found new collaboration partners in the process. Firm B used involvement in funded research projects to initiate development projects with customers that will secure its future if they materialize. The research projects became grounds for establishing relationships with potential customers for product testing. Having interacted with a consultant and considered which parts of the firm could be sold, Firm C is returning to the initial business concept of selling to the private-boat market. Even though they did not necessarily return to the exact same actors or (potential) customers, all three firms repositioned by returning to history in the sense that they again sought a context they were part of in earlier phases for initiating new relationships. For two of the start-ups this context was a development context, while it was more of selling again to a certain market segment for the third start-up.

All three firms seem to constantly consider and reconsider their offering and who to sell to, and this has consequences for the relationships they develop. However, the scope of this consideration is very different. Firm C is open to selling the whole firm, while the product has been more or less the same. Firm A is considering selling the rights to one of its products and has spun off certain parts of the firm, while Firm B has a narrower scope in their reconsideration in terms of focusing on continuously testing the product in new applications. For all three firms, it is the combination of history and future that enables them to see opportunities for developing their offering and new relationships in the present.

The repositioning identified in the empirical material is also related to network imprinting (Milanov and Fernhaber, 2009; Johnson, 2007). Even though the start-ups are not spin-offs, their behavior also resembled reimprinting (Ferriani et al., 2012). In particular, the emphasis on utilizing history in terms of the structures of networking, rather than the relationships as such, strengthened the relation to network imprinting. However, the present chapter has argued that it is possible to some extent to move away from the pattern of network imprinting.

One aspect of the pattern is the importance of being able to initiate relationships on a continuous basis (La Rocca et al., 2013). It is the possibility of continuous relationship initiation that directs the firms' repositioning. Firms see the possibility of continuing to initiate relationships in the intended direction from their present position. If it is not possible to initiate relationships either in the intended direction or sideways in the network with, for example, other collaboration partners, the firm moves backwards in time in order to be able to initiate relationships again using familiar network structures.

CONCLUSIONS AND IMPLICATIONS

In order to contribute to research on the process aspect of entrepreneurial networks, the present chapter addressed how start-ups can overcome the loss of all their customer relationships through repositioning. The chapter shows that, even though the three start-ups are very young, they can utilize their history by initiating new relationships using networking patterns that they have used before in order to find a new way forward.

We thereby extend arguments such as those by Birley (1985), who argues that it is during the initiation of the firm that its elements are set and that an entrepreneur is likely to re-create elements of previous employment. The extension that this chapter makes is that network structures that have previously been useful may be remembered and used again later. Furthermore, Greve and Salaff (2003) argued that the successful transition between development phases for an entrepreneurial firm depends on the ability to develop its network and on the initial network position. In the present chapter we agree with this statement and show that it holds in extreme situations.

This chapter has highlighted the need for a bifocal view (Slotte-Kock and Coviello, 2010) using both the business network approach and the social network approach in studying entrepreneurial network processes. The business network approach used in this chapter had the benefits of providing insights into how history could be utilized in present networking. Using the social network approach may have provided additional insights into how social networks somehow bridged the networking in the past and the present. We therefore hope that researchers who are experts in the social network approach will conduct similar studies in the future to 'complete the story'. We also suggest that future studies based on the present chapter should focus on in-depth studies of the roles of different types of past and present relationships. From the present chapter it seems clear that there are relationships that are important to have had in the past in order to move further in the present through repositioning. A clarification of important characteristics of these past relationships and network structures could provide important managerial implications for developing more robust networks and firms. In addition, future studies are needed of Firms A, B and C in order to find out whether these firms continued to develop or if they failed later, and how the repositioning shaped their development.

Research limitations include the limited data material. The current chapter thereby becomes more of a conceptual chapter based on empirical observations. We leave it to future studies to test the findings on larger samples and in other contexts than the Nordic. However, the chapter still makes an important contribution in challenging situations currently facing many companies and start-ups, and few studies have so far been made on how to overcome them.

REFERENCES

Aaboen, L., Dubois, A. and Lind, F. (2011), 'Start-ups starting up – firms looking for a network', *IMP Journal*, **5**(1), 42–58.

Aaboen, L., Dubois, A. and Lind, F. (2012), 'Capturing processes in longitudinal multiple case studies', *Industrial Marketing Management*, **41**(2), 235–46.

Anderson, A.R., Dodd, S.D. and Jack, S. (2010), 'Network practices and entrepreneurial growth', *Scandinavian Journal of Management*, **26**(2), 121–33.

Anderson, A.R., Dodd, S.D. and Jack, S. (2012), 'Entrepreneurship as connecting: some implications for theorising and practice', *Management Decision*, **50**(5), 958–71.

Andries, P. and Debackere, K. (2007), 'Adaptation and performance in new businesses: understanding the moderating effects of independence and industry', *Small Business Economics*, **29**, 81–99.

Birley, S. (1985), 'The role of networks in the entrepreneurial process', *Journal of Business Venturing*, **1**(1), 107–17.

Cantù, C., Corsaro, D. and Snehota, I. (2012), 'Roles of actors in combining resources in complex solutions', *Journal of Business Research*, **65**, 139–50.

Dodd, S.D., Anderson, A. and Jack, S. (2013), 'Being in time and the family owned firm', *Scandinavian Journal of Management*, **29**(1), 35–47.

Dubois, A. and Gibbert, M. (2010), 'From complexity to transparency: managing the interplay between theory, method and empirical phenomena in IMM case studies', *Industrial Marketing Management*, **39**(1), 129–36.

Easton, G. (2010), 'Critical realism in case study research', *Industrial Marketing Management*, **39**(1), 118–28.

Ferriani, S., Garnsey, E. and Lorenzoni, G. (2012), 'Continuity and change in a spin-off venture: the process of reimprinting', *Industrial and Corporate Change*, **21**(4), 1011–48.

Greve, A. and Salaff, J.W. (2003), 'Social networks and entrepreneurship', *Entrepreneurship Theory and Practice*, **28**(1), 1–22.

Håkansson, H. and Snehota, I. (1989), 'No business is an island', *Scandinavian Journal of Management*, **5**(3), 187–200.

Håkansson, H. and Waluszewski, A. (2002a), *Managing Technological Development*, London: Routledge.

Håkansson, H. and Waluszewski, A. (2002b), 'Path dependence: restricting or facilitating technical development?', *Journal of Business Research*, **55**, 561–70.

Håkansson, H., Ford, D., Gadde, L.-E., Snehota, I. and Waluszewski, A. (2009), *Business in Networks*, Chichester, UK: John Wiley & Sons.

Halinen, A., Medlin, C.J. and Törnroos, J.-Å. (2012), 'Time and process in business network research', *Industrial Marketing Management*, **41**(2), 215–23.
Hernes, T., Simpson, B. and Söderlund, J. (2013), 'Managing and temporality', *Scandinavian Journal of Management*, **29**(1), 1–6.
Hoang, H. and Antoncic, B. (2003), 'Network-based research in entrepreneurship: a critical review', *Journal of Business Venturing*, **18**(2), 165–87.
Jack, S.L. and Anderson, A.R. (2002), 'The effects of embeddedness on the entrepreneurial process', *Journal of Business Venturing*, **17**, 467–87.
Jack, S., Dodd, S.D. and Anderson, A.R. (2008), 'Change and the development of entrepreneurial networks over time: a processual perspective', *Entrepreneurship & Regional Development*, **20**(2), 125–59.
Jack, S., Moult, S., Anderson, A. and Dodd, S. (2010), 'An entrepreneurial network evolving: patterns of change', *International Small Business Journal*, **28**(4), 315–37.
Jahre, M., Gadde, L.-E., Håkansson, H., Harrison, D. and Persson, G. (eds) (2006), *Resourcing in Business Logistics – The Art of Systematic Combining*, Malmö: Liber and Copenhagen Business School.
Johanson, J. and Mattsson, L.-G. (1992), 'Network positions and strategic action – an analytical framework', in B. Axelsson and G. Easton (eds), *Industrial Networks: A New View of Reality*, London: Routledge, pp. 205–14.
Johnson, V. (2007), 'What is organizational imprinting? Cultural entrepreneurship in the founding of the Paris Opera', *American Journal of Sociology*, **113**(1), 97–127.
Kim, T.-Y., Oh, H. and Swaminathan, A. (2006), 'Framing interorganizational network change: a network inertia perspective', *The Academy of Management Review*, **31**(3), 704–20.
La Rocca, A., Ford, D. and Snehota, I. (2013), 'Initial relationship development in new business ventures', *Industrial Marketing Management*, **42**(7), 1025–32.
Lechner, C. and Dowling, M. (2003), 'Firm networks: external relationships as sources for the growth and competitiveness for entrepreneurial firms', *Entrepreneurship & Regional Development*, **15**(1), 1–26.
Marquis, C. (2003), 'The pressure of the past: network imprinting in intercorporate communities', *Administrative Science Quarterly*, **48**(4), 655–89.
Milanov, H. and Fernhaber, S.A. (2009), 'The impact of early imprinting on the evolution of new venture networks', *Journal of Business Venturing*, **24**(1), 46–61.
Mu, J. (2013), 'Networking capability, new venture performance and entrepreneurial rent', *Journal of Research in Marketing and Entrepreneurship*, **15**(2), 101–23.
Ragin, C.C. (1992), '"Casing" and the process of social inquiry', in C.C. Ragin and H.B. Becker (eds), *What is a Case? Exploring the Foundations of Social Inquiry*, Cambridge: Cambridge University Press, pp. 217–26.
Semrau, T. and Werner, A. (2014), 'How exactly do network relationships pay off? The effects of network size and relationship quality on access to start-up resources', *Entrepreneurship Theory and Practice*, **38**(3), 501–25.
Slotte-Kock, S. and Coviello, N. (2010), 'Entrepreneurship research on network processes: a review and ways forward', *Entrepreneurship Theory and Practice*, **34**(1), 31–57.
Yin, R.K. (2003), *Case Study Research Design and Methods*, 3rd edn, Thousand Oaks, CA: Sage Publications.

PART II

Formal Networks: A New Research Agenda?

5. Business and professional networks: scope and outcomes in Oxfordshire, UK*

Helen Lawton Smith and Saverio Romeo

INTRODUCTION

The growing demand for networks has been identified as one of the distinctive features of the evolution of high-tech economies. Saxenian (1994) and later Benner (2003) have argued that the success of Silicon Valley's economy since the 1950s is fundamentally linked with the dense social networks that exist across organizational boundaries. The argument for the significance of networks per se is that they are 'key mechanisms through which external economies benefit local firms and are ultimately responsible for the emergence, growth and success of a cluster of innovative firms' (Breschi and Malerba, 2005, p. 5). Even though Benner's setting is that of professional networks, his emphasis is on the informal social networks that develop within them rather than on outcomes of formal associations.

This chapter focuses on the scope and outcomes of formal business and occupationally based professional (OBP) networks. They are important because exposure to a range of new contacts in these networks results 'in an increased capacity to access new resources' (Huggins, 2010, p. 343). Here it is shown that, although the number of such networks is rising, they are not geographically evenly distributed in respect of either when they were established or their numbers or type. Their extent, membership and utilization reflect differences not only in economic activity in particular locations, but also the expectations of national and local public authorities that subsidize them.

Formal networks need to be understood not solely as a paradigm about functional, socially underpinned business interconnections, but also from the perspective of the role of place in determining networking activity. Where they occur reflects a demand for the resources they potentially offer. The chapter adapts a framework by Bennett (1998), who identified two broad categories of demand for business associations: the logic of services and the logic of influence. Here the idea of different logics is used to consider how formal networks generate different types of value and how this varies with place. These are: (1) network logics: why do individuals/firms engage in particular kinds of networks?; (2) networks as a service: what do they seek to procure from these networks?; and (3) networks as a resource: what value do they provide?

To answer these questions, the chapter draws on two bodies of evidence. The first is a review of formation by type, age profile and function of business and OBP networks in Oxfordshire and in comparison with the rest of the Oxfordshire–Cambridge (O2C) Arc. The second is a survey of members of networks in Oxfordshire. Both types of evidence suggest that growth in formalized networking activity provides an indication that informal networking does not necessarily give access to new suppliers and customers, technology and knowledge (Bessant and Tidd, 2007). The original study followed a chance remark that there were too many networks in Oxfordshire, meaning that the sheer proliferation meant too many choices between competing networks. From an examination of the evidence of network formation and utilization, it is proposed that there is a three-stage process in the development of network density: (1) a rise in the number of networks; (2) institutionalization of networks; and (3) rationalization and consolidation. The chapter proceeds by outlining the rationale for the research questions. It then discusses these networks in practice in Oxfordshire. It concludes with an assessment of what such networks reveal about the importance of place in formal networking.

BUSINESS AND PROFESSIONAL NETWORKS IN THEORY

Networks provide varying types of value in different places. 'Value' can be understood as arising from three different logics relating to their formation, utilization and outcomes. The first is network logics: the reasons firms engage in particular types of networks and why they vary by place. The second is the logic of services: the value that they are expected to provide as a means of achieving competitive advantage, and how this is influenced by local industrial structures. The third is the logic of resources: the value that they actually provide as a local resource to their participants and the region.

Network Logics

The first question is why firms and individuals engage in particular types of formal business and OBP networks. The answer is related to what and where they are. The criterion for defining both is that participants attend events or otherwise meet with other business or professional people (such as through online networks) because they expect a return on the time and other resources invested. Networks vary by sector, by function, costs of membership, when they meet, and entry criteria. Some networks are very formal, having officers, bye-laws, dues and regular meetings (Besser et al., 2006). Not all charge a membership fee, while some charge non-members more than members for specific events. Some are open to all, while others, particularly OBP networks, have restrictions on membership. Certain types of networks provide specialist services; others facilitate general introductions.

Generally the logic of formal networking is translated into seven types of activity:

(i) sector-specific membership organizations of firms and associated professionals;
(ii) gender-specific, for example women-only networks;
(iii) functionally specific, with cross-sector activity with specific functions such as business-angel-type networks;
(iv) OBP networks: meetings where professionals meet each other. In some cases membership is limited to specific criteria, such as university-based networks, which are open only to current members and alumni of the university;
(v) general networks cross-cutting sectors and activities;
(vi) breakfast, lunch and dinner clubs, which have general membership;
(vii) virtual networks – cross-cutting membership; some also host events.

Alongside these are events run by 'network hosts'. These include universities, firms of solicitors, and business and science parks. In the UK, universities' involvement in such networking activities reflects the current political agenda for their greater involvement in local and regional economies (Kitson et al., 2009). Participants at events, in addition to business people, include professionals such as lawyers, patent agents and policy makers.

Business networks exist because firms and individuals lack access to certain types of resources and services (Bennett, 1998; Huggins, 2010). Access can most effectively be gained by meeting or in other ways being in formal contact with other firms and professionals in a region where they would not otherwise meet (Bennett, 1998). Johannisson (1998) found that individuals such as academic entrepreneurs may join networks as a way of gaining legitimacy in the business community while maintaining legitimacy in the academic community. Professional networks are also useful to founders of companies as a way of keeping in touch with their educational origins.

The expectation of value that networks offer to members can be a reflection of the stage of business development: resource needs of start-up businesses are different from those of established businesses (Besser et al., 2006). Participation has been found to be particularly significant in pre-firm formation and subsequent entrepreneurial behaviour. Starr and MacMillan (1990) found that networks provide a means of mobilizing social resources as a way of organizing new business activity. Accordingly, nascent entrepreneurs are often to be found as members as well as owner-managers (Chell and Baines, 2000), directors of companies and so on. Moreover, particular phases of the innovation process are significant in the propensity of firms to network in order to gain access to commercially useful information (Rutten and Boekma, 2004). Firm size is also relevant. Although advantages of network membership accrue to large and small firms, the more limited resources of small ones may mean that membership is important for survival.

The importance of place is indicated by the number, rate of formation of networks and the form that network events take. Each location has its own set of networks reflecting past and present industrial structures (see Bathelt and Boggs, 2003). Some types are prevalent in most regions, such as those organized by chambers of commerce. Local branches of national organizations such as the Athena Network for Business Women and the Institute of Directors (IOD) are present in some places. Specialized networks, for example for the biotech industry, reflect current local sectoral concentrations of firms. Other networks are place-based and are part of the service provided by the providers of infrastructure such as science parks and incubators: they run events for their tenants that are also open to other participants.

That some places are more collaborative than others seems to be related to the type and stage of regional development. Huggins and Johnston (2009) found, and this is supported by this study, that in successful regions, particularly high-tech ones, demand for formal networks is higher (network thick). Less competitive regions lacking both a high density of knowledge-based firms able to absorb new knowledge from external sources and a networked business culture are 'network thin' – demand is lower.

In successful regions such as Silicon Valley (Benner, 2003), new networks form where firms' and professionals' interests have been underrepresented. For example, the rapid increase in the number of women-only networks in the UK since 2000 recognizes that there are needs for women in business that are not being fulfilled (Miller et al., 2007). In the USA, Benner (2003) drew attention to the lack of the 'good ol' boys' networks that women in

Silicon Valley faced, which led to the formation of Silicon Valley Webgrrls in 1997. The geography of new networks is therefore indicative of expectations translated into a demand for networking opportunities (stage one). 'Network thick' similarly applies to the quality and range of organizations that host business networks in particular locations to meet this demand. The leverage they provide as a service derives from their attractiveness to business and professional people. The stronger the pull, the greater the distance people will travel to meetings, based on their expectations of the quality of the experience.

The advantage of network density for both participants and a region is that, if a regional environment is full of information ties (Saxenian, 1994), it will be better able to diffuse new knowledge than regions without dense ties (Huggins and Johnston, 2009). Formal networks are a type of locally based cross-firm 'communities of practice' (Wenger, 1998) and 'networks of practice' (Brown and Duguid, 2000). Both allow for the cumulative effects of face-to-face knowledge accumulation and sharing, and embody the economic motivation for local and specialized membership (information exchange) involving a range of occupations and professions. Social relationships are a key component of formal networking activities.

Logic of Services

The second question is: what value do participants in networks value as the service they give to their business or professional interests, and why does place matter? The answer to the first part is that they provide solutions to problems of resource procurement and environmental uncertainty (Besser et al., 2006). Resources are the key to firms' capacity to innovate and to their competitiveness. In the resource-based view (RBV), firms are defined as bundles of unique resources (financial, physical, human capital and organizational) that lead to competitive advantage (Barney, 1991; Hessels and Terjesen, 2010) and to sustained superior long-term performance. The RBV has been used to explain what firms want from formal networks. For example, Parilli and Sacchetti (2008, p. 391) draw on Penrose's (1959) competence-view perspective, a variation of the RBV, to explain that interfirm linkages, such as through business networks, arise from the need to 'access external complementary competences and abilities, which may or not be found in their closest neighbours' and as instruments that will expand their own competences.

Formal networks as a service represent two interpretations of relational aspects of four types of resources: material (including inputs and infrastructure), knowledge, power and social capital (Bathelt and Glucker, 2005, p. 1545). First, 'resources are relational as their generation, interpretation and use' are dependent on the particular institutional structures, social relations, knowledge contexts and mental models of agents involved. Second, 'some types of resources such as power and social capital' are collective and built by routine social practices. Networks in this latter interpretation of providing the means for accessing the returns to resources are connected conceptually to Granovetter's work (1973, 1985) on weak and strong ties and on embeddedness (also Bathelt and Glucker, 2005 and Huggins and Johnston, 2009) and to trust (see also Woolcock and Narayan, 2000 on networks and social capital, and Rutten and Boekma, 2004 on the links between social capital and innovation).

Granovetter (1985) identified that economic actions are embedded within social relationships. Business relationships span the range of weak or strong ties between firms. Strong ties take the form of contractual joint ventures and supply chain networks (Besser and Miller, 2011) (institutional structures), whereas weak ties, bridging social capital, are part of a wide range network of information ties that help an individual make contact. Weak ties enable individuals to draw on information, advice and assistance from personal relationships outside the strong ties of family and close personal relationships. Granovetter (1994) also emphasized the importance of formal context in weak ties, identifying that firms can be connected by business groups, which are legally separate firms bound together in persistent formal and/or informal ways. Here formal networks are examples of institutional structures, providing the setting for both the development of informal functional as well as contractual relationships.

Smangs (2006) argues that social capital and trust make resource exchanges possible. Successful networks require honesty and reliability from members, relationships and trust between members, and willingness to share resources (Sherer, 2003; Inkpen and Tsang, 2005; Smangs, 2006). Both soft, that is, affective and relational, as well as hard trust, for example, reliability, are needed (Bennett and Ramsden, 2007).

Gulati's (2007) concept of 'network resources' (firms gain access to resources through interfirm networks) can be seen as expressing similar notions of dependence on external organizations and social relationships needed to operationalize resource acquisition. Huggins (2010, p. 339), however, finds Gulati's concept too vague and instead introduces the concept of 'network capital' to identify 'investments in calculative relations by firms through which they gain access to knowledge to enhance economic returns'. This is a similar idea to the use made by Bennett (1998) of Dasgupta's (1988) concept of 'calculative trust', which refers to the way that business associations are judged on the costs and benefits of the services they deliver (Cooke et al., 2005). Effectiveness is based on the quality of the experience at meetings and on subsequent outcomes compared to expectations.

Place is important from a resource acquisition perspective because of the availability of potential participants with expertise, status and calibre to make attending a network meeting and establishing social relationships worthwhile. Networks need to be of optimal size (Phillipson et al., 2006) and quality in order for resources to be obtained. In network-thick places the expectation of return is likely to be high because of the number and type of people with appropriate tradable resources, such as diversity of business age, size and sector, as well as the demographics of individual owners and managers (Besser and Miller, 2011). This includes support from member CEOs (Sherer, 2003) and others who have positions of importance within the member firms, or are seen as worth knowing professionally. For example, high-tech places are characterized by high densities of R&D-intensive business and educational and professional qualifications (Lawton Smith and Waters, 2011).

Also important is the quality of network leadership in creating structures that facilitate trust and resource exchanges. There is the likelihood of the highly skilled participating in formal networks, increasing their attractiveness (stage two). In other words, weak ties and social capital in particular places are calculative and in turn are related to the quality of the business and professional environment. Moreover, there is no assumption here that participation in formal networks is available to all. Even in network-thick places entrepreneurs and professionals can be constrained from network participation by a lack of relevant ties to other organizations that will help them overcome market failures in supply – for example for raising external finance (Zhang and Wong, 2008).

Networks as a Resource

The third question is: what do formal networks provide and why is network capital (Huggins, 2010) stronger in some places than in others? Studies have shown that the stock of formal networks is not constant and they are not equally successful. Criteria for effectiveness of a business network identified by Besser and Miller (2011, p. 115) include the network's contribution directly to the 'short term success of members' business interests through knowledge transfer and resource exchanges'. The authors identify other indicators of impact, such as personal and social support for the business owner, and the ability to influence government policy making and regulations.

Place matters in the number and range of successful networks and in the extent to which they provide the opportunity for firms and professionals to access resources. Spatial concentration of 'potential co-actors' implies a better matching of potential resource acquisition (Rutten et al., 2010, p. 867). Moreover, where participants in networks and hosted events have geographically extensive business and professional contacts, gains to firms and individuals are achieved through a process whereby networks act as 'open gates' that can bring new ideas and practices to the local economy as a whole (Eraydin and Armatlı-Köroğlu, 2005). Extra-local links, especially international ones, may be more important than local interactions in leading-edge firms' knowledge acquisition portfolios (Malmberg and Power, 2005). Crouch (2006) emphasizes the important role of formal institutions in reinforcing the industrial fabric of a region.

Formal networking opportunities thereby reinforce processes of regional change (Johannisson et al., 1994; Storper, 1997) because of the collective gains of inflows of ideas and contacts. A secondary effect is that formal networks may contribute to the economic climate of region (Besser and Miller, 2011) comprising an element of local business infrastructures and providing significant regional competitive advantages (Wolfe and Gertler, 2004).

Availability of networks is also related to the extent of public and private sector support for formal networks and events. The expectation of contributing to local economic development can be a factor in public funding. Private sponsorship enables accountancy and law firms, for example, to raise their profile with potential customers. Sometimes sources of funding dry up, for example those funded by national, regional or local policy bodies, due to political changes and pressures, not an uncommon feature of institutionalized activity (see Bennett and McCoshan, 1993).

Network churn (stage three) is also caused by other factors. For example, closure of a network may reflect the decline of its effectiveness over time. This can result from mistakes in the original structure or social processes (Miles and Snow, 1992). The markets that networks serve may have changed, or the motivation for organizations hosting networks becomes less important over time, irrespective of the value of the event to participants. Churn has the advantage of avoiding 'lock-in' whereby resources are dedicated to activities that no longer serve their original function.

To summarize: formal networking offers additional resources over and above formal networks. Place matters because of differences in prevalence of networks in different places due to differences in economic history, more recent specializations, and quantity and quality of participants. Services offered by business and occupationally based professional networks are indicative of forms of resource development in particular places.

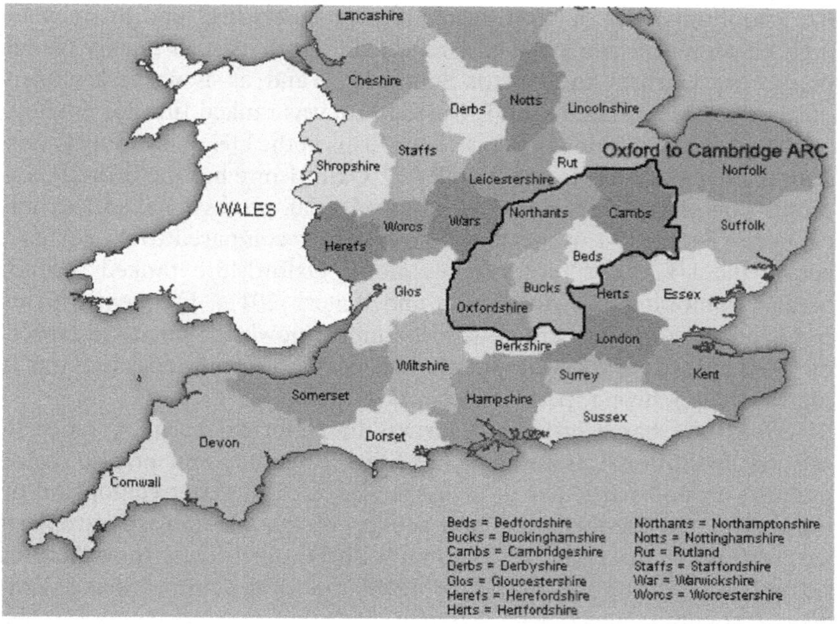

Source: The O2C Arc.

Figure 5.1 The Oxford to Cambridge Arc

FORMAL NETWORKS IN PRACTICE IN OXFORDSHIRE

The O2C Arc, before its demise in 2009, was marketed as a band of counties to the north and west of London from Cambridgeshire to Oxfordshire, and acted as a focus for driving forward innovation-led economic development (Figure 5.1). It was funded by the three regional development agencies (RDAs)[1] with counties comprising the Arc region: South East England Regional Development Agency (SEEDA); East of England Development Agency (EEDA); and East Midlands Development Agency (EMDA). A central remit of the O2C Arc programme was to increase collaboration between organizations in or near to Oxford and Cambridge and to link the two city-regions with the innovation community of the central area – its universities, high technology companies, entrepreneurs and skilled labour force.[2]

The case-study county, Oxfordshire, is one of Europe's leading centres of innovation-led economic development. Since the mid-1980s it has had, like Cambridgeshire, a growing number of enterprises and an increasingly entrepreneurial science base reflected in both its high-quality labour market (see Garnsey and Lawton Smith, 1998) and, as shown here, numerous business networks. In 2007, Oxfordshire was ranked fifth for employment and sixth for number of high-tech firms in the UK. Clustering is very strong in sectors such as scientific R&D. Oxfordshire has the fifth-highest proportion of residents employed in managerial, professional and technical occupations (just over half – 51 per cent – compared to 44 per cent across the UK). For professionals alone, Oxfordshire ranked second, behind Cambridge (Lawton Smith and Waters, 2011). Frequently, firms in Oxfordshire are concerned with the most knowledge-intensive aspects of these industries, for example in biotech. As in Cambridgeshire, this is represented by strong specialist networks.

Oxfordshire has a history of formal and informal business networking. Its institutional assemblage (coalition of public and private sector interests around particular growth agendas) and the interrelationship of innovation and the formation and activity of that assemblage have been key features of its high-tech economy. The Oxford Trust (now Science Oxford) was during the 1980s and 1990s the focal point of that assemblage through its networking activities, engaging with private and public sector organizations including Oxford University (Lawton Smith, 2003). It was established by the founders of Oxfordshire's leading high-tech firm, Oxford Instruments, in 1985. This was three years later than the Cambridge Europe Technology club (1982) but earlier than the St John's Innovation Centre established in 1987, which developed similar functions for the Cambridgeshire high-tech economy (Waters and Lawton Smith, 2002). The Oxford Trust introduced initiatives such as the Oxfordshire Investment Opportunity Network (OION) in 1994 (a technology business-angel network that links investors with entrepreneurs seeking early-stage funding) and Oxfordshire BiotechNet in 1997. More recently, the scope of formal networking has expanded as the high-tech economy has grown, with other organizations playing an increasing role.

Methodology

Evidence is drawn from two types of data. The first is information on number and type of networks in Oxfordshire. The second is an online survey. The study of business networks in Oxfordshire was conducted in 2006. A follow-up study was later funded by the O2C Arc, with coverage of the rest of the Arc. Here the discussion of the larger study is confined to the numbers of networks in each constituent local economic partnerships, the geographical unit of analysis for the study.

BOX 5.1 QUESTIONNAIRE CONTENT IN OXFORDSHIRE SURVEY

1. Company profile.
2. Value of business networking.
3. Where business networking happens.
4. Type of network(s) used.
5. Which were used most.
6. Relative importance of formal and informal networks to other ways of making contact.
7. What networks deliver to members.
8. What initiatives could be traced back to participation in a network.
9. Limitations/gaps of networks and opportunities to improve practical operational efficiency.

Information on the number of networks, their function and their membership, and network hosts in each location was gathered from an extensive range of sources. Locally known networks from previous studies and local organizations such as the Oxford Trust and the Oxfordshire Economic Partnership were contacted. This was followed by a snowballing technique of asking networks for further information on other networks. Information on membership (numbers and cost of membership), activities and frequency of meetings on each network's website was collated and network organizers were contacted for additional information. Each network was asked to send an email to their members asking them to participate. Follow-up requests were made for the networks by phone calls and emails to send reminders to their members to participate. A total of 114 usable questionnaires was completed from 28 members of networks, including 5 breakfast and lunch clubs. Information gathered through the questionnaire is shown in Box 5.1.

Most respondents were from business networks, with only two from OBP networks (the local branch of the IOD and the Oxford Business Alumni). Sectors represented included general business (retail, service, construction and consultancy), law- and finance-associated businesses, engineering and electronics, biotechnology, pharmaceuticals and medical, education and research, media and publishing, information and communications technology, and non-governmental organizations (NGOs). Only two replies were received from women-only networks.

The majority of respondents were based in Oxford. Around half were members of networks. Exceptions to this pattern were events and meetings organized by the IOD, which were primarily attended by members (13 out

Table 5.1 Networks in each economic partnership across the O2C Arc showing populations using 2001 Census data

County	Number of networks	Population	Head of population per network
Oxfordshire	65	605492	9315
Cambridgeshire	59	552655	9367
Milton Keynes	38	207063	5449
Bedfordshire	23	381571	16590
Northamptonshire	20	629676	31483
Buckinghamshire	16	479028	29939
Total	221	2855485	12920

Source: Oxfordshire Economic Observatory (OEO), http://oeo.geog.ox.ac.uk.

of 17), whereas of respondents who attended OION events, only 8 out of 25 were members.

Network Logics

Some 221 business networks were found to operate in the Arc (Table 5.1). Areas within the Arc can be classified in two categories. The first includes two high-tech regions where demand for networks is high, Oxfordshire and Cambridgeshire, and the unitary authority Milton Keynes. All three are relatively 'network thick'. Milton Keynes has a much higher proportion of networks per size of population than the other two, being one-third of the size of Oxfordshire. Although it has a research university (the Open University) and aspirations for developing high-value, knowledge-based sectors,[3] its economy is more diverse and its relatively dense set of networks offers less specialized services. For example, the Sparc Technology network[4] is 'managed by the Milton Keynes Enterprise Hub and run by knowledge-based organisations for technology-led individuals and organisations who are seeking to develop face-to-face networking opportunities, whether they are in academia, a start up or existing business or an incoming business'.

Other locations, that is, Aylesbury and Luton, are in transition from economies based on traditional industries to more knowledge-based economies. Northamptonshire's economic strategy has a strong focus on inward investment.[5] Each is characterized as 'network thin', suggesting that formal networks are less of a collective resource. Buckinghamshire, however, in spite of a higher than the national average number of new businesses starting up each year and flagship economic activities such as the British motor sport industry,[6] Pinewood studios[7] and international companies such as GE Healthcare, Volvo and Martin Baker Aircraft,[8] has one of the lowest densities of networks in the Arc.

The earliest networks were hosted by chambers of commerce. Both kinds of network, particularly smaller business networks (breakfast, lunch and dinner clubs), have become much more popular since the mid-1990s (Table 5.2). The Oxfordshire Chamber is the oldest (1906). The figure also shows that the demand for specialist networks started earlier in Oxfordshire and Cambridgeshire than elsewhere.

In the middle of the Arc, the majority of networks have been established since 2000, consistent with the argument that networks and networking are associated with particular stages of economic development (Rutten and Boekma, 2004; Boschma and Frenken, 2006). This reflects a shift towards economies becoming more 'knowledge-based' – that is, the number of networks increases as the demand for material as well as knowledge-accessing resources and services rises (see Parilli and Sacchetti, 2008).

Alongside and part of these developments is the involvement of knowledge-based networking activities by 'knowledge-based' organizations such as universities. Until the late 1990s, Oxford University did not formally participate in initiatives designed to support the Oxfordshire high-tech economy (Lawton Smith, 2003). More recently it has hosted events and networks, particularly OBP networks. Since 1999, Oxford University's Saïd Business School Science Enterprise Centre has acted as a host for networking events such as Venturefest (an annual fair for bringing entrepreneurs and funders together) and other high-profile networking seminars. Oxford Business Alumni is 'Oxford's official global business alumni network'.[9] While Cambridge similarly hosts networks such as Biology in Business,[10] the Open University, Cranfield and Bedfordshire universities were not mentioned as network hosts in this study. OBP networks exist independently in the middle of the Arc. For example, the Chartered Institute of Marketing, Milton Keynes Branch, aims to lead the development of professional standards and practice, and champion the big issues and new ideas in the marketing world.[11]

Size of networks varies, although that does not necessarily indicate their importance for participants. For example, Science Oxford has around 400 members and the Oxfordshire Chambers of Commerce has some 1400 members. The Oxford Innovation-run family of business-angel networks (OION, Oxford Early Investments and Thames Valley Investment Network) had over 150 members. The Oxford Construction Training Network had 50 members.

Networks can be non-profit, private or joint public–private partnerships. In Oxfordshire, excluding breakfast/lunch clubs, out of 31 formal business networks in Oxfordshire, 21 were private (funded by membership

Table 5.2 Chronology of networks

	Oxfordshire	Cambridgeshire	Milton Keynes	Buckinghamshire/ Northamptonshire	Bedfordshire
1900	1906 Oxfordshire Chamber of Commerce and Trade 1979 Oxford Chamber of Commerce		Chamber of Commerce	1917 Northamptonshire Chamber Bucks Chamber of Commerce	Chamber of Commerce
1980	1985 The Oxford Trust 1987 Oxford Innovation 1987 The Oxford Biotech Net 1988 ISIS Innovation	1982 Cambridge Europe and Technology Club 1987 Cambridge Hi-Tech Network of SMEs 1989 Cambridge Business Women's Network	1981 Stony Stratford Business Association		
1990	1990 ISIS Business Angels ISIS Angels Network 1990 Oxford Innovation Society 1991 Oxfordshire Bioscience Network				

	1994 Oxfordshire Construction Training Group	1993 Women in Science Group 1994 Cambridge Association for Women in S&E	1993 The Milton Keynes Media Circle		
	1995 The Oxfordshire Investment Opportunity Network	1995 Biology in Business			1995 Ampthill & Flitwick Business Breakfast Club
	1998 Oxford Business Alumni 1998 Oxlt Cluster	1997 ERBI 1998 Cambridge Network 1998 Enterprise Link 1998 Medilink East 1999 WiSETI			
2000	2000 Be Your Boss Club		2000 Central Innovation Network		
	2001 Oxford Science Enterprise	2001 i10 Network 2001 PROWESS 2002 Winning Connections for Women	2000 Connection MK 2002 Teabag Talent 2002 MKP Anet	2001 Cross Reference	2001 i10 Network 2001 PROWESS
	2003 Oxford Entrepreneurs 2003 Thames Valley Investments Network			2004 Be Your Own Boss 2004 BizNet 2004 Aylesbury Business Club	2004 Bedford SME Breakfast Club

Table 5.2 (continued)

	Oxfordshire	Cambridgeshire	Milton Keynes	Buckinghamshire/ Northamptonshire	Bedfordshire
	2005 Oxford Private Equity Network 2005 Oxford Early Investments 2005 Oxford Town Chambers Network	2005 Enterprising Women			
			2006 MK Enterprise Gateway 2007 SPARC Tech Network 2007 Women's Business Starter Network		2004 South Beds SME Breakfast Club 2006 Wyboston SME Breakfast Club

fees supplemented by donations and sponsors including accountancy firms and investment banks). The rest were either joint private–public partnerships or non-profit organizations. Investment networks are funded through members, sponsors, fees and activities.

Sponsorship by public authorities is important. In the middle of the Arc, public funding for business networks is significant in sustaining networks. For example, the i10 Network was funded by EEDA to allow partnerships between graduates, job seekers and industry, while the Mid-Beds Business Breakfast Club was sponsored by Bedfordshire County Council. SEEDA, however, in 2005 recognized the need to make networks more effective and avoid duplication of activities. Following a review, the number of networks supported was reduced. Focus moved to innovative growth sectors, originally based on six sector consortia, which were business-led, not-for-profit organizations. None was based in the Arc. This process of policy review is similar to that found in the 1970s by Bennett and Krebs (1993).

OBN, managed by Oxford Brookes University between 2006 and 2008, replaced the Oxfordshire BiotechNet, following removal of SEEDA funding. OBN has grown from local to regional network hosting international events. Its members come from across the South East. This change indicates the importance of formal networks to the sector, but also that sometimes the organizing body needs to change.

Network logics are different across the Arc, even between Oxfordshire and Cambridgeshire, as well as in network-thick Milton Keynes, for example in the number of women-only networks and investment networks. Although the number of women-only networks has increased, particularly, as in Silicon Valley (Benner, 2003), in Cambridge, where there are at least five. Examples include 'Enterprising Women', a business network for 'women living and working in and around Cambridge' and 'The Cambridge Graduate Women's network', an OPB network, both established in 2005. At the time of the study there was one in Oxfordshire and four in Milton Keynes.

Another difference is in the incidence of investment networks. There are now five in Oxfordshire, all of which support high-tech and innovative companies with high growth potential, but none were found in Cambridgeshire nor in Milton Keynes. Oxfordshire's oldest, OION, is 'Europe's most successful technology business-angel network that links investors with entrepreneurs seeking early stage funding'. Since 2001, OION has helped close nearly 100 deals, raising over £21.5m for companies.[12] Oxford Innovation has since established four more specialist investment networks. Among them, Oxford Early Investment (2006) is a business-angel network helping innovative companies at early stages of technical and commercial development raise investment capital of up to £150 000. Similarly, Thames Valley Investment Network funds high-tech companies with £50 000–£500 000. In Cambridge, business-angel and other forms of finance appear to be available through other routes. The St John's Innovation Centre (St John's College) has a business-angel database and runs training programmes (Waters and Lawton Smith, 2002).

Virtual networks exist in the three network-thick locations. Science Oxford, like the Cambridge Network,[13] provides an online newsletter and notification of events, job vacancies and so on. The Central Innovation Network based in Milton Keynes is a 'network of networks'[14] 'intended to increase the success and prestige of the Central part of the Oxford to Cambridge Arc'.

Logic of Services

The survey investigated respondents' expected objectives from membership and/or attending events. These are shown in Figure 5.2. This shows that expectation of gaining access to new customers was the prime motivation for membership. Potential contractual, structural relationships that provide entry into new markets involving 'hard trust' (Bennett and Ramsden, 2007) were therefore the primary target for making contact with other companies. Information sharing was second and making contacts in

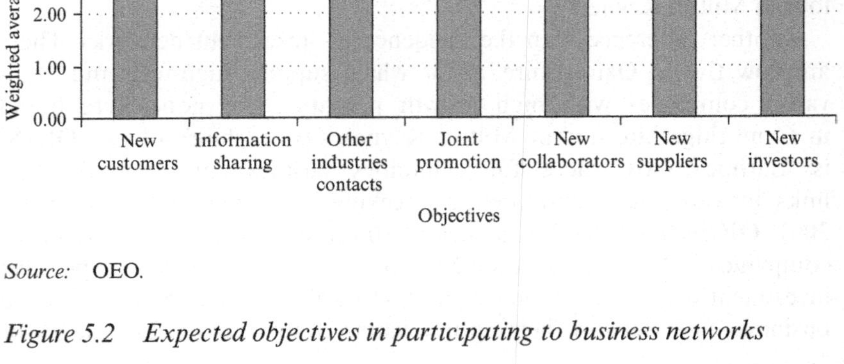

Source: OEO.

Figure 5.2 Expected objectives in participating to business networks

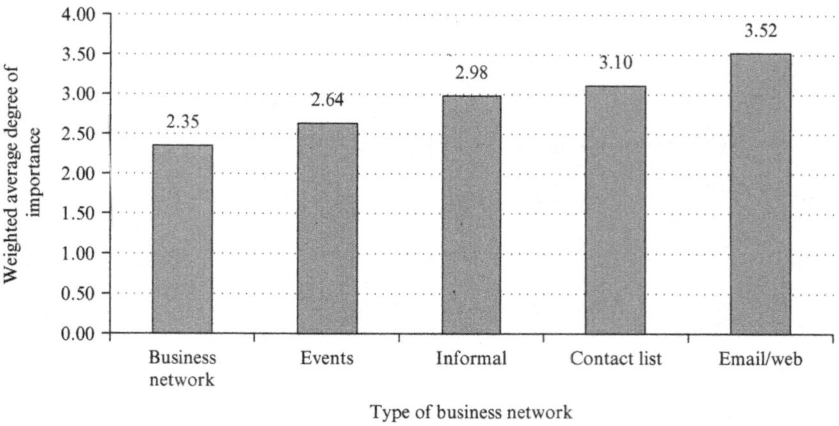

Note: Scale of importance is 1: most important to 5: least important.

Source: OEO.

Figure 5.3 Types of business networks and degree of importance

other industries was third. Gaining access to new investors was the least important.

Business networks and events are the two most important in a portfolio of networking activities. They are ahead of events and informal networks (Figure 5.3). Other forms include companies' contacts lists, Internet searches, business referrals, targeted research and advertising. Email and web-based interactions were the least important of the main forms of activity, suggesting that they had a less direct influence than face-to-face contact on inter-company/interfirm interaction. Therefore social relations or social capital (Woolcock and Narayan, 2000; Besser and Miller, 2011) can be inferred as being important in the expectation of value from participation.

Networks as a Resource

The ability of the networks to meet the expected objectives of their members is shown in Figure 5.4. Responses were overwhelmingly positive: only four respondents replied that networks have not delivered significant outcomes for their companies. This suggests that investment decisions on participation based on 'calculative trust' (Bennett, 1998) and 'network capital' (Huggins, 2010) paid off. While the expectation of meeting new clients appears to be satisfied, it seems that the main outcome

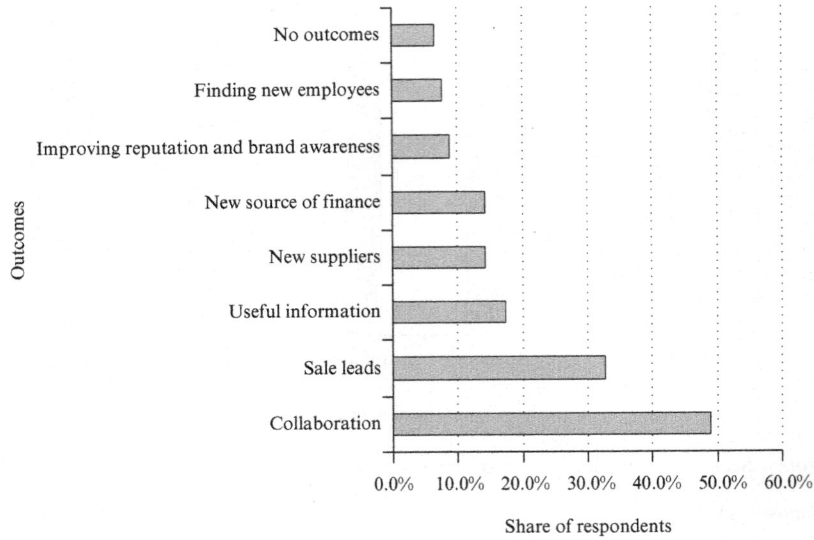

Source: OEO.

Figure 5.4 Outcomes from participation in business networks

was collaboration with other firms. Over two-thirds rated this as most important and over one-third used networks for this purpose, suggesting that Oxfordshire is a highly collaborative place. Information sharing, while scoring high on expected outcomes, in contrast with what might be expected from the learning-region literature (see Lawson and Lorenz, 1999; Benner, 2003), was of less importance, at least in Oxfordshire.

Encountering diverse people from different industries to access complementary competences and abilities across sectoral boundaries was significant for over half of the sample, but was not ranked by many as the prime benefit. That this might be the means of providing value to participants is supported by the status of people who responded to the questionnaire. Respondents were overwhelmingly senior people in the companies, for example directors (42 per cent), managers (13 per cent), business owners and traders (12 per cent), and CEOs and chairmen (9 per cent). Hence the prospect of value is increased by the kinds of people who attend. This is in turn a function of place because of the potential number of highly skilled people attending events.

Networks do not seem to be particularly useful resources for finding new employees, improving brand reputation/awareness or for finding finance. The low ranking of access to finance, however, had a sectoral bias. It was particularly important for the high-tech companies within the biotechnology, pharmaceuticals and medical, and engineering sectors, suggesting demand for specialist funding. The evidence on the importance of representation of interests to outside organizations was mixed. It scored low on being most important but was similarly ranked with other advantages of networks. Hence there is some support for Bathelt and Glucker's (2005) notion that influence in formal networks is a resource for their members, providing leverage on external organizations – Bennett's (1998) 'logic of influence'.

The survey also revealed sectoral differences in what networks delivered. Business networks were identified as being very important for all 11 respondents within the biotechnology, pharmaceuticals and medical sector. As well as new investors, services provided included facilitating international collaboration, mentoring, fundraising, collaborators and customers. For example, one company secured 'one major international collaboration and five new and currently active leads through business networks'. All other respondents gave examples of successful contacts/projects. OBN and the Oxford Trust were highlighted as key organizations.

Within the engineering and electronics sector, participants viewed networks positively, as providing good business and professional opportunities. Among others, the Oxford Trust, Connect4Success, Institute of Business Advisors, MNT network (national network of UK micro- and nanotechnology sector) and TVIN were among those highlighted as key facilitators. Within sectors such as IT, media and publishing, and research and education, business networks provided general opportunities for finding collaborators, customers, suppliers and client referrals. For example, for a publishing company, 'approximately 98% of our current business is achieved through networking and referrals'.

Tips with business referrals were one of the most important outcomes for the general business sector, which included service and retail, construction and consultancy industries. For example, one construction company secured 'contracts, totalling over 340k in three years, traceable back to referrals from members of networking groups'.

Advertising and profile-raising were among the most significant outcomes within the law and finance sector. One bank noted that 'they [networks] are good for raising our profile within the technology sector, which improves our knowledge and credibility, which in turns results in more companies choosing our bank as their banking partner'. All four NGO/charity organizations replied that business networks had provided their organization with the possibility of fundraising.

Networks are therefore established particularly for material advantages

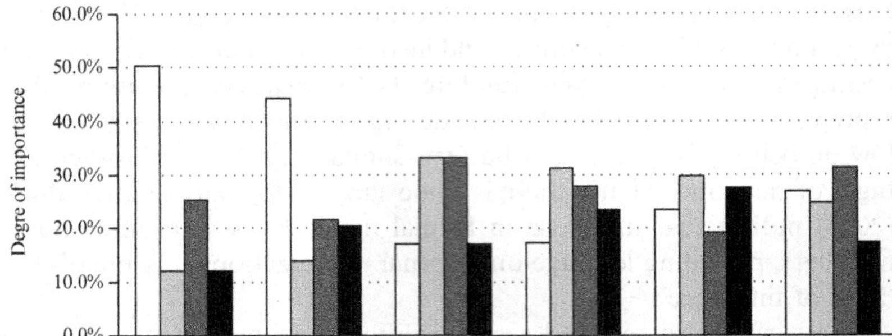

	Available labour	Good infrastructure	Prestige	Access to university	Access to local business services	Suppotive local government
□ More important	50.5%	44.1%	17.0%	17.2%	23.4%	26.9%
▨ Less important	12.1%	14.0%	33.0%	31.2%	29.8%	24.7%
▩ No opinion	25.3%	21.5%	33.0%	28.0%	19.1%	31.2%
■ Same	12.1%	20.4%	17.0%	23.7%	27.7%	17.2%

Factors

Source: OEO.

Figure 5.5 Importance of business networks compared to other local factors

and to a lesser extent as conduits of information. These findings are consistent with Granovetter's (1994, 2005) arguments about the importance of formal contexts in the making and utilization of social ties.

In order to put the importance of networks in perspective, firms were asked about the relative importance of business networks compared with other aspects of Oxfordshire as a place to do business (Figure 5.5). More important than networks were available labour, good infrastructure and supportive local government. Less important than networks were prestige of the location, accessing local business services and linking to universities. Responses to this question, however, revealed a surprising level of no opinion on some indicators, particularly that of locational prestige and the value of local government.

Nearly one-third said there were too many networks (28 per cent) and one-fifth (21 per cent) found gaps in network coverage. Others reported that there were not enough members (17 per cent), and they did not provide enough business opportunities (17 per cent). Some smaller firms unsurprisingly reported that network membership was too expensive. Over half (68) responded to the question of how networks could be improved. The main suggestions were: better coordination to reduce overlap; improved publicity about events; and more information on the content and objectives of events. Several responded that they should attract more relevant market players, and networking modes could be better.

Recently a number of networks have disappeared. As suggested earlier, a lack of success is not the only reason for this. Some had run their course. For example, the Chamber of Commerce high-tech network, RESBIG (REsearch and Science Based Industry Group, Oxfordshire Chamber of Commerce), organized network meetings in conjunction with the Oxford Science Park. The last meeting that used the RESBIG name was in January 2008, when some 60 people attended. The Oxfordshire BiotechNet had been very successful up to the mid-2000s, but was deemed by SEEDA to have become unsuccessful. Oxmedia.net and OXIT, although there were positive comments in the survey, did not attract members and have since disappeared.

CONCLUSIONS

This chapter set out to contribute to a better understanding of the formation and utilization of various types of formal networks in different places. It is argued that the 'network paradigm' that emerged in the 1990s (Simmie, 2008) and is now pervasive in learning-region and cluster literatures underplays the importance of formal networks. The chapter adopted a threefold framework: network logics, what they are and where they are; services logic, a demand for making business and professional contacts, what they value in those contacts; and a resource logic, the outcomes of networking activity. These are understood from the perspective of the role of place in determining network patterns and types of networks.

The logic of networks is that they exist to provide specialist and generalist events, and other contact points for people with similar business and professional interests to meet. They vary by sector, function, activity and organization. The importance of place in this logic arises from the stage of development of businesses, sectors and careers, and associated industrial structures. The geography of formal networking activity appears to be associated with particular phases in economic development and coexisting particular socioeconomic circumstances. Networks are formed because the chance of meeting people with appropriate resources needs to be improved by formal settings. In innovation-led economies, demand for business and OBP networks is high (stage one in a process of new network formation). Moreover, as this study shows, the number and diversity of organizations that host business networks is also increasing. The universities of Oxford and Cambridge are in the van of this trend. Even so, networks are not evenly distributed by type of network, even in what might appear to be places with similar economies such as Oxfordshire and Cambridgeshire.

What participants expect from networks, networks as a service, is to provide solutions to problems of resource procurement and environmental uncertainty (Besser and Miller, 2011). This is consistent with the RBV through accessing services from other organizations (collaboration, information) (Bennett, 1998). In this sense, resources gained through networks can be understood as being relational (Bathelt and Glucker, 2005), their use being contingent on particular institutional structures, social relations and knowledge contexts (stage two).

Networks as resource was demonstrated as expectations and outcomes were largely matched; that is, investments in calculative relations (Huggins, 2010) had paid off. Demand centred on the need to gain access to new customers, a demand that does not appear to be made though informal networks (stage three). Consolidation and coordination (churn) of networks is also part of this stage. As in this study, closure of networks results from decisions made by public and private agencies to stop funding them, a feature of institutionalized activity identified by Bennett and McCoshan (1993).

In sum, formal networking should be seen in the broader context of expectations and demand resource development in firms, individuals and regions. In network-thick regions (Huggins and Johnston, 2009), formal networks form geographically focused and distinctive business practices that contribute to local business infrastructures and hence to the competitiveness of the region (see Wolfe and Gertler, 2004).

Finally, while this study has identified certain patterns, it has a number of limitations. Accordingly, there is scope for further work that examines how formal networking behaviour differs in varying geographical contexts.

ACKNOWLEDGEMENTS

The Oxfordshire Economic Observatory and the O2C Arc are thanked for sponsoring the studies. The authors are indebted to Professors Bob Bennett, Daniele Archibugi, John Slater and Robert Huggins for their helpful comments, and to the referees and the editor on a previous version of this chapter.

NOTES

* An earlier version of this paper was published as H. Lawton Smith, S. Romeo and M. Virahsawmy (2012), 'Business and professional networks: scope and outcomes in Oxfordshire', *Environment and Planning A*, **44**(8), 1801–18.

1. RDAs were discontinued in 2010, following a change of UK government.
2. http://www.oxford2cambridge.net/ (accessed 9 April 2008).
3. http://www.mkelp.co.uk/mkelp-home/DisplayArticle.asp?ID=36819 (accessed 8 February 2011).
4. http://www.sparcmiltonkeynes.com/PagePreview.aspx?web_id=42.
5. http://www.northamptonshireenterprise.ltd.uk/whatwedo/inwardinvestment.asp (accessed 7 June 2008).
6. www.silverstone-circuit.co.uk/html/.
7. www.pinewoodshepperton.com.
8. http://www.buck-ep.co.uk/bucks_economy.asp.
9. http://www.oba.co.uk/OBA/NonSecure/External/EventsHome.aspx?operation=forthcoming.
10. http://www.biologyinbusiness.org/.
11. http://www.cim.co.uk/.
12. http://www.oion.co.uk/.
13. http://www.cambridgenetwork.co.uk/.
14. http://www.centralinnovation.co.uk/aboutus/index.htm.

REFERENCES

Barney, J.B. (1991), 'Firm resources and sustained competitive advantage', *Journal of Management*, **17**, 99–120.

Bathelt, H. and Boggs, J.S. (2003), 'Towards a reconceptualisation of regional development paths: is Leipzig's media cluster a continuation of or a rupture with the past?', *Economic Geography*, **79**(3), 265–93.

Bathelt, H. and Glucker, J. (2005), 'Resources in economic geography: from substantive concepts towards a relational perspective', *Environment and Planning A*, **37**, 1545–63.

Benner, C. (2003), 'Learning communities in a learning region: the soft infrastructure of cross-firm learning networks in Silicon Valley', *Environment and Planning A*, 1809–30.

Bennett, R.J. (1998), 'Business associations and their potential contributions to competitiveness of SMEs', *Entrepreneurship and Regional Development*, **10**, 243–60.

Bennett, R.J. and McCoshan, A. (1993), *Enterprise and Human Resource Development: Local Capacity Building*, London: Paul Chapman Publishing.

Bennett, R. and Krebs, G. (1993), 'Chambers of commerce in Britain and Germany: the challenges of the Single Market', in R.J. Bennett, G. Krebs and H. Zimmermann (eds), *Chambers of Commerce in Britain and Germany and the Single European Market*, London: Anglo-German Foundation, pp. 1–38.

Bennett, R. and Ramsden, M. (2007), 'The contribution of business associations to SMEs: strategy, bundling or reassurance?', *International Small Business Journal*, **25**(1), 49–76.

Bessant, J. and Tidd, J. (2007), *Innovation and Entrepreneurship*, Chichester, UK: John Wiley & Sons.

Besser, T.L. and Miller, N. (2011), 'The structural, social and strategic factors associated with successful networks', *Entrepreneurship and Regional Development*, **23**(3–4), 113–34.

Besser, T.L., Miller, N. and Perkins, R.K. (2006), 'For the greater good: business networks and business social responsibility to communities', *Entrepreneurship & Regional Development*, **18**(4), 321–40.

Boschma, R.A. and Frenken, K. (2006), 'Why is economic geography not an evolutionary science?', *Journal of Economic Geography*, **6**, 273–302.

Breschi, S. and Malerba, F. (2005), 'Clusters, networks, and innovation: research results and new directions', in S. Breschi and F. Malerba (eds), *Clusters, Networks and Innovation*, Oxford: Oxford University Press, pp. 1–28.

Brown, J.S. and Duguid, P. (2000), *The Social Life of Information*, Boston, MA: Harvard Business School Press.

Chell, E. and Baines, S. (2000), 'Networking, entrepreneurship and microbusinesses', *Entrepreneurship and Regional Development*, **12**, 195–215.

Cooke, P., Clifton, N. and Oleaga, M. (2005), 'Social capital, firm embeddedness and regional development', *Regional Studies*, **39**(8), 1065–78.

Crouch, C. (2006), 'Specialisation and networking in medium-sized cities', in *Competitive Cities in the Global Economy*, Paris: OECD, pp. 317–28.

Dasgupta, P. (1988), 'Trust as a commodity', in D. Gambetta (ed.), *Trust: Making and Breaking Cooperative Relations*, Oxford: Basil Blackwell, pp. 49–72.

Eraydin, A. and Armatlı-Köroğlu, B. (2005), 'Innovation, networking and the new industrial clusters: the characteristics of networks and local innovation capabilities in the Turkish industrial clusters', *Entrepreneurship & Regional Development*, **17**(4), 237–66.

Garnsey, E. and Lawton Smith, H. (1998), 'Proximity and complexity in the emergence of high technology industry: the Oxbridge comparison', *Geoforum*, **29**(4), 433–50.

Granovetter, M. (1973), 'The strength of weak ties: a network theory revisited', *Sociological Theory*, **1**, 201–33.

Granovetter, M. (1985), 'Economic action and social structure: the problem of embeddedness', *American Journal of Sociology*, **91**(3), 481–510.

Granovetter, M.S. (1994), 'Business groups', in N.J. Smelser and R. Swedberg (eds), *Handbook of Economic Sociology*, Princeton NJ: Princeton University Press, pp. 453–75.

Granovetter, M. (2005), 'The impact of social structure on economic outcomes', *Journal of Economic Perspectives*, **19**(1), 33–50.

Gulati, R. (2007), *Managing Network Resources: Alliances, Affiliations, and Other Relational Assets*, Oxford: Oxford University Press.

Hessels, J. and Terjesen, S. (2010), 'Resource dependency and institutional theory perspectives on direct and indirect export choices', *Small Business Economics*, **34**, 203–20.

Huggins, R. (2010), 'Forms of network resource: knowledge access and the role of inter-firm networks', *International Journal of Management Reviews*, **12**(3), 335–52.

Huggins, R. and Johnston, A. (2009), 'Knowledge networks in an uncompetitive region: SME innovation and growth', *Growth and Change*, **40**(2), 227–59.

Inkpen, A.C. and Tsang, E.W.K. (2005), 'Social capital, networks and knowledge transfers', *Academy of Management Review*, **30**(1), 146–65.

Johannisson, B. (1998), 'Personal networks in emerging knowledge-based firms: spatial and functional patterns', *Entrepreneurship & Regional Development*, **10**(4), 297–312.

Johannisson, B., Alexanderson, O., Nowicki, K. and Senneseth, K. (1994),

'Beyond anarchy and organization: entrepreneurs in contextual networks', *Entrepreneurship and Regional Development*, **6**, 329–56.
Kitson, M., Howells, J., Braham, R. and Westlake, S. (2009), 'The connected university', http://www.nesta.org.uk/the-connected-university, accessed 20 October 2009.
Lawson, C. and Lorenz, E. (1999), 'Collective learning, tacit knowledge and regional innovative capacity', *Regional Studies*, **33**, 305–17.
Lawton Smith, H. (2003), 'Local innovation assemblages and institutional capacity in local high-tech development: the case of Oxfordshire', *Urban Studies*, **40**(7), 1353–69.
Lawton Smith, H. and Waters, R. (2011), 'Scientific labour markets, networks and regional innovation systems', *Regional Studies*, **45**(7), 961–78.
Malmberg, A. and Power, D. (2005), 'On the role of global demand in local innovation processes', in P. Shapiro and G. Fuchs (eds), *Rethinking Regional Innovation and Change*, Dordrecht: Kluwer Academic Publishers, pp. 273–90.
Miles, R.E. and Snow, C.C. (1992), 'Causes of failure in network organizations', *California Management Review*, Summer, 53–72.
Miller, N., Besser, T.L. and Rive, J.V. (2006), 'Do strategic business networks benefit male and female owned small community businesses?', *Journal of Small Business Strategy*, **17**(2), 53–74.
Parilli, M.D. and Sacchetti, S. (2008), 'Linking learning with governance in networks and clusters: key issues for analysis and policy', *Entrepreneurship & Regional Development*, 387–408.
Penrose, E. (1959), *The Theory of the Growth of the Firm*, New York: John Wiley.
Phillipson, J., Gorton, M. and Laschewski, L. (2006), 'Local business cooperation and the dilemmas of collective action: rural microbusiness networks in the north of England', *Sociologia Ruralis*, **46**(1), 40–60.
Rutten, R. and Boekma, F. (2004), 'The spatial dimension of inter-firm learning: case study and conceptualisation', in P. Cooke and A. Piccaluga (eds), *Regional Economies as Knowledge Laboratories*, Cheltenham, UK and Northampton, MA, USA: Edward Elgar, pp. 181–96.
Rutten, R., Westlund, H. and Boekema, F. (2010), 'The spatial dimension of human capital', *European Planning Studies*, **18**(6), 863–71.
Saxenian, A. (1994), *Regional Advantage: Culture and Competition in Silicon Valley and Route 128*, Cambridge, MA: Harvard University Press.
Sherer, S.A. (2003), 'Critical success factors for manufacturing networks as perceived by network coordinators', *Journal of Small Business Management*, **41**(4), 325–45.
Smangs, M. (2006), 'The nature of the business group: a social network perspective', *Organisation*, **13**(6), 389–409.
Simmie, J. (2008), 'The contribution of clustering to innovation: from Porter I agglomeration to Porter II export base theories', in C. Karlsson (ed.), *Handbook of Research on Innovation and Clusters*, Cheltenham, UK and Northampton, MA, USA: Edward Elgar, pp. 19–32.
Starr, J.A. and MacMillan, I.C. (1990), 'Resource co-optation via social contracting: resource acquisition strategies for new ventures', *Strategic Management Journal*, **11**, 79–92.
Storper, M. (1997), *The Regional World: Territorial Development in a Global Economy*, New York: Guilford Press.
Waters, R. and Lawton Smith, H. (2002), 'RDAs and local economic development:

scale and competitiveness in Oxfordshire and Cambridgeshire', *European Planning Studies*, **10**(5), 633–49.

Wenger, E. (1998), *Communities of Practice: Learning, Meaning, and Identity*, Cambridge: Cambridge University Press.

Wolfe, D.A. and Gertler, M.S. (2004), 'Ontario's regional innovation system: the evolution of knowledge-based institutional assets', in Philip Cooke, Martin Heidenreich and Hans-Joachim Braczyk (eds), *Regional Innovation Systems*, 2nd edn, London: Taylor & Francis, pp. 91–124.

Woolcock, M. and Narayan, D. (2000), 'Social capital: implications for development theory, research, and policy', *World Bank Research Observer*, **15**(2), 225–50.

Zhang, J. and Wong, P.K. (2008), 'Networks vs. market methods in high-tech venture fundraising: the impacts of institutional environment', *Entrepreneurship & Regional Development*, **20**, 409–30.

6. Women entrepreneurs and the process of networking as social exchange

Claire M. Leitch, Richard T. Harrison and Frances M. Hill

INTRODUCTION

Since the 1970s, the potential contribution of entrepreneurial activities to economic development has been increasingly recognized (Fritsch, 2011a), particularly in view of the shift from a 'managed' economy to an 'entrepreneurial' economy (Audretsch et al., 2011). Two general recommendations for an entrepreneurship-based, regional development policy have been identified (Acs et al., 2009; Fritsch, 2011b): first, government should not interfere with the market selection process, for example by picking winners, as it runs a high risk of being resource inefficient (Acs, 2011); and, second, government should instead concentrate on creating conditions favourable for entrepreneurship in the regions. It can do so in three ways (Fritsch, 2011b, p. 8): first, the development of a knowledge base as a precondition for the emergence of entrepreneurial firms (Boekema et al., 2000); second, the construction of framework conditions (including an appropriate regulatory and competitive environment and access to the core competencies essential to support the emergence and growth of new ventures (Eliasson, 1997; Eliasson and Eliasson, 2006)) conducive to entrepreneurial activity; third, the development of an entrepreneurial culture (Sternberg, 2011).

Given that entrepreneurship is a social process embedded in a social and regional context, the network-founding hypothesis (Brüderl and Preisendörfer, 1998) emphasizes the positive effect on entrepreneurial activity of involvement in a network (Hanson and Blake, 2009; Nijkamp, 2003). Although the empirical evidence on this is not consistent, at least in the case of nascent entrepreneurship (Davidsson and Honig, 2003), the presence of supportive networks, both formal and informal, is generally positively associated with regional differences in the economic impact of entrepreneurship (Fritsch, 2011c, p. 98). Those regions where entrepreneurs have extensive informal, personal and social networks as well as a high level of role models perform better. On the other hand, in regions where entrepreneurs have less extensive informal networks, economic development agencies have stimulated the formation of formal networks as a catalyst to the development of an entrepreneurial culture to provide entrepreneurs and would-be entrepreneurs with access to relevant knowledge, expertise, support and role models. Specifically, over the last decade, successive governments have introduced a range of policy initiatives designed to encourage more women's entrepreneurship including the development of formal, women-only business networks to promote networking and to offer support and encouragement to those starting their own ventures (Marlow et al., 2008).

In this chapter, we examine the implications of this policy using a case study of the establishment of formal entrepreneurial networks in one region in the UK, with a particular focus on the nature of entrepreneurs' networking behaviour. This addresses something of a gap in the literature, where most work has tended to consider the informal network and specifically the social network of the entrepreneur (Robson et al., 2008). In looking at networking within the context of participation in purposively designed formal networks, we recognize that entrepreneurs can receive both formal and informal advice. Specifically, we seek to enhance understanding of how women business owners engage in the process of networking within formal networks. This extends understanding of women's entrepreneurship that occurs within, and contributes to, socially constructed systems of gendered beliefs and relations (Jennings and Brush, 2013). The research addresses three questions: what are women's motivations for participating in formal business networks and their expectations of such participation? What networking behaviours do they engage in, especially regarding the initiation, development and maintenance of contacts and relationships? What are the potential and actual benefits that they perceive to accrue from networking?

NETWORKS AND NETWORKING: STRUCTURE AND PROCESS

There is an extensive body of literature on networks (for reviews, see Phillips et al., 2013; Vissa, 2012; Slotte-Kock and Coviello, 2010; Jack, 2005; Hoang and Antoncic, 2003). Research on networks and networking is challenging in three respects (Coviello, 2005): a lack of clarity about the terms used (networks and networking); the units of analysis employed (individual, group or organization); and the focus of research (structure or process). Specifically, networks can be classified as either formal or informal (Ibarra, 1992), where formal networks can be more beneficial to their members than informal ones because they more likely to include more weak ties and structural holes (Watson, 2011). Informal networks primarily comprise business contacts, family and personal relationships. Formal networks, by contrast, include professional relationships such as accountants, banks, lawyers and trade associations (Littunen, 2000). Central to the analysis in this chapter is an investigation of formal networks, either trade associations or structures specifically established, for example, by economic development agencies, to stimulate networking activity. Using these formal networks as a framework, the focus is on the process and outcomes of networking itself, which is 'concerned with the actual behaviour of people developing, entering, maintaining, altering and leaving social networks' (Benschop, 2009, p. 221).

Network research has also employed different units of analysis (O'Donnell et al., 2001; Jack et al., 2010). At a macro-level, this includes considering networks to exist *sui generis* and, through counting linkages and situating connections, understanding them as social structures that are distinct from their participants. At a more micro level, the nature of ties between members has been investigated (Iacobucci and Zerrilo, 1996; Larson, 1992; Hite, 2005), as well as the significance of actors' positions in networks (Burt, 2000; Uzzi, 1996). Nevertheless, irrespective of the focus of research, for clarity, it is important that a study's unit of analysis is stated explicitly (Jack et al., 2010; O'Donnell et al., 2001). Here, the formal network established the context while the networking activities of individual entrepreneurs are the primary consideration.

Even though authors such as Neergaard et al. (2005) have called for social interaction to be addressed as an important element of networks, research continues to be dominated by a concentration on their structural elements (Benschop, 2009). Indeed, the 'player–structure duality' has been identified as one of the paradoxes inherent in network theory (Parkhe et al., 2006, p. 561): behaviour is interpreted in terms of structural constraints on activity in which people are the vehicles for structurally induced action (Burt, 1992; Wellman, 1988). Within entrepreneurship these structural elements include transactional content (what is exchanged by actors); the nature of links (the strength and qualitative characteristics of the relationship between two actors); and structural features (the overall pattern of relationships) (Tichy et al., 1979). Through counting linkages and situating connections, the morphology of a network can be established (O'Donnell et al., 2001; Neergaard et al., 2005), which, from a social network theory perspective, determines not only the resource opportunities available to participants but also their access to them (Uzzi, 1996).

Building up a network map provides understanding of its properties as a social structure but it is a fairly limited representation for two main reasons. First, the assumption that such structures are static has resulted in the majority of studies adopting a cross-sectional approach (Aldrich and Reese, 1993), with the result that any modifications in an entrepreneur's network over time in line with changes in their business resource needs has received insufficient attention. Hite and Hesterly (2001) propose that firms' evolution will be reflected in changes in entrepreneurs' networks over time, from identity-based to more calculative ones. The former they define as 'egocentric networks that have a high proportion of ties where some type of personal or social identification with the other actor motivates or influences economic actions' (Hite and Hesterly, 2001, p. 278). Calculative networks are those in which an actor's ties are mainly based on expected economic benefits (Williamson, 1993). Second, viewing networks as being *in situ* (Jack, 2005) ignores the fact that they are not exogenous but are created (Portes, 1998), as well as the impact of human agency on their generation and development (Stevenson and Greenberg, 2000). Thus our understanding of the process of networking (Jack et al., 2010; Jack, 2010), including 'how individuals generate networks in the first place', remains restricted (Nebus, 2006, p. 615). However, there is a growing debate about whether understanding of networks is increased by considering the ties that comprise their structures, or by exploring the interactions between and among the ties (Jack et al., 2010). Such a choice, we believe, is unnecessary, as adopting a 'both/and' approach instead of an 'either/or' one has the potential to produce interesting insights that can yield holistic knowledge and understanding, as part of the development of a process-oriented perspective to network research that allows for the study of dynamic changes in the phenomenon (Parkhe et al., 2006, p. 563; Kim et al., 2006; Koka et al., 2006).

To increase knowledge of networking, O'Donnell et al. (2001) suggest that a deeper appreciation of individuals' motivations, expectations and outcomes of network participation is required (Curran et al., 1993). Network research in entrepreneurship has for the most part adopted social network theory as a framework for analysing the structure of whole social entities (Wasserman and Faust, 1994). Social network theory considers issues of network structure and the dynamic between these at micro-, meso- and macro-levels of analysis (Mitchell, 1974). However, in determining how individuals go about networking, social network theory on its own is unable to address adequately the process issue of how networks are initiated, developed and maintained over time, an area where concentrated research attention is still needed (Parkhe et al., 2006). Indeed, given the expansion of social network theory across a wide range of disciplines and research contexts, it is perhaps better viewed as a perspective on research rather than an integrated theoretical framework in which 'indiscriminate proliferation of the network concept threatens to relegate it to the status of an evocative metaphor, applied so loosely that it ceases to mean anything' (Nohria, 1992, p. 3). However, as Carsrud and Johnson (1989, p. 26) have observed, 'reciprocity and social exchange occur in social interactions with others. This exchange involves the reciprocation of tangible and intangible outcomes that are seen as valuable . . . It is these exchanges that are the basis of networking by entrepreneurs'. We propose, therefore, that if social exchange is key to entrepreneurial networking, then social exchange theory is a complementary, valuable lens through which to investigate this process. Whitten and Wolfe (1974) are in no doubt, asserting that, without exchange theory, which highlights interpersonal exchange relationships, the notion of network would appear quite abstract, divorced from the realities of human life, in specific social and cultural settings.

In social exchange theory the exchange relation is the primary unit of analysis (Cook, 1982) and it is this, and its development, that is emphasized rather than the transactional content, the nature of links within, or structural characteristics of, a network (Table 6.1). Molm (2003) demonstrates the significance of this by arguing that both social and economic exchanges are based on a fundamental reality of life, namely, that much of what we need and value can only be gained from others. This includes goods, services, information, support and companionship, and broadly equates to social capital.

WOMEN AND NETWORKING

Thus far in the entrepreneurship literature, the discourse on women,[1] networks and networking has been limited (Watson, 2011; Foss, 2010; Brush et al., 2009; Renzulli et al., 2000; Ibarra, 1993, 1997) and it is only recently that the role that the female–male distinction may, or may not, play in such activity has been explored more fully (Foss, 2010; Díaz García and Carter, 2009; Neergaard et al., 2005). Knowledge remains incomplete due to a number of theoretical and methodological limitations (Foss, 2010). In particular, Neergaard et al. (2005) have noted a scarcity of empirical evidence, both on the types of networks in which women entrepreneurs are embedded and on their networking, that is, how they establish, maintain and use networks for business purposes. Three issues in particular in the extant entrepreneurship literature restrict current discourse in this area (Jennings and Brush, 2013). First, an andocentric perspective dominates and is reflected in the pervasiveness of the normative male model that has

Table 6.1 Summary of main features of social network theory and social exchange theory

Main features	Social network theory	Social exchange theory
Focus	Linkages between a defined set of individuals (Mitchell, 1969) and, in particular, the structure of these which is the primary unit of analysis	Interpersonal relationships; the exchange relation is the primary unit of analysis (Cook, 1982; Molm, 2003)
Assumptions	Founded on the proposition that understanding group composition is important for understanding social life (Simmel, 1955; Smith-Doerr and Powell, 2005; Slotte-Kock and Coviello, 2010) – The social networks within which individuals and groups are embedded have significant consequences for the success/failure of their endeavours (Ibarra et al., 2005)	Much of what we need and value in life can only be gained from others (Molm, 2003, 2007) – All types of social exchange take place within structures of mutual dependence in which actors are mutually, or reciprocally, dependent on one another for valued outcomes (Molm, 2007) – Interdependence and reciprocity are defining characteristics of social exchange (Cropanzano and Mitchell, 2005)
Key elements	Encompasses both (formal) inter-organizational networks and (informal) personal networks (O'Donnell et al., 2001; Brown and Butler, 1993; Johannisson, 1986) – Proposes various network properties: • Content (what is exchanged by social actors) • Nature of links (strength and qualitative nature of relationship between two actors) • Structural characteristics (overall pattern of	Exchanges may be both negotiated (via explicit bargaining) and reciprocal (one actor's actions contingent on another's behaviour) (Cook and Emerson, 1978; Cook et al., 1983; Molm, 2000, 2003) – Involves dyadic and collective relations (3+ parties involved) (Molm et al., 2007) – In dyadic relations, exchange is direct or productive; in collective relations, exchange is generalized, involving

Table 6.1 (continued)

Main features	Social network theory	Social exchange theory
	relationships between actors including clustering, network density and centrality) (Tichy et al., 1979; Granovetter, 1973; Burt, 1998)	relationships between > 2 actors, benefits flow unilaterally and reciprocity is indirect (Molm et al., 2007)
	– Argues that the type of network in which an organization/individual is embedded defines the opportunities potentially available, while their position in the structure and nature of ties developed/maintained defines access to those opportunities (Uzzi, 1996)	– Assumes risk and uncertainty not only require trust but also promote trust (Molm, 2003) – Suggests indirect reciprocity in generalized exchange enhances social solidarity and commitment to a network (Molm et al., 2007)
	– Suggests individuals in a network are competing for resources (Burt, 2000) (negatively connected relations – Molm, 2003); thus relative power is significant, determining whether actors' exchanges produce equal or unequal benefits (Marsden and Laumann, 1977)	– Due to trust, cooperation and solidarity among network members (positively connected relations); SET suggests they may not compete with each other, thus relative power has little significance (Molm, 2003)

influenced, and continues to influence, how research is conducted and findings are explained. Second, there is a tendency to treat men and women as homogeneous groups that can be compared with each other. Third, there is a preponderance of research designs employing quantitative methods.

Even though Foss (2010, pp. 84 and 86) cautions that neither men nor women are homogeneous in nature and so we should 'be sceptical of treating them as two groups with distinct and coherent patterns of behaviour', researchers have tended to compare the networks of female and male entrepreneurs to determine sex- and gender-based disparities, as well as the effects of any variations on entrepreneurial success. Research has also tended to focus on differences between men and women at the expense of similarities, while overlaps have been ignored (Ahl, 2004).

On the basis of a meta-analysis of psychological research on men and women, Ahl (2006, p. 597) observed that 'the differences between individuals within the same sex are invariably much larger than the average differences, if any, between the sexes'. This resonates with Harrison and Mason's (2007) belief that in women's entrepreneurship a lack of attention has been paid to within-sex differences, due to a preoccupation with between-sex ones based on a supposition of gender polarity (Fine and Gordon, 1989; Riger, 1992).

In her review of the literature, Foss (2010) identifies three guiding hypotheses: women networked less than men as their networks were smaller with fewer weak ties; the only criterion on which women were expected to score highly was on contact with friends and kin, identified in the literature as an ineffective means of securing resources for a business; and that women do not benefit from the inclusion of other women in their networks. Essentially, all of this research used the networks of men as the standard against which to measure and assess women. However, adopting a 'gender-as-variable' approach can be problematic, as researchers are more inclined to document differences between men's and women's networks instead of determining the cause of patterns that have emerged (Foss, 2010).

RESEARCH DESIGN AND PROCESS

On this basis, it is, therefore, vital to identify and question such suppositions so that the limits of particular discourses are revealed. Moreover, Foucault (1972) suggests that it is especially important to challenge the assumptions underlying the practices that shape the research process, as these 'influence the research questions asked, the methods chosen and the answers received' (Ahl, 2006, p. 598). We propose that one method of doing this is to conduct more studies that investigate women and men separately from each other, as opposed to merely adding to the existing pool of comparative ones.

The production of rich, in-depth knowledge requires researchers to adopt diverse ontological and epistemological positions and draw on a range of theoretical and practice traditions from both the social sciences and the humanities (Leitch et al., 2010; Easterby-Smith et al., 2008; Gephart, 2004). While extant research, though dominated by cross-sectional surveys (Foss, 2010), has provided significant understanding of networks, such as in Neergaard et al. (2005), we believe that methodological variety would provide additional insights. This would help overcome Foss's (2010, p. 88) assertion that we do not need more of the same stories

(Haraway, 1988), in other words, 'studies conducted in the same manner and reporting more or less the same findings'. The danger of recycling existing, rather than creating new, knowledge is that accepted assumptions are less likely to be challenged.

In planning this research we were particularly cognizant of the dominance of androcentrism in entrepreneurship in which women are represented 'as blemished men who must be assisted to become honorary men, [who] will then achieve within the existing paradigm of entrepreneurship' (Marlow, 2002, p. 83) and the related trend towards comparative studies between male and female business owners (Watson, 2011). In this, men and women are assumed to be homogeneous groups: comparisons are made between men and women, with the former comprising the norm or standard against which women are measured and assessed; and excessive emphasis is placed on between-group differences to the neglect of within-group differences. This has led to many assumptions about women's entrepreneurship remaining unchallenged (Foss, 2010). It is on this basis that Aldrich (1989) developed a conceptual argument for the analysis of women's entrepreneurship on its own terms rather than adopting male/female comparative research designs. Despite this, little work has been conducted from this perspective (Hanson and Blake, 2009). As this potentially diminishes our comprehension of femaleness (Hill et al., 2006), we have, instead, deliberately sought to give 'voice' to women's experiences as intrinsically interesting in their own right. Thus all the participants in this study were women business owners.

Context

This study was undertaken in Northern Ireland, where entrepreneurship in general, and female entrepreneurship in particular, is low (Hill et al., 2010). At the time this research was conducted, Northern Ireland was ranked bottom of the 12 UK regions in terms of the rate of early-stage entrepreneurial activity among women (Hart, 2008). Further, although significant female entrepreneurial activity is a long-standing but largely invisible phenomenon (Jennings and Brush, 2013), research into this is more recent (Gatewood et al., 2009), and it appears that women-owned businesses are generally younger than those of men (Greene et al., 2001; Hill et al., 2006). Following wider UK initiatives (Marlow et al., 2008), in order to increase numbers of women engaging in entrepreneurship, the regional economic development agency, Invest NI, has introduced a number of initiatives aimed at improving the low levels of entrepreneurial activity in addition to the quality of start-ups by women. These include the cultivation of role models, as well as the development of formal, women-only business networks to promote networking and to offer support and encouragement to those starting their own ventures:

> A key element of government's drive to increase entrepreneurial activity is supporting more women to become involved in business and business start-up and unlocking their wealth creating potential. Women are the largest under-represented group when it comes to enterprise in Northern Ireland and there is enormous benefit to be realized for our economy if more women are encouraged to maximize the use of their skills in new business start-up . . . We know that women are influenced by other women and that strong role models are an important element in creating a stronger culture of entrepreneurship among women. (www.investni.com/femaleentrepreneurs, 9 March 2007, accessed 27 April 2011)

Participant Selection

A purposive approach to participant selection was adopted to access women's experiences of networking (Neergaard, 2007). Accordingly, women who were members of formal business networks and who had knowledge, understanding and experience of networking in their professional capacity were targeted. Participants were drawn from five networks, two that were mixed-gender and three women-only. All the networks are formally constituted, with a board or committee structure. The women-only networks established by Invest NI tend to be relatively small and are administered by part-time coordinators who are also entrepreneurs, while the mixed-gender ones have full-time staff. All provide a range of facilities and services for members. Data were collected from two categories of participant: inexperienced, early-stage entrepreneurs whose businesses were aged less than three years ($n = 8$) (Aldrich et al., 1987) and more experienced individuals with businesses aged three years or more ($n = 10$). The purpose of having these two categories was to explore changes in behaviour over time, in the absence of an opportunity to conduct a real-time, longitudinal study (Benschop, 2009, p. 244), as networking is a dynamic process (Jack, 2005).

Data Collection

Network processes are too subtle to capture and understand using questionnaires (Neergaard et al., 2005; Dubini and Aldrich, 1991). Furthermore, our unit of analysis is the individual and the focus is on their self-understandings (Shapiro and Wendt, 2005). Accordingly, an interpretivist perspective was adopted (Leitch et al., 2010). Specifically, qualitative, semi-structured interviews were conducted. These do not necessarily have to take place on a one-to-one basis (Saunders et al., 2009) and, indeed, Easterby-Smith et al. (2008, p. 343) observe that 'for some types of investigation group interviews can be very useful'.[2] These were employed in this research for two reasons. First, the involvement of two or more participants in an interview permits a range of perspectives to emerge and for these to be challenged (Saunders et al., 2009). All individuals have the opportunity of engaging with the issues under consideration, leading to a broad and in-depth participatory discussion (Boddy, 2005). Second, this method provides an efficient way for researchers to interact with a larger number of individuals than would be the case with one-to-one interviews (Easterby-Smith et al., 2008). Accordingly, in this study five group interviews (one group of six participants, two groups of three and two dyadic interviews) were conducted. Two participants were unable to participate in the group interviews and were interviewed individually.

A topic guide was designed, comprising the themes to be explored while also permitting unforeseen issues to emerge (Easterby-Smith et al., 2008). The use of such a template encourages participants to provide detailed accounts of their own experiences in what are essentially 'guided' conversations (Rubin and Rubin, 2005). Although initially shaped by the researchers the course of the dialogue was largely set by the participants (Thompson et al., 1989). The initial themes included:

- the women's motivations for participating in formal business networks, both women-only and mixed-gender, and their expectations of such participation (which influence behaviours);
- the networking behaviours they engage in, especially regarding the initiation, development and maintenance of contacts and relationships;
- the potential and actual benefits that they perceive to accrue from network participation, and whether or not these differ in relation to women-only and mixed-gender networks.

Participants were interviewed in surroundings that they perceived as relaxed and unthreatening (Easterby-Smith et al., 2008), and so all the sessions were hosted at the network venues. Two of the research team were present at all interviews to allow full concentration on the process and ensure that data were fully and accurately recorded. The interviews lasted between 60 and 90 minutes and were audio-taped with the permission of all the participants, who were also provided with background information about the project, offered the opportunity to opt out at any time and given a guarantee of confidentiality.

Data Analysis

Analysing qualitative data is a difficult, intuitive, creative and dynamic process, the aim of which is to understand the assumptions, categories and relationships that constitute the experiences of the participants (Shaw, 1999; Basit, 2003; Gephart, 2004; Gremler, 2004). However, few interpretivist studies elaborate on the principles of data analysis (Bryman, 2004), which involves 'working with data, organizing it, breaking it into manageable units, synthesizing it, searching for patterns, discovering what is important and what is to be learned, and deciding what you will tell others' (Bogdan and Biklen, 1982, p. 145). As 'it is difficult to specify exactly *what* interpretive analysis actually entails, particularly as the specifics of it will vary from study to study' (Braun and Clarke, 2006, p. 93), there is an obligation on researchers to demonstrate the integrity and trustworthiness of their work. This is achieved by being transparent and describing in detail how each step was undertaken. Drawing on guidelines for conducting interpretivist research in entrepreneurship (Leitch et al., 2010), Table 6.2 describes the approach to thematic analysis adopted in this study.

RESULTS

The findings are structured around three *a priori* themes derived from the literature: motivations and expectations; networking behaviours; and potential and actual benefits perceived to accrue from networking (O'Donnell et al., 2001; Neergaard et al., 2005; Curran et al., 1993). In exploring these we were guided by the distinction in social exchange theory between, on the one hand, direct (unilateral, dyadic) and productive (dyadic bilateral exchange of contribution and benefit) exchange, and, on the other, generalized exchange (multi-actor, where the benefits are unilateral and the exchange is indirect).

Motivations and Expectations

The motivations for joining formal business networks may be divided into two categories (Table 6.3): instrumental motivations, concerning the early-stage and subsequent development of a business; and social motivations, those primarily related to relationships with others. The differences between the motivations of the early-stage and more established entrepreneurs were less than anticipated. Instrumentally, early-stage entrepreneurs were primarily focused on making contacts and keeping up to date with the business environment (A1), while more established entrepreneurs were

Table 6.2 Phases of thematic analysis

Phases	Description of the process
1. Development of the initial thematic template	Following a review of the relevant literature, identification of *a priori* themes to inform the development of the initial thematic template
2. Familiarization with data and gaining insights	Close reading and re-reading of the interview transcripts to develop an understanding of the data and noting down of initial observations
3. Labelling and categorization	Coding or labelling of bits of data and the subsequent allocation of interesting ones in a systematic fashion across the entire data set and relating these to the *a priori* themes or issues deemed important for interpretation
4. Checking and refining coding	Checking of allocated data to ensure appropriate coding
5. Identification of emergent themes	Revisiting unallocated data to identify patterns across the transcripts and subsequent coding of bits of unattributed data to capture emerging themes
6. Reviewing themes	Checking all data were allocated appropriately – to the *a priori* themes
7. Defining and naming themes	Ongoing analysis to further refine and define each theme and starting to create the overall story from the analysis
8. Interpretation, writing up and contribution to theory	Final analysis and structuring of outcomes according to the topics and issues important to the participants. Selection of illustrative quotations, relating the analysis back to the research questions and literature and identification of new avenues for research

Source: Adapted from Kempster and Cope (2010); Leitch et al. (2010, p. 78); Braun and Clarke (2006, p. 87); King (2004, pp. 256–7).

concerned with gaining credibility in the business community through association with a respected business network; gaining the support of a specific business community; and finding out 'who's who and for people to find out who I am and what I do' (see also A2). Further, a more experienced participant explained that, when seeking government funding,

Table 6.3 Motivations for and expectations of joining formal business networks

A: Motivations	B: Expectations
A1: I want to see who's doing what and how successful they are and what the success rate is and what the feedback is . . . And also I'm looking for contacts. (Early-stage entrepreneur)	B1: I think that XXXX [a women-only network] needs . . . more visits with women's enterprise organizations internationally, women's enterprise organizations specifically focused on women's development and women's business development, women's business skills, personal development – all of that is required. (Early stage entrepreneur)
A2: For me, I think it was an imperative to join . . . as it was not a question of 'do I like them, or do I not?' . . . it's part of my business and needs to be done because an awful lot of my business is about credibility. (More established entrepreneur)	B2: So it's just conversation for me and it's nearly a bonus if business comes out of it, I'm not there to sell, I'm there to meet like-minded people who may or may not then do business with me further down the line. (More established entrepreneur)
A3: Basically the main reason I joined was I wanted to be with like-minded people and entrepreneurs etcetera so it was more inquisitive but I also wanted to be part of a women's group so to speak because the industry I am in is completely male dominated. (More established entrepreneur)	

applicants are often asked to identify those formal networks to which they belong. As the majority of networks included in this research were initiated and/or funded by the local economic development agency, this suggests that membership of a network was seen as both a sign of legitimacy and commitment on the part of the entrepreneur as well as an indication of their eligibility for business development support.

From a socially oriented perspective, some early-stage and more established entrepreneurs identified formal network participation as a social outlet and an opportunity to interact with other women, especially when operating in a male-dominated sector (A3), while one of the more established entrepreneurs considered that the relaxed social environment of a women-only network was conducive to the personal/professional development of women. However, as she owns a large and mature beauty business, such an environment would also help her in promoting it to fellow network members. This demonstrates not only a relational but also a strategic and tactical aspect to women's networking (Foss, 2010). While participation in formal networks may be motivated by instrumental considerations ('what can I get out of it?'), most participants were also interested in developing social relationships in addition to those already in their existing social networks. This is particularly so in women-only networks.

Regarding participants' expectations of membership of a formal business network, the early-stage entrepreneurs believed that the services provided by such bodies should help women to develop both business and networking skills (B1). One more established entrepreneur also had high expectations of the services she believed should be provided, including speed networking, introductions and the promotion of the network and participant businesses within it. As most of the networks in this research, especially the women-only ones, tend to have small budgets, such expectations may be unrealistic but, if not met, may have implications for members' continued participation and the development of their networking skills. One early-stage and a more established entrepreneur both stated that making sales was not necessarily a priority (B2). Given that these women are investing time, energy and money (Katz and Williams, 1997) in network participation, this shows their commitment to social exchange within a network structure of mutual dependence in which the actors are reciprocally dependent on one another for valued outcomes (Molm, 2007; Cropanzano and Mitchell, 2005).

Networking Behaviours

Entrepreneurs' motivations and expectations are potentially significant influences on their networking behaviours and how they go about building their professional and social networks (Ibarra, 1997) (Box 6.1). Given that many participants had instrumental motivations for joining a formal business network, it is perhaps not surprising that both early-stage and more established entrepreneurs appreciated the need for proactivity in networking (C1). Further, a number of participants were tactical in the development of contacts (C2–C3), and there was political awareness among some of the more established entrepreneurs regarding whom they should interact with (C4).

To raise one's profile in a formal network, one of the more established entrepreneurs suggested that offering to provide an event on an issue related to one's business prompted interested parties to initiate contact with the speaker. This instrumental and tactical approach to networking

BOX 6.1 NETWORKING BEHAVIOURS

C: Networking Behaviours

C1: You attend events . . . and once you go into that event then there's the opportunity to move around those people that are there, exchange cards, really get to know what their business is and what they are looking for and hoping that it will grow your own business. (Early-stage entrepreneur)

C2: I try not to run in there just to make a sale. I'd sooner get to know people, see how the land lies, find out what's happening and then, months down the line, I'll know how I fit into this and how I'm getting benefit from it. (Early-stage entrepreneur)

C3: Some people definitely go in there with a plan. They get out the list and they know who they want to approach and so on. There's no one best way but it probably is a good idea to do that. (More established entrepreneur)

C4: When you join these organizations, make sure you know who's the head, who's the committee, who's the proactive people so you make yourself aware of them, you introduce yourself to them and then you are building a relationship with these people. (More established entrepreneur)

C5: I think it is useful to quickly get a contact with somebody but you are not establishing a relationship with that person you are talking to . . . you quickly make contact with somebody and understand what they do and say a quick 'hello'. You then have to follow it up. (More established entrepreneur)

C6: I feel quite strong about building business friends. That's where you go along and you've got your network of friends there in the business context and that's the way it should be, to build those relationships. (More established entrepreneur)

C7: I've always been of the opinion what you give out, you get back and I've found that a lot of people that I've given a lot of business have given me nothing back but that doesn't prevent me from still giving because I know it comes back to me long-term . . . you are connected with certain groups of people and they may not all help you. They help you and you may benefit, there may be something small that you could benefit from . . . and we all learn, evolve and grow . . . I'm happy with that and content as a human being. (More established entrepreneur)

C8: To me, it's [membership of a women-only network] a very informal thing: you know, chatting, sharing experiences . . . it's a relief to just talk to other women, it's absolutely brilliant. I don't really get that in my day-to-day life because they're all guys that I deal with . . . so, in my less formal working life, if you want to include the network as that, yes, I can do that and it's nice and I get a lot from it . . . it lightens the load. (Early-stage entrepreneur)

C9: I think there is a sense of solidarity. I remember when I was feeling really completely overwhelmed, I used to think oh no I've got to go to XXX meeting or whatever! It relaxed me hugely, it really relaxed me – for no tangible reason – it's just really being in a community of other people who are self-employed and everybody has got the same problems and you are not on your own. (More established entrepreneur) contradicts one of the hegemonic statements identified by Foss (2010), namely that women cannot network effectively. While some participants made a clear distinction between an initial contact and the subsequent development of a relationship (C5–C6), most seemed to focus on building up a 'bank of contacts'. As one early-stage entrepreneur stated: 'I suppose it's like keeping a mental Rolodex, so you always know who to go to when you've a particular need.' This suggests that there is less interest in the development of dyadic relations where exchange is bilateral and direct or productive than in collective relations where exchange is generalized and involves relationships with more than two actors in which benefits flow unilaterally and reciprocity is indirect (Molm et al., 2007).

Specifically, a more established entrepreneur observed that, to be useful, contacts and relationships need to be reciprocal: 'It's up to you what you put into it. If you don't put something into it you are not going to get anything back out again.' Accompanying this, though, is the risk of exploitation: 'but I find I've given a phenomenal amount of business and contacts to a lot of other people and I've got very little back' (see also C7). Although some authors have suggested that reciprocity is a universal norm or principle (Malinowski, 1932; Gouldner, 1960; Mauss, 1969; Tsui and Wang, 2002; Wang et al., 2003), Cropanzano and Mitchell (2005) observe that not everyone values it to the same degree, and those with a strong exchange orientation are more likely to reciprocate than those with a weaker one. On the other hand, Molm (2003) argues that the risk and uncertainty inherent in reciprocal interdependence not only require trust but also promote it. Therefore, as the risk of exploitation is lower, members of social groups should not fear entering into exchange relations with unfamiliar others (C8). Indeed, social exchange theory advocates that indirect reciprocity in generalized exchange enhances social solidarity and commitment to a network (Molm et al., 2007) and, in so doing, encourages cooperation rather than competition (Molm, 2003) (C9).

Another hegemonic view evident in the entrepreneurship literature on networks is that women are more likely to report strong ties, which is a drawback, whereas weak ties are believed to be the source of men's success (Foss, 2010). From this study of women's networking behaviour, few participants mentioned the development of close dyadic relationships, even for those whose articulated motivations for participating in a formal business network were social in nature. Consequently, they did not expect to be involved in direct social exchanges, but rather they focused on building a collective body of contacts perceived to be potentially helpful, either in the short or longer term (Uzzi, 1996). Where the majority of women in the networks are engaging in these behaviours, it demonstrates a tacit understanding of interdependence and the need for collective indirect exchange.

Further, it is likely that, although some contacts may remain latent and dormant (Jack, 2005) and may never be activated, those that are will be activated at different times, suggesting that the pattern of each entrepreneur's professional and social networks is not static but fluid, changing over time according to their needs (Klyver and Grant, 2010).

Potential and actual benefits perceived to accrue from networking

Potential benefits of participation in entrepreneurial networks include: enhancing one's image; gaining acceptance and credibility; accessing diverse and useful information; support; and locating a range of resources (Díaz García and Carter, 2009; Mitton, 1984; Ibarra, 1997). From the data, the benefits perceived to accrue from networking can be divided into two categories, tangible and intangible (Box 6.2). For early-stage entrepreneurs, intangible benefits identified included sharing experiences, companionship, emotional support and mentoring; information and advice; learning; motivation; and confidence (D1). For more established entrepreneurs, intangible benefits included companionship and solidarity; overcoming isolation and establishing links; problem-sharing; knowledge, information, ideas and advice; credibility; business development; and confidence: 'working together or just things that help my business grow' (early-stage entrepreneur). This suggests that, for early-stage entrepreneurs, intangible benefits tend to relate to personal development, while for more established

BOX 6.2 POTENTIAL AND ACTUAL BENEFITS PERCEIVED TO ACCRUE FROM NETWORKING

D: Benefits

D1: Motivational and confidence. When you . . . go out, even if you've nothing specific to your business, it does sort of lift you again and give you another boost till the next time. (Early stage entrepreneur)

D2: there is confidence in being with other like-minded women where there is no pressure and your opinion is as valid as the person sitting beside you and you are kind of all in on it together. (More established entrepreneur)

D3: Well I think the advantages . . . are that they can . . . look particularly at women's development, women's education, women's opportunities and women's place on corporate boards, women's role in society, and women's participation in politics. (More established entrepreneur)

D4: and the advantage of the mixed [gender] thing is you are dealing with a mixed bag in your business anyway . . . and you have to think and learn how to think like men and play the game and that's the way they operate. (Early-stage entrepreneur)

entrepreneurs these are to do with both personal and business development, indicating some change in focus over time (Leitch et al., 2009, 2013).

Concerning tangible benefits, early-stage entrepreneurs identified the value of services, such as access to information, the database of members, training events, referrals, contacts and leads. 'I have got leads, you know . . . and business contacts.' In addition to these, more established entrepreneurs also mentioned the importance of 'three-minute pitches' and talks. Neither category of entrepreneur identified sales as a particularly important benefit, though, for some, this appeared in line with their expectations, 'If sales come out of it then well and good but that is not the overriding factor.' However, others clearly found this disappointing, 'but in terms of business, absolutely nothing'.

While all the participants, whether members of women-only, mixed-gender networks, or of both, perceived benefits to accrue from networking, some felt particularly comfortable networking with other women (D2). One participant stated that women-only networks are not just concerned with business matters, but with a broad range of women's issues (D3). Women belonging to such networks gravitated towards them mainly to interact with other like-minded women, for support and because they felt secure in such an environment. Although one woman accepted this, she perceived it to be a limitation of women-only networks (D4), highlighting that operating in a homophilous environment may be disadvantageous. This perspective is consistent with Nebus's (2006, p. 615) conclusion that, while existing relationships provide 'a convenient pool of advice contacts . . . they also act as a constraint limiting the scope of the advice search by substituting for experts who would provide better advice'. This reinforces Burt's (1998) observation that cohesive contacts of individuals strongly connected to each other are likely to share similar information and therefore provide redundant rather than additive information benefits. From a policy perspective in the case-study region – Northern Ireland – the presence of homophily (McPherson et al., 2001) and cultural propinquity (Kogut and Singh, 1998) can be problematic. This is likely to be more evident in relatively small rural areas, where some of the networks were deliberately established, since members of these communities tend to interact with each other regularly, whether or not they belong to the same formal networks.

DISCUSSION

Shaw (1999) observes that the term 'network' has at times been loosely applied in entrepreneurship research, resulting in a general failure to recognize that 'networks' and 'networking' are in fact different constructs. Essentially the former is the outcome of the latter, for as Jack et al. (2010, p. 316) note, a network exists through the actions of individuals and the process of networking, either at the individual and personal level or at a more formal, inter-organizational one (Brown and Butler, 1993; Johannisson, 1986; O'Donnell et al., 2001). Our focus in this chapter has been on formal networks established to support women's entrepreneurship, and specifically on the behaviours, outcomes and exchanges of the women who participate in them.

We have argued that, while the literature on entrepreneurial networking, though limited, is growing (see Jack, 2005), to date little attempt has been made to investigate women's approaches to networking and their networking behaviours (Watson, 2011; Hanson and Blake, 2009). The gendered nature of the entrepreneurship literature is widely recognized (Jennings and Brush, 2013; Ahl, 2004; Marlow et al., 2008; Ogbor, 2000). In this, men and women are assumed to be homogeneous groups: comparisons are made between men and women, with the former comprising the norm or standard against which women are measured and assessed; and excessive emphasis is placed on between-group differences to the neglect of within-group differences. This has led to many assumptions about women's entrepreneurship remaining unchallenged (Foss, 2010). It is on this basis that Aldrich (1989) developed a conceptual argument for the analysis of women's entrepreneurship on its own terms rather than adopting male/female comparative research designs. Despite this, little work has been conducted from this perspective (Hanson and Blake, 2009).

Our results throw light on the process of social exchange as it occurs in formal networks. Social exchange involves a series of interactions that generate obligations (Emerson, 1976), which are usually seen as interdependent and contingent upon the actions of another person (Blau, 1964). Thus, in social exchange relationships actors are directly, or reciprocally, dependent on one another for valued outcomes (Molm et al., 2007, p. 207). As actors are motivated to obtain more of the outcomes they value and that others control, they engage in recurring exchanges in which what is received via the exchange relation by an actor is contingent on what s/he provides in that relationship (Molm and Cook, 1995; Emerson, 1972a; Molm et al., 2007). To illustrate, an action by one party results in a response by another, so that if A provides B with a benefit, then B is expected to provide a benefit to A (direct exchange) (Cropanzano and Mitchell, 2005; Gergen, 1969). Since outcomes are based on a combination of each actor's efforts, interdependence is also considered a defining characteristic of social exchange (Cropanzano and Mitchell, 2005).

Exchanges may be both negotiated and reciprocal. In the former, the parties negotiate rules in the hope of achieving mutually beneficial outcomes (Cook and Emerson, 1978; Cook et al., 1983). In the latter, there is no explicit bargaining (Molm, 2000, 2003) and one actor's actions are contingent on another's behaviour. This, Molm (1994) has argued, reduces risk and encourages cooperation because, although risk provides the opportunity for exploitation, it also permits the demonstration of trustworthiness. Reciprocal exchanges are facilitated by the principle of reciprocity, or repayment in kind, described by Cropanzano and Mitchell (2005, p. 875) as the best-known rule or guideline of exchange. In addition, over time a series of interdependent transactions can produce some kind of interpersonal attachment (Cropanzano and Mitchell, 2005). In terms of the development of exchange relations, this takes place within certain structures of mutual dependence: direct exchange, productive exchange and generalized exchange (Molm, 2003). While both direct exchange between two actors (see above) and productive exchange, whereby both actors in the relation must contribute something in order for each to obtain benefits, are relevant to dyadic relationships, generalized exchange involves relationships among more than two actors in which benefits flow unilaterally and reciprocity is indirect. As Molm et al. (2007) explain, in generalized exchange involving social communities such as networks, each actor gives benefits to another and will eventually receive benefits from another, but not from the same actor. Thus exchange is unilateral and indirect.

Indirect reciprocity in generalized exchange seems to enhance social solidarity and commitment to a network, irrespective of size. Solidarity comprises subjective feelings of trust, affective regard, social unity and feelings of commitment to other actors, all of which increase the probability that actors will enter into exchanges with others (Molm et al., 2007) and reduce the risk of exploitation. However, in social network theory, there is an assumption that individuals are competing with each other for resources (see, e.g., Burt, 2000), which Molm (2003) terms 'negatively connected relations'. In such circumstances the issue of whether actors have equal or unequal power is significant, as this determines whether their exchanges produce equal or unequal benefits. According to Emerson (1962, 1972a, 1972b), power is a function of dependence, which is determined by two factors: access to alternative sources of valued resources; and the relative value to each actor of the resources exchanged.

From social network theory, power is a function of position in the structure, where, for example, those at the centre of a network on whom more peripheral actors depend are considered the most powerful (Marsden and Laumann, 1977), while those who 'broker relations between people otherwise disconnected in a social structure' (Burt, 1998, p. 8), or who assist with external linkages (Tichy et al., 1979), gain both information and control advantages. However, in social exchange theory positively connected relations, in which actors exchange benefits that flow across relationships and build cooperation and solidarity, are considered at least as common in social life as negatively connected ones (Molm, 2003). Accordingly, in the case of positively connected networks, such as those examined in this chapter, the absence of competition means that power has little significance. All this helps to explain why those setting up or growing a business are willing to invest valuable time and energy (Katz and Williams, 1997) participating in networks that, from a different perspective, may appear to involve potentially risky collective, indirect exchange.

Based on our results, we argue that social exchange is key to entrepreneurial networking and that entrepreneurs' networks involve not only dyadic but also collective relationships that are reflected in direct, productive and generalized exchange. Social exchange theory, therefore, is a potentially valuable additional lens through which to examine not only how individuals build and, over time, extend their personal networks, but also how they behave in them. The research reported here reflects a shift in focus from structure to process, from networks to networking and from social network theory to social exchange theory as more congruent with a processual perspective. Thus we have explored participants' motivations and expectations in joining and participating in formal networks and identified how these are reflected in the behaviours in which they engage. Given that a major theme in social exchange theory is indirect reciprocity in generalized exchange, these motivations and behaviours are associated with issues such as the development of trust, commitment, social unity, affective regard, solidarity and cooperation. It is on the basis of the development of these that participants identify benefits, including the acquisition of, or access to, valuable resources.

The point of departure for this research has been the argument that more attention should be paid to process than to the analysis of network structure (Benschop, 2009), to networking rather than networks per se, where the exchange relation becomes the primary unit of analysis (Cook, 1982; Molm, 2003), and to the use of social exchange theory as a complement to the more prevalent social network theory (Molm, 2007). Through the study of women's networking motivations, behaviours and outcomes we have demonstrated that, even within the context of formal networks, women identify these as structures of mutual dependence within which reciprocal rather than negotiated exchanges take place. While for some participants network membership is engaged in transactionally, with a clear view as to the expected benefits, for most this is overlain by a belief that network participation confers membership of a community, which enhances social solidarity, trust and cooperation (Molm et al., 2007). Furthermore, it also emerges from this research that for many of the participants these networks provided a forum for social exchange and interaction through the development of collective relations that were not available to them in their existing professional and social networks. As such, this suggests that the distinction between formal and informal networks (Ibarra, 1992) may be less clear cut than often presented, and that the process of social exchange in formal networks may, in fact, be more beneficial because these networks are more likely to include weak ties (Watson, 2011).

CONCLUSION

This chapter makes three contributions to entrepreneurship research: first, it demonstrates the relevance of a social exchange theory perspective as the theoretical basis for entrepreneurial networks research; second, it illuminates additional aspects of the role of gender in the networking process; and, third, it provides the foundation for the design and implementation of regional economic development initiatives.

Central to social exchange theory is the recognition of collective relationships involving three actors or more (Emerson, 1976), indirect generalized exchange (Molm, 2007) and the notion of positively connected relations (Molm, 2003), which implies that benefiting from social exchange does not necessarily require the formation of close dyadic ties. Rather, in generalized exchange, benefits flow unilaterally and reciprocity is indirect; thus a member of a social grouping who provides a benefit to another will almost certainly receive a benefit in return, though not necessarily from that same individual. In other words, the development of a wide range of contacts and relationships with whom one is prepared to exchange reciprocally as necessary is the equivalent of 'saving for a rainy day'. This indirect reciprocity in generalized exchange seems to enhance solidarity and commitment to a network, which can lead to the development of positively-connected relations through which benefits flow both within and across relationships. In such circumstances there is no perception of competition or concern with power, both of which can impede social exchange. This is reflected in the apparently high level of trust among the network members, a lack of concern for potential exploitation and little evidence of competition between them.

The predominant framework for the analysis of entrepreneurial networks, with its focus on structure, argues that the type of network in which an individual is embedded defines the opportunities potentially available to them, while their position in the structure and the nature of the ties they develop, or maintain, define access to those opportunities (Uzzi, 1996).

From a social exchange theory perspective, this insight is complemented by a more detailed analysis of the process of networking itself as it occurs within both formal and informal networks.

In relation to the gendered nature of the entrepreneurial literature and the *de facto* assumption of men and women belonging to homogeneous, but different, groups, this research adopted an interpretive approach to the study of the self-reported, lived experience of women entrepreneurs. These women had joined formal networks with a variety of motivations and expectations, which were reflected in their various behaviours. This demonstrates that, if women are studied in their own right rather than in comparison with men, not only do within-group differences become more apparent, but also the tendency towards androcentrism may be tempered and hegemonic statements such as those identified by Foss (2010) invalidated. Specifically, our findings suggest that some women entrepreneurs use social networks strategically; some women, like some men, are effective networkers, while others may be less so; women do not necessarily favour the development of strong ties as opposed to weak ones; and only a small minority were concerned with developing relationships rather than contacts.

A common theme in both the entrepreneurship research literature and in the practice of regional development policy is that networks play a critical role in influencing the entrepreneurial process, shaping entrepreneurial outcomes and facilitating business development through the provision of information, resources and contacts (Robson et al., 2008, p. 296; Hanson and Blake, 2009). In particular, the creation of networking groups as an instrument of regional economic development policy is undertaken on the basis that it would lead to the creation of opportunities (Lockett et al., 2012; Farr-Wharton and Brunetto, 2007). It is clear that in practice this does not happen. Instead, this research demonstrates that women use formal networks to provide support and a sense of community that appear not to be available from their own existing informal networks. This poses a specific challenge for policymakers, for if the benefits of formal network membership are indirect and longer term, they are different from, and go beyond, those that were intended. As a result, network design and evaluation will need to recognize that creating opportunities and supporting measurable business development may not be the most appropriate performance indicators by which to assess the success of formal networks. What we do not yet have, however, is a detailed evaluation of the extent to which, if at all, there are differences between women-only and mixed networks. Notwithstanding the potential constraints of cultural propinquity (Kogut and Singh, 1998) and homophily (McPherson et al., 2001) in restricting the variety of experiences women may have, this study suggests that these constraints would appear to be outweighed by the benefits of participating in such networks. From a policy perspective, therefore, the establishment of women-only networks should not be seen as the instrumental creation of opportunities but instead as the development of regionally based social capital required to underpin successful women's entrepreneurship.

ACKNOWLEDGEMENT

This work was supported by the British Academy (Grant No. SG 47047).

NOTES

1. In the entrepreneurship literature this discourse is normally couched in terms of gender. However, the shift from women's studies to gender studies is associated with a displacement of research focus that allows the study of difference between the sexes to replace that investigating the role of women in society (Evans, 1990), and in which gender is most often reduced to a fixed category or label for individuals (Bradley, 2007).
2. It is important to note that these group interviews were not designed and run as focus groups: 'the hallmark of a focus group is the explicit use of the group interaction to produce data and insights that would be less accessible without the interaction found in a group' (Morgan, 1988, p. 12).

REFERENCES

Acs, Z.J. (2011), 'High-impact firms: gazelles revisited', in M. Fritsch (ed.), *Handbook of Research on Entrepreneurship and Regional Development*, Cheltenham, UK and Northampton, MA, USA: Edward Elgar, pp. 133–74.

Acs, Z.J., Audretsch, D.B. and Strom, R.J. (eds) (2009), *Entrepreneurship, Growth, and Public Policy*, Cambridge: Cambridge University Press.

Ahl, H. (2004), *The Scientific Reproduction of Gender Inequality*, Copenhagen: Copenhagen Business School.

Ahl, H. (2006), 'Why research on women entrepreneurs needs new directions', *Entrepreneurship Theory and Practice*, September, 595–621.

Aldrich, H.E. (1989), 'Networking among women entrepreneurs', in O. Hagan, C. Rivchun and D. Sexton (eds), *Women-Owned Businesses*, New York: Praeger, pp. 103–32.

Aldrich, H.E. and Reese, P.R. (1993), 'Does networking pay off? A panel study of entrepreneurs in the research triangle', in N.C. Churchill, S. Birley, J. Doutriaux, E.J. Gatewood, F.S. Hoy and W.E. Wetzel, Jr (eds), *Frontiers of Entrepreneurship Research*, Wellsley, MA: Babson College, pp. 325–99.

Aldrich, H.E., Rosen, B. and Woodward, B. (1987), 'The impact of social networks on business foundings and profit: a longitudinal study', in N.C. Churchill, S. Birley, J. Doutriaux, E.J. Gatewood, F.S. Hoy and W.E. Wetzel, Jr (eds), *Frontiers of Entrepreneurship Research*, Wellesley, MA: Babson College, pp. 154–68.

Audretsch, D.B., Grilo, I. and Thurik, A.R. (2011), 'Globalization, entrepreneurship, and the region', in M. Fritsch (ed.), *Handbook of Research on Entrepreneurship and Regional Development*, Cheltenham, UK and Northampton, MA, USA: Edward Elgar, pp. 11–32.

Basit, T.N. (2003), 'Manual or electronic? The role of coding in qualitative data analysis', *Educational Research*, **45**(2), 143–54.

Benschop, Y. (2009), 'The micro-politics of gendering in networking', *Gender, Work and Organization*, **16**(2), 217–37.

Blau, P.M. (1964), *Exchange and Power in Social Life*, New York: Wiley & Sons.

Boddy, C. (2005), 'A rose by any other name may smell as sweet but "group discussion" is not another name for a "focus group" nor should it be', *Qualitative Market Research: An International Journal*, **8**(3), 248–55.

Boekema, F.W.M., Morgan, K., Bakkers, S.H.P. and Rutter, R.P.J.H. (2000), 'Introduction to learning regions: a new issue for regional analysis', in F.W.M. Boekema, K. Morgan, S.H.P. Bakkers and R.P.J.H. Rutten (eds), *Knowledge, Innovation and Economic Growth. The Theory and Practice of Learning Regions*, Cheltenham, UK and Northampton, MA, USA: Edward Elgar, pp. 3–17.

Bogdan, R.C. and Biklen, S.K. (1982), *Qualitative Research for Education: An Introduction to Theory and Methods*, Boston, MA: Allyn & Bacon.

Bradley, H. (2007), *Gender*, Cambridge: Polity Press.

Braun, V. and Clarke, V. (2006), 'Using thematic analysis in psychology', *Qualitative Research in Psychology*, **3**, 77–101.

Brown, B. and Butler, J.E. (1993), 'Networks and entrepreneurial development: the shadow of borders', *Entrepreneurship and Regional Development*, **5**, 101–16.

Brüderl, J. and Preisendörfer, P. (1998), 'Network support and the success of newly founded businesses', *Small Business Economics*, **10**, 213–25.

Brush, C.G., De Bruin, A. and Welter, F. (2009), 'A gender-aware framework for women's entrepreneurship', *International Journal of Gender and Entrepreneurship*, **1**(1), 8–24.

Bryman, A. (2004), 'Qualitative research on leadership: a critical but appreciative review', *Leadership Quarterly*, **15**, 729–69.

Burt, R.S. (1992), *Structural Holes: The Social Structure of Competition*, Cambridge, MA: Harvard University Press.

Burt, R.S. (1998), 'The gender of social capital', *Rationality and Society*, **10**(1), 5–46.

Burt, R.S. (2000), 'The network entrepreneur', in R. Swedberg (ed.), *The Social Science View*, Oxford: Oxford University Press, pp. 281–307.

Carsrud, A.L. and Johnson, R.W. (1989), 'Entrepreneurship: a social physiological perspective', *Entrepreneurship and Regional Development*, **1**(1), 21–31.

Cook, K.S. (1982), 'Network structures from an exchange perspective', in P.V. Marsden and N. Lin (eds), *Social Structure and Network Analysis*, Beverly Hills, CA: Sage, pp. 177–218.

Cook, K.S. and Emerson, R.M. (1978), 'Power, equity and commitment in exchange networks', *American Sociological Review*, **43**, 721–39.

Cook, K.S., Emerson, R.M., Gilmore, M.R. and Yamagishi, T. (1983), 'The distribution of power in exchange networks: theory and experimental results', *American Sociological Journal*, **89**, 275–305.

Coviello, N.E. (2005), 'Integrating qualitative and quantitative techniques in network analysis', *Qualitative Marketing Research: An International Journal*, **8**(1), 39–60.

Cropanzano, R. and Mitchell, M. (2005), 'Social exchange theory: an interdisciplinary review', *Journal of Management*, **31**(6), 874–900.

Curran, J., Jarvis, R., Blackburn, R.A. and Black, S. (1993), 'Networks and small firms: constructs, methodological strategies and some findings', *International Journal of Small Business*, **11**(2), 34–45.

Davidsson, P. and Honig, B. (2003), 'The role of social and human capital among nascent entrepreneurs', *Journal of Business Venturing*, **18**(3), 301–31.

Díaz García, C. and Carter, S. (2009), 'Resource mobilization through business owners' networks: is gender an issue?', *International Journal of Gender and Entrepreneurship*, **1**(3), 226–52.

Dubini, P. and Aldrich, H. (1991), 'Personal and extended networks are central to the entrepreneurial process', *Journal of Business Venturing*, **6**, 305–13.

Easterby-Smith, M., Thorpe, R. and Jackson, P.R. (2008), *Management Research*, 3rd edn, London: Sage Publications.

Eliasson, G. (1997), 'Competence blocks and industrial policy in the knowledge based economy', *Science Technology Industry Review*, **22**, 209–41.

Eliasson, G. and Eliasson, A. (2006), 'The Pharmacia story of entrepreneurship and as a creative technical university – an experiment in innovation, organizational break up and industrial renaissance', *Entrepreneurship and Regional Development*, **18**, 393–420.

Emerson, R.M. (1962), 'Power–dependence relations', *American Sociological Review*, **27**(1), 31–41.

Emerson, R.M. (1972a), 'Exchange theory, part I: a psychological basis for social exchange', in J. Berger, M. Zelditch and B. Anderson (eds), *Sociological Theories in Progress, Volume Two*, Boston, MA: Houghton Mifflin, pp. 38–57.

Emerson, R.M. (1972b), 'Exchange theory, part II: exchange relations and network structures', in J. Berger, M. Zelditch and B. Anderson (eds), *Sociological Theories in Progress, Volume Two*, Boston, MA: Houghton Mifflin, pp. 58–87.

Emerson, R.M. (1976), 'Social exchange theory', *Annual Review of Sociology*, **2**, 335–62.

Evans, M. (1990), 'The problem of gender for Women's Studies', *Women's Studies International Forum*, **13**, 457–62.

Farr-Wharton, R. and Brunetto, Y. (2007), 'Women entrepreneurs, opportunity recognition and government-sponsored business networks: a social capital perspective', *Women in Management Review*, **22**(3), 187–207.

Fine, M. and Gordon, S.M. (1989), 'Feminist transformations of/despite psychology', in M. Crawford and M. Gentry (eds), *Gender and Thought: Psychological Perspectives*, New York: Springer-Verlag, pp. 146–74.

Foss, L. (2010), 'Research on entrepreneur networks: the case for a constructionist feminist theory perspective', *International Journal of Gender and Entrepreneurship*, **2**(1), 83–102.

Foucault, M. (1972), 'The discourse on language (L'ordre du discourse)', in M. Foucault, *The Archaeology of Knowledge*, New York: Pantheon Books, pp. 215–37.

Fritsch, M. (ed.) (2011a), *Handbook of Research on Entrepreneurship and Regional Development*, Cheltenham, UK and Northampton, MA, USA: Edward Elgar.

Fritsch, M. (2011b), 'The role of new businesses in regional development', in M. Fritsch (ed.), *Handbook of Research on Entrepreneurship and Regional Development*, Cheltenham, UK and Northampton, MA, USA: Edward Elgar, pp. 1–10.

Fritsch, M. (2011c), 'The effect of new business formation on regional development: empirical evidence, interpretation and avenues for further research', in M. Fritsch (ed.), *Handbook of Research on Entrepreneurship and Regional Development*, Cheltenham, UK and Northampton, MA, USA: Edward Elgar, pp. 58–106.
Gatewood, E.J., Brush, C.G., Carter, N.M., Greene, P.G. and Hart, M.M. (2009), 'Diana: a symbol of women entrepreneurs' hunt for knowledge, money and the rewards of entrepreneurship', *Small Business Economics*, **32**(2), 129–44.
Gergen, K.J. (1969), *The Psychology of Behavior Exchange*, Reading, MA: Addison-Wesley.
Gephart, R.P. (2004), 'From the editors: qualitative research and the *Academy of Management Journal*', *Academy of Management Journal*, **47**(4), 454–62.
Gouldner, A.W. (1960), 'The norm of reciprocity: a preliminary statement', *American Sociological Review*, **25**, 161–78.
Granovetter, M. (1973), 'The strength of weak ties', *American Journal of Sociology*, **78**(6), 1360–80.
Greene, P.G., Brush, C.G., Hart, M.M. and Saparito, P. (2001), 'Patterns of venture capital funding: is gender a factor?', *Venture Capital: An International Journal of Entrepreneurial Finance*, **3**(1), 63–83.
Gremler, D.G. (2004), 'The critical incident technique in service research', *Journal of Service Research*, **7**(1), 65–89.
Hanson, S. and Blake, M. (2009), 'Gender and entrepreneurial networks', *Regional Studies*, **43**(1), 135–49.
Haraway, D.J. (1988), 'Situated knowledges – the science question in feminism and the privilege of particle perspective', *Feminist Studies*, **14**(3), 575–99.
Harrison, R.T. and Mason, C. (2007), 'Does gender matter? Women business angels and the supply of entrepreneurial finance', *Entrepreneurship Theory and Practice*, **31**(3), 445–72.
Hart, M. (2008), *Global Entrepreneurship Monitor, Northern Ireland Summary*, Belfast: Invest Northern Ireland.
Hill, F.M., Leitch, C.M. and Harrison, R.T. (2006), 'Desperately seeking finance? The demand for finance by women-owned and -led businesses', *Venture Capital: An International Journal of Entrepreneurial Finance*, **8**(2), 159–82.
Hill, F.M., Leitch, C.M. and Harrison, R.T. (2010), 'Growing a high-tech business: gender, perceptions and experiences in Northern Ireland', in C.G. Brush, A.M. de Bruin, E.J. Gatewood and C. Henry (eds), *Women Entrepreneurs and the Global Environment for Growth: A Research Perspective*, Cheltenham, UK and Northampton, MA, USA: Edward Elgar.
Hite, J.M. (2005), 'Evolutionary processes and paths of relationally embedded network ties in emerging entrepreneurial firms', *Entrepreneurship Theory and Practice*, **29**(1), 113–44.
Hite, J.M. and Hesterly, W.S. (2001), 'The evolution of firm networks: from emergence to early growth of the firm', *Strategic Management Journal*, **22**(3), 275–86.
Hoang, H. and Antoncic, B. (2003), 'Network-based research in entrepreneurship: a critical review', *Journal of Business Venturing*, **18**(2), 165–87.
Iacobucci, D. and Zerrillo, P.C. Sr (1996), 'Multiple levels of relational marketing phenomena', in D. Iacobucci (ed.), *Networks in Marketing*, Thousand Oaks, CA: Sage Publications, pp. 387–409.
Ibarra, H. (1992), 'Homophily and differential returns: sex difference in network structure and access in an advertising firm', *Administrative Science Quarterly*, **37**, 422–47.

Ibarra, H. (1993), 'Personal networks of women and minorities in management: a conceptual framework', *Academy of Management Review*, **18**(1), 56–88.
Ibarra, H. (1997), 'Paving an alternative route: gender differences in managerial networks', *Social Psychology Quarterly*, **60**(1), 91–102.
Ibarra, H. Kilduff, M. and Tsai, W. (2005), 'Zooming in and out: individual and collectivities at the frontiers of organizational network research', *Organization Science*, **6**(4), 359–71.
Invest NI (2010), http://www.investni.gov.uk, accessed 20 September 2010.
Jack, S.L. (2010), 'Approaches to studying networks: implications and outcomes', *Journal of Business Venturing*, **25**(1), 120–37.
Jack, S.L. (2005), 'The role, use and activation of strong and weak ties: a qualitative analysis', *Journal of Management Studies*, **42**(6), 1233–60.
Jack, S.L., Moult, S., Anderson, A.R. and Dodd, S. (2010), 'An entrepreneurial network evolving: patterns of change', *International Small Business Journal*, **28**(4), 315–37.
Jennings, J. and Brush, C. (2013), 'Research on women entrepreneurs: challenges to (and from) the broader entrepreneurship literature?', *Academy of Management Annals*, **7**(1), 633–715.
Johannisson, B. (1986), 'Network strategies: management technology for entrepreneurship and change', *International Small Business Journal*, **5**(1), 19–30.
Katz, J.A. and Williams, P.M. (1997), 'Gender, self-employment and weak-tie networking through formal organizations', *Entrepreneurship and Regional Development*, **9**, 183–97.
Kempster, S. and Cope, J. (2010), 'Learning to lead in the entrepreneurial context', *International Journal of Entrepreneurial Behaviour and Research*, **16**(1), 6–35.
Kim, T.-Y., Oh, H. and Swaminathan, A. (2006), 'Framing interorganizational network change: a network inertia perspective', *Academy of Management Review*, **31**(3), 704–20.
King, N. (2004), 'Using interviews in qualitative research', in C. Cassell and G. Symon (eds), *Essential Guide to Qualitative Methods in Organizational Research*, London: Sage, pp. 256–70.
Klyver, K. and Grant, S. (2010), 'Gender differences in entrepreneurial networking and participation', *International Journal of Gender and Entrepreneurship*, **2**(3), 213–27.
Kogut, B. and Singh, H. (1998), 'The effect of national culture on the choice of entry mode', *Journal of International Business Studies*, **19**, 411–32.
Koka, B.R., Madhavan, R. and Prescott, J.E. (2006), 'The evolution of interfirm networks: environmental effects on patterns of network change', *Academy of Management Review*, **31**(3), 721–37.
Larson, A. (1992), 'Network dyads in entrepreneurial settings: a study of the governance of exchange relationships', *American Science Quarterly*, **37**, 76–104.
Leitch, C.M., McMullan, C. and Harrison, R.T. (2009), 'Leadership development in SMEs: an action learning approach', *Action Learning: Research and Practice* (Special Issue on Action Learning and SMEs), **6**(3), 243–64.
Leitch, C.M., Hill, F.M. and Harrison, R.T. (2010), 'The philosophy and practice of interpretivist research in entrepreneurship: quality, validation and trust', *Organizational Research Methods*, **13**(1), 67–84.
Leitch, C.M., McMullan, C. and Harrison, R.T. (2013), 'The development of entrepreneurial leadership: the role of human, social and institutional capital', *British Journal of Management*, **24**(3), 347–66.

Littunen, H. (2000), 'Networks and local environmental characteristics in the survival of new firms', *Small Business Economics*, **15**(1), 59–71.
Lockett, N., Jack, S.L. and Larty, J. (2012), 'Myths, motivations and challenges of network formation for economic purposes: a dual perspective', *International Small Business Journal*, **31**(8), 866–89.
Malinowski, B. (1932), *Crime and Custom in Savage Society*, London: Paul, Trench & Trubner.
Marlow, S. (2002), 'Women and self-employment; a part of or a part from theoretical construct?', *International Entrepreneurship and Management Journal*, **3**(2), 83–91.
Marlow, S., Carter, S. and Shaw, E. (2008), 'Constructing female entrepreneurship policy in the UK: is the US a relevant benchmark?', *Environment and Planning C; Government and Policy*, **26**, 335–51.
Marsden, P.V. and Laumann, E.O. (1977), 'Collective action in a community elite: exchange, influence resources and issue resolution', in R.J. Liebert and A. Imershein (eds), *Power, Paradigms and Community Research*, London: ISA/ Sage Publications, pp. 199–250.
Mauss, M. (1969), *The Gift: Forms and Functions of Exchange in Archaic Societies*, London: Cohen & West.
McPherson, M., Smith-Lovin, L. and Cook, J.M. (2001), 'Birds of a feather: homophily in social networks', *Annual Review of Sociology*, **27**, 415–44.
Mitchell, J.C. (1969), 'The concept and use of social networks', in J.C. Mitchell (ed.), *Social Networks in Urban Situations*, Manchester, UK: Manchester University Press, pp. 1–50.
Mitchell, J.C. (1974), 'Social networks', *Annual Review of Anthropology*, **3**, 279–99.
Mitton, D.G. (1984), 'No money, know-how, know-who: formula for managing venture success and personal wealth', *Frontiers of Entrepreneurship Research*, Wellesley, MA: Babson College.
Molm, L.D. (1994), 'Dependence and risk: transforming the structure of social exchange', *Social Psychology Quarterly*, **57**, 163–76.
Molm, L.D. (2000), 'Theories of social exchange and exchange networks', in G. Ritzer and B. Smart (eds), *Handbook of Social Theory*, Thousand Oaks, CA: Sage Publications, pp. 260–72.
Molm, L.D. (2003), 'Theoretical comparison of forms of exchange', *Sociological Theory*, **2**, 1–17.
Molm, L.D. (2007), 'Building solidarity through generalized exchange: a theory of reciprocity', *American Journal of Sociology*, **113**(1), 205–42.
Molm, L.D., Collett, J.L. and Schaefer, D.R. (2007), 'Building solidarity through generalized exchange: a theory of reciprocity', *American Journal of Sociology*, **113**(1), 205–42.
Molm, L.D. and Cook, K.S. (1995), 'Social exchange and exchange networks', in K.S. Cook, G.A. Fine and J.S. House (eds), *Sociological Perspectives on Social Psychology*, Needham Heights, MA: Allyn & Bacon, pp. 209–35.
Morgan, D. (1988), *Focus Groups in Qualitative Research*, London: Sage Publications.
Nebus, J. (2006), 'Building collegial information networks: a theory of advice network generation', *Academy of Management Review*, **31**(3), 615–37.
Neergaard, H. (2007), 'Sampling in entrepreneurial settings', in H. Neergaard and J. Parm Ulhøi (eds), *Handbook for Qualitative Research Methods in Entrepreneurship*, Cheltenham, UK and Northampton, MA, USA: Edward Elgar, pp. 253–78.

Neergaard, H., Shaw, E. and Carter, S. (2005), 'The impact of gender, social capital and networks on business ownership – a research agenda', *International Journal of Entrepreneurial Behaviour and Research*, **11**(5), 338–57.

Nijkamp, P. (2003), 'Entrepreneurship in a modern network economy', *Regional Studies*, **37**, 395–405.

Nohria, N. (1992), 'Is a network perspective a useful way of studying organizations?', in N. Nohria and R.G. Eccles (eds), *Networks and Organizations: Structure, Form and Action*, Boston, MA: Harvard Business School Press, pp. 1–22.

O'Donnell, A., Gilmore, A., Cummins, D. and Carson, D. (2001), 'The network construct in entrepreneurship research: a review and critique', *Management Decision*, **39**(9), 749–60.

Ogbor, J.O. (2000), 'Mythicizing and reification in entrepreneurial discourse: ideology critique of entrepreneurial studies', *Journal of Management Studies*, **35**, 605–35.

Parkhe, A., Wasserman, S. and Ralston, D.A. (2006), 'New frontiers in network theory development', *Academy of Management Review*, **31**(3), 560–68.

Phillips, N., Tracey, P. and Karra, N. (2013), 'Building entrepreneurial tie portfolios through strategic homophily: the role of narrative identity work in venture creation and early growth', *Journal of Business Venturing*, **28**(1), 134–50.

Portes, A. (1998), 'Social capital: its origins and applications in modern sociology', *Annual Review of Sociology*, **24**, 1–24.

Renzulli, L.A., Aldrich, H. and Moody, J. (2000), 'Family matters: gender, networks and entrepreneurial outcomes', *Social Forces*, **79**(2), 523–46.

Riger, S. (1992), 'Epistemological debates, feminist voices: science, social values, and the study of women', *American Psychologist*, **47**, 730–40.

Robson, P.J.A., Jack, S.L. and Freel, M.S. (2008), 'Gender and the use of business advice: evidence from firms in the Scottish service sector', *Environment and Planning C: Government and Policy*, **26**, 292–314.

Rubin, H. and Rubin, I. (2005), *Qualitative Interviewing: The Art of Hearing Data*, 2nd edn, London: Sage.

Saunders, M., Lewis, P. and Thornhill, A. (2009), *Research Methods for Business Students*, 5th edn, Harlow, Essex: Pearson Education.

Shapiro, I. and Wendt, A. (2005), 'The difference that realism makes: social science and the politics of consent', in I. Shapiro (ed.), *The Flight from Reality in the Human Sciences*, Princeton, NJ: Princeton University Press, pp. 19–50.

Shaw, E. (1999), 'A guide to the qualitative research process: evidence from a small firm study', *Qualitative Market Research: An International Journal*, **2**(2), 59–70.

Simmel, G. (1955), *Conflict and the Web of Group Affiliations*, New York: Free Press.

Slotte-Kock, S. and Coviello, N. (2010), 'Entrepreneurship research on network processes: a review and ways forward', *Entrepreneurship Theory and Practice*, **34**(1), 31–57.

Smith-Doerr, L. and Powell, W.W. (2005), 'Networks and economic life', in N.J. Smelser and R. Swedberg (eds), *The Handbook of Economic Sociology*, 2nd edn, Princeton, NJ: Russell Sage Foundation/Princeton University Press, pp. 379–402.

Sternberg, R. (2011), 'Regional determinants of entrepreneurial activities – theories and empirical evidence', in M. Fritsch (ed.), *Handbook of Research on Entrepreneurship and Regional Development*, Cheltenham, UK and Northampton, MA, USA: Edward Elgar, pp. 33–57.

Stevenson, W.B. and Greenberg, D. (2000), 'Agency and social networks: strategies of action in a social structure of position, opposition and opportunity', *Administrative Science Quarterly*, **45**, 651–78.
Thompson, C.J., Locander, W.B. and Pollio, H.R. (1989), 'The lived meaning of free choice: an existential–phenomenological description of everyday consumer experiences of contemporary modern women', *The Journal of Consumer Research*, **17**(3), 346–61.
Tichy, N.M., Tushman, M.L. and Fombrun, C. (1979), 'Social network analysis for organizations', *Academy of Management Review*, **4**(4), 507–19.
Tsui, A.S. and Wang, D.X. (2002), 'Employment relationships from the employer's perspective: current research and future directions', in C.L. Cooper and I.T. Robertson (eds), *International Review of Industrial and Organizational Psychology*, Chichester, UK: Wiley, pp. 111–14.
Uzzi, B. (1996), 'The sources and consequences of embeddedness for the economic performance of organizations: the network effect', *American Sociological Review*, **61**(4), 674–98.
Vissa, B. (2012), 'Agency in action: entrepreneurs' networking style and initiation of economic exchange', *Organization Science*, **23**(2), 492–510.
Wang, D., Tsui, A.S., Zhang, Y. and Ma, L. (2003), 'Employment relationships and firm performance: evidence from an emerging economy', *Journal of Organizational Behavior*, **24**(5), 511–35.
Wasserman, S. and Faust, K. (1994), 'Social network analysis in the social and behavioral sciences', in *Social Network Analysis: Methods and Applications*, Cambridge, UK: Cambridge University Press, pp. 1–27.
Watson, J. (2011), 'Networking: gender differences and the association with firm performance', *International Small Business Journal*, **30**(5), 536–58.
Wellman, B. (1988), 'Structural analysis: from method and metaphor to theory and substance', in B. Wellman and S.D. Berkowitz (eds), *Social Structures: A Network Approach*, New York: Cambridge University Press.
Whitten, N.E. and Wolfe, A.W. (1974), 'Network analysis', in J.J. Honigman (ed.), *The Handbook of Social and Cultural Anthropology*, Chicago, IL: Rand MacNally, pp. 717–46.
Williamson, O.E. (1993), 'Calculativeness, trust and economic organization', *Journal of Law and Economics*, **36**, 453–86.

7. Cooperation versus coordination relations in SME networks: a new view of collective strategy dynamics

Christophe Leyronas and Stéphanie Loup

1. INTRODUCTION

Many studies have highlighted the importance of collective dynamics in the development of companies. These can take different names depending on the references and theoretical approaches employed: alliances, clusters, networks of companies, collective strategies and so on. One way that small businesses can boost their development is through participation in collectives. The concept of collective action and the importance for companies of acting together have long been shown. A collective strategy is defined as the joint mobilization of resources and the formulation of joint actions within communities of organizations (Hawley, 1950). In 1965, Alderson highlighted the importance for organizations of working together. In the same year, Emery and Trist (1965) observed that multilateral organizations were an effective way to develop a strategy in a turbulent environment. Thus, as noted in the work largely inspired by Astley and Fombrun (1983), the individual destiny of a company depends to a greater or lesser degree on a collective destiny (Le Roy and Guillotreau, 2002). From this it becomes clear that the strategic development of companies relies increasingly on relational practices (Grenier, 2002).

Collective action is becoming an important issue for companies, but many questions remain regarding the analysis of its mode of operation. While the question of 'Why?' has been dealt with at some length, the question of 'How?' and therefore of its operation remains open. There have been studies of the modalities of organization and monitoring, but they only partially help us understand the operation of these collectives and grasp their dynamics. This issue has been addressed by examining interactive behaviour between the actors: opportunism, trust, reciprocity, equity/fairness, truthfulness and solidarity (Gulati et al., 2012). While these aspects are important for understanding the nature of the relations between the actors in the framework of a collective strategy or action, they do not examine the content of the exchange. It is important to analyse the content of relations between actors in order to understand their dynamics, but also in order to grasp how these relational dynamics generate, enrich or modify the way the collective functions.

More generally, collective strategy is a systemic response formulated by a group of organizations, in the sense that a system has properties independent of its component parts (Astley and Fombrun, 1983). We can assume that the characteristics of the parties and those resulting from the links between the parties both contribute to the way the system operates. An analysis of the content of the relations between pairs of actors (dyads) would shed light on the way they affect the collective dynamics and highlight a new element as an explanatory factor of the way collective actions develop. An analysis based on the way the collective is organized through an examination of the activities undertaken, together with the relations between the actors, both as they exist and in their content, should enable a better understanding of their dynamics. It is therefore necessary to identify the content as well as the conditions under which this content is implemented. An analysis of the collective actions and strategies means addressing the issue of the dynamics of these actions, organized both statically and dynamically. This requires an understanding of how the objectives, the content and the organization evolve in response both to the strategies of the different actors and to the external constraints and opportunities.

We first discuss the analysis of the collective dynamic by highlighting the importance of studying the links between the actors through the dyads in order to grasp how, when pairs of companies develop relationships involving cooperation and exchange, they are able to develop new resources and skills that can provide content for the collective. To see how this works, however, it is first necessary to analyse the content of these dyadic ties. We propose to introduce the distinction between cooperation-based and coordination-based relations, in order to understand why dyadic ties influence the collective only in certain cases. Second, we try to apply the fruits of this analysis to the case of Revel, where 17 companies in the furniture sector have formed a collective. After presenting the sector, the collective and the research methodology, we show how the application of the distinction between cooperation and coordination sheds new light on the dynamics of this collective. Finally, we investigate how collective dynamics can be understood through an analysis of the content of the relations. For this purpose we emphasize the role of the strategic choices of the actors as well as the forms of organization of the collective in the implementation of the collective dynamic.

2. AN APPROACH TO COLLECTIVE DYNAMICS BY AN ANALYSIS OF THE RELATIONS BETWEEN ACTORS

An analysis of collective actions and strategies once again raises the question of relations between strategy and structure (Chandler, 1962; Ansoff, 1968) by presenting structure in a new way, as it is not analysed at the level of the company but at the collective level. In their seminal article, Astley and Fombrum (1983) raise the question of structures in the analysis of collective strategies but from the perspective of the rules governing coordination and control or, quoting Commons and Parsons (1950), of working rules for collective action. To a certain extent it may be considered that this requires an analysis of the structure of the relations contributing to a collective strategy.

How can we best grasp this structure or these structures? The best way to approach inter-organizational analysis may be to consider the situation at multiple levels, multiple dimensions, or perhaps both (Osarenkhoe, 2010). To comprehend these different levels and dimensions we first consider the different contributions of structural analysis through networks of relationships. To mitigate the limitations of this analysis, which does not take the real content of interactions and exchanges into consideration, we then introduce the distinction between cooperation-based and coordination-based relations through an analysis of resources. New resources (whether collective or not) can only be created through cooperation; coordination does no more than provide an organizational framework for the collective strategy, without contributing to joint action.

2.1 An Analysis of the Dyads as a Way of Understanding the Collective

Different methodologies have been applied to study the structural dimension of collective strategies. It should be remembered that, whatever the method, analysing a collective strategy involves taking two levels of analysis into account: the collective as an organization, that is, organized and organizing (Heinman, 1980), and the companies. The link between the companies and the collective is an essential element for grasping the dynamics of these relations. Indeed, if the individual company appears as the entry point for analysing intra- and inter-organizational processes (Alter, 1990), the individual–collective or company–collective link remains a fundamental element. This link is useful both through the two levels of analysis it requires and by taking account of the interactions. Thus, by taking into account the collective dimensions and not just the dyadic relations, we are better able to understand the nature as well as the effects of networks of relationships (Madhavan et al., 1998; Dyer and Singh, 1998; Ahuja, 2000; Gulati et al., 2000).

Several major approaches have been employed to explain relations between enterprises, resource dependence, embeddedness or strategic actions (Ozcan and Eisenhardt, 2009). Our analysis is in line with this latter position, although analysis has mostly focused on the influence of the position in the network on strategic action, and not the reverse (Powell et al., 1996; Hallen, 2008; Santos and Eisenhardt, 2009). Analysing a company's network of relations can explain why the company is able to establish links (Hallen, 2008) in terms of resources and capacity. This ability to forge links has an impact on the ability of companies to identify, access and mobilize external resources (Stam and Elfring, 2008; Adler and Kwon, 2002). These authors examine the question of the existence, the intensity or the evolution of dyadic links but without extending their vision to include the overall structure of these links.

The analysis of interactions between companies has been addressed in very different ways in the literature: 'The methodological approach based on network analysis used in this study operationalizes the collective strategy framework and links homogeneity of organizational characteristics to the location or position of organizations in a field relative to one another' (Olivier, 1988, p. 544). This approach makes it possible to analyse the structural dimensions, which represent 'the nested structure of inter-organizational linkages from the micro-level, through organizations and networks up to the meso- and macro-level of inter-organizational linkages' (Tang and Xi, 2006, p. 189). We here attempt to understand collective strategy by taking relations between companies into account as measured by the network of relations between the actors.

By using the concepts and tools of the sociology of networks to develop models and methods borrowed from graph theory, it is possible to model relationship systems and map exchange flows[1] (Lazega, 2007) in a collective. The sociology of networks provides a way of seeing the positions of companies in relation to each other and of mapping the complete set of relations between participants. We can thus determine and analyse a company's network (egocentric network) by measuring the direct links the company maintains with the other companies participating in the collective strategy. The aggregation of dyadic relations provides a representation of the full set of relations (Das and Teng, 2002) and, by extension, a representation of the collective. We make the assumption that the nature of micro-level links (dyad) has an effect on the dynamics of macro-level links (map of all relations between the different actors). At the macro-level, one of the issues discussed was that of the link between the properties of the network resulting from the choices and behaviour of actors, and the network's performance. Thus Meagher and Rogers (2004) insist on the density of relations, and Stuart (1998) and Ahuja (2000) on the strength of the relationships. This has been understood to reflect a quantitative view of a relationship where we can measure the flow.

There has been little investigation into the nature of this, whereas it can be assumed that this qualitative aspect also has an undoubted impact on the dynamics of relationships. While structural analysis is a promising approach for analysing how the strategies and positioning of companies (centrality) in the collective enable them to derive certain benefits (access to information, power etc.), it does not really help us grasp the nature of the collective as such, and especially the link between the individual and the collective. Despite the existence of links that may reflect relations of interdependence, this approach still broadly reduces the collective to a juxtaposition of the interests of individual companies rather than taking the collective dimensions into account (Astley, 1984). How can we attempt to answer this question, which has already been raised many times? We propose to update the analysis by introducing an analysis of the content of relations.

2.2 Looking inside the Black Box of Relations: Cooperation versus Coordination

Many approaches have been developed for identifying the factors or variables that have an impact on the development of cooperation-based relations, such as conflicts of interest (Doz, 1996), an analysis of the impact of confidence (Ring and Van de Ven, 1994; Uzzi, 1997; Zaheer et al., 1998), approaches analysing the structure of relations (Gulati, 1995; Robinson and Stuart, 2007), among others. These approaches have often dealt with these issues so as to avoid the issues of negative incentives that can appear in the framework of these cooperative relationships (Gulati et al., 2012). Yet, even in situations where interests are aligned and there are positive incentives to cooperate, relations do not always develop.

To answer this question, Gulati et al. (2012) highlight an approach focusing on the mechanisms, the nature and the content of relations. Too often the approaches developed have focused solely on cooperation, whereas these authors note that if an approach to relations includes issues of coordination, this allows 'organization design, communication, and process management' to be studied simultaneously (Gulati et al., 2012, p. 533). In order to ensure consistency in their reasoning, they consider relations that can be described as 'collaboration' and include an analysis of cooperation and coordination in the same framework. Coordination is then defined as the junction, the network structure, the synchronization or the extent to which actions are consistent with one another (Aiken et al., 1975; Okhuysen and Bechky, 2009). Gulati et al. (2012, p. 537) state that 'Coordination typically involves the specification and operation of information-sharing, decision-making, and feedback mechanisms in the relationship to unify and bring order to partners' efforts, and to combine partners' resources in productive ways'. Organizations tend to develop coordination when they perceive a need for resources that would enable them to achieve their goals (Van de Ven and Walker, 1984).

The idea of considering coordination-based relations separately from cooperation-based ones in the framework of collective strategies is not new in itself, and many authors have raised the issue of coordination-based relations (Galbraith, 1977; Argote, 1982; Gulati et al., 2012) to explain some of the dynamics of alliances. However, they address the question from the point of view of the coordination of firms in the alliance (Puranam et al., 2012), whereas it would seem appropriate to study collective strategies also at the dyadic level. Coordination even appears inseparable from cooperation, as indicated in the following definition: 'Several organizations may decide to implement a collective strategy, for instance, to coordinate their activities for product development or product promotion' (Bresser and Harl, 1986, p. 411). This definition highlights a dual logic in collective strategies: coordination of activities and/or creation of new resources at the level of the collective. Cooperation, coordination and the question of the specificity of the assets have often been discussed in the context of research on the analysis of interorganizational relations (Payan, 2007). Too many studies have failed to examine coordination and cooperation at the same time (Gulati et al., 2012).

The first studies taking on the issue of coordination concentrated on intra-organizational relations via the coordination of departments (Van de Ven and Walker, 1984). Some authors even consider the two notions as synonymous (Alter and Hage, 1993; Morgan and Hunt, 1994; Anderson et al., 1994), which explains why many studies seem to deal with only one of the two concepts (Payan and Svensson, 2007). It is not easy to explain the distinction between the two. Sivadas and Dwyer (2000) consider coordination as a component of cooperation because they see cooperative competency as a second-order factor.

There is, however, a difference between the two concepts because coordination issues can arise outside any context of cooperation (Day and Klein, 1987). Many authors have tried to introduce distinctions between these two concepts (Dabholkar et al., 1994; Mulford and Rogers, 1982). They are based on criteria such as the nature of normative objectives versus outcome orientation (Day and Klein, 1987), on behaviour (Alter and Hage, 1993; McNeilly and Russ, 1992) or on an organization's goal orientations/decision rules (Mulford and Rogers, 1982).

Varadarajan and Jayachandran (1999) propose to analyse coordination strategies by distinguishing three levels: 'content', to see how relations are related to resources and the resources used; 'formulation', to see how coordination enables the development of activities and with what efficiency; and, finally, 'implementation', to analyse the implementation of actions and activities.

Even so, any analysis of the content of relationships remains at the level of relations between the partners. While this approach is interesting, it remains inadequate for the analysis of collective strategies because these are often less structured in terms of organization and management than alliances, mainly due to the multiplicity of actors and the less formalized nature of collective strategies. This is particularly the case with collective strategies in which there is no one company or small group of companies taking the lead. In these conditions it appears necessary to start from the analysis of the dyads in order to understand how the companies work together and to what extent these relations have an impact on the collective dynamic. Not only will it be necessary to identify the dyads but also to qualify them to see if the contents of dyadic relations can be an explanatory variable for the development of collective actions. We thus propose to introduce a distinction between cooperation-based and coordination-based relations in the analysis of dyadic links to help us understand the collective dynamic.

This distinction can be established by analysing the resources generated/mobilized by the actors of the collective strategy. Participation in the collective will have the effect of revealing resources (Barney, 1991) or even giving access to new resources. The creation, development and/or the mobilization of resources would not have been possible without participation in the collective (Das and Teng, 2000). It enables companies to exchange information, knowledge, different forms of capital and so on (Koka and Prescott, 2002).

Thus cooperation involves an exchange of resources whose objective is to increase access to both resources and expertise; coordination means pooling or exchanging resources at a given time without any increase in the stock of resources or expertise of the companies in the relationship. Unlike cooperation, coordination does not generate new resources/skills in the companies themselves.

3. CASE STUDY: THE FURNITURE SECTOR IN REVEL

The town of Revel contains a large variety of trades and craftsmen. Our approach focuses only on the companies working in artistic furniture production, many of whom are specialized in cabinetmaking/marquetry. All these businesses are members of the association 'Les Artisans Réunis', which testifies to their willingness to act together. For our case study, we undertook several phases of data collection and processing in order to analyse the relations between the actors.

3.1 Presentation of the Case Study

The reputation of Revel for artistic furniture originates from the desire of a businessman at the end of the nineteenth century to develop know-how related to cabinetmaking. The quality of local work (reproduction furniture, personal creations) was quickly recognized. The customer base expanded rapidly, enabling many apprentices to set up their own workshops. The second half of the twentieth century saw a new expansion, with greater recognition of the know-how associated with Revel, and the establishment of a training centre. From the 1950s, a group of companies decided to promote Revel's expertise to counter European competition. In addition, in order to avoid competition between them based on price, the companies in the group agreed on a collective review of the prices of their products. This collective will was also strengthened by the Artisans' Union, created in 1960, as well as by the creation of the 'Hall du Meuble' (furniture showroom). The Union rapidly became the 'Association for the Promotion of Artistic Furniture' from Revel with the aim of promoting Revel by organizing various events and through a dedicated exhibition and sales centre, the 'Espace Art et Meubles'. At the beginning, all the companies in the network were from the cabinetmaking sector, but in response to the drop in membership (barely 15 today compared with 40 in 1960), the Association opened its doors to companies with complementary activities, but always in relation to furniture. Cabinetmaking none the less remains the network's core business (nine companies). At the end of the 1980s, the Association organized the first trade fair for artistic furniture; then, three years later, the Biennale of Artistic Furniture and Decoration, to showcase the specificity and quality of local know-how (cabinetmakers, marquetry specialists, sculptors, gilders on wood, bronze smelters and engravers, upholsterers and marble masons) in the face of national and international competition in the reproduction, the renovation and the creation of traditional or contemporary furniture. Today, Revel has the largest concentration of skilled

French craftsmen in artistic furniture. It has become one of the main training centres for the furnishing trades in France, as regards both initial training, with its high school specializing in arts and crafts, wood and furniture, and training for adults, with the adult training centre of the Institute of Arts and Crafts Trades. The craftsmen interviewed considered that Revel's arts and crafts sector forms a high-quality cluster, which has existed for nearly a century, possessing substantial know-how and a variety of professions related to the furniture sector. The proximity of fellow craftsmen is important because it helps to present customers with a more concentrated range of goods, as well as sustaining the network over time. Most of the members, mainly small businesses each with slightly different market positions, joined the Association to obtain a higher profile, but also to develop synergies and collective actions. 'Les Artisans Réunis' is made up of small businesses specializing in trades related to furniture production. It therefore includes cabinetmakers (creators and restorers), ironworkers, upholsterers and stained-glass specialists. The companies work together as regards relations with sub-contractors, customers, exchange of information and ideas, and also on joint ad hoc projects such as large commissions or exhibitions. Revel's companies contribute different skills, depending on their speciality. Furniture production may require that different businesses work together on a given project. They also pool their resources to give themselves better visibility. As active local players, they also influence training, together with support structures in order to gain access to the resources and skills necessary for their development. Several companies thus use the resources available in Revel, notably by hiring trainees from the local training centres.

3.2 Research Methodology and Design

As observed by Yami (2006), a qualitative approach offers the best way of grasping the complexity of collective strategies, using an in-depth case study. This should be an extensive study of a single case but with multiple levels of analysis (Yin, 1989; Eisenhardt, 1989). Our analysis is based on an in-depth study of the association for the 'Promotion of Artistic Furniture from Revel' for historical reasons and to ensure legitimacy, because it brings together virtually all the businesses in Revel involved in artistic furniture and also because it enables us to establish clear limits on the actions and actors concerned. In order to carry out this study, we identified all the companies taking part in collective actions proposed by the association. We collected data from multiple sources in three phases (see Table 7.1).

The network data were collected by the sociometrics technique (Wasserman and Faust, 1994). We submitted the list of companies in the network to each person interviewed and asked them to describe their

Table 7.1 Phases of the methodological approach

Phases of research	Methodology
Phase 1 – Overview of the context and the main actors	8 semi-directive interviews with company directors organized around 4 themes (the company and its director; the Revel cluster; the Association; and the institutional environment) – duration between 30 minutes and 1 hour. These interviews were recorded.
Phase 2 – Identification and analysis of relations within the cluster	13 questionnaires administered to company directors around 6 themes (cooperative links; customer–supplier relations; links of competition; personal links; institutional links; and relational breakdowns) and collection of additional data
Phase 3 – Qualification of links	Use of secondary sources and data from Phases 1 and 2 + supplementary interviews

relationship with each of these companies. As a result, we obtained information on their interactions. The responses to the questionnaire enabled us to form matrices of relationships. These matrices were analysed to calculate the centrality indices and to map the relations. The validity of the data was ensured by the use of the 'key informant' approach (Huber and Power, 1985; Kumar et al., 1993); we were also able to validate the data in part through individual interviews and partly by the constitution of the matrix of relations. We cross-checked the data by verifying the information through other available sources (company and association websites; books on the history of Revel; interviews with players related to the networks – institutions such as the town council, training centres, chambers of trades etc.). This method enabled us to obtain sufficient data for our analysis, both on the network and on each of the companies, and allowed us to characterize the content of the relations.

During the first phase, we were able to interview the main actors of the collective strategy face to face (8 out of the 17 firms that then made up the Association). They were selected because they were playing an active role in the life of the Association (participation in events on behalf of the Association). Following this first phase, we were able to draw up a questionnaire to assess and then to measure the links between the actors. It was submitted to all the member companies of the Association, but only 13 managers out of the 17 responded. Concerning the second phase, the themes indicated were chosen to enable us to map the relations. In the

Table 7.2 Elements for the analysis of relations

Identification of partners	With which companies or institutions do you have cooperative links (both in the region of Revel and outside this region)?
Duration and evolution of relations	Date the relationship began Evolution of the relationship over time (strengthening, maintenance, cessation etc.) and, if cessation, identification of the reasons
Content of relations	Nature of the relationship (personal network, business network, information network) Nature of joint actions (training, commercial initiative, technical innovation etc.) Identification of the competitive relationships between the members, and measurement of their intensity
Type of relationship	Sub-contracting, customer–supplier relations, cooperation Development of joint activities in a sustainable manner, grouped offers in response to customer requests
Intensity and hierarchy of relationships	Intensity of the relationship with this company Degree of importance of those you consider as being the most important in terms of cooperation

third phase we analysed the existing relations between the actors in order to identify whether each was a cooperation-based or a coordination-based relationship. We also used different information (see Table 7.2) in addition to that collected for Phases 1 and 2.

3.3 Analysis of the Case

Based on the different phases of the investigation, we were able to analyse the relations between the members using different indicators of centrality – degree of centrality (Nieminem, 1974) and degree of 'betweenness' (Freeman, 1979) – and to map the relations. The data were processed with the UCINET software package, Version 6.392 (Borgatti et al., 2002).

Only 13 companies out of the 17 responded to the interviews and questionnaires of Phase 2 that we used to map relations. The absence of certain responses makes it difficult to analyse the network of relations because complete networks are necessary for a structural analysis (Saglietto, 2006). For our analysis we were able to process the data because we had an acceptable representation of the relations for several reasons. The first reason was the number of respondents. With 13 respondents out of 17, we were able to identify the set of relations even if it was not possible to check their

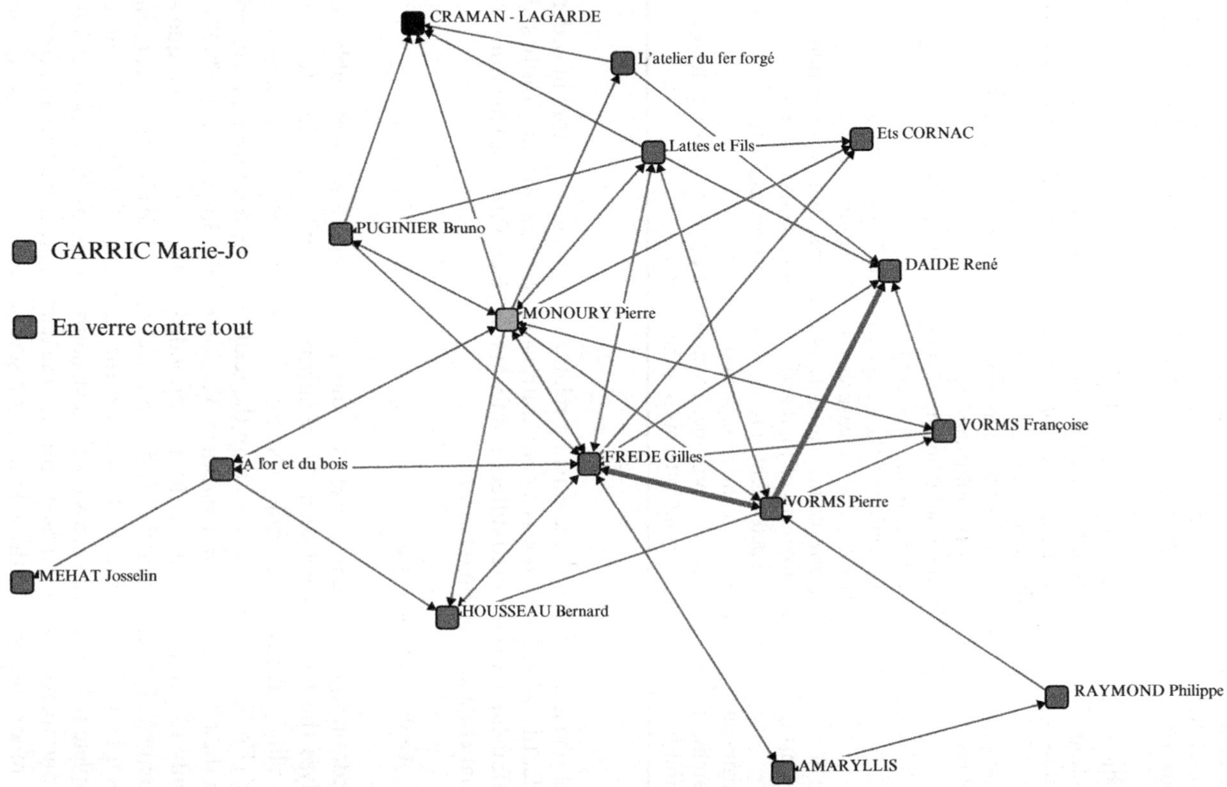

Figure 7.1 Map of relations between the actors

symmetry in every case. The matrix of relations obtained from the respondents is not asymmetrical if you are asking respondents only to declare whether or not they have a cooperation-based relationship. If we examine what the companies say about the intensity of the relationships, there are variations, even if these are limited on the whole. On a scale measuring this intensity according to seven criteria, there is often a slight degree of variation in the perception of the intensity, depending on which respondent you ask. The symmetry observable in the matrix of relations and their intensity suggests that the 13 respondents adequately represent the overall situation regarding relations. In addition, some of the non-respondents in Phase 2 were interviewed in Phase 1. The qualitative data collected in the first phase thus enabled us to validate a number of relationships even when we did not have input from both parties. The use of data concerning the structure measured by the questionnaire together with the qualitative data enabled us to represent relations between the actors. A square matrix of relations was prepared from which to construct a map (see Figure 7.1). In the case of these relations the position cannot be explained by the size of the firms, as shown by Avenel et al. (2007), because the distribution of sizes of enterprises is fairly homogeneous across all the possible positions of the network.

The cooperation-based relations are mostly within the Association, because, concerning 'extraversity' (Lechner and Leyronas, 2012), that is, their cooperation-based relations outside the network, very few members reported having any relations with firms outside the network. The Association is therefore the relevant framework for analysing these relationships. However, they are polymorphic because there are also competition-based relationships between them. The cabinetmakers rarely call on other cabinetmakers for their own creations, either for technical assistance or advice on how to work the wood. According to their statements, the majority of the members of the Association are passionate about their profession as cabinetmakers, working the wood with their own styles and specific techniques. There is a desire to both maintain their specificities in terms of production and avoid entering into competition with the others. The intensity of competition between the members is perceived as low within the network, but the presence of a certain degree of competition undoubtedly has an impact on the density of the network.

Our analysis identifies several activities developed in common (see Table 7.3).

If we introduce the content of relations between the actors, we can identify the following items (see Table 7.4).

An analysis of the nature of the relations between the actors (see Table 7.4) at the dyadic level shows, except in one relationship qualified as collaboration-based, that all the existing relationships involve

Table 7.3 Collective activities developed in the framework of the Association

Marketing and sales	A 600m² sales area, owned by the Association. The purpose of this area is not to make a profit but to showcase the network, according to the store manager
	Organizing and participating in shared events, including trade fairs, and finding subsidies to help finance them
	Communicating about the network and its actions
Optimizing costs	Reducing some management costs
	Pooling the customer portfolio of each by exchanging customers between the members of the network according to the needs of the latter (these exchanges are possible because of the strong complementarity of the membership)
	Using apprentices and trainees from the training centres in Revel[a]
Developing companies[b]	Developing new business opportunities – responding to calls for tender
	Discussing knowledge and professional skills, communicating and developing affinities

Notes:

[a] Apprentices are an important factor, because virtually all businesses have them. Some workshops count on them heavily. As an example, between 2006 and 2010 one workshop had two full-time employees, and between eight and 12 apprentices.

[b] Concerning the sales of these companies, approximately half of them increased turnover between 2006 and 2010, while turnover declined or stagnated for the other half. In all cases, all the companies surveyed had made a profit every year over the previous five years.

either sub-contracting for specialist services, or customer–supplier relationships in which businesses work together but where each continues to produce its own creations as a function of its own know-how. In addition, if we refer to the intensity of the links between the actors, in only 10 cases out of the 45 links identified between the enterprises of the collective, the relationship obtains a score of at least 4 on a scale ranging from 1 to 6.[2] In all other cases the relationship is regarded as not very intense because exchange-based relations between companies are limited, which can be explained by the nature of the relations among them (customer–supplier, sub-contracting etc.). The analysis of the dyads shows that, in this collective, relationships mainly concern the coordination of activities or know-how and are not really cooperation-based with specific aims, such as developing new concepts, product lines, methods of supply and the like. Finally, we note that any labour-based relations between companies are only dyadic and that there are

Table 7.4 Content of relations between the actors

	1	2	3	4	5	6	7	8	9	10	11	12	13	14	15	External collaboration
1						ST (1)	ST (1)			ST (1)	ST (2)					
2						CT (1)							CT (2)			
6	ST (1)	ST (2)		ST (1)	ST (4)		ST (1)		ST (2)		ST (6)				ST (1)	
7						ST (1)										
8			ST (3)	C (5)												EA (5) Discussion and advice
9			CT (2)	CT (3)	CT (3)	CT (4)					CT (4)	CT (3)			CT (3)	
11	ST (2/3)		ST (3/4)			ST (6)		ST (1)						ST	ST (4)	
12			ST (1)			ST (1)					ST (1)					
13		C–F (4)													C–F (3)	
14				CT (6)		CT (3)					CT (1)				CT (6)	

Table 7.4 (continued)

	1	2	3	4	5	6	7	8	9	10	11	12	13	14	15	External collaboration
15			CT/ ST (1)			ST (1)	CT (1)		CT (2)		CT/ ST (1)			CT (2)		EB EC ED EE
16																EF – CT (6) EG – CT (4) EH EI – ST (3) EJ – ST (3)

Notes:
The table should be read line by line. The external companies are coded from EA to EJ.
ST = sub-contracting relationship as either originator or sub-contractor.
C–F = customer–supplier relations.
CT = co-contracting: a joint response to the markets, sharing customers or work.
C = collaboration.
The number in parentheses gives the intensity of cooperation measured on a scale of 1 to 6.

Table 7.5 Satisfaction and desired developments of the collective strategy

Companies	Satisfaction with the collective	Change desired
0.	Satisfied	Increase
1.	Satisfied	No
2.	Not satisfied (no benefit)	No response
3.	No response	No response
4.	No response	No response
5.	Satisfied	Increase
6.	Satisfied	Improvement
7.	No response	No response
8.	Satisfied	No
9.	No response	No response
10.	Highly satisfied	Increase
11.	No response	No response
12.	Satisfied	Increase
13.	Satisfied	No
14.	No response	No response
15.	Satisfied	Increase

no projects involving more than two firms. Furthermore, if we look at whether or not actors are satisfied with the collective strategy and their desire for change (strengthening or improving the collective, keeping the status quo, slackening off the collective), we note that many of them are satisfied and that six of them wish for an increase or a strengthening of collective aspects (see Table 7.5). The most central companies, measured by their direct relations, also perform the administrative roles in the Association. Their involvement in the associative structure and the intensity of their cooperation show their commitment to the cooperation project. It should be noted, however, that although those with the most relationships are the most satisfied, we cannot conclude that there is a causal link.

In the case of Revel, we note that there is a willingness to expand the scope of the collective among the firms most involved in the Association and in dyadic working links. However, a closer look at the evolution of this collective shows that there has been no change in the actions implemented by the companies. The companies most involved and most in search of assistance have not been able to develop a sub-network to meet their expectations. In fact, the case of Revel is more about the allocation of overall resources than about actually creating new resources (they share costs in order to minimize marketing/communication expenses). Observation of the relations between the actors involved in the Association shows that they pursue a strategy of coordination rather than dyadic cooperation. They do not create any new resources jointly, but are attracted by the possibility of accessing the resources of others in order to help them fulfil an order requiring input from different trades. Coordination at the dyadic level is therefore the predominant strategy. The absence of cooperation-based relations at the level of the dyads means that individual strategies have little to do with the strategy of the collective. Furthermore, some important actors are pursuing a wait-and-see policy (Company 3). In the light of the various data gathered in the different phases of the study, it would seem that the lack of sufficiently important cooperation-based dyadic relations is not conducive to the development of a collective strategy. This is more like an agreement on means, as described by Bourgeois (1980).

4. DISCUSSION: UNDERSTANDING THE COLLECTIVE DYNAMIC BY ANALYSING IT IN TERMS OF BOTH CONTENT AND ORGANIZATION

The difficulty in interpreting this case with the tools of structural analysis means that we need to adapt this approach by analysing not only the links but also their content. In addition, the organizational structure influences the transfer of resources and skills from the dyads to the collective, helping the collective evolve.

4.1 The Importance of the Content of Relationships

If we accept the distinction introduced by Varadarajan and Jayachandran (1999) about coordination strategies, in our case the 'content' shows us that there is resource-sharing between actors that have links, while the 'formulation' shows that there is no development of activities other than those at the origin of the collective project. Coordination has remained at the dyadic level and has not led to any developments in the collective as a whole. This dyadic coordination has not helped create new resources but has just provided access to resources (attraction) that already existed elsewhere in the network or has enabled the pooling of resources for individual projects handled jointly by a few actors at a given time. This is market-driven coordination in the sense that the pooling of resources and expertise enables suppliers to meet the needs of their customers. It does not bring about long-term projects; nor does it lead to innovation in ways of working, in the development of new models and so on. There is no sharing of experience between the actors who could make contributions beyond the given case to try to perpetuate and generalize the resources and skills. Thus the last level – 'implementation' – shows that the dyadic actions and activities performed have not led to any change in the collective.

If we refer to the resource based view (RBV), only a limited number of resources have been developed collectively and these are of limited strategic value. The question of resources and how they are shared is a key point in the framework of collective strategies. It was one of the first elements put forward to justify collective strategies: resource-sharing has become a primary explanation for inter-organizational cooperation (Borys and Jemison, 1989; Hamel, 1991) by bringing together complementary assets owned by different organizations (Nohria and Garcia-Pont, 1991) in order, for example, to acquire the assets needed to turn an innovation into a commercial success (Hagedoorn, 1993; Teece, 1986).

We could apply this analysis concerning the acquisition of resources, which assumes that the company 'trades' existing resources against the attraction of access to resources, implying that it can call on resources at will without having to actually acquire them (Lechner and Leyronas, 2009). The collective strategy seems to be based primarily on the attractiveness of being able to access resources easily, but at the same time if the company does not want to risk being copied or even to be exposed too strongly to competition from the other companies in the cluster, it needs either to develop internal resources or to acquire or attract resources from outside.

In these conditions, the companies in a collective can exchange standard resources that are of some value to them but not key resources with a high strategic value. This question is all the more important if the company is seeking to establish an individual identity. Thus, in a collective marked by relations involving the coordination of activities, there is no creation of new resources and skills in the individual companies and little or no transfer (regardless of the strategy followed by the firms) at the collective level. So there is only allocation of resources between the actors, and no creation of new resources that could be of benefit to the entire collective.

We can therefore consider that the coordination-based relations at the level of the dyads do not result in the generation of new resources, and that these would not be transferred to the collective. In fact, if we ask whether or not the collective strategy is driven by the actors on the basis of their dyadic experiences, the absence of cooperation-based inter-company relations makes it difficult to either develop or strengthen the collective on this basis.

Although the question of resources is fundamental to a consideration of the creation of value (Makadok, 2003), many studies following the RBV approach also highlight the question of the motivation of actors. Thus Bridoux et al. (2011), using an approach centred on the collective creation of value in organizations, show that in recent work based on the RBV a number of authors have addressed the question of the diversity of motivations, to shed light on the behaviour of directors. They suggest studying the interaction between individuals within and not between organizations. They note (p. 712) that 'Recent RBV studies explicitly advocate introducing behavioural microfoundations at the individual level to explain firms' collective value creation (Felin and Foss, 2005; Felin and Hesterly, 2007; Foss, 2007)'. Through these approaches, the RBV allows us to grasp not only the question of resources and their impact on the creation of collective value, but in its fine-grained ('micro') approach it addresses the issues of the motivations of actors and could improve our understanding of the brakes on the development of the collective, beyond the lack and weakness of cooperation-based links.

4.2 The Importance of the Organizational Structure of the Collective

An analysis of the content of dyadic relations, especially the distinction between cooperation and coordination, requires a 'micro' approach, as a way of getting to grips with the operating principles of the overall collective ('macro' level). It might also be considered that the reverse is true. That means that the way the collective is organized may have consequences for 'micro' relationships and particularly for the transferability between the 'micro' and the 'macro'.

The collective project calls on a form of socioeconomic organization. These organizations can take different forms, in terms of legal status and governance. In the case under study we can characterize the form of organization as a 'heterarchy',[3] which can be defined as 'an organizational form of distributed intelligence in which units are laterally accountable according to diverse principles of evaluation' (Stark, 2009, p. 19). Indeed, in the case of Revel, power is distributed equitably even if some companies are more involved than others, without this giving rise to hierarchical links between those that are more involved and the rest. Heterarchy describes the situations of different actors who take a collegial approach to the coordination of a given collective action, and is thus the opposite of the term hierarchy. The most active members act more as initiators than as leaders of the collective. To quote Hofstadter (1979, p. 134), 'A program which has a structure in which there is no single "highest level" or "monitor" is called a heterarchy.'

To follow the analysis by Steward (1999) on the question of coordination, this is the distinction made by March and Simon (1958), which emphasized two major approaches to coordination: 'coordination by feedback' and 'coordination by plan', the first being coordination based on interaction whereas the second follows pre-established plans or routines. A heterarchical system is most likely to use the former mode of coordination, which makes it difficult to perpetuate and organize coordination between the actors.

The absence of elements of hierarchy and control is explained by the very nature of a system characterized by 'loose coupling' (Orton and Weick, 1990) in order, among other reasons, to allow partners to have expectations which are not necessarily identical, even if it is obviously in their interest to cooperate. These loose couplings can be regarded as integral to these collective strategies: several authors explain the success of cooperative projects by the fact that the partners have different goals (Auster, 1987). To a certain extent, heterarchy results in the passage from structural power to 'resource power' (Stark, 2009, p. 19), which can involve collective resources, individual resources and resources developed in the context of dyadic relations. When the organizational form is seen to depend on 'resource power', this demonstrates the relevance of analysing the content of relations beyond the mere identification of the structure of relations.

5. CONCLUSION

The RBV sheds further light on the structural analysis and helps us understand the dynamics of collective strategies. This dimension requires a methodology for coupling the structural analysis with a qualitative analysis of the content of relations.

Analysing the dynamics of collective action by introducing the content of resources through the distinction between coordination and cooperation lends support to the other reasons why, despite the number of favourable factors, a collective strategy is not or is only slightly developed. It helps understand the reasons for its strengthening, weakening or stagnation.

Our approach enriches the analysis of collective strategies on the basis of a modified dyadic analysis by an analysis of the content through the distinction between cooperation and coordination. The organizational model of the collective project acts as a 'moderator' on the coordination/cooperation relationship. However, if the framework of the case had been different, with actions that were more 'push' than 'pull', the impact of coordination in the relations would have been different. In a model with a more hierarchical structure, there would doubtless have been greater transferability between the dyadic level and the collective level.

NOTES

1. It has traditionally (Ibarra, 1993; Burt, 1992; Tsai, 2001; Zaheer and Bell, 2005) been based on the notion of centrality (Coleman, 1988; Burt, 1992) or on the study of direct and indirect linkages (Ahuja, 2000) through the notion of 'structural holes' (Burt, 1982).
2. In measuring the intensity of the relationship, 1 represents a low-intensity relationship and 6 a very close relationship.
3. The term 'heterarchy' was first employed in informatics in an article by W. McCulloch (1945), who opposed the idea of hierarchy to that of neural networks. He used it to describe the circular organization in the neural networks composed of three neural connections A, B and C. A influences B and B influences C. If A has an impact on C, then A is at the top of the hierarchical organization; if C has an influence on A, then the whole forms a heterarchical system.

REFERENCES

Adler, P.S. and Kwon, S.W. (2002), 'Social capital: prospects for a new concept', *The Academy of Management Review*, **27**(1), 17–40.

Ahuja, G. (2000), 'The duality of collaboration: inducements and opportunities in the formation of interfirm linkages', *Strategic Management Journal*, **21**(March), Special Issue, 317–43.

Aiken, A., Dewar, R., DiTomaso, N., Hage, J. and Zeitz, G. (1975), *Coordinating Human Services*, San Francisco, CA: Jossey-Bass.

Alderson, W. (1965), *Dynamic Marketing Behaviour*, Homewood, IL: Richard D. Irwin.

Alter, C. (1990), 'An exploratory study of conflict and coordination in interorganizational service delivery systems', *Academy of Management Journal*, **33**(3), 478–502.

Alter, C. and Hage, J. (1993), *Organizations Working Together*, Newbury Park, CA: Sage Publications.

Anderson, J.C., Håkansson, H. and Johanson, J. (1994), 'Dyadic business relationships within a business network context', *The Journal of Marketing*, 1–15.

Ansoff, I. (1968), *Business Strategy*, New York: Penguin.

Argote, L. (1982), 'Input uncertainty and organizational coordination in hospital emergency units', *Administrative Science Quarterly*, **27**(3), 420–34.

Astley, W.G. (1984), 'Toward an appreciation of collective strategy', *Academy of Management Review*, **9**(3), 526–35.

Astley, W.G. and Fombrun, C.J. (1983), 'Collective strategy: social ecology of organizational environments', *The Academy of Management Review*, **8**(4), 576–87.

Auster, E.R. (1987), 'International corporate linkages: dynamic forms in changing environments', *Columbia Journal of World Business*, **22**(2), 3–6.

Avenel, E., Favier, A.V., Ma, S., Mangematin, V. and Rieu, C. (2007), 'Diversification and hybridization in firm knowledge bases in nanotechnology', *Research Policy*, **36**(6), 864–70.

Barney, J.B. (1991), 'Firm resources and sustained competitive advantage', *Journal of Management*, **17**(1), 99–120.

Borgatti, S.P., Everett, M.G. and Freeman, L.C. (2002), *Ucinet for Windows: Software for Social Network Analysis*, Harvard, MA: Analytic Technologies.

Borys, B. and Jemison, D.B. (1989), 'Hybrid arrangements as strategic alliances: theoretical issues in organizational combinations', *Academy of Management Review*, **14**(2), 234–49.

Bourgeois, L.J. (1980), 'Performance and consensus', *Strategic Management Journal*, **1**(3), 227–48.

Bresser, R.K. and Harl J.E. (1986), 'Collective strategy: vice or virtue?', *Academy of Management Review*, **11**(2), 408–27.

Bridoux, F., Coeurderoy, R. and Durand, R. (2011), 'Heterogeneous motives and the collective creation of value', *Academy of Management Review*, **36**(4), 711–30.

Burt, R.S. (1982), *Toward a Structural Theory of Action: Network Models of Social Structure, Perception and Action*, New York: Academic Press.

Burt, R.S. (1992), *Structural Holes: The Social Structure of Competition*, Cambridge, MA: Harvard University Press.

Chandler, A.D. (1962), *Strategy and Structure*, Cambridge, MA: MIT Press.

Coleman, J.S. (1988), 'Social capital in the creation of human capital', *American Journal of Sociology*, No. 94, 95–121.

Dabholkar, P.A., Johnston, W.J. and Cathey, A.S. (1994), 'The dynamics of long-term business-to-business exchange relationships', *Journal of the Academy of Marketing Science*, **22**(2), 130–45.

Das, T.K. and Teng, B. (2002), 'Alliance constellations: a social exchange perspective', *Academy of Management Review*, **27**, 445–56.

Day, G.S. and Klein, S. (1987), 'Cooperative behaviour in vertical markets: the influence of transaction costs and competitive strategies', *Review of Marketing*, 39–66.

Doz, Y.L. (1996), 'The evolution of cooperation in strategic alliances: Initial conditions or learning processes?', *Strategic Management Journal*, **17**, 55–83.

Dyer, J.H. and Singh, H. (1998), 'The relational view: cooperative strategy and sources of interorganizational competitive advantage', *Academy of Management Review*, **23**(4), 660–79.

Eisenhardt, K.M. (1989), 'Building theories from case study research', *Academy of Management Review*, **14**(4), 532–50.

Emery F.E. and Trist, E. (1965), 'Causal texture of organizational environments', *Human Relation*, **18**, 21–32.

Felin, T. and Foss, N.J. (2005), 'Strategic organization: a field in search of micro-foundations', *Strategic Organization*, **3**, 441–55.

Felin, T. and Hesterly, W.S. (2007), 'The knowledge-based view, heterogeneity, and the individual: philosophical considerations on the locus of knowledge', *Academy of Management Review*, **32**, 195–218.

Foss, N.J. (2007), 'The emerging knowledge governance approach: challenges and characteristics', *Organization*, **14**, 29–52.

Freeman, L.C. (1979), 'Centrality in social networks: conceptual clarification', *Social Networks*, **1**, 215–39.

Galbraith, J.R. (1977), *Organization Design*, Reading, MA: Addison-Wesley.

Grenier, C. (2002), 'Comment gérer l'articulation paradoxale individuel/collectif pour favoriser les pratiques cooperatives?', *Economies et Sociétés, Série Economie de l'entreprise*, K, **36**(5), 793–819.

Gulati, R. (1995), 'Social structure and alliance formation patterns: a longitudinal analysis', *Administrative Science Quarterly*, 619–52.
Gulati, R., Nohria, N. and Zaheer, A. (2000), 'Guest editors' introduction to the special issue: "Strategic Networks"', *Strategic Management Journal*, **21**(3), 199–201.
Gulati, R., Wohlgezogen, F. and Zhelyazkov, P.L. (2012), 'The two facets of collaboration: cooperation and coordination in strategic alliances', *The Academy of Management Annals*, **6**(1), 531–83.
Hagedoorn, J. (1993), 'Understanding the rationale of strategic technology partnering: inter-organizational modes of cooperation and sectoral differences', *Strategic Management Journal*, **14**, 371–85.
Hallen, B.L. (2008), 'The causes and consequences of the initial network positions of new organizations: from whom do entrepreneurs receive investments?', *Administrative Science Quarterly*, **53**(4), 685–718.
Hamel, G. (1991), 'Competition for competence and interpartner learning within international strategic alliances', *Strategic Management Journal*, **12**(S1), 83–103.
Hawley, A.H. (1950), *Human Ecology: A Theory of Community Structure*, New York: The Ronald Press Company.
Heinman, S. (1980), *Aspects économiques de la révolution scientifique et technique*, Moscow: Edition du Progrès.
Hofstadter, D. (1979), *Gödel, Escher, Bach. An Eternal Golden Braid*, New York, Basic Books.
Huber, G.P. and Power, D.J. (1985), 'Retrospective reports of strategic-level managers: guidelines for increasing their accuracy', *Strategic Management Journal*, **6**, 171–80.
Ibarra, H. (1993), 'Network centrality, power, and innovation involvement: determinants of technical and administrative roles', *Academy of Management Journal*, **36**(3), 471–501.
Koka, B.R. and Prescott, J.E. (2002), 'Strategic alliances as social capital: a multidimensional view', *Strategic Management Journal*, **23**(9), 795–816.
Kumar, N., Stern, L.W. and Anderson, J.C. (1993), 'Conducting interorganizational research using key informants', *Academy of Management Journal*, **36**(6), 1633–51.
Lazega E. (2007), *Réseaux sociaux et structures relationnelles*, Que-sais-je? collection, Paris: Presses Universitaires de France.
Le Roy, F. and Guillotreau, P. (2002), 'Contester la domination des leaders de marché en changeant les règles du jeu: le cas de l'industrie thonière française', *Management International*, **6**(2), 29–41.
Lechner, C. and Leyronas, C. (2009), 'Small-business group formation as an entrepreneurial development model', *Entrepreneurship Theory and Practice*, **33**(3), 645–67.
Lechner, C. and Leyronas, C. (2012), 'The competitive advantage of cluster firms: the priority of regional network position over extra-regional networks – a study of a French high-tech cluster', *Entrepreneurship and Regional Development*, **24**(5–6), 457–73.
Madhavan, R., Koka, B.R. and Prescott, J.E. (1998), 'Networks in transition: how industry events (re)shape interfirm relationships', *Strategic Management Journal*, **19**(5), 439–59.
Makadok, R. (2003), 'Doing the right thing and knowing the right thing to do: why the whole is greater than the sum of the parts', *Strategic Management Journal*, **24**, 1043–55.

March, J.G. and Simon, H.A. (1958), *Organizations*, New York: Wiley.
McCulloch, W. (1945), 'A heterarchy of values determined by the topology of nervous nets', *Bulletin of Mathematical Biophysics*, **7**(2), 89–93.
McNeilly, K.M. and Russ, F.A. (1992), 'Coordination in the marketing channel', *Advances in Distribution Channel Research*, **1**(1), 161–186.
Meagher, K. and Rogers, M. (2004), 'Network density and R&D spillovers', *Journal of Economic Behavior & Organization*, **53**(2), 237–60.
Morgan, R. and Hunt, S. (1994), 'The commitment-trust theory of relationship marketing', *Journal of Marketing*, **58**(July), 20–38.
Mulford, C.L. and Rogers, D.L. (1982), 'Definitions and models', in D.L. Rogers and D.A. Whetten (eds), *Interorganizational Coordination: Theory, Research and Implementation*, Ames, IA: Iowa State University Press, pp. 9–31.
Nieminem, J. (1974), 'On centrality in a graph', *Scandinavian Journal of Psychology*, **15**(1), 322–36.
Nohria, N. and Garcia-Pont, C. (1991), 'Global strategic linkages and industry structure', *Strategic Management Journal*, **12**(S1), 105–24.
Okhuysen, G.A. and Bechky, B.A. (2009), 'Coordination in organizations: an integrative perspective', *Academy of Management Annals*, **3**, 463–502.
Olivier, C. (1988), 'The collective strategy framework: an application to competing predictions of isomorphism', *Administrative Science Quarterly*, **33**, 543–61.
Orton, J.D. and Weick, K.E. (1990), 'Loosely coupled systems: a reconceptualization', *Academy of Management Review*, **15**(2), 203–23.
Osarenkhoe, A. (2010), 'A study of inter-firm dynamics between competition and cooperation – a coopetition strategy', *Journal of Database Marketing & Customer Strategy Management Journal*, **17**, 201–21.
Ozcan, C.P. and Eisenhardt, K.M. (2009), 'Origins of alliance portfolios: entrepreneurs, network strategies, and firm performance', *Academy of Management Journal*, **52**(2), 246–79.
Payan, J.M. and Svensson, G. (2007), 'Co-operation, coordination, and specific assets in inter-organisational relationships', *Journal of Marketing Management*, **23**(7–8), 797–813.
Payan, J.M. (2007), 'A review and delineation of cooperation and coordination in marketing channels', *European Business Review*, **19**(3), 216–33.
Powell, W.W., Koput, K.W. and Smith-Doerr, L. (1996), 'Interorganizational collaboration and the locus of innovation: networks of learning in biotechnology', *Administrative Science Quarterly*, **41**, 116–45.
Puranam, P., Raveendran, M. and Knudsen, T. (2012), 'Organization design: the epistemic interdependence perspective', *Academy of Management Review*, **37**(3), 419–40.
Ring, P.S. and Van de Ven, A.H. (1994), 'Developmental processes of cooperative interorganizational relationships', *Academy of Management Review*, **19**(1), 90–118.
Robinson, D.T. and Stuart, T.E. (2007), 'Network effects in the governance of strategic alliances', *Journal of Law, Economics, and Organization*, **23**(1), 242–73.
Saglietto, L. (2006), 'Quelques points de repères sur l'étude des réseaux par la théorie des graphes', *Network and Communication Studies Netcom*, **20**(1–2), 195–216.
Santos, F.M. and Eisenhardt, K.M. (2009), 'Constructing markets and shaping boundaries: entrepreneurial agency in nascent fields', *Academy of Management Journal*, **52**(4), 643–71.

Sivadas, E. and Dwyer, F.R. (2000), 'An examination of organizational factors influencing new product success in internal and alliance-based processes', *Journal of Marketing*, **64**(1), 31–49.

Stam, W. and Elfring, T. (2008), 'Entrepreneurial orientation and new venture performance: the moderating role of intra- and extra-industry social capital', *Academy of Management Journal*, **51**(1), 97–111.

Stark, D. (2009), *The Sense of Dissonance. Accounts of Worth in Economic Life*, Princeton, NJ: Princeton University Press.

Steward, M.D. (1999), 'A typology of coordination strategies employed by business-to-business salespeople', *Marketing Management Journal*, **19**(1), 7–45.

Stuart, T.E. (2000), 'Interorganizational alliances and the performance of firms: a study of growth and innovation', *Strategic Management Journal*, **21**(8), 791–811.

Tang, F. and Xi, Y. (2006), 'Exploring dynamic multi-level linkages in inter-organizational networks', *Asia Pacific Journal of Management*, **23**(2), 187–208.

Teece, D.J. (1986), 'Profiting from technological innovation: implications for integration, collaboration, licensing and public policy', *Research Policy*, **15**(6), 285–305.

Tsai, W. (2001), 'Knowledge transfer in intraorganizational networks: effects of network position and absorptive capacity on business unit innovation and performance', *The Academy of Management Journal*, **44**(5), 996–1004.

Uzzi, B. (1997), 'Social structure and competition in interfirm networks: the paradox of embeddedness', *Administrative Science Quarterly*, 35–67.

Van de Ven, A.H. and Walker, G. (1984), 'The dynamics of interorganizational coordination', *Administrative Science Quarterly*, **29**(December), 598–621.

Varadarajan, P.R. and Jayachandran, S. (1999), 'Marketing strategy: an assessment of the state of the field and outlook', *Journal of the Academy of Marketing Science*, **27**(2), 120–43.

Wasserman, S. and Faust, K. (1994), *Social Networks Analysis*, Cambridge: Cambridge University Press.

Yami, S. (2006), 'Fondements et perspectives des stratégies collectives', *Revue Française de Gestion*, **8**(167), 91–104.

Yin, R.K. (1989), *Case Study Research: Design and Methods*, Newbury Park, CA: Sage.

Zaheer, A. and Bell, G.G. (2005), 'Benefiting from network position: firm capabilities, structural holes, and performance', *Strategic Management Journal*, **26**(9), 809–25.

Zaheer, A., McEvily, B. and Perrone, V. (1998), 'Does trust matter? Exploring the effects of interorganizational and interpersonal trust on performance', *Organization Science*, **9**(2), 141–59.

PART III

Context: A Benign Neglect?

8. The competitiveness of entrepreneurial firms from a network perspective

Christian Lechner

1. THE COMPETITIVENESS OF FIRMS

Why do some firms perform better than others? Common to strategy research is the question of firm performance (Meyer, 1991). Strategy for management is commonly understood (see Porter, 1980) as the art of gaining and sustaining a competitive advantage leading to above average returns. Strategic entrepreneurship has been defined as the creation of competitive advantage through the identification of new opportunities (Ireland et al., 2003). This overriding definition does not distinguish between firm types but adds to the classical definition of strategic management the concept of a particular way of advantage seeking, namely through new opportunities. While this definition has been rightfully criticized as an almost hostile takeover of the entrepreneurship domain (see, e.g., Verstraete, 2003), it builds somehow a bridge between strategic management and entrepreneurship through the idea of advantage seeking.

In its vaguest form, entrepreneurship is about the emergence of new companies (Gartner, 1995). Why is the distinction between entrepreneurial and established firms important? Because the context of entrepreneurial firms is different. The entrepreneurial venture (and therefore its management) is a distinct form and is characterized by liability of newness, resource poverty and the liability of adolescence; it is linked to a life-cycle perspective. The development of an entrepreneurial firm has it its own life-cycle perspective: first, there is the entrepreneurial process that leads to the start of the firm; second, there is the development towards the mature, established large firm. Entrepreneurship refers therefore to the entrepreneurial process and to the development that eventually leads to an established company. Theoretically, it contributes the missing piece to management theory. Potentially and ideally an entrepreneurial firm will one day become an established firm through the growth of the firm. The notion of growth is central to entrepreneurship. To some extent, entrepreneurial strategy is the art of growing without resources (or with very few resources). Growth, however, is not possible without strategy. Thus it appears that entrepreneurial firms need to assure firm survival (as a minimum goal) and then realize substantial growth through an opportunity orientation that is linked to advantage-seeking behavior. In any case, two questions emerge: why do some firms perform better than others? And why do some firms survive while others do not?

A basic condition for a firm's performance is competitiveness. Competitiveness can be understood as the productivity with which human and other resources are used by a firm, region or nation (Porter, 2005). Three components determine the competitiveness of a firm as drivers of productivity: effectiveness, efficiency and innovativeness. Effectiveness means that a firm is able to deliver a desired output (Jarillo, 1993). Efficiency means that a company is able to perform the same activities better than its competitors (Porter, 1996). Innovation can drive both effectiveness and efficiency. To be competitive, a firm needs to achieve both effectiveness and efficiency, but effectiveness and efficiency are not sufficient to achieve a competitive advantage (Porter, 1996). A firm gains a competitive advantage by being unique in fulfilling the three determinants (effectiveness, efficiency, innovativeness) leading to differential firm performance.

The competitiveness of a firm depends obviously on its resource base (Penrose, 1959; Wernerfelt, 1984; Barney, 1991; Conner, 1991; Mahoney and Pandian, 1992; Amit and Schoemaker, 1993; Peteraf, 1993; Barney, 1996). It defines the performance potential on the business unit level in isolation from all other factors that might influence firm performance (Peteraf and Barney, 2003).

Firms are, however, not islands. They are embedded in larger socioeconomic systems through relationships with other firms, through their location in a specific geographical area (Richardson, 1972), and through their 'membership' in industries (Porter, 1980; Rumelt, 1984). The competitiveness of firms cannot be fully understood if the firm's embeddedness in larger socioeconomic systems is ignored (Lorenzoni, 1992). Apart from firm-level effects, there exists thus a variety of factors that can drive firm-level performance (Meyer, 1991).

The question 'Why do some firms perform better than others?' or 'Why do some firms survive and others not?' is thus complex. For matters of simplicity, we can distinguish between three levels of effects on firm performance (see Lechner, 2000):

1. firm-level effects;
2. firm-constellation effects;
3. regional- or national-level effects.

Firm-level effects are industry effects, business strategy effects and corporate effects (Rumelt, 1984; McGahan and Porter, 1997; Bowman and Helfat, 2001). Firm-constellation effects can be summarized under the relational view (Dyer and Singh, 1998), and they include positive effects that firms can achieve through relationships with other firms: through joint ventures, alliances, co-opetition, networks and so on (Meyer, 1991). Finally, there are effects that stem from a firm's embeddedness in even larger socioeconomic systems such as a firm's ecosystem, region or nation through, for example, beneficial national innovation systems (Porter, 1990; Dodgson et al., 2005).

The study of relational effects for a firm's competitiveness can be distinguished from firm-level effects insofar as it concerns the performance effects that arise through the relationships with other constituencies leading to relational resources rather than firm resources (e.g. while firms can access information through relations with another firms and while this information can be integrated into the firm, the resource ceases to exist with the end of the relationship); that is, they constitute a resource base outside the firm's boundaries that is dependent on the existence of the relationship. In the same sense, the relational view, if applied to a spatial dimension, can be distinguished from economic geography and agglomeration economics (e.g. Krugman, 1991). The relational view of regions investigates the effects stemming from relationships that are spatially defined; this view helps to clarify the understanding of regional dynamics. Analysis, however, becomes more difficult and more sophisticated. Regional networks shift the attention from agglomeration to relations, therefore requiring the analysis of relations that are enacted by firms (Lechner, 2000). However, if firm-constellation effects are important for understanding firm performance and what firms are actually doing, then one can also understand the relational view from an organizational perspective (Lorenzoni, 1992). Networks of firms are to be understood as an organizational field (DiMaggio, 1986). This organizational field starts from a central unit and comprises all nodes of interaction with other firms. An organizational perspective of interfirm relations introduces the notion of organizational contingencies on the link between a firm's strategy and performance. In this sense a central question is how different competitiveness effects are related, for example, firm-competitiveness effects and firm-constellation effects, and how this interplay is effected by processes in time.

2. THE ROLE OF INTERFIRM RELATIONSHIPS IN OVERCOMING FIRM LIABILITIES

Survival, performance and development of the entrepreneurial firm are at the heart of entrepreneurship research (Gartner, 1985; Bygrave and Hofer, 1991; Virtanen, 1997; Shane and Venkataraman, 2000). Entrepreneurial firms are characterized by a lack of internal resources and other start-up handicaps, as expressed in the theoretical constructs of liability of newness (Stinchcombe, 1965) and liability of smallness (Baum, 1996). The strategic use of external resources through interfirm networks in many different industries (Powell, 1987; Lorenzoni and Ornati, 1988; Jarillo, 1989) that are often embedded in regional clusters (Boari and Lipparini, 2000; Lechner and Dowling, 2000) is regarded as one effective means for overcoming these liabilities. In this context, interfirm networks are considered an important model of organization development (Richardson, 1972; Powell, 1987, 1990) to enable an entrepreneurial firm to grow and survive (Jarillo, 1988; Lorenzoni and Ornati, 1988; Nohria, 1992; Johannisson, 1998; Venkataraman and Van de Ven, 1998; Freel, 2000).

There is a long history of research on networks in the management and organization theory literature. Networks can be defined as a specific set of linkages between a defined set of actors characterized by the linkages as a whole being used to interpret the social behavior of the actors involved (Mitchell, 1969; Alba, 1982; Lincoln, 1982). Different types of relations define different types of networks, even if the same units are connected (Knoke and Kuklinsky, 1983). Network research distinguishes three components in order to explain the role of networks in firm performance: network content, network structure and network governance. According to the theory of structural embeddedness, network structure and a firm's or a person's network position are considered to be both opportunities and constraints (Aldrich and Zimmer, 1986). Favorable positions are regarded as network resources (Granovetter, 1974, 1985; Burt, 1992; Easton, 1992); over-embeddedness, however, ('trapped in your own net') can lead to an inability to act (Uzzi, 1997; Gargiulo and Benassi, 2000). A rich literature suggests that networks are a particular form of governance in which the development of trust plays a major role in influencing resource exchange and costs, compared to market coordination or integration of activities (Richardson, 1972; Thorelli, 1986; Powell, 1987, 1990). In this sense, interfirm networks constitute a third way of organizing the business, which is neither by markets nor by hierarchies (DiMaggio, 1986; Powell, 1990; Lorenzoni, 1992; Jarillo, 1993).

In the last decade, the importance of networks has become popular as part of the 'small-world phenomenon' and the 'six-degrees-of-separation' based on Milgram's initial experiments (Milgram, 1967), the mathematical description of the phenomenon by Watts and Strogatz (1998), and an increasing body of experiments and studies (for an overview see, e.g., Barabasi, 2003; Newman et al., 2006; Christakis and Fowler, 2009). The small-world phenomenon describes how any person on this planet is connected to anyone else on this planet through intermediary connections with other people and comes to the conclusion that on average people are connected to each other through five links to other people.

I will try to explain this social phenomenon in a simple form: the world of human relations is 'organized' into 'grapes' and 'bridges'. Grapes are local and dense networks in which basically everyone is connected with everyone. Granovetter was able to show that strong ties are often characterized by a high level of similarity among the players. Friends like and do similar things, and therefore also have similar information (Granovetter, 1973, 1974). A strong tie offers a great depth of knowledge (close friends know almost everything about each other) but little diversity of knowledge (C tells me all about a movie he saw, which B had also seen and already told me about). Strong ties between one player and other players also tend to establish at least weak ties between these players (if A has friendship relations with B and C, it is likely that B and C know each other and sometimes meet each other), leading therefore to the establishment of redundant ties (Granovetter, 1974; Burt 1992). Granovetter argues with his famous phrase, the 'strength of weak ties', that only weak ties can offer access to diverse information because they link a player to a new set of (in itself) strong relations by a bridging tie (Granovetter, 1973). The relationship between grapes and bridges can be easily explained through a verbal and a graphic example. Grapes are the outcomes of strong ties and might also be membership-based. Bridges can be linked to the fact that people are 'members' of different grapes or somehow linked to different grapes. Imagine a businessman who wants to get divorced. He is a member of a small tennis club in which everyone has known everyone for years. One of the tennis partners of the businessman is a lawyer specializing in business law. Besides being a tennis partner, he is also assisting the businessman in business matters (as a result of the tennis relationship). The lawyer is naturally a member of another 'grape' (grape 2), the multi-service law firm he works in, in which the specialist in labor relations is married to a divorce lawyer (grape 3). Generally, people reach other people by a few steps within a grape, while bridges are the links to other grapes. As a consequence, a few steps within grapes and, in an extreme case only, one or a few bridges explain the 'small-world phenomenon'.

For entrepreneurs, the small-world phenomenon would mean that they have access to valuable network resources through a few intermediate connections. However, Aldrich and Kim (2007) question this simple logic in their article: 'Small worlds, infinite possibilities? How social networks affect entrepreneurial team formation and search'. Reviewing and criticizing the network literature, they first question the universality of the small-world phenomenon and, second, the simple application of this phenomenon for entrepreneurs. As Granovetter (1973) already noted, strong ties arise from similarities since similarity leads to likening, a well-known concept in sociology called 'homophily' (Aldrich and Kim, 2007). If people mainly form networks on the basis of homophily, then they build networks with people who are similar, that is, who share the same background (and often competencies). So, if, in an extreme case, start-up teams are formed on the basis of homophily, how can they reach out to the world?

So, while empirical research has shown an association between the development and transformation of relationships, size and growth of a firm's interfirm networks and firm growth (Jarillo, 1989; Zhao and Aram, 1995; Ardichvili and Cardozo, 2000; Delmar et al., 2003; Hoang and Antoncic, 2003; Sawyer et al., 2003), the question arises: how do entrepreneurs develop functional and valuable networks if they do not possess them already? What types of relationships help to develop relationships further? What types of relationships matter most for entrepreneurial firms, and when and where can they be found? How can firms enable relationships that increase their competitiveness?

3. THE SPATIAL DIMENSION OF NETWORK EMBEDDEDNESS

Firm networks have a spatial collocation. Industry clusters, understood as an agglomeration of firms within one particular industry in a specific geographical area, are a prominent feature of economic activity across industries and nations (Krugman, 1991; Porter, 2000) and an important element for understanding firms' and regions' competitiveness through positive externalities (Porter, 1998). In this sense, a region's competitiveness will also influence the competitiveness of the firms located in this region. The understanding of this phenomenon is important for policymakers with an interest in strengthening a region's and (on a larger scale) a nation's competitiveness. The so-called Lisbon strategy was outlined for the European Union: 'The Union has today set itself a new strategic goal for the next decade: to become the most competitive and dynamic knowledge-based economy in the world, capable of sustainable economic growth with more and better jobs and greater social cohesion' (European Parliament, 2000, p. 2). In order to reach these goals by 2010 (which were largely not attained), cluster development was seen as one of the key drivers favoring policies in favor of cluster initiatives (see Sölvell et al., 2003; Lafitte et al., 2007). In 2008, a European Cluster Policy Group (ECPG) was established by the European Commission in order to advise the Commission and member states on how better to support the development of more world-class clusters in the EU.

Strategic management research on clusters failed, however, to distinguish between general agglomeration effects (Shaver and Flyer, 2000), on the one hand, and advantages derived from social interaction (Harrison, 1992), on the other. So, how co-location of entrepreneurial firms makes a difference is a core question in both cluster and entrepreneurship research. The key idea is that entrepreneurial firms affected by liabilities of newness and smallness need to gain access to knowledge and resources and to develop reputation. Cluster research stemming from an agglomeration economics perspective assumes that there is a series of positive spillover effects caused by proximity (Alcacer and Chung, 2007; Audretsch and Lehmann, 2006; Freel, 2003; Macpherson and Holt, 2007). However, physical proximity alone is not sufficient; social, cognitive but also intra-organizational factors are also considered important mediators of spillover effects (Presutti et al., 2011; Funk, 2014). Research on social networks suggests that the interaction between firms (facilitated by proximity) is the key driver for the acquisition of knowledge, resources and reputation, and thus also for understanding the functioning of clusters (Boari and Lipparini, 2000; Corno et al., 2000). In this sense, successful clusters can be characterized by the regional networks that constitute the cluster (Lechner and Dowling, 2000; Lechner and Leyronas, 2007).

In general, research on the performance of firms co-located in proximity are mixed (Tallman, 2004; Presutti et al., 2011), but the focus on average differences between firms located within and outside clusters might be misleading since it tends to ignore the characteristics of the specific regional networks and the relationships firms within clusters can have with other organizations outside the cluster, and to assume that performance variance within clusters is low (Lechner and Leyronas, 2012). Thus it becomes relevant to understand how performance differences between firms located within the same cluster can be explained by differences in social networks, thus contributing to the question of how co-location of firms matters. That is, the focus shifts from variance between different locations to variance within locations.

Given their limited internal resource base (including reputation and knowledge), external relationships have been considered as crucial for the successful development of entrepreneurial firms (Neck et al., 2004; Presutti et al., 2011; Lechner and Dowling, 2003, Lechner et al., 2006;

Johannisson, 2000). However, it is not the sheer number of relationships constituting the organizational interfirm networks that is decisive, but the quality and the structure of these networks.

4. DIFFERENTIAL FIRM PERFORMANCE IN REGIONAL NETWORKS

Research on interfirm networks has largely focused on the number of direct collaborative ties of a firm and its performance (Hoang and Antoncic, 2003; Slotte-Kock and Coviello, 2010). In general, these studies have associated size of interfirm networks with firm performance, some assuming a straight-linear relationship (Johannisson, 2000) and others a curve-linear relationship (Deeds and Hill, 1996). Research on network embeddedness and research on regional networks, while being strongly intertwined, have hardly been integrated and applied to full populations – a necessary condition for these theoretical concepts. From these research streams emerges the following question: does a firm's privileged position within a regional network lead to superior performance?

However, cluster research has largely ignored the relationships between cluster members and between cluster members and outside firms, leading to the general assumption that all firms benefit in the same way from their cluster location, and that performance differences between firms within the cluster are less important (Tallman et al., 2004). This leads us to believe that there are no relevant differences between a region's competitiveness and the competitiveness of the regional firms, an assumption disconfirmed by empirical research (Powell et al., 2012): differential firm performance within clusters exists.

From a perspective of advantage-seeking network research it can be inferred that networks rich in structural holes should positively influence firm performance (Burt, 1992). A structural hole is an opportunity, an unserved space in a network that can be exploited as a result of brokering connections between disconnected segments. If actor A is connected with actor B and actor C but B and C are not connected with each other, then actor A possesses a structural hole: actor A possesses two non-redundant ties. A network rich in structural holes is considered an effective network. An effective network will give a firm autonomy of action and power. Structural holes are opportunities to coordinate action and to access valuable and exclusive resources. An absence of non-redundant ties, however, means that the autonomy of the firm is heavily restricted, since each decision taken by a firm is subject to the acceptance and influence of all the interconnected firms or because resources are shared among many other firms (Burt, 1992). Networks that have predominantly redundant ties therefore restrict a firm's autonomy and lead to a phenomenon that is called over-embeddedness: a firm is trapped in it own net (Gargiulo and Benassi, 2000). In essence, favourable positions are regarded as network resources (Burt, 1992; Easton, 1992; Granovetter, 1974, 1985; Zaheer and McEvily, 1999); over-embeddedness, however, can lead to inability to act (Gargiulo and Benassi, 2000; Uzzi, 1997). However, a different perspective focuses on the benefits of network closure favoring trust and in-depth knowledge flow (Coleman, 1988), with dedicated research on the the benefits of cohesive networks for innovation (Obstfeld, 2005; Reagans and McEvily, 2003). Regional clusters are characterized by knowledge spillovers between the firms. Spillover requires some degree of network closure, meaning that member firms know each other and interact with each other, which allows for strong information flows between them. All cluster companies can benefit from general knowledge spillovers. While the collective knowledge spillover hypothesis can explain why firms in clusters are in an advantageous position compared with non-cluster firms based on some degree of closure, it cannot explain the differential performance of firms within the same cluster. In order to gain competitive advantage within a cluster, firms need to access proprietary knowledge advantages, which can derive from selective partnerships. The role of brokerage in innovation networks should thus lead to firm-specific advantages (Graf, 2011; Graf and Kruger, 2011). Therefore networks rich in structural holes should help to establish firms within clusters to develop a competitive advantage.

While research broadly emphasized the role of structural holes in explaining differential performance (Burt, 2005; Lechner and Leyronas, 2007; Graf, 2011; Graf and Kruger, 2011), a different element complements the question of competitiveness of firms embedded in regional networks (Burt, 2010; Lechner and Leyronas, 2012; Powell et al., 2012). First, while research generally assumes that firms in clusters can all basically access a cluster's public benefits by being located in the cluster, the authors argue that the access to a cluster's public benefits is a question of connectivity, that is, how well connected a firm is within the regional network. While simple network centrality is usually used as a measure, only counting a firm's direct relationships does not capture the firm's potential to capture regional knowledge spillover, which depends on the contacts of a firm's contacts. It thus fails to measure access to a cluster's common knowledge base. If firms want to benefit from the diverse knowledge and resources that reside in the cluster, it is important for them to be so connected that they can access a maximum of resources with relative ease. As a consequence, the authors propose a new measure for a firm's connectedness that better reflects access to a regional network's public benefits. The research shows finally that access to public benefits within clusters is already more distributed than globally assumed, and that differential firm performance in clusters is partially driven by connectiveness (and thus differential access to common benefits). The research also confirms the importance of structural holes for firm performance.

On the other hand, research confirms that brokerage roles in networks drive firm performance (Graf, 2011; Graf and Kruger, 2011). Exclusiveness of networks within regional networks is key for differential performance (Lechner and Leyronas, 2012). It seems that, within regional clusters where knowledge spillover appear to be frequent, firms can gain proprietary advantages through various networks rich in structural holes. In this sense, there are potential common benefits deriving from regional networks of interfirm relationships: for example, firms with a high degree of connectedness can access important information regarding ongoing innovation projects and so on (Morrison, 2008). A high degree of connectedness assures access to a maximum of information. The value of connectedness from a network structure point of view depends on the structure of the regional network (Burt, 2007). If many firms have relationships with each other (i.e. high network density), then it is less important for an actor to have many relationships since a few relationships are sufficient to access relevant information within the regional network. Thus the denser the regional network, the more common benefits are available to most of the cluster firms. Common benefits can create an advantage for firms located inside clusters relative to firms located outside. In this sense, a region's competitiveness influences firms' competitiveness. Research on the emergence of clusters shows similarities between successfully developed clusters in contrast with those that did not take off despite favorable starting conditions (Whittington et al., 2009). While survival of firms within the dynamic clusters did not differ from those outside, the surviving firms benefited from knowledge spillovers. Unsuccessful clusters are generally characterized by sparse networks (Powell et al., 2012): start-up rate and increasing network density are thus key to a cluster's competitiveness. Potential common benefits, however, create performance differentials within the cluster only if there is some variance in the degree of firms' connectedness.

However, firms need to realize private benefits from interfirm relations. This is possible if they can engage in rather exclusive relationships; as a consequence, firms access resources hardly available to other firms. These relationships can create performance differentials within the cluster. Again, research found that, despite general cluster advantages (public benefits), only a few winners exist in given industries, but that these winners emerge from successful clusters (Powell et al., 2012). This implies that successful firms acquire private benefits. The structural representation of the existence of private benefits lies in structural holes (Burt, 2007). Therefore the competitiveness of firms located in clusters can be understood as a function of common and private benefits accruing to firms through interfirm relationships. In our research, we focused on private benefits expressed by the concept of structural holes. We could also interpret our findings in the following sense: under-investment in structural holes means that disadvantages in private benefits offset advantages of common benefits.

The pattern of private and common benefits appears consistent for different networks, but also for networks that served as antecedents of other networks if we consider brokerage as the main driver of private benefits. In this sense, the existence of structural holes in different types of networks gives rise to opportunities for accessing other value-creating networks. This could mean that there is a consistent pattern of network opportunities or network disadvantages. A firm receiving only common information about partnering options has a higher probability of entering partnering networks giving mainly common benefits, leading finally to mediocre performance. Firms with private information benefits should be able to use them for higher-order private partnerships benefits, leading to higher performance. Even clusters in general can benefit from structural holes in networks as the boundary spanners of structural holes connect to a higher variety of resources and the corresponding knowledge will at least partially spill over to other firms (Powell et al., 2012).

Performance within clusters is highly distributed: clusters are made up of high- and low-performing firms. These performance differences appear to be a precondition for cluster development. It is the role model of high-performing firms that attracts new firms. High-performing firms are those that maximize benefits from interfirm relationships, while lower-performing firms tend to suffer from 'liability of unconnectedness' (Podolny and Page, 1998, p. 63; Malmberg and Maskell, 1999). The potential for regional network advantages also depends on the opportunity for firms to be able to span structural holes and, thus, to realize private benefits from interfirm relationships. The potential to do so is a function of the regional networks' density. We could advance the following proposition: in regional networks with low density, regional competitiveness influencing firm competitiveness is restricted to general agglomeration advantages; in regional networks with high density, regional competitiveness influencing firm competitiveness is influenced by general agglomeration advantages and a maximum of common benefits accruing to an increasing number of well-connected regional firms; that is, regional competitiveness is comparable to firms' competitiveness. In networks characterized by intermediate density, firm performance is a function of regional competitiveness and private network benefits.

General and increasing networking activities in clusters combined with a reduced entrepreneurship activity would make regional networks denser and thus reduce opportunities for private benefits, which in turn would reduce cluster dynamics. This pattern means in conclusion that regional network structure leads to an interplay of individual firm performance and cluster development. We argued that the competitiveness of firms located in clusters can be understood as a function of common and private benefits. Private benefits are expressed by the concept of structural holes, while we took the level of overall network density as given. According to our arguments, cluster development is based on variance in firm performance within clusters and depends on network dynamics. Network dynamics are driven by the rate of entrepreneurial activity, network density and the existence of structural holes. More complex drivers of cluster development appear to exist, such as the degree of variety of actors forming a cluster, the role of some central actors linking different sub-communities (core–periphery structure), and specific regional networks' composition, which creates both cluster dynamism and resilience (Powell et al., 2012).

One way to further the interplay between these factors could be through network simulations of various degrees of new entry and network density. Another way could be by comparing existing research where density measures are available or computable. Preliminary results of network simulation (Lechner and Znidarsic, 2014) appear to support this reasoning. From this simulation it emerges that a high level of entrepreneurial activity, a sufficient number of unconnected actors and a sufficient number of connected actors are key ingredients for dynamic clusters. It is hypothesized that an optimal strategy for cluster dynamics derives from a relatively high level of network density; that is, unconnected clusters do not even provide the minimum public benefits for clusters. Lack of structural holes, however, reduces entrepreneurial activities and would prevent start-ups from successful development, with negative influences on cluster development. Interestingly, start-up companies did relatively well in clusters with medium-high density compared to low-density clusters, assuming a threshold level of entrepreneurial activity. In essence it appears that network structures, entrepreneurial activities and entrepreneurial opportunities, and thus also differential firm performance, are vital conditions for dynamic clusters.

5. OUTLOOK AND CONCLUSION: PUBLIC AND PRIVATE BENEFITS AND NETWORK DYNAMICS

Firm competitiveness cannot sufficiently be explained by extracting a firm from its context as if it were an island. Firm networks both on the individual (ego-networks) and global (regional or full networks) level contribute to a better understanding of firm competitiveness. Recent research from different disciplines on networks appears to converge on a few points:

1. Network advantage is local and individual (on the personal and organizational level): advantage can be built actively through direct networks rich in structural holes (Burt, 2010). Direct connectivity matters. Research in different industries and settings largely confirms this view (Burt, 2010; Lechner and Leyronas, 2007; Graf, 2011; Graf and Kruger, 2011).
2. Network advantage is local first. Cluster dynamics depend on the development of functional local or regional networks before outside connections become valuable (Lechner and Leyronas, 2012; Powell et al., 2012). Points 1 and 2 taken together mean that some degree of closure is necessary in local networks to assure overall connectivity. Closure leads to local sticky knowledge that spills over locally (Burt, 2010).
3. Differential advantage in regions becomes a function of public and private benefits. If we extend the logic of the first two points to a dynamics perspective, we can conclude the following. The direct and indirect relationships of organizations define overall regional connectivity. Indirect relationships are those that the direct relationships of an ego hold with other organizations. In relatively dense networks, this social capital creates the regionally sticky knowledge that spills over regionally. This type of knowledge can constitute a cluster advantage, that is, the public benefits accruing to cluster firms, but does not lead to differential advantages for organizations within a specific cluster.

Closure and the addition of new members through entrepreneurship lead to a core and periphery structure where varying degrees of connectivity lead to the emergence of structural holes. Structural holes create opportunities for differential advantage, that is, private benefits for some organizations within clusters. In this sense, the accumulated body of research on networks and clusters suggests that dynamic and vital clusters appear to be partially a function of network closure, new entry and subsequent emergence of structural holes in a continuous loop.

In conclusion, the competitiveness of firms is a central question for managers but also for policymakers. The aggregation of the competitiveness of firms leads to the competitiveness of regions and nations, and is thus key to the economy. The inverse perspective can also be applied: the general competitiveness of nations and regions also has impacts on an individual firm's competitiveness. While research in strategy has been characterized for a long time by a firm-as-an-island perspective, the relational view has made important contributions towards understanding a firm's competitiveness (as well as a region's or nation's competitiveness).

Thus competitiveness research benefits from:

1. adopting a relational view and thus extending the sources of competitiveness for a firm;
2. studying influences of aggregated constructs (regions, nations) on a firm's competitiveness;
3. analyzing the effects of firm competitiveness for aggregated constructs; and
4. adopting a contingency view for network effects that includes space and time.

In particular, integrating dynamic network processes should help to understand the dynamics of firm competitiveness.

REFERENCES

Alba, R.D. (1982), 'Taking stock of network analysis: a decade of results', in S.B. Bachran (ed.), *Research in the Sociology of Organizations*, vol. 1, Greenwich, CT: JAI, pp. 39–74.

Alcacer, J. and Chung, W. (2007), 'Location strategies and knowledge spillovers', *Management Science*, **53**(5), 760–76.

Aldrich, H. and Kim, P. (2007), 'Small worlds, infinite possibilities? How social networks affect entrepreneurial team formation and search', *Strategic Entrepreneurship Journal*, **1**, 147–65.

Aldrich, H. and Zimmer, C. (1986), 'Entrepreneurship through social networks', in D. Sexton and R. Smilor (eds), *The Art and Science of Entrepreneurship*, New York: Ballinger, pp. 3–23.

Amit, R. and Schoemaker, P. (1993), 'Strategic assets and organizational rent', *Strategic Management Journal*, **14**, 33–46.

Ardichvili, A. and Cardozo, R. (2000), 'A model of the opportunity recognition process', *Journal of Enterprising Culture*, **8**(2), 103–19.

Audretsch, D. and Lehmann, E. (2006), 'Entrepreneurial access and absorption of knowledge spillovers: strategic board and managerial composition', *Journal of Small Business Management*, **44**, 155–66.

Barabasi, A.-L. (2003), *Linked*, Harmondsworth, UK: Penguin Books.

Barney, J. (1991), 'Firm resources and sustained competitive advantage', *Journal of Management*, **17**, 99–120.

Barney, J. (1996), *Gaining and Sustaining Competitive Advantage*, Reading, MA: Addison-Wesley.

Baum, J. (1996), 'Organizational ecology', in S. Clegg, C. Hardy and S. Nord (eds), *Handbook of Organization Studies*, London: Sage, pp. 77–114.

Boari, C. and Lipparini, A. (2000), 'Networks within industrial districts: organising knowledge creation and transfer by means of moderate hierarchies', *Journal of Management and Governance*, **99**(3), 339–60.

Bowman, E. and Helfat, C. (2001), 'Does corporate strategy matter?', *Strategic Management Journal*, **22**, 1–23.

Bygrave, W. and Hofer, C. (1991), 'Theorizing about entrepreneurship', *Entrepreneurship Theory and Practice*, **16**(2), 13–22.

Burt, R. (1992), *Structural Holes*, Cambridge, MA: Harvard University Press.

Burt, R. (2005), *Brokerage & Closure*, Oxford: Oxford University Press.

Burt, R. (2007), 'Secondhand brokerage: evidence on the importance of local structure for managers, bankers, and analysts', *Academy of Management Journal*, **50**(1), 119–48.

Burt, R. (2010), *Neighbor Networks*, Oxford: Oxford University Press.

Christakis, N. and Fowler, J. (2009), *Connected*, New York: Little, Brown and Company.

Conner, K. (1991), 'A historical comparison of resource-based theory and five schools of theory within industrial organization economics: do we have a new theory of the firm?', *Journal of Management*, **17**, 121–54.

Corno, F., Reinmoeller, P. and Nonaka, I. (2000), 'Knowledge creation within industrial systems', *Journal of Management and Governance*, **3**(4), 379–94.

Deeds, D. and Hill, C. (1996), 'Strategic alliances and the rate of new product development: an empirical study of entrepreneurial biotechnology firms', *Journal of Business Venturing*, **11**(1), 41–55.

Delmar, F., Davidsson, P. and Gartner, W. (2003), 'Arriving at the high-growth firm', *Journal of Business Venturing*, **18**(2), 189–216.

DiMaggio, P. (1986), 'Structural analysis of organizational fields: a blockmodel approach', *Research in Organizational Behavior*, **8**, 335–70.

Dodgson, M., Gann, D. and Salter, A. (2005), *Think, Play, Do: Technology, Innovation, and Organization*, Oxford: Oxford University Press.

Dyer, J. and Singh, H. (1998), 'The relational view: cooperative strategy and sources of interorganizational competitive advantage', *The Academy of Management* Review,**23**(4), 660–79.

Easton, G. (1992), 'Industrial networks: a review', in B. Axelsson and G. Easton (eds), *Industrial Networks: A New View of Reality*, London: Routledge, pp. 1–27.

European Parliament (2000), Lisbon European Council 23 and 24 March 2000, Presidency Conclusions, http://www.europarl.europa.eu/summits/lis1_en.htm#a.

Freel, M. (2000), 'External linkages and product innovation in small manufacturing firms', *Entrepreneurship and Regional Development*, **12**, 245–66.

Freel, M. (2003), 'Sectoral patterns of small firm innovation, networking and proximity', *Research Policy*, **32**, 751–70.

Funk, R. (2014), 'Making the most of where you are: geography, networks, and innovation in organizations', *Academy of Management Journal*, **57**(1), 193–222.

Gargiulo, M. and Benassi, M. (2000), 'Trapped in your own net? Network cohesion,

structural holes, and the adaptation of social capital', *Organization Science*, **11**(2), 183–96.
Gartner, W. (1985), 'A conceptual framework for describing the phenomenon of new venture creation', *Academy of Management Review*, **10**, 696–706.
Gartner, W. (1995), 'Aspects of organizational emergence', in I. Bull, H. Thomas and G. Willard (eds), *Entrepreneurship – Perspectives on Theory Building*, Oxford: Oxford University Press, pp. 67–86.
Graf, H. (2011), 'Gatekeepers in regional networks of innovators', *Cambridge Journal of Economics*, **35**, 173–98.
Graf, H. and Kruger, J. (2011), 'The performance of gatekeepers in innovator networks', *Industry and Innovation*, **18**(1), 69–88.
Granovetter, M. (1973), 'The strengths of weak ties', *American Journal of Sociology*, **78**(6), 1360–80.
Granovetter, M. (1974), *Getting a Job: A Study of Contacts and Careers*, Boston, MA: Harvard University Press.
Granovetter, M. (1985), 'Economic action and social structure: the problem of embeddedness', *American Journal of Sociology*, **91**(3), 481–510.
Harrison, B. (1992), 'Industrial districts: old wine in new bottles?', *Regional Studies*, **26**(5), 469–83.
Hoang, H. and Antoncic, B. (2003), 'Network-based research in entrepreneurship: a critical review', *Journal of Business Venturing*, **18**, 165–87.
Ireland, R., Hitt, M. and Sirmon, D. (2003), 'A model of strategic entrepreneurship: the construct and its dimensions', *Journal of Management*, **29**(6), 963–89.
Jarillo, Carlos J. (1988), 'On strategic networks', *Strategic Management Journal*, **9**, 31–41.
Jarillo, J. (1989), 'Entrepreneuship and growth: the strategic use of external resources', *Journal of Business Venturing*, **4**, 133–47.
Jarillo, C. (1993), *Strategic Networks*, Oxford: Butterworth Heinemann.
Johannisson, B. (1998), 'Personal networks in emerging knowledge-based firms: spatial and functional patterns', *Entrepreneurship and Regional Development*, **10**, 297–312.
Johannisson, B. (2000), 'Networking and entrepreneurial growth', in D. Sexton and H. Landstrom (eds), *Handbook of Entrepreneurship*, New York: Wiley-Blackwell, pp. 368–86.
Krugman, P. (1991), *Geography and Trade*, Cambridge, MA: MIT Press.
Knoke, D. and Kuklinsky, I. (1983), *Network Analysis*, Beverly Hills, CA: Sage.
Lafitte, P., Aho, E., Danneels, L., Evrard, J., Meyer zu Kocker, G., Mingasson, J.P., Monks, G., Sandberg, O., Sandri, S., Simon, P. and Subira, A. (2007), 'The European cluster memorandum', www.clusterobservatory.eu.
Lechner, C. (2000), *The Competitiveness of Firm Networks*, New York: Gabler.
Lechner, C. and Dowling, M. (2000), 'The evolution of industrial districts and regional networks: the case of the biotechnology region Munich/Martinsried', *Journal of Management and Governance*, Special Issue, **3**(99), 309–38.
Lechner, C. and Dowling, M. (2003), 'Firm networks: external relations as sources for the growth and competitiveness of entrepreneurial firms', *Journal of Entrepreneurship and Regional Development*, **1**, 1–26.
Lechner, C. and Leyronas, C. (2007), 'A new model for cluster dynamics: from strategic to regional networks', Special Issue on Europe, *International Journal of Entrepreneurship and Small Business*, **4**(3), 341–60.
Lechner, C. and Leyronas, C. (2012), 'The competitive advantage of cluster

firms: the priority of regional network position over extra-regional networks', *Entrepreneurship & Regional Development*, **24**(5–6), 457–73.
Lechner, C. and Znidarsic, A. (2014), 'An optimal cluster strategy: start-up rate, density and entrepreneurial opportunities', Working Paper, Bolzano.
Lechner, C., Dowling, M. and Welpe, I. (2006), 'The network perspective: the relational mix and the growth of the entrepreneurial firm', Special Issue on Alliances and Networks, *Journal of Business Venturing*, **21**(4), 514–40.
Lincoln, J.R. (1982), 'Intra- (and inter-) organizational networks', in S. Bachararan (ed.), *Research in the Sociology of Organizations*, vol. 1. Greenwich, CT: JAI, pp. 1–38.
Lorenzoni, G. (1992), *Accordi, reti e vantaggio competitivo*, Milano: Etas libri.
Lorenzoni, G. and Ornati, O. (1988), 'Constellations of firms and new ventures', *Journal of Business Venturing*, **3**, 41–57.
Macpherson, A. and Holt, R. (2007), 'Knowledge, learning and small firm growth: a systematic review of the evidence', *Research Policy*, **36**(2), 172–92.
Mahoney, J. and Pandian, R. (1992), 'The resource-based view within the conversation of strategic management', *Strategic Management Journal*, **13**, 363–80.
Maskell, P. and Malmberg, A. (1999), 'The competitiveness of firms and regions and the importance of localized learning', *European Urban and Regional Studies*, **6**, 9–25.
McGahan, A. and Porter, M. (1997), 'How much does industry matter really?', *Strategic Management Journal*, Summer Special Issue, **18**, 15–30.
Meyer, A. (1991), 'What is strategy's distinctive competence?', *Journal of Management*, **17**(4), 821–33.
Milgram, S. (1967), 'The small world problem', *Psychology Today*, **2**, 60–67.
Mitchell, J.C. (1969), 'The concept and the use of social network', in J.C. Mitchell (ed.), *Social Networks in Urban Situations*, Manchester, UK: Manchester University Press, pp. 1–32.
Morrison, A. (2008), 'Gatekeepers of knowledge within industrial districts: who they are, how they interact', *Regional Studies*, **42**(6), 817.
Neck, H., Meyer, G., Cohen, B. and Corett, A. (2004), 'An entrepreneurial system view of new ventures creation', *Journal of Small Business Management*, **42**, 190–208.
Newman, M., Barabasi, A.-L. and Watts, D. (2006), *The Structure and Dynamics of Networks*, Princeton, NJ: Princeton University Press.
Nohria, N. (1992), 'Is a network perspective a useful way of studying organisation?', in R. Eccles (ed.), *Networks and Organisations*, Boston, MA: Harvard Business School Press, pp. 1–22.
Obstfeld, D. (2005), 'Social networks, the tertius iungens orientation, and involvement in innovation', *Administrative Science Quarterly*, **50**(1), 100–130.
Penrose, E. (1959), *The Theory of the Growth of the Firm*, New York: Wiley.
Peteraf, M. (1993), 'The cornerstones of competitive advantage: a resource-based view', *Strategic Management Journal*, **14**(3), 179–91.
Peteraf, M. and Barney, J. (2003), 'Unraveling the resource-based tangle', *Managerial and Decision Economics*, **24**(4), 309–23.
Podolny, J. and Page, K. (1998), 'Network forms of organization', *Annual Review of Sociology*, 57–76.
Porter, M. (1980), *Competitive Strategy*, New York: Free Press.
Porter, M. (1990), *The Competitive Advantage of Nations*, London: Macmillan.
Porter, M. (1996), 'What is strategy?', *Harvard Business Review*, **74**(6), 61–78.

Porter, M. (1998), 'Clusters and the new economics of competition', *Harvard Business Review*, November–December, 77–90.
Porter, M. (2000), 'Location, competition, and economic development: local clusters in a global economy', *Economic Development Quarterly*, **14**, 15–34.
Porter, M. (2005), 'What is competitiveness?', *Notes on Globalization and Strategy*, **1**(1), 2–3.
Powell, W. (1987), 'Hybrid organizational arrangements: new form or transitional development?', *California Management Review*, Fall, 67–87.
Powell, W. (1990), 'Neither market nor hierarchy: network forms of organization', *Research in Organizational Behavior*, **12**, 295–336.
Powell, W., Packalen, K. and Whittington, K. (2012), 'Organizational and institutional genesis: the emergence of high-tech clusters in the life sciences', in J. Padgett and W. Powell (eds), *The Emergence of Organizations and Markets*, Princeton, NJ: Princeton University Press, pp. 1247–330.
Presutti, M., Boari, C. and Majocchi, A. (2011), 'The importance of proximity for the start-ups' knowledge acquisition and exploitation', *Journal of Small Business Management*, **49**(3), 361–89.
Reagans, R. and McEvily, B. (2003), 'Network structure and knowledge transfer: the effects of cohesion and range', *Administrative Science Quarterly*, **48**, 240–67.
Richardson, G. (1972), 'The organisation of industry', *Economy Journal*, 883–96.
Rumelt, R. (1984), 'Towards a strategic theory of the firm', in R.B. Lamb (ed.), *Competitive Strategic Management*, Englewood Cliffs, NJ: Prentice-Hall, pp. 566–70.
Sawyer, O., McGee, J. and Peterson, M. (2003), 'Perceived uncertainty and firm performance in SMEs – the role of personal networking', *International Small Business Journal*, **21**(3), 269–90.
Shane, S. and Venkataraman, S. (2000), 'The promise of entrepreneurship as a field of research', *Academy of Management Review*, **25**, 217–26.
Shaver, J. and Flyer, F. (2000), 'Agglomeration economies, firm heterogeneity, and foreign direct investment in the United States', *Strategic Management Journal*, **21**(12), 1175–93.
Slotte-Kock, S. and Coviello, N. (2010), 'Entrepreneurship research on network processes: a review and ways forward', *Entrepreneurship Theory and Practice*, **34**(1), 31–57.
Sölvell, Ö., Lindqvist, G. and Ketels, C. (2003), *The Cluster Initiative Greenbook*, Stockholm: Bromma tryck AB.
Stinchcombe, A. (1965), 'Social structure and organizations', in J. March (ed.), *Handbook of Organization*, Chicago, IL: Rand McNally, pp. 142–93.
Tallman, S., Jenkins, M., Henry, M. and Pinch, S. (2004), 'Knowledge, clusters, and competitive advantage', *Academy of Management Review*, **29**(2), 258–71.
Thorelli, H. (1986), 'Networks: between markets and hierarchies', *Strategic Management Journal*, **7**(1), 37–51.
Uzzi, B. (1997), 'Social structure and competition in interfirm networks: the paradox of embeddedness', *Administrative Science Quarterly*, **42**, 35–67.
Venkataraman, S. and Van de Ven, A. (1998), 'Hostile environmental jolts, transaction set, and new business', *Journal of Business Venturing*, **13**, 231–55.
Verstraete, T. (2003), 'On the singularity of entrepreneurship as a research domain', *Annual Review of Progress in Entrepreneurship*, Brussels: EFMD, pp. 10–64.
Virtanen, M. (1997), 'The role of different theories in explaining entrepreneurship', *Journal of Best Papers*, ICSB 42nd World Conference.

Watts, D. and Strogatz, S. (1998), 'Collective dynamics of "small-world" networks', *Nature*, **393**(4), 440–42.

Wernerfelt, B. (1984), 'A resource-based view of the firm', *Strategic Management Journal*, **5**, 171–80.

Whittington, K., Owen-Smith, J. and Powell, W. (2009), 'Networks, propinquity and innovation in knowledge intensive industries', *Administrative Science Quarterly*, **54**(1), 90–122.

Zaheer, A. and McEvily, B. (1999), 'Bridging ties: a source of firm heterogeneity in competitive capabilities', *Strategic Management Journal*, **20**(12), 1133.

Zhao, L. and Aram, J. (1995), 'Networking and growth of young technology-intensive ventures in China', *Journal of Business Venturing*, **10**, 349–70.

9. The role of family members in entrepreneurial networks: beyond the boundaries of the family firm*

Alistair R. Anderson, Sarah L. Jack and Sarah Drakopoulou Dodd

INTRODUCTION

The sister disciplines of entrepreneurship and family business scholarship have, with some notable exceptions, addressed themselves to the study of two separate conceptualizations of independent business. Entrepreneurship has focused on the pursuit of opportunities through the creation and growth of business organizations, paying special attention to the individuals and teams that undertake such activities, and the industrial, economic and social environments in which they are located. Family business scholarship has concentrated on the governance, management, development and succession of the family firm. Whilst relevant literature has periodically breached the gulf between the two fields, there are clear indications that the two fields are moving ever closer together. Evidence for this trend can be seen in the recent (2003) special issues of leading entrepreneurship journals dedicated to the family business (*Journal of Business Venturing*, **18**(4–5) and *Entrepreneurship Theory and Practice*, **27**(4)), as well as in its inclusion as a theme in major entrepreneurship conferences (2001 Babson Kauffman Conference). The increasing recognition of the significance of family matters to entrepreneurship has its roots in theoretical developments concerning the sociocultural context of entrepreneurship, perhaps embodied most clearly in the research stream dealing with entrepreneurial networks. It is therefore not surprising that it is the doyen of entrepreneurial networks scholarship, Howard Aldrich, who has made the strongest call for recognition of the role of the family in entrepreneurship:

> The family embeddedness perspective on entrepreneurship implies that researchers need to include family dimensions in their conceptualizing and

modeling, their sampling and analyzing, and their interpretations and implications. (Aldrich and Cliff, 2003, p. 574)

At the same time as entrepreneurship has begun the process of embracing the family embeddedness perspective, the field of family business scholarship has also been challenging the traditional boundaries of its research, in particular questioning the necessity of a dichotomous approach to definitions of the family firm (Astrachan and Shanker, 2003; Astrachan et al., 2002). The upshot of these two trends is that there is a convergence of interest in the interplay of the family and independent business, and in the interstices between the two disciplines. The present study attempts to peer into this gap, to examine the influence of family on those entrepreneurial businesses that fall outside the traditional definitions of the family firm. To achieve this objective, we utilize the theoretical concepts of the entrepreneurial network, focusing especially on the role of family members in these sets of social relationships. The chapter continues with a short introduction to the issue of defining the family firm, before progressing to discuss extant material on the role of family in supporting independent enterprise, particularly through entrepreneurial networks. From this literature review, we next develop exploratory research questions, which we empirically investigate in a multi-method study. Our findings indicate that, for our Scottish sample, about one quarter of key entrepreneurial network ties were kin, and that most of these family contacts worked outside the family firm. These ties provided a range of very important resources, both professional and affective in nature. Family are frequently integrated into entrepreneurial businesses, even when their involvement falls outside the broadest definition of the family firm. The study also makes a practical contribution, by demonstrating that the family as virtual enterprise offsets some of the liabilities of the family firm, while retaining its strengths.

BEYOND DICHOTOMY: EXTENDING DEFINITIONS OF THE FAMILY FIRM

Although family business is now a major field of inquiry, there is no generally accepted definition of what is meant by the term 'family business' (Litz, 1995; Fox et al., 1996). Various definitions have been offered in the literature, but ambiguities exist. Most researchers tend to adopt a pragmatic definition, viewing family involvement as ownership and management and/or the owner-managers' perception that a business is a family business (Westhead and Cowling, 1996; Handler, 1989). Upton and

Petty (2000) define the family business as a firm owned and operated by two or more family members. Carsrud (1994) defines a family business as one in which ownership and policymaking are dominated by members of an 'emotional kinship group'. James (1999, p. 45) defines a family firm as a privately held company that will be inherited and controlled by one or more of the proprietor's children on his retirement. Researchers generally agree that family involvement in the business is what makes the family business different (Miller and Rice, 1967). Conventional definitions of family firms can thus be seen to concentrate on those owned and operated by two or more family members and where 'ownership and policymaking are dominated by members of an emotional kinship group'. Family businesses are presented as a bounded entity, restricted to those businesses directly involving family members. This definitional issue is not merely semantic, but reflects upon the unit of analysis for empirical work; shapes the conceptual framework underpinning family business research; and may have implications for support policies. The lack of a clear definition also inhibits cross-study comparisons. Two recent solutions to this problem have been proposed, both of which move away from dichotomous definition of what is, or is not, a family firm.[1]

The F-PEC scale (Astrachan et al., 2002) avoids the dangers of a Boolean yes/no definition of the family firm by developing a series of instruments allowing researchers to position firms according to three key variables: power, experience and culture. This permits robust comparisons across studies and samples, as well as a more detailed examination of the relationship between family and business, even for those firms not included in any of the traditional definitions of family business. Our study is in the spirit of such inquiry, and represents an attempt to move beyond received definitional family-firm boundaries to study the role of family in the entrepreneurial firm.

Astrachan and Shanker (2002) propose a set of three definitions of the family firm – narrow, middle and broad – which are successively more inclusive of family participation. Their broad definition of the family firm encompasses those businesses where a family controls the strategic direction of the firm, and also participates in the business. In the middle definition, additionally, the business is run by a founder or descendant, and is intended to remain in the family. For the narrowest definition of the family firm, the extra criteria of multiple-generation participation in business, and more than one member of the owner's family having management responsibility, are added. These three definitions are diagrammatically arranged in a target-like format of concentric circles, with the narrow definition at the centre of the target, the 'bull's eye'.

Definitions of both family business and entrepreneurship have until recently been mutually exclusive. This has led to a conceptual gap between the two areas of study, with the impact of the family on entrepreneurial firms being sadly under-explored. By extending the bull's-eye model, so as to move still further beyond the constraints of traditional definitions, this study adds a new conceptual dimension to the study of the interrelationship of family and entrepreneurship.

This model can provide a conceptual basis for linking together the two research fields of entrepreneurship and family business scholarship, for modelling family-firm interactions in a wider sense, and for highlighting under-researched areas. The role of the family in the entrepreneurial business is, as already mentioned, an even more important research topic. A fine example of such work is Birley et al.'s (1999) typology of relationships between the family and the entrepreneurial business. Following a survey of more than 500 entrepreneurs, three types of family-business cluster were identified. One group, 'Family Rules', saw the family and business as a single unit, while for the 'Family Out' cluster, the two should be kept as far apart as possible. The third group, 'Family Jugglers' was concerned to balance the interests of both parties, and maximum formal family involvement was restricted to the employment of a few kin in the firm. None the less they were comfortable with, and accepting of, some degree of overlap between the two domains.

Relating this typology to the Astrachan and Shanker bull's-eye model, the following observations can be made: the 'Family Rules' group encompasses the first (narrow definition), second (medium definition) and third (broad definition) circles of the model. The 'Family Jugglers' group is clearly beyond the scope of the three circles, since its enterprises cannot be classified as family firms, even under the terms of the broadest definition. None the less, the role of kin for these entrepreneurs may be substantial. Finally, the 'Family Out' group rejects all links between family and business, and, again, cannot be mapped on to the bull's-eye model. By extending the bull's-eye model to incorporate Birley et al.'s typology, we can show two additional possibilities for the interaction of family and business. The first of these two new circles, 'Family Jugglers', makes informal use of family members in the running of the firm. The second, 'Family Out', avoids all interaction of family and firm. Figure 9.1 shows the extended bull's-eye model in diagrammatic form. The diagram also helps to focus attention on a serious research gap: entrepreneurship is guilty of spending, until very recently, far too much attention on those in the outer circle ('Family Out'), or, worse still, assuming that most entrepreneurs fall into this group. Family business studies have, not surprisingly, given the definitional issues involved, focused on the inner three circles, the 'Family In' group. The

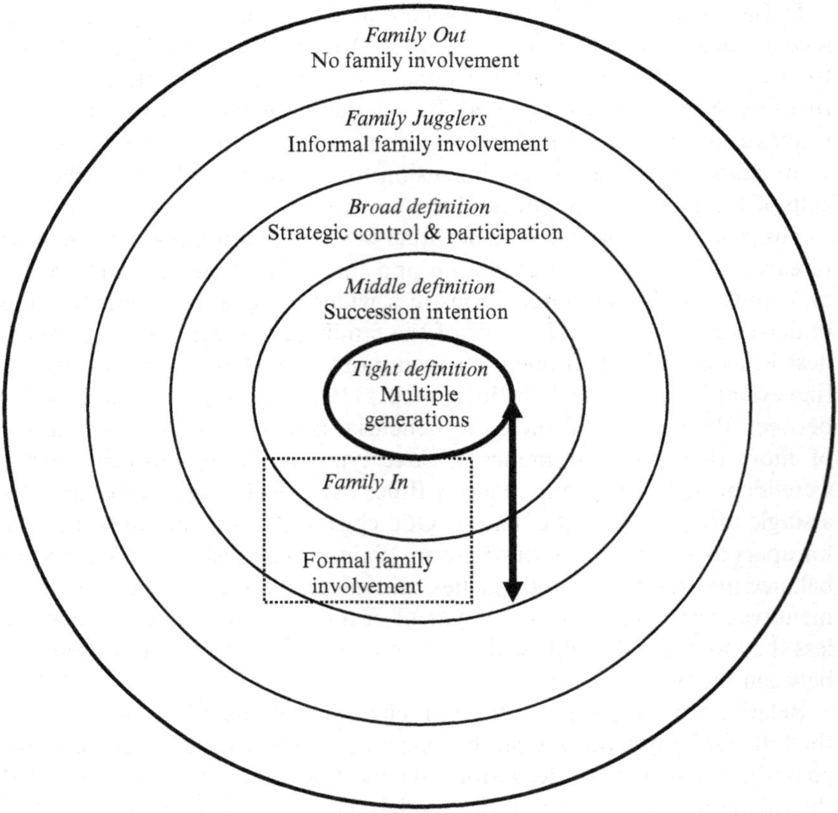

Figure 9.1 A continuum of family–enterprise interactions extending Astrachan and Shanker's bull's-eye model

'Family Jugglers' group, which Birley et al. estimated to include about a third of all entrepreneurs, has been woefully neglected. The aim of this study is to redress this neglect by exploring the nature, extent and impact of informal family contributions to the entrepreneurial firm, using the lens of entrepreneurial networks as the means to do so. In other words, we intend to examine the role of family members in entrepreneurial networks, beyond the formal boundaries of the family firm. The following theoretical discussion builds on extant literature to develop a set of research questions contrasting the commercial benefits and hazards encountered through family-business interrelationships, for the 'Family Jugglers' and 'Family In' groups respectively.

THE ROLE OF FAMILY IN SUPPORTING INDEPENDENT ENTERPRISE

As with many studies of entrepreneurial networks, the approach we adopted focused on the 'ego-centred network' of the entrepreneur (Greve and Salaff, 2003, p. 9; see also Barnir and Smith, 2002, p. 221; Burt and Minor, 1983; Knoke and Kuklinski, 1982; Suitor et al., 1997). The ego-centred approach is especially appropriate for samples where those studied have a diverse network, not contained within a single social structure. This is certainly the case for entrepreneurs, as has been repeatedly shown, with their networks containing a mixture of business, friendship and kin ties. Entrepreneurial networks are thus a complex mixture of multiplex social and professional ties, all of which tend to contain both affective and instrumental elements, bonded by trust. We concentrated our study on the five main personal network contacts of our sample, for both the quantitative and qualitative phases of the study, since evidence shows that recall is strong for these relationships (Greve and Salaff, 2003, p. 9; Burt and Ronchi, 1994). In Granovetter's terms, then, we were interested in the 'strong ties' of our entrepreneurial sample, or, to use Uzzi's similar concept, 'embedded ties', those with whom entrepreneurs regularly discussed their business, and where relationships are tightly coupled amalgams of the personal and the professional (Uzzi, 1996, p. 682). The governing mechanism of such networks is trust:

> trust is a governance structure that resides in the social relationship between and among individuals and cognitively is based on heuristic rather than calculative processing . . . trust is fundamentally a social process, since these psychological mechanisms and expectations are emergent features of a social structure that creates and reproduces them through time. (Uzzi, 1997, p. 45)

Although there has been scant direct research into the informal interrelationship between family and business in entrepreneurship, none the less, studies do exist that highlight the importance of kin to enterprise creation and development. Ram (2001) has emphasized family culture, its influence on social relations in small firms, and the importance of the 'family' in creating and sustaining such businesses. For example, dependence on family members for labour within small firms is common and, within the UK, recent work indicates that this is the norm rather than the exception (Rosa et al., 1994; Baines and Wheelock, 1998).

> The initial capital . . . generally comes from personal and family assets . . . In some instances, an entrepreneur's family or extended family not only provides needed capital, but provides other resources such as access to markets, sources

of supply, technology, and even new ideas. (Dyer and Handler, 1994, pp. 73–4; see also Reynolds et al., 2004)

It is the growing interest in the sociocultural context of entrepreneurship, though, that has led to heightened awareness of the importance of familial relationships to the entrepreneur, and especially those studies that take a network perspective. All economic activity is embedded in social context (Granovetter, 1973), but this is especially so for entrepreneurship, where the person of the entrepreneur provides the focus, the decision-making centre, the information-gathering hub – the embodiment – of the firm. Entrepreneurs have a strong tendency to personalize their business activities, working with and through other people to identify and validate business ideas (Hill et al., 1999; de Koning 1999), to access resources (Ostgaard and Birley, 1994), to manage supplier and customer systems (Larson, 1992; Uzzi, 1996, 1997), to interrogate the wider commercial environment, and to both develop and implement strategies (Burt, 1992; Hills et al., 1997). The slowly developing set of relationships that entrepreneurs enact, as they carry out these highly personalized processes, are termed 'entrepreneurial networks'. In general, the literature distinguishes between two types of network tie, both of which are needed in an effective entrepreneurial network (Granovetter, 1973). Strong-tie network contacts are those people with whom the entrepreneur has a close personal relationship, and with whom they interact quite frequently. Weak ties, on the other hand, are more distant emotionally, and may only be activated infrequently. Strong-tie contacts are often friends or family, whereas weak ties are more likely to be defined as business associates. Strong ties have been found to provide very high-quality resources – especially information – that is often not commercially available, and that is focused sharply on the specific needs of the entrepreneur and their business. However, because family and friends tend to move in the same circles as the entrepreneur, these resources may not offer much beyond the entrepreneur's own scope; that is, they may not be adequately diverse in nature. The main benefit of weak ties is that they can access heterogeneous information (and other resources), acting as a bridge across social structural holes (Singh et al., 1999).

Literature on the changing nature of enterprises suggests that the boundaries around organizations have become much more permeable, with concepts such as strategic alliances, networks and virtuality replacing clear delineation of organizational limits. Building on relationships with individuals and organizations beyond formal firm boundaries is increasingly seen as essential in generating optimum business performance. This is especially so of entrepreneurial, independently owned and managed businesses – a category that includes the vast majority of family firms (see, especially, Szarka, 1990), as the foregoing discussion of entrepreneurial networks has shown. Business assistance provided by those outside the firm can also be conceived of in terms of virtuality. In a virtual organization, physical proximity and formal ownership/employment ties are rejected in favour of exchange relationships based on trust, mutual benefit and a sense of belonging (Barnatt, 1997; Alexander, 1997). Boundaries are permeable, and must be managed so that advantages are not outweighed by corresponding disadvantages from impaired interaction relationships (Alexander, 1997, p. 124). Trust plays a major role in the successful management of such relationships (Larsen and McInerney, 2002; Nonaka and Takeuchi, 1995; Handy, 1995). Again, it seems feasible to argue that appropriate kin outside the formal boundaries of the family firm, working in physically and organizationally distinct places, may prove excellent virtual members of a family firm. Trust, and a sense of belonging, are provided by the family context, which also mediates relationship interactions in a positive manner. The benefits that these possible kin network contacts, or virtual members of the family firm, provide to the family firm are likely to be enhanced by their emotional commitment and long-term understanding of the firm. Informal interrelationships between strong-tie family network contacts and the entrepreneurial firm can thus be argued to provide flexibility and diversity in their resource provision, beyond that which can be provided by family employees, but with greater levels of trust and commitment than those exhibited by non-family strong-tie contacts.

As we have seen, the family plays a crucial role in the development of new firms, and this is not least because kinship relationships provide the strongest of strong ties. Stewart (2003) provides the most detailed review of work that examines the role of kin in entrepreneurial networks, although he focuses on kin employed within the family business. Stewart lists the benefits of kin-based network ties as including commitment, extensive tacit knowledge, access to information, reliability, and a willingness to make sacrifices in terms of time, money and effort. (This list can be seen as a heightened version of that describing the benefits of strong-tie network contacts in general.) We would argue that these benefits would also obtain for kin-based network ties with those relatives who are not formally employed within the family firm. Indeed, the very fact of their following a different career path may also proffer a more diverse and richer range of resources to their family's business. However, the liabilities of strong ties may also accrue to these relationships, most especially homogeneity and sterility in terms of resource provision. Indeed, these liabilities are likely to be especially pronounced for family strong-tie network contacts, given the high degree of social, educational and professional homophily within immediate kinship groups.

The foregoing discussion allows us to draw the following tentative conclusions. The literature suggests that informal interrelationships between strong-tie family members and the entrepreneurial firm will deliver many of the benefits associated with strong-tie family employees, including the provision of high-quality, well-focused, low-cost resources in a timely fashion. However, it is also likely that these informal interrelationships will particularly exhibit the liabilities of strong-tie network couplings, including excessive homogeneity, and sterility of resource provision. Notwithstanding this point, the potential contributions of family members outwith the organizational borders of the firms are likely to deliver greater diversity than those within its formal employ.

Beyond these theoretical arguments, little is known about the scale and character of kin strong-tie network contacts employed outwith the entrepreneurial venture. A series of international studies into entrepreneurial ventures, discussed in more detail below, indicates that between 13 per cent (Ireland, Japan) and 31 per cent (Greece) of an entrepreneur's five most important network contacts are family members. However, we do not yet know what proportion of these work outside the family firm, what kinds of assistance they provide, nor the relevance and quality of this support. Since so little information is available, it is not yet viable to develop formal testable hypotheses, but rather to develop a series of exploratory research questions. Research attempting to generate understanding, *verstehen*, is required, before more specific *erklärung* studies can analyse the details of cause and effect. In order to begin developing our understanding of 'Family Jugglers', and to build on the theoretical discussion above, the following research questions need to be addressed:

RQ 9.1: What is the extent of informal family support for entrepreneurs as members of their strong-tie network?

RQ 9.2: How do kin-based strong-tie network contacts differ from non-kin contacts?

RQ 9.3: What is the nature of support provided by family strong-tie network contacts outside the boundaries of the family firm?

RQ 9.4: What is the quality of this support provision?

METHODOLOGY

A Multi-method Approach

Literature-driven theoretical considerations led to the selection of entrepreneurial networks as a potentially rewarding perspective from which to study the impact of family on entrepreneurial firms. Having used the literature to generate four research questions, the next stage in the project was to design a method to address these issues. Several considerations needed to be borne in mind at this stage, including generalizabilty, data requirements, methodological rigour and operationalizability. These requirements led to the development and implementation of a two-stage research project, which utilized both quantitative and qualitative techniques.

So as to be able to extrapolate our findings to a wider population, we elected to utilize a well-established research instrument, specifically a questionnaire into entrepreneurial networks that has formed the basis of a number of international studies (Aldrich et al., 1989 – the USA and Italy; Aldrich and Sakano, 1995 – Japan; Birley et al., 1991 – Northern Ireland; Drakopoulou Dodd and Patra, 2002 – Greece; Greve and Salaff, 2003 – Norway; Johannisson and Nilsson, 1989 – Norway; Staber and Aldrich, 1995 – Canada). Comparing our findings to extant international results permits the similarities and differences between our sample and its international counterparts to be laid bare, and thus for strong arguments to be made regarding possible generalizability. The internationally recognized survey instrument is especially well suited to eliciting data with regard to network structure, compositio, and content. We followed Drakopoulou Dodd and Patra (2002) in adding several further questions relating to the content of network exchanges. Simple quantitative analysis was carried out on data derived from the survey to establish the size, scale and significance of informally linked strong-tie family network contacts.

Many argue that richer and deeper data of the dynamics, processes and complexities of networks are best accessed through qualitative methodologies, (Chell and Haworth, 1992; O'Donnell et al., 2001; Hill et al., 1999; Hoang and Antoncic, 2003; Johannisson, 1996; Johannisson and Monsted, 1997; Larson, 1992; Lechner and Dowling, 2003; Uzzi, 1997; Zeleny, 2001). Our hypotheses address both types of data, and therefore required both methodologies. The second stage of the study involved qualitative research, using semi-structured interviews to probe in more detail into the relationship between family and entrepreneurship, paying special attention to the 'Family Jugglers' group.

Stage 1: the quantitative study

Our sample frame was derived from the 1997 edition of the *Grampian Business Directory*, a local government publication that provides a comprehensive listing of all firms in the Grampian region. Grampian was selected as the locus for the study because it is an economic environment in which the three authors are well embedded, and because it represents a discrete, geographically bounded area. The selection of a single cognate region was intended to limit the effects of social and economic geography on the data. Grampian, in the North East of Scotland, is centred around the City of Aberdeen, the 'oil capital' of Europe. The city has a long history of international trade and merchant venturing dating back (at least) to the Middle Ages. It is also, however, physically distant from the Central Scotland belt (Glasgow, Stirling and Edinburgh), and has retained a distinct character. Grampian combines some oil-related industries with the more traditional whisky, fishing, food-processing and textiles sectors.

The regional business directory details the size and sector of firms, and provides some indication of ownership/legal status. The directory was used to generate a total regional population of 786 owner-managed firms, with between zero and 200 employees. We then randomly selected somewhat over one-third of this population and thereby arrived at our final sample of 271 entrepreneurial firms. All these firms were contacted in a telephone survey carried out between May and June 2000, and their entrepreneurs were invited to participate in the survey by responding to the extended questionnaire over the telephone. The survey generated 68 useable responses, equating to a 25 per cent response rate for the sample. While this is a fairly low response rate, it is not untypical for studies of networks, which entrepreneurs often show a marked reluctance to discuss (Johannisson and Monsted, 1997). Furthermore, the telephone survey method reduces response rate by requiring that the respondent deals with the survey at a given moment in time, which is especially difficult for busy entrepreneurs. Nevertheless, the multi-method nature of the study, and the representativeness of our sample to the overall regional population, provide assurances of the quality of the data, low response rate notwithstanding.

Stage 2: the qualitative study

In the second stage of our empirical study, we applied a qualitative methodology to conduct a series of 12 extended in-depth interviews to generate a fuller, richer appreciation of the dynamics of the family in business. All respondents to the telephone survey were invited to participate in the second stage of the study. From this group, 12 respondents were purposefully selected for in-depth interviews. This purposeful sampling method, recommended for qualitative studies, enabled the researchers to use their judgement to select respondents and cases that were particularly informative (Neuman, 1991) and that would help to achieve the objectives of the research (Saunders et al., 1997). We used information provided during the quantitative survey to identify a set of respondents who, between them, represented the complete continuum of family-business relationships, and who also mirrored the wider regional population in terms of gender, age, sector and business size. Each respondent was interviewed for between two and four hours at various times throughout the summer of 2000. Interviews were carried out at the respondents' premises, since relaxed and open discussion is facilitated by familiar surroundings (Hill et al., 1999, p. 75; O'Donnell et al., 2001, p. 756). The interviews were carried out by two of the researchers. Questions were asked and explanations sought about the types of network ties used, the areas that respondents tended to discuss with each strong tie, the kind of help these people provided, and how often, where and when they interacted with their ties. Respondents were also invited to describe the relationship they had with each strong tie, and to recount the history of these relationships, with special emphasis on their relevance for the entrepreneurial venture. Questions were not asked in any specific order, but were governed instead by the actual situation (Gummesson, 2000).

Interview tapes were transcribed verbatim, and examined using well-established qualitative data analysis methods (Miles and Huberman, 1994; Glaser and Strauss, 1967), which have become the accepted approach for handling entrepreneurial network analysis (Human and Provan, 1996; Hill et al., 1999, p. 76). Specifically, the transcripts were read and re-read, with notes on emergent themes contemporaneously entered into a research diary (Easterby-Smith et al., 1999). The research diary was reviewed to clarify these emergent themes, and we then revisited the transcripts for initial coding. This revistitation continued until few new insights occurred (Human and Provan, 1996). The initial coding was discussed and clarified by the research team, and categories agreed. Next, the transcripts were surveyed again for complete identification of examples matching the agreed thematic categories. We followed Hill et al.'s technique of physically cutting and pasting these examples into separate files (1999, p. 76) to facilitate examination. Completing the laborious task of categorization, replete with illustrative examples, we simultaneously continued the interrogation of the data in relationship to the four research questions developed from the literature. Finally, we produced an illustrated summary of the major themes and the relationships between them, presented below.

We recognize that these research techniques have some inherent limitations. The study area was restricted, and both the small number of respondents to the quantitative survey, and the nature of qualitative methodologies, inhibit generalizability (Larson, 1992). Conducting both quantitative and qualitative studies, as well as comparing our findings to other extant work from the literature stream, mitigates some of these limitations by triangulating findings. The use of a well-established survey instrument also allows us to position our findings in their international context. Furthermore, the value of qualitative research design lies in its capacity to provide insights, rich detail and thick description (Geertz, 1973) and to produce a grounded model that can generate hypotheses for further testing (Larson, 1992). This is an especially valuable contribution for such an underresearched area.

FINDINGS

Quantitative Findings – Network Composition

The quantitative data were used to provide an indication of overall trends. Respondents were asked to name up to five main personal network contacts, the people with whom they most frequently discussed their business. Background information on these contacts was elicited, including the nature of their relationship to the entrepreneur and their occupation. In terms of international comparisons, our Scottish sample reported spending more time on maintaining their existing tight circle of strong ties than on developing new relationships. Their networks were relatively small, and contained about the same proportion of kin (24 per cent) as their European neighbours (Greece, 31 per cent; Italy: 23 per cent; Sweden 24 per cent), although considerably more than entrepreneurs from other nations (Canada, 18 per cent; Ireland, 13 per cent; Japan, 13 per cent; USA, 14 per cent[2]). As Table 9.1 shows, these family ties were more likely

Table 9.1 Nature of strong tie, and occupation of strong-tie contact

	Family ties	Friendship ties	Business ties
% of total ties	24	15	61
N = 182	*N* = 44	*N* = 28	*N* = 111
Occupation of strong-tie contact by nature of tie, %			
Professionals	4	7	31
Partners/co-directors	25	10	34
Entrepreneurs	16	39	3
Employed (external)	42	32	22
Employee (internal)	2	4	6
Other	11	7	4
Total	100	99	100
Occupational locus of strong-tie contact by nature of tie, %			
Internal/quasi-internal	31	21	73
External	69	78	27
Total	100	100	100

to be employees of another firm than either friends or business associates. Given the small cell sizes, statistical testing is not appropriate in this case, but the data point to clear trends, nevertheless.

Table 9.1 also shows that family ties were fairly heterogeneous, in terms of professional locus, with 69 per cent working in a different business, either for themselves or someone else. Well over two-thirds of the family members to whom entrepreneurs turned for help with their business work were outside the formal boundaries of the family firm, confirming once again the importance of such relationships. Friendship ties, although a much smaller overall percentage, are even more externally focused (78 per cent). Compare this to the business ties, where 73 per cent are either internal (partners/co-directors and employees), or quasi-internal (closely linked professionals). These family members – named among the five most important personal network contacts of the sample respondents, perhaps because of their heterogeneous working environment – were reported as providing a wide and diverse range of assistance to the business throughout its existence.

Nature of the help provided

Respondents were asked to identify, from a list of 12 possible areas, which management areas they discussed with their contacts and, from a list of 7 potential types of help, what type of help was provided. We examined discussion content, and type of support provided, by nature of tie (business, family or friend). We calculated the importance of each discussion topic, and support type, as a percentage of the total reported for each of the three groups. Table 9.2 shows the findings of the analysis of discussion content, which are then illustrated graphically in Figure 9.2.

Table 9.2 Discussion content by nature of tie, %

	Business	Family	Friend
Finding new customers	11.7	9.5	12.9
Selecting suppliers	8.0	8.0	6.5
Recruiting employees	8.1	7.6	3.2
Seeking finance	8.5	8.4	7.5
Business growth	12.8	11.6	15.1
Export possibilities	5.4	3.6	6.5
Accounting and credit management	7.0	6.9	5.4
Tax issues	6.7	8.0	6.5
Advertising and promotion	7.8	10.2	11.8
Managing production and operations	7.8	9.5	7.5
Legal issues	7.6	7.6	10.8
Managing staff	8.6	9.1	6.5

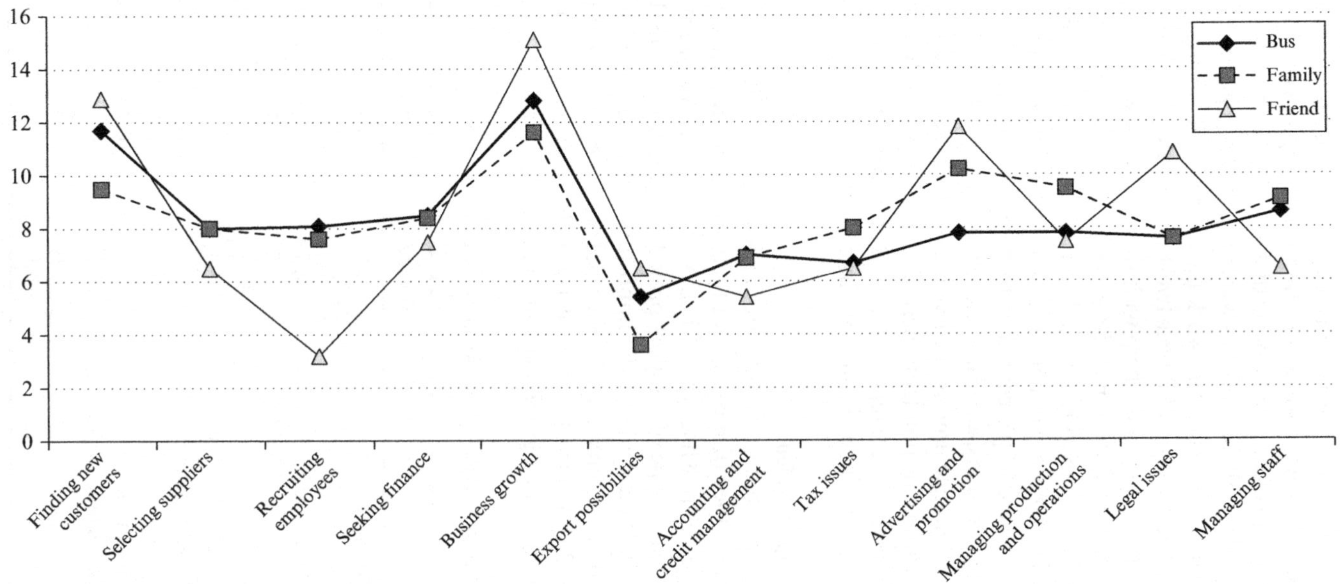

Figure 9.2 Discussion content by nature of tie

These data show that, while content discussed with friends varies somewhat from the overall trend, the findings for family and business ties are very similar in many respects. Whilst the small sample size prevents any meaningful statistical analysis from being carried out, the trend is strong enough to take seriously, and is especially evident in Figure 9.2. Our respondents were as likely to discuss a range of highly instrumental and functional topics with their family contacts as with their business contacts. Indeed, for some topics, they were more likely to seek discussion with family than with business ties. These subjects were found to be tax issues, advertising and promotion, managing production and operations and managing staff. However, in general, the data showed a great similarity between the ways family and business ties were used.

There are two possible explanations for this finding. On the one hand, it may be that entrepreneurs choose to discuss a range of functional issues with their family, regardless of family members' expertise and experience. If this is so, the content of discussions with family members may be a hazard for the entrepreneur and his/her business, given the possible low-calibre nature of the information and advice thus provided. A more positive reading of the data would suggest that, where experience and expertise in a given area are available within the family circle of the entrepreneur, advice and information will be solicited from this source, rather than from business contacts. One of the reasons that we embarked on the second phase of the qualitative study was to address this issue more directly.

When we turn to the type of help provided, again, there is less difference between family and business ties than might have been expected. Figure 9.3 shows these findings, which indicate that, as expected, family help is more likely to be emotional support than is help from business contacts, although assistance provided by friends is still more likely to be emotional in nature. Family help is also often in the form of advice, problem solving and information provision. Again, family support for the entrepreneur seems to be almost as practical in nature as that provided by business contacts.

Summary

The picture that our quantitative study allowed us to develop, then, was one in which the assistance provided by family members to the entrepreneur appeared to be focused and functional in nature. We have already reported that the vast majority of these family ties, unlike the business ties, were external to the firm, thereby offering better potential for accessing otherwise unavailable resources and information (technically termed 'the bridging of structural holes'). As strong ties, family contacts would also be expected to provide help at negligible cost, with a high degree of

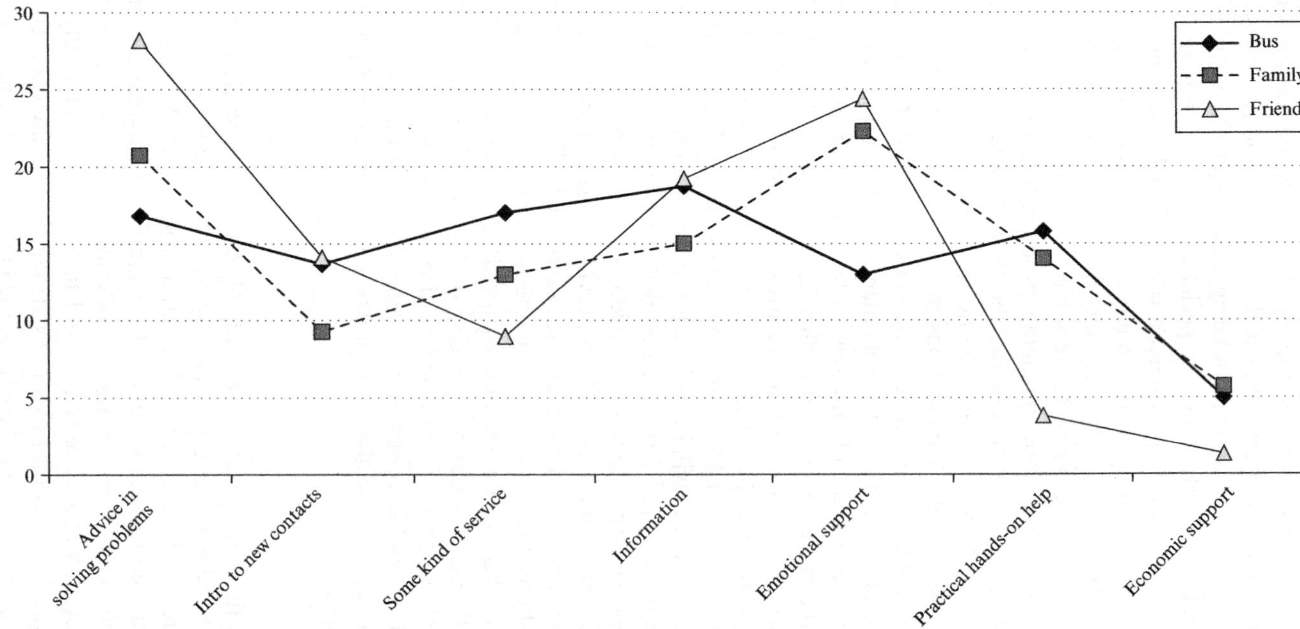

Figure 9.3 Type of help provided by nature of tie

attention, and in a timely and proactive fashion. The entrepreneur's family would be functioning as a cost-effective, high-quality, virtual business. The quantitative study provides some answers to our research questions: family strong-tie contacts are indeed an important element of entrepreneurial networks, and they provide a range of professional support to the firm. They differ from friendship ties, counter-intuitively, in being used to provide commercial support, and from business ties in being – again, counter-intuitively – located mostly outside the formal boundaries of the entrepreneur's business.

However, the quantitative instrument used did not permit us to assess the quality of support provided by specific family ties, and this is clearly a crucial issue in assessing their value to the firm.

Qualitative Findings

The family in business

The findings from the qualitative study confirmed the earlier findings that most entrepreneurs made extensive use of family members in the running of the business. This was often so, even when there was no formal involvement of family members with the firm. Using Birley et al.'s (1999) typology, we found that five of the 12 entrepreneurs we interviewed had chosen to employ members of their family formally, and/or to encourage family equity stakes in the business. These entrepreneurs have chosen the 'Family In' grouping. Two of the entrepreneurs studied were firmly opposed to any form of family involvement in the firm, and did not even discuss work at home over dinner in the evening! It would be hard to find clearer examples of the 'Family Out' group. The third group of five entrepreneurs was the most interesting for the purposes of this study. Although there was no formal family link to the business, either through employment or ownership, nevertheless kin constituted an important part of the entrepreneurs' networks. Table 9.3 presents short overviews of the 12 respondents and their businesses.

Start-up help

Our findings confirmed, as Dyer and Handler (1994) suggested, the importance of family involvement at the start-up phase. Critical forms of family support as businesses were created were promotion of the entrepreneurial concept, help with opportunity identification and, especially, provision of finance. For the 'Family In' group, entry to entrepreneurship had been especially facilitated by kin, either through inheritance or very extensive provision of finance and other resources. One respondent, Nigel, founded his first business in his very early twenties and faced all the usual

Table 9.3 Overview of respondents' businesses

Respondent	Activity	Date firm started	Background and route to entrepreneurship	No. of employees
'Family In' group				
Nigel	Freight forwarder	1992	Freight forwarding, set up own business in competition with in-laws	35
Shaun	Stationery supplies	1983	Took over family business	2
Grant	Chemical supplies	1981	Accounting and business degree. Gradually taking over family business	5
William	Light engineering	1973	New venture based on technical innovation	5
Bill	Light engineering	1989	University, professional career, then creation of 'lifestyle' business	1
'Family Out' group				
Barry	Computing services	Various dates	Originally employed in oil industry; then started a number of businesses	160
Tony	Construction	1974	Management buy-out	100
'Family Jugglers' group				
Mary	Counselling services	1997	Housewife who identified need through own experience	0
Graeme	Computing services	1990	Worked for major oil company, allowing him to recognize related opportunities	19
Stuart	Language school	1995	Various jobs on leaving university. Turned hobby into business	1
Kathy	Video production	1985	Sales and marketing, set up business with partner when employer (same industry) went into liquidation	15
Adam	Manufacturing	1977	Identified a local opportunity	25

legitimacy-gap problems of the very young entrepreneur. His father-in-law allowed him to use the name of his own business to generate credibility, which in turn delivered 'recognition, good credit standing . . . a cheap office', as well as providing one salary-free member of staff from his own business (his daughter, now the entrepreneur's wife).

Interestingly, however, kin had played a highly significant start-up role for the 'Family Jugglers' group of sample entrepreneurs, providing entrepreneurial stimulus, finance, advice and other resources. As an example of the type of help offered to the jugglers, let us tell the story of another respondent, Adam. Adam's father-in-law had enjoyed a career as one of the country's top businessmen, and remained exceptionally influential and well connected in the commercial world. It is hard to imagine a more appropriate and high-quality tie for a new, young entrepreneur. Adam told us how his father-in-law conceived the original business idea, provided technical expertise and access to a network of contacts and had acted as a 'business sage': 'Father-in-law was saying, "why don't you start your own business", which was a bloody stupid idea! I had no money, no assets, nothing . . . He convinced me you don't need money . . . and away we went.'

As a contrasting case, Kathy's husband had lent her money to start her business, and her father had guaranteed a bank loan. Both husband and father provided advice and support during these early days. Mary's husband had been a key initiator of her business, bought her a computer and trained her in the basic skills needed to produce marketing materials. He had also introduced her to several of her early clients. Stuart's parents had acted as important sources of support and some finance. Stuart also emphasized how important it had been for him to know that they were happy with and proud of his move into entrepreneurship.

Assistance from relatives at the start-up point is perhaps understandable. When the business has no track record, it is difficult for the entrepreneur to leverage resources and information from the marketplace. Family, however, already trust each other and usually have a desire to see each other succeed. Assistance in the very early stages of the new firm's life was thus especially important to the entrepreneurs in both the 'Family In' and 'Jugglers' groups.

Continuing support

Although family help was especially important at the start-up stage, in later years family members outside the business continued to act as key network contacts and provided a range of assistance to entrepreneurs. For the 'Family In' group, this is not surprising, as kin continued to be formally involved with the firm as employees and investors. In some cases, additional family members took on informal roles, or moved between formality and informality. For example, retired parents continued to provide hands-on assistance, helping with day-to-day business tasks in pressing times.

The 'Family Jugglers' also continued to make extensive use of their relatives, in the provision of professional advice, as links to other people, and as sounding boards for entrepreneurs to bounce ideas off. The nature of their support has developed and changed, in line with the dynamics of the entrepreneur's needs, so that Adam's father-in-law is now helping him by 'talking in more detail, ins and outs, balance sheet details . . . the conversation has moved'. Similarly, Kathy told us that since her business is now so much larger than her father's had been, she uses him for more general, less specific advice. More important for her now is the specialist advice provided by her sister, 'an extremely high-flying HR senior consultant'. Her husband also acts as a 'good sounding board . . . this can provide you with the reassurance about whether your ideas are reasonable'.

The benefits of external family support

Our respondents ascribed several key benefits to the support provided by family members outwith the formal borders of the firm. The most important of these were: the high quality of the help provided; the heterogeneity of resources and viewpoints made available; the rapidity of the service provided and its low or non-existent cost. Much of the assistance provided by external family members was explicitly and spontaneously praised by our respondents for its quality: 'Well it's easy really, my brother-in-law is an accountant, so I get the best advice for my business' (William). Kathy's HR consultant sister 'knows her stuff inside-out and upside-down'.

Network theory suggests that a danger of strong ties is the likelihood of homogeneity, which in turn dilutes the richness of information and other resources available to the entrepreneur. Conversely, we found many instances where respondents valued the heterogeneity of family ties. The family members filled an additional role of offering diverse ways of viewing issues, or access to technical, organizational or interpersonal skills that the entrepreneurs lacked. Kathy explained about her husband: 'He comes from a completely different angle – he's an engineer, and as you know, engineers think in a completely different way from normal people'. Graeme, talking about his wife's impact on the business, said: 'A woman's view on the sort of stuff we do is tremendous; in fact, it's made me . . . I describe myself as a recovering engineer . . . if I go back there I'll start thinking like that again'.

The rapidity of family response to the entrepreneur's needs is also mentioned frequently as a benefit by our sample, who often said, 'I just have to pick up the phone'. Similarly, the fact that these services were not only made available quickly, but at virtually no cost, was seen as a major benefit by several respondents: 'it's also cheaper talking to her about legalities and so on' (Kathy).

Hazards of family involvement

In our interviews, just two examples of family conflict were raised, both of these in the 'Family In' group. Stuart's relationship with his parents-in-law, who had done so much to help start the business, have deteriorated to the point where very serious arguments have taken place. William had extreme difficulties managing a family employee, and had to rely on an external (non-family) adviser to resolve the situation. None of the 'Family Jugglers' group reported any conflict with their relatives related to their business. Interestingly, the reasons that the two 'Family Out' respondents gave for maintaining the boundaries between work and home/family were derived from the desire to avoid typical family-firm conflicts. Barry had refused to allow his son to join his business, because he did not want any nepotism in the firm and because he thought it would damage his son's development. Tony explicitly referred to the high failure rate of second-generation firms as his reason for not involving his offspring in the business.

DISCUSSION OF FINDINGS

Our first research question asked: what is the extent of informal family support for entrepreneurs, as members of their strong-tie network? The quantitative survey findings indicate strongly that family outside the boundaries of the firm are indeed very important for entrepreneurs. A quarter of the most important network contacts in our survey were kin, and the majority of them worked outside the family's company. The qualitative stage of our research revealed that these external family ties were especially important for the 'Family Jugglers' group, the 'missing middle' in entrepreneurship and family business research.

How do kin-based strong-tie network contacts differ from non-kin contacts? While family involvement is indeed of special importance at the start-up stage, family members who do not work for the family firm also continue to provide a wide range of help and assistance to entrepreneurs in later years.

What is the nature of support provided by family strong-tie network contacts outside the boundaries of the family firm? Their help was typically instrumental and functional in nature, very similar to that of business ties.

What is the quality of this support provision? Entrepreneurs placed special value on the high quality of the help provided by kin; the heterogeneity of resources and viewpoints; the rapidity of the service provided and its low or non-existent cost. No conflicts were revealed by the 'Family Jugglers' group of respondents, although some had indeed occurred within the boundaries of traditional family firms. Their avoidance was why some entrepreneurs had self-selected the 'Family Out' grouping.

What are the implications of these findings? For those advising entrepreneurs in traditional family firms, our findings indicate that many of the hazards associated with this type of organization can be mitigated by the adoption of more fluid boundaries between family and business. There are also many benefits for the family firm in promoting the development of a strong network of family members outside its boundaries. Similarly, 'Family Out' entrepreneurs may find the middle path to their benefit, since it permits family involvement in their firm without risking the hazards they so fear. The quality and reliability of kin-based virtual organizations, as well as their cost implications, have much to offer family and non-family entrepreneurs alike. Indeed, the very high quality, rapidity and flexibility of the resource provision offered by these especially strong ties make them a highly strategic asset for the entrepreneurial firm. Furthermore, and in contrast to the predictions of the literature, these family strong-tie contacts were found to be helpfully heterogeneous from their entrepreneurial relatives, so that the anticipated liabilities of extreme homophily did not prevail.

For entrepreneurship scholars, the study highlights the importance of the recent move towards taking family issues seriously. The study also indicates that the neglected middle ground between entrepreneurship and family business research is worth considerable further investigation. Our exploratory work provides the basis for other scholars to develop testable hypotheses on the interrelationship between non-employee family members and the entrepreneurial firm using quantitative surveys. However, in order to fully appreciate the dynamic nature of these processes, longitudinal studies are likely to be of special value, especially those adopting qualitative techniques that permit privileged access to these complex phenomena.

CONCLUSIONS

Family members outside the (family) firm offer a range of very important resources to entrepreneurs, which are both professional and affective in nature. They offer many benefits of the benefits of the traditional family firm, while not incurring their hazards.

Extending Astrachan and Shanker's bull's-eye model to encompass the full range of potential family–business interrelationships provided a strong conceptual basis for this study. It also highlighted how fertile the no-man's land is between entrepreneurship and family business scholarship, drawing attention to a significant research agenda for both disciplines.

This study has demonstrated that, in the interstices between the traditional interests of entrepreneurship and family business, there is indeed a 'missing middle' that merits analysis. Our extension of the bull's-eye model to cover all family–enterprise relationships, from the most intense to the loosest, is hence provided some initial validation. Additionally, we have shone some light on the nature of family–enterprise interactions, using network approaches, for the hitherto 'missing middle' group. Clearly, this is an area that merits further substantial research.

NOTES

* This chapter was previously published as an article in the *Family Business Review*, June 2005, **18**(2), 135–54. The authors would like to acknowledge the Editor of the *Family Business Review*, Professor Pramodita Sharma, and thank her for her kindness and support throughout the process of its production. Special thanks are also due to Sue Birley, for trusting us with the networks survey, and to the most valuable comments made by two anonymous referees and the editor of the *Family Business Review*.

1. These articles also provide a more detailed review of family-firm definitions than space permits here.
2. See Drakopoulou Dodd and Patra (2002) for a summary of these international studies, and the methodology section for a full set of references. Drakopoulou Dodd et al. (2002) provide a detailed overview of the comparison between this Scottish sample and their international counterparts.

REFERENCES

Aldrich, H. and Cliff, J. (2003), 'The pervasive effects of family on entrepreneurship: toward a family embeddedness perspective', *Journal of Business Venturing*, September, 573–96.

Aldrich, H. and Sakano, T. (1995), 'Unbroken ties: how the personal networks of Japanese business owners compare to those in other nations', in M. Fruin (ed.), *Networks and Markets: Pacific Rim Investigations*, New York: Oxford University Press, pp. 17–45.

Aldrich, H., Reese, P.R., Dubini, P., Rosen, B. and Woodward, B. (1989), 'Women on the verge of a breakthrough: networking between entrepreneurs in the United States and Italy', *Entrepreneurship and Regional Development*, **1**, 339–56.

Alexander, M. (1997), 'Getting to grips with the virtual organization', *Long Range Planning*, **31**(1), 122–4.

Astrachan, J. and Shanker, M. (2003), 'Family businesses' contribution to the U.S. economy: a closer look', *Family Business Review*, **XVI**(3), 211–19.

Astrachan, J., Klein, S. and Smyrnios, K. (2002), 'The F-PEC scale of family

influence: a proposal for solving the family business definition problem', *Family Business Review*, **XV**(1), 45–58.
Baines, S. and Wheelock, J. (1998), 'Working for each other: gender, the household and micro-business survival and growth', *International Small Business Journal*, **17**(1), 16–31.
Barnatt, C. (1997), 'Virtual organisation in the small business sector: the case of Cavendish Management Resources', *International Small Business Journal*, **15**(4), 36–48.
Barnir, A. and Smith, K. (2002), 'Interfirm alliances in the small business: the role of social networks', *Journal of Small Business Management*, **40**(3), 219–32.
Birley, S., Cromie, S. and Myers, A. (1991), 'Entrepreneurial networks: their emergence in Ireland and overseas', *International Small Business Journal*, **9**(4), 56–74.
Birley, S., Ng, D. and Godrey, A. (1999), 'The family and the business', *Long Range Planning*, **32**(6), 598–608.
Burt, R.S. (1992), *Structural Holes*, Cambridge, MA: Harvard University Press.
Burt, R.S. and Minor, M.J. (1983), *Applied Network Analysis: A Methodological Introduction*, Beverly Hills, CA: Sage Publications.
Burt, R. and Ronchi, D. (1994), 'Measuring a large network quickly', *Social Networks*, **16**(2), 91–135.
Carsrud, A.L. (1994), 'Meanderings of a resurrected psychologist or lessons learned in creating a program', *Entrepreneurship Theory and Practice*, **19**(1), 39–48.
Chell, E. and Haworth, J.M. (1992), 'The development of a research paradigm for the investigation of entrepreneurship: some methodological issues', UIC/AMA Research Symposium on Marketing and Entrepreneurship, INSEAD, France.
De Koning, Alice J. (1999), 'Opportunity formation from a socio-cognitive perspective', paper presented at the Babson College/Kauffman Foundation Entrepreneurship Research Conference, Columbia, SC, May.
Drakopoulou Dodd, S. and Patra, E. (2002), 'National differences in entrepreneurial networking', *Entrepreneurship and Regional Development*, **14**, 117–34.
Drakopoulou Dodd, S., Jack, S. and Anderson, A.R. (2002), 'Scottish entrepreneurial networks in the international context', *International Small Business Journal*, **20**(2), 213–19.
Dyer, W.G. and Handler, W. (1994), 'Entrepreneurship and family business: exploring the connections', *Entrepreneurship Theory and Practice*, **19**(1), 71–84.
Easterby-Smith, M., Thorpe, R. and Lowe, A. (1999), *Management Research: An Introduction*, London: Sage Publications.
Fox, M., Nilakant, V. and Hamilton, R.T. (1996), 'Managing succession in family-owned businesses', *International Small Business Journal*, **15**(1), 15–26.
Geertz, C.A. (1973), *The Interpretation of Culture*, New York: Basic Books.
Glaser, B.G. and Strauss, A.L. (1967), *The Discovery of Grounded Theory: Strategies for Qualitative Research*, New York: Aldine.
Granovetter, M. (1973), 'The strength of weak ties', *American Journal of Sociology*, **78**(6), 1360–80.
Greve, A. and Salaff, J. (2003), 'Social networks and entrepreneurship', *Entrepreneurship: Theory & Practice*, **28**(1), 1–23.
Gummesson, E. (2000), *Qualitative Methods in Management Research*, Thousand Oaks, CA: Sage.
Handler, W.C. (1989), 'Methodological issues and considerations in studying family businesses', *Family Business Review*, **4**(2), 257–76.

Handy, C. (1995), 'Trust and the virtual organization', *Harvard Business Review*, **73**(3), 40–50.

Hill, J., McGowan, P. and Drummond, P. (1999), 'The development and application of a qualitative approach to researching the marketing networks of small firm entrepreneurs', *Qualitative Market Research*, **2**(2), 71–81.

Hills, G.E., Lumpkin, G.T. and Singh, R.P. (1997), 'Opportunity recognition: perceptions and behaviours of entrepreneurs', in *Frontiers of Entrepreneurship Research*, Wellesley, MA: Babson College, pp. 203–18.

Hoang, H. and Antoncic, B. (2003), 'Network-based research in entrepreneurship: a critical review', *Journal of Business Venturing*, **18**(2), 165–87.

Human, S. and Provan, K. (1996), 'External resource exchange and perceptions of competitiveness within organizational networks: an organizational learning perspective', in *Frontiers of Entrepreneurship Research*, Wellesley, MA: Babson College, pp. 240–67.

James, H.S. (1999), 'Owner as manager, extended horizons and the family firm', *International Journal of the Economics of Business*, **6**(1), 41–53.

Johannisson, B. (1986), 'Network strategies: management technology for entrepreneurship and change', *International Small Business Journal*, **5**(1), 19–30.

Johannisson, B. and Monsted, M. (1997), 'Contextualizing entrepreneurial networking', *International Journal of Management and organization*, **27**(3), 109–37.

Johannisson, B. and Nilsson, A. (1989), 'Community entrepreneurs: networking for local development', *Entrepreneurship and Regional Development*, **1**(1), 3–19.

Knoke, D. and Kuklinksi, J.H. (1982), 'Network analysis', Sage University Papers No. 28, Newbury Park, CA.

Larsen, K.T.R. and McInerney, C.R. (2002), 'Preparing to work in the virtual organisation', *Information Management*, **39**, 445–56.

Larson, A. (1992), 'Network dyads in entrepreneurial settings: a study of the governance of exchange relationships', *Administrative Science Quarterly*, **37**(1), 76–104.

Lechner, C. and Dowling, M. (2003), 'Firm networks: external relationships as sources for the growth and competitiveness of entrepreneurial firms', *Entrepreneurship and Regional Development*, **15**, 1–26.

Litz, R.A. (1995), 'The family business: towards definitional clarity', *Family Business Review*, **VIII**(1), 71–81.

Miles, M.B. and Huberman, A.M. (1994), *Qualitative Data Analysis*, London: Sage Publications.

Miller, E.J. and Rice, A.K. (1967), *Systems of Organizations*, London: Tavistock.

Neuman, W.L. (1991), *Social Research Methods*, London: Allyn & Bacon.

Nonaka, I. and Takeuchi, H. (1995), *The Knowledge-Creating Company: How Japanese Companies Create the Dynamics of Innovation*, New York: Oxford University Press.

Ostgaard, T.A. and Birley, S. (1994), 'New venture growth and personal networks', *Journal of Business Research*, **36**, 37–50.

Ram, M. (2001), 'Family dynamics in a small consultancy firm: a case study', *Human Relations*, **54**(4), 395–418.

Reynolds, P., Bygrave, W., Autio, E. et al. (2004), *GEM 2003 Global Report*, Kansas City, MO: Kauffman Foundation.

Rosa, P., Hamilton, D., Carter, S. and Burns, H. (1994), 'The impact of gender on small business management: preliminary findings of a British study', *International Small Business Journal*, **12**(3), 25–32.

Saunders, M., Lewis, P. and Thornhill, A. (1997), *Research Methods for Business Students*, London: Pitman.
Singh, R., Hills, G.E., Hybels, R.C. and Lumpkin, G.T. (1999), 'Opportunity recognition through social network characteristics of entrepreneurs', in *Frontiers of Entrepreneurship Research*, Wellesley, MA: Babson College, pp. 168–82.
Staber, U. and Aldrich, H. (1995), 'Cross-national similarities in the personal networks of small business owners: a comparison of two regions in North America', *Canadian Journal of Sociology*, **20**(4), 441–65.
Stewart, J. (2003), 'Help one another, use one another: toward an anthropology of family business', *Entrepreneurship Theory and Practice*, Summer, 383–96.
Suitor, J.J., Wellman, B. and Morgan, D.L. (1997), 'It's about time: how, when and why networks change', *Social Networks*, **19**(1), 1–17.
Szarka, J. (1990), 'Networking and small firms', *International Small Business Journal*, **8**, 10–22.
Upton, N. and Petty, W. (2000), 'Venture capital investment and US family business', *Venture Capital*, **2**(1), 27–39.
Uzzi, B. (1996), 'The sources and consequences of embeddedness for the economic performance of organizations: the network effect', *American Sociological Review*, **61**, 674–98.
Uzzi, B. (1997), 'Social structure and competition in interfirm networks', *Administrative Science Quarterly*, **42**(1), 37–70.
Westhead, P. and Cowling, M. (1998), 'Family firm research: the need for a methodological rethink', *Entrepreneurship Theory and Practice*, **32**(1), 31–54.
Zeleny, M. (2001), 'Autopoiesis (self-production) in SME networks', *Human Systems Management*, **20**, 201–7.

10. Social network structures of nascent entrepreneurs: an exploratory study of advisor networks in MENA countries

Sarfraz A. Mian and Shahid Qureshi

INTRODUCTION

It is now widely recognized that entrepreneurs increasingly embed their business decisions in social networks around them (Reynolds, 1991; Starr and Macmillan, 1990). The network approach to studying how nascent entrepreneurs use these networks to shape their entrepreneurial intentions (Klyver and Schott, 2011) and get advice and resources to launch a business is gaining scholarly attention (Reynolds, 2011; Granovetter, 1992; Jenssen and Koenig, 2002). However, the limited extant literature on this subject implies that entrepreneurs in diverse cultural settings access their social relations in somewhat similar ways to get these resources (Wellman, 1999). We also note that establishing a business requires different contacts and resources in different phases of the dynamic business development process.

To understand these concepts in detail, this research investigates the use of social networks in the new venture creation process starting from the opportunity recognition, startup and growth stages of the business. The comparison of various entrepreneurial characteristics during various entrepreneurial stages will decipher the way entrepreneurs use their networks during opportunity recognition and resource acquisition. The objective of this research is to investigate the common features that distinguish the entrepreneur's advisory networks in different countries of the MENA (Middle East and North Africa) region having diverse cultural and economic backgrounds. This research work is focused on filling the gap in networking literature with regard to how entrepreneurs leverage various types of advisory networks to start and grow a business in the MENA region.

Data for this research were obtained from the Global Entrepreneurship Monitor (GEM) project carried out during the period 2009–11. The GEM project is carried out on a yearly basis to measure various entrepreneurial indicators such as entrepreneurial activity, aspirations and attitudes of individuals in countries all over the world. The representative sample in each country for the GEM research is obtained from adults in the age bracket 18–64. The participants in the survey are interviewed using a detailed questionnaire. The networks-related data are obtained through 20 sub-elements with binary responses. These sub-elements are then further used to form five scales labeled private, work, professional, market and international advisory networks (Schott, 2013).

The primary purpose of this chapter is to examine the relationship between typical patterns of advisor networks used by fledgling entrepreneurs and their country of origin. The construction of advisor networks is an important component of the complex dynamic process of planning, starting and operating a new business. While the construct of entrepreneurial networks has yet to be clearly defined and universally accepted (Mian and Hattab, 2013), the search for a small set of homogeneous clusters of individuals and the varying multi-country profiles appear to be a promising contribution to our understanding of such network types and shapes. This study is an important exploratory step in understanding the function of advisor networks in international entrepreneurship.

LITERATURE REVIEW

Earlier research states that entrepreneurship is socially embedded and that networks play an important role in promoting entrepreneurship (Borch, 1994; Starr and Macmillan, 1990). The networks enable firms to access knowledge, skills and other resources (Kogut and Zander, 1992; Looman and Farrag, 2009) and allow them to look for new perspectives on problems and enhance their learning through new combinations of knowledge (Kogut and Zander, 1992). The networking literature suggests that successful business owners have a special networking behavior that helps them in resource acquisition and mobilization in creative and resource parsimonious ways needed to start and grow the business. Johannisson (2000) posits three ways that describe the relationship ties within networks: informational, exchange and influence. Informational ties provide business information, exchange ties provide access to resources, and influence-related ties legitimize the business owner's activities and create barriers to entry for competitors. The assets thus created through social interaction can be leveraged to gain and maintain a competitive advantage. The networks are instrumental in gaining access to information, knowledge, advice and resources that expedite the entrepreneurial activities (Toledano et al., 2010; Hoang and Antoncic, 2003). One of the most important functions of these networks is support for opportunity recognition and refinement (Khakbaz and Aghazadeh, 2012). The networks also help build legitimacy, credibility, skill development and enhancement, and provide access to finance (Klyver et al., 2008).

Another dimension of networks is gaining trust and strength. Trust is proven to be a key element in their success and effectiveness (Toledano et al., 2010). Huff and Kelley (2003) have investigated the role of trust and how it differs among nations. Harris and Dibben (1999) report a significant difference in managers' propensity to trust partners and other collaborators between US and Asian countries. Toledano et al. (2010) investigated family businesses in Spain and conclude that trust is a basic requirement for networking leading to entrepreneurial activities. Networks based on trust thus lead to better and more cooperative relationships within and outside the firm. Family networks play a major role in opportunity identification and persuasion, as in some societies these networks are stronger than in others (Chrisman et al., 2002). Toledano et al. (2010) posit that ventures develop and crystallize out of personal networks, which continue to play a significant role in the growth of these ventures. GEM-based studies have shown that having an entrepreneur in the family enhances the probability of initiating an entrepreneurial activity (Klyver et al., 2008).

Firms need creative ideas and knowledge to enhance innovation capabilities (Bell and Pavitt, 1997). These creative ideas and knowledge in many cases lie outside the firm. Brown and Duguid (1991) posit that innovation and search for knowledge constitute an interactive process between different people embedded in networks that can draw on their diverse expertise, and embeddedness within networks has significant positive effects on innovation performance. Tiessen (1997) posits that entrepreneurship consists of two major functions, that is, innovation and resource leverage, which in turn benefit from different cultural orientations. The individualism dimension of cultural orientation enhances innovation generation in contrast to collectivism, which is pivotal for resource leverage. These two cultural phenomena are based on values that lead to different network behaviors in different countries. Dodd (2002) reports that Greek entrepreneurs belonging to a collectivist culture use strong-tie networks based on family and friends rather than business contacts. In contrast, US entrepreneurs use more business contacts within their networks (Birley et al., 1991). Similar findings are reported by Zali et al. (2012), positing that entrepreneurs in collectivist cultures use the family and friends network, whereas those in individualistic cultures use business and job networks. Zali et al. (2013) further posit that network effects on innovation are mediated by culture as expressed in social norms.

FakhrElDin et al. (2013) report differences in entrepreneurial behavior between different cultures, and find that national culture motivates certain behaviors and attitudes through values and beliefs that are idiosyncratic to a society (Hayton et al., 2002). Cultural values lead to entrepreneurial forms that are unique to a society's history and values (Russell, 1997). Two positions on networking have been taken in the literature. One is that social networking is generic and universal, independent of culture and industry (Klyver et al., 2008). In contrast, the other position is that social networking is context dependent; that is, networking differs a great deal and depends on the culture and the industry in which the entrepreneur operates. Klyver and Foley (2012) investigated three case studies on three diverse cultural groups to understand how culture influences entrepreneurial networks. It was reported that the networking of entrepreneurs is neither uniform nor universal, and there is a difference in networking in minority and dominant cultures. The study further explains that culture defines the norms and rules of the society and can limit the people with whom a person can interact. If someone interacts in contravention of the norms and rules, they will be or at least feel that they are being expelled from their culture. And therefore the need for social acceptance moderates the way entrepreneurial networking is carried out (Klyver and Foley, 2012).

Wilken (1979) was the first to state that there are three phases in the establishment of enterprises: innovation, planning and establishment. Entrepreneurs explore the possibility of starting their own businesses on a low level with close contacts. If they expand their network at the very beginning, it will be harder for them to withdraw from a losing course of action (Birley, 1986). The second phase is the starting phase. As the entrepreneurs get ready for the new venture they need to acquire information, new skills and resources, and thus must mobilize a larger social network. They generally contact a large number of people to find the relevant ones. The third phase is the operating phase. Entrepreneurs concentrate their network on key persons who are valuable and helpful in providing access to resources and information (Hansen, 1995).

ENTREPRENEURIAL NETWORK COMPOSITION IN MENA COUNTRIES

The GEM study incorporated 20 different advisors surrounding entrepreneurs to understand the composition of entrepreneurial networks. These different advisors have been regrouped into five separate categories: private, work, professional, market and international (Schott, 2013). In addition to the composition of the advisors' network, the GEM study also investigated the phases of the entrepreneurial process: prospective, startup and operating. The entrepreneurs are thus divided into the above-mentioned three categories: future startups, startups and owners of established businesses. GEM data on the adult population survey from 2009 to 2011 is used in this research. Around 44 334 respondents participated in the survey in the respective countries, out of whom 13 212 respondents selected themselves as entrepreneurs in one of the three entrepreneurial phases.

Table 10.1 describes the percentage of entrepreneurs who use different types of advisory networks in the MENA region countries. The majority of the entrepreneurs (85 percent) in the MENA region get advice from a private network, followed by their workplace network (49 percent). The private and workplace networks are therefore valued more in the MENA

Table 10.1 Entrepreneurs' network composition in the MENA region

Network type	Usage (%)	Sub-categories	Usage* (%)
Private	85	Partners	60
		Family or relatives	59
		Friends	58
		Spouse or life partner	44
Workplace	49	Current work colleagues	32
		Somebody with much business experience	32
		Somebody who is starting a business	23
		Current boss	13
Market	26	Customer	20
		Supplier	13
		Firm That You Collaborate With	12
		Firm That You Compete With	7
Professional	22	Researcher or inventor	80
		Bank	80
		Lawyer	80
		Possible investor	11
		Accountant	11
International	15	Somebody in another country	11
		Somebody who has come from abroad	10

Note: * There is an overlap among the overall and sub-category percentages.

Source: GEM data.

region. Table 10.1 also gives details of the various components of the advisory network groups. Parents, family and friends are the important parts of the private network. Current colleagues and people with business knowhow are the major components of the workplace network.

The following sub-sections break down the five environments into their components to provide an accurate means to compare and contrast the diverse countries that make up this data analysis.

Private Network

Danis et al. (2011) have investigated the impact of close social networks and their importance in developing countries as opposed to developed countries. They report that such networks are more important in developing countries due to weak and insufficient institutional frameworks to promote entrepreneurship in these countries. Smith and Lohrke (2008) highlight the importance of trust in networks and further posit that trust is built over time through repeated actions. According to Hoang and Antoncic (2003), social networks are important for entrepreneurs as they provide not only tangible but also intangible benefits in the form of emotional support, which is needed in the startup phase. Klyver et al. (2008) posit that entrepreneurial ventures run by entrepreneurs from family businesses have a low probability of failure. Entrepreneurs from countries such as Yemen, Palestine, Saudi Arabia, Egypt, Algeria and Pakistan consult their life partners and parents the most, as compared to the other MENA countries. The Palestinians and the Saudis score high in terms of consulting their relatives and family members. Algerians and Saudi Arabians score highest in contacting friends. This dependence on the private network in the form of spouse, family and friends indicates that there is a great deal of financial and emotional support from these networks.

Workplace Network

Workplace networks are reported to be important as they provide access to talent, information and other intangible resources (Hoang and Antoncic, 2003). Information and services are provided through informal channels (Witt, 2004). Syria, UAE (United Arab Emirates), Saudi Arabia, Egypt and Algeria are the highest utilizers of the advisor network based on current work colleagues, bosses, someone starting a business and someone with business experience. Tunisia and Lebanon are relatively very low in utilization of these advisory networks. The data reveal that work-environment-based advisory networks are less consulted as compared to the family-based advisory network. This point is supported by the fact that trust is the main attribute responsible for the use of these types of advisory networks.

Professional Network

The entrepreneur's professional network consists of people who are researchers, investors and professionals such as bankers, lawyer and accountants. These professionals are much less frequently consulted as they charge fees for their advice. Hoang and Antoncic (2003) posit that these people possess talent and key information regarding business and financing in the various stages of the business. Zali et al. (2012) report that these actors provide valuable information not available in other forms of networks. However, in many developing nations the infrastructure supporting entrepreneurs' professional networks is available to a lesser degree (Danis et al., 2011).

UAE turns out to be the largest user of professional advisors' networks. It is the only country in the MENA region considered as having an innovation-driven economy. Tunisia, Jordan and Lebanon are very small users of this resource. The above-mentioned facts highlight the great opportunity for the public sector organizations to increase their profile and build trust to help entrepreneurs in the pre-launch and launch stages to promote entrepreneurship and contribute to the economic development of the country.

Market Network

The market network of an entrepreneur consists of firms that collaborate and compete as suppliers and customers. Many new ideas for innovation in product and service design, placement and promotion come from the market network. UAE and Saudi Arabia are the largest users of this network. Tunisia and Jordan use this resource least. This explains the low utilization rate of the market-based advisory network.

International Network

The international network consists of someone who is in another country or who has come from abroad. This network helps develop the international orientation of the entrepreneur and supports him/her in opportunity recognition and finding customers. International networks help in the marketing and growth of the firm (Coviello and Munro, 1995). UAE, Syria, Saudi Arabia and Algeria are high in utilizing their international networks. Iran and Tunisia are reported to use this resource the least.

METHODS AND ANALYSIS

We applied an individual differences (weighted) Euclidean distance model using a multidimensional scaling procedure to determine dimensionality and relationships between 20 potential member types of entrepreneurs' advisory networks, based on GEM data of the population (aged 18–64) of 10 247 entrepreneurs who responded to the GEM survey in 14 MENA nations and Denmark. We then examined the configuration of the entrepreneurs' countries in the space defined by the GEM variables in order to understand differences between the advisor networks of entrepreneurs who live in different countries.

We decided to analyze the country-level networks of starting and operating entrepreneurs separately, as there is evidence that the networks differ by phase at the individual level. We did not include prospective entrepreneurs in the study, since the data for these individuals were unavailable for a number of countries. The first step in the analyses was to aggregate the individual-level binary network data to country-level data. During the collection of the GEM data, respondents were presented with a list of 20 potential advisors and were asked: 'Various people may give you advice on your new business. Have you received advice from any of the following?' They responded 'yes' or 'no' to each of the items. To aggregate these data, we calculated the percentage of respondents in each of the 15 countries in the GEM sample who received advice from each potential advisor. We built two country-level aggregated data sets – one for starting entrepreneurs and the other for operating entrepreneurs.

We subjected each data set to a hierarchical cluster analysis to identify maximally homogeneous groups of countries on the basis of their advisor characteristics. While the percentages allow a country-by-country comparison of the convergences and divergences between the advisors, cluster analysis produces structurally similar groups of countries and allows a more refined probe into country entrepreneurial profiles. The exploratory nature of this study and the absence of predefined clusters and the small country sample size (n = 15) made hierarchical cluster analysis an appropriate analytic procedure. We submitted the advisor percentages to Ward's (hierarchical) algorithm (SPSS, 2009), which produces clusters whose centroids differ maximally based on minimum within-cluster variance. We then standardized the percentages (z-scores) so that their variances are similar and they contributed equally to cluster formation. The Ward's hierarchical algorithm begins by treating each observation as a separate cluster and all variance is between-group variance. The algorithm then joins the two most similar observations into one cluster, thus reducing the number of clusters by one in each step until all the observations are contained in a

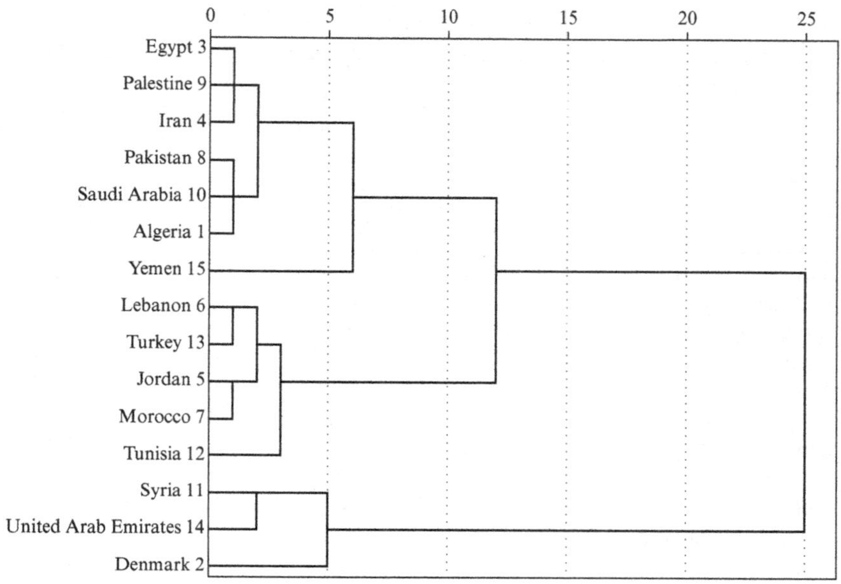

Figure 10.1 Hierarchical cluster analysis of the network characteristics of entrepreneurs in the startup phase

single cluster and all variance is within-group variance. Once the clusters were identified, we examined the characteristic profiles of the advisors to describe their similarities and differences. Then we examined the mean scores on the GEM framework variables to establish the links between the clusters and the country cultural and economic characteristics.

Starting Entrepreneurs

We began by conducting a hierarchical cluster analysis of the network characteristics in the 15 countries in the sample. An examination of Figure 10.1 suggests that there were three clusters of countries with similar startup networks. Little would be accomplished by increasing the number of clusters, since it would result in removing a single country from a cluster.

The clusters were labeled as follows:

- Factor economy driven: Algeria, Egypt, Iran, Pakistan, Palestine, Saudi Arabia and Yemen.
- Efficiency economy driven: Jordan, Lebanon, Morocco, Tunisia and Turkey.
- Innovation economy driven: Denmark, Syria and UAE.

Table 10.2 Network profiles of startups along country clusters

Networking with (%)	Ward method			
	Factor economy driven	Innovation economy driven	Efficiency economy driven	Total
	Mean	Mean	Mean	Mean
spouse or life-partner	52.4	41.6	31.4	43.2
parents	67.9	48.5	48.5	57.5
other family or relatives	66.2	47.9	48.2	56.5
friends	66.2	71.0	53.3	62.9
current work colleagues	38.4	45.9	22.8	34.7
a current boss	19.2	21.1	8.4	16.0
somebody who is starting a business	25.6	41.6	19.4	26.7
somebody with much business experience	38.0	66.3	25.8	39.6
a researcher or inventor	8.0	15.8	6.1	8.9
a possible investor	13.8	26.7	8.1	14.5
a bank	6.8	14.6	5.2	7.8
a lawyer	8.0	20.8	6.2	10.0
an accountant	11.2	30.0	7.5	13.7
a public advisory service for business	12.5	9.6	4.2	9.2
a firm that you collaborate with	13.4	28.7	6.1	14.0
a firm that you compete with	8.9	15.7	2.5	8.1
a supplier	16.9	30.6	6.1	16.1
a customer	26.9	44.2	15.6	26.6
somebody in another country	15.1	35.1	9.1	17.1
somebody who has come from abroad	12.5	26.1	12.4	15.2

An examination of the mean percentage of startup entrepreneurs from each cluster using each advisor (Table 10.2) suggests that those from factor-economy-driven countries tend to rely on family advisors more than other countries. Entrepreneurs from innovation-economy-driven countries, while still consulting with family advisors, are far more likely than startups from other countries to use advisors from the workplace, professional, market and even international environments. Finally, startup entrepreneurs from efficiency-economy-driven countries tended to use fewer advisors, of all types, than those from other countries. It would have been desirable to be able to use tests of statistical significance to guide the analysis, but the small sample size (n = 15) made that option problematic.

We examined the mean cultural and economic values for each cluster of countries to validate them (Table 10.2). Again, the samples size (n = 15) was too small to justify tests of statistical significance. The most striking differentiating variable was the level of trust prevailing in the country. Innovation-economy-driven countries had the highest level, efficiency-economy-driven the lowest, and factor-economy-driven countries came between them. This link between the characteristic profile of a country's network for startup entrepreneurs and the level of trust as assessed by experts in an independent sample provides evidence that clusters do not exist in isolation.

The innovation- and efficiency-driven economies are high in terms of entrepreneurship support policies, programs, entrepreneurship education, technology transfer and commercial and physical infrastructure. They are also high in terms of individualism, opportunities and esteem of the entrepreneurial vocation. The innovation-based economies are highest in terms of entrepreneurial skills in the population, policies towards growth and receptiveness towards innovation.

Operating Entrepreneurs

Since there was reason to believe that entrepreneurial phases influence the nature of advisor networks on the individual, we replicated the previous analysis on entrepreneurs who were in the operating phase, as described in Figure 10.2. Again we identified three clusters of countries with similar patterns of advisor networks. In this case the clusters were very well defined.

The composition of the three clusters of countries was as follows:

- Factor economy driven: Algeria, Egypt, Iran, Pakistan, Palestine and Yemen.
- Innovation economy driven: Denmark, Saudi Arabia, Syria and UAE.
- Efficiency economy driven: Jordan, Lebanon, Morocco, Tunisia and Turkey.

One country shifted its cluster membership. Saudi Arabia moved from the factor-driven-economy cluster in the startup phase to the innovation-driven-economy cluster in the operating phase. When we examined them,

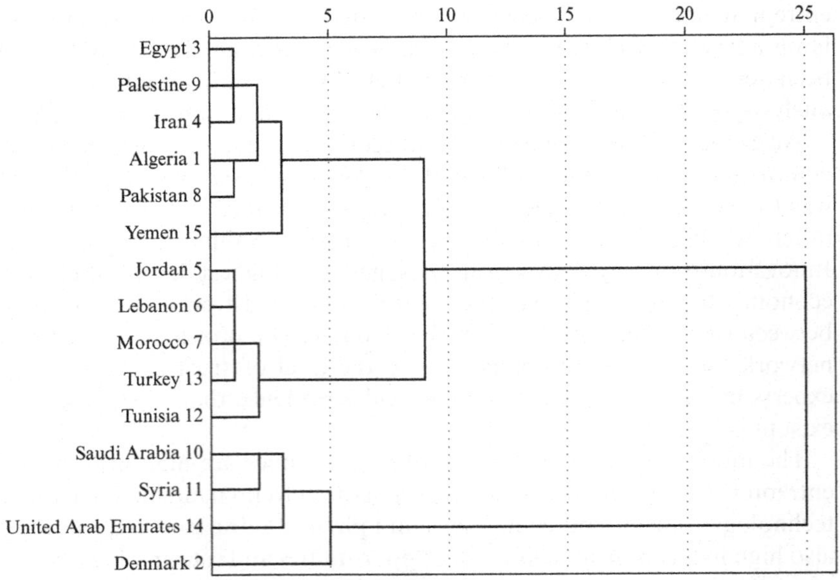

Figure 10.2 Hierarchical cluster analysis of the network characteristics of entrepreneurs in the operating phase

the mean percentages of operating entrepreneurs from each cluster were similar to those of startup entrepreneurs using each advisor at the country level, suggesting that they are quite similar to those of startup entrepreneurs (Table 10.3). Operating entrepreneurs from factor-economy-driven countries still tend to rely on family advisors more than those in other clusters. Operating entrepreneurs from innovation-driven economy countries demonstrate an even more extensive and balanced assemblage of advisors, while operating entrepreneurs from efficiency-driven-economy countries tended to be more isolated than they were as startups.

CONCLUSION AND IMPLICATIONS

While advisor networks are known to be idiosyncratic and primarily dependent on the characteristics of the entrepreneur and the enterprise, we were curious as to whether network profiles differed from country to country and, if so, if the collective profiles could be explained. We were surprised to find that the countries in the three network clusters corresponded to a well-known economic typology: factor-, efficiency- and innovation-driven-economy nations. Homogeneous clusters of countries

Table 10.3 Characteristic economic and cultural profiles of startups

Entrepreneurial framework conditions	Ward method			
	Factor economy driven	Innovation economy driven	Efficiency economy driven	Total
	Mean	Mean	Mean	Mean
Trust prevailing in country	62.3	86.3	34.7	57.9
Financing	2.48	2.75	2.58	2.57
Support policies	2.49	2.81	3.06	2.74
Support programs	2.22	2.68	2.76	2.49
Entrepreneurship education	2.06	2.40	2.27	2.2
Technology transfer	2.19	2.38	2.42	2.31
Commercial legal infrastructure	2.97	3.32	3.13	3.09
Market openness	2.80	2.90	2.83	2.83
Physical infrastructure	3.58	3.81	3.78	3.69
Individualism	2.71	3.03	2.81	2.81
Opportunities	3.32	3.60	3.48	3.43
Entrepreneurial skills in population	2.52	2.83	2.53	2.59
Esteem of the entrepreneurial vocation	3.39	3.60	3.61	3.51
Intellectual property rights	2.15	2.89	2.68	2.47
Proportion of women	2.68	3.35	3.4	3.05
Policies promoting growth	2.72	3.38	3.08	2.97
Receptiveness to innovation	3.19	3.50	3.29	3.29
Human Development Index	0.61	0.75	0.67	0.663
Life expectancy at birth (years)	70.5	77.0	72.8	72.6
Mean years of schooling	6.3	8.1	6.8	6.8
Expected years of schooling	11.4	13.0	12.7	12.2
Gross national income (GNI) per capita	8346	33057	9079	13532
Non-income HDI	0.652	0.761	0.704	0.691
Secular-rationalism	−1.43	−0.34	−1.4	−1.2
Self-expressionism	−0.48	0.08	−0.8	−0.47

provide a more parsimonious design than using large numbers of individual countries in advisor network research.

Country-level advisor networks, while relatively weak constructs, are obviously linked to the framework variables, suggesting that the clusters are valid and are linked to collective economic and cultural variations of nations. As a policy implication, the policy makers in these countries can devise programs and develop institutional frameworks to encourage and train entrepreneurs to move beyond family networks into workplace, market, professional and international networks to grow their businesses.

ACKNOWLEDGMENT

The authors would like to thank IDRC for funding the MENA networking research project, which relies on data collected in the Global Entrepreneurship Monitor (GEM) program. However, sole responsibility for the analysis and interpretation rests with the authors. A preliminary version of this chapter was presented in the 2014 Babson College Entrepreneurship Research Conference, London, Ontario, Canada. The authors gratefully acknowledge the help of Robert Schell in the data analysis.

REFERENCES

Bell, M. and Pavitt, K. (1997). 'Technological accumulation and industrial growth: contrasts between developed and developing countries', *Technology, Globalisation and Economic Performance*, 83–137.

Birley, S. (1986). 'The role of networks in the entrepreneurial process', *Journal of Business Venturing*, **1**(1), 107–17.

Birley, S., Cromie, S. and Myers, A. (1991). 'Entrepreneurial networks: their emergence in Ireland and overseas', *International Small Business Journal*, **9**(4), 56–74.

Borch, O.J. (1994). 'The process of relational contracting: developing trust-based strategic alliances among small business enterprises', *Advances in Strategic Management*, **10**(1), 113–35.

Brown, J.S. and Duguid, P. (1991). 'Organizational learning and communities-of-practice: toward a unified view of working, learning, and innovation', *Organization Science*, **2**(1), 40–57.

Chrisman, J.J., Chua, J.H. and Steier, L.P. (2002). 'The influence of national culture and family involvement on entrepreneurial perceptions and performance at the state level', *Entrepreneurship Theory and Practice*, **26**(4), 113–30.

Coviello, N.E. and Munro, H.J. (1995). 'Growing the entrepreneurial firm: networking for international market development', *European Journal of Marketing*, **29**(7), 49–61.

Danis, W.M., De Clercq, D. and Petricevic, O. (2011). 'Are social networks more

important for new business activity in emerging than developed economies? An empirical extension', *International Business Review*, **20**(4), 394–408.
Dodd, S.P.E. (2002). 'National differences in entrepreneurial networking', *Entrepreneurship and Regional Development*, 117–54.
FakhrElDin, H., Skoko, H. and Cheraghi, M. (2013). 'The effect of national culture on entrepreneurs' networks: a comparison of the MENA region and Denmark', *International Journal of Business and Globalisation*, **11**(4), 353–66.
Granovetter, M. (1992). 'Problems of explanation in economic sociology', *Networks and Organizations: Structure, Form, and Action*, **25**, 1–56.
Hansen, E.L. (1995). 'Entrepreneurial networks and new organization growth', *Entrepreneurship Theory and Practice*, **19**, 7–20.
Harris, S. and Dibben, M. (1999). 'Trust and co-operation in business relationship development: exploring the influence of national values', *Journal of Marketing Management*, **15**(6), 463–83.
Hayton, J., George, G. and Zahra, S. (2002). 'National culture and entrepreneurship: a review of behavioral research', *Entrepreneurship Theory and Practice*, 33–52.
Hoang, H. and Antoncic, B. (2003). 'Network-based research in entrepreneurship: a critical review', *Journal of Business Venturing*, **18**(2), 165–87.
Huff, L. and Kelley, L. (2003). 'Levels of organizational trust in individualist versus collectivist societies: a seven-nation study', *Organization Science*, **14**(1), 81–90.
Jenssen, J.I. and Koenig, H. (2002). 'The effect of social networks on resource access and business start-ups', *European Planning Studies*, **10**(8), 1039–46.
Johannisson, B. (2000). 'Networking and entrepreneurial growth', in D. Sexton and H. Landstrom (eds), *Handbook of Entrepreneurship*, New York: Wiley-Blackwell, pp. 368–86.
Khakbaz, P.P. and Aghazadeh, L. (2012). 'An investigation into the impact of social networks on entrepreneurial opportunities', *Journal of Social & Development Sciences*, **3**(3), 85–8.
Klyver, K. and Foley, D. (2012). 'Networking and culture in entrepreneurship', *Entrepreneurship & Regional Development*, **24**(7–8), 561–88.
Klyver, K. and Schott, T. (2011). 'How social network structure shapes entrepreneurial intentions', *Journal of Global Entrepreneurship Research*, **1**, 3–19.
Klyver, K., Hindle, K. and Meyer, D. (2008). 'Influence of social network structure on entrepreneurship participation – a study of 20 national cultures', *International Entrepreneurship and Management Journal*, **4**(3), 331–47.
Kogut, B. and Zander, U. (1992). 'Knowledge of the firm, combinative capabilities, and the replication of technology', *Organization science*, **3**(3), 383–97.
Looman, W.S. and Farrag, S. (2009). 'Psychometric properties and cross-cultural equivalence of the Arabic Social Capital Scale: instrument development study', *International Journal of Nursing Studies*, **46**(1), 45–54.
Mian, S.A. and Hattab, H.W. (2013). 'How individual competencies shape the entrepreneur's social network structure: evidence from the MENA region', *International Journal of Business and Globalisation*, **11**(4), 399–412.
Reynolds, P.D. (1991). 'Sociology and entrepreneurship: concepts and contributions', *Entreprenurship Theory and Practice*, **16**(2), 47–70.
Reynolds, P.D. (2011). 'Informal and early formal financial support in the business creation process: exploration with PSED II data set', *Journal of Small Business Management*, **49**(1), 27–54.
Russell, R.D. (1997). 'The impact of national culture on the emergence of

entrepreneurship', paper presented at the USASBE Annual National Conference 'Entrepreneurship: The Engine of Global Economic Development', San Francisco, CA.

Schott, T. (2013). 'Components of a network around an actor', in *Encyclopedia of Social Network Analysis and Mining*, Heidelberg: Springer Verlag.

Smith, D.A. and Lohrke, F.T. (2008). 'Entrepreneurial network development: trusting in the process', *Journal of Business Research*, **61**(4), 315–22.

SPSS (2009). PASW Statistics for Windows, Version 18.0, Released 2009, Chicago, IL: SPSS Inc.

Starr, J.A. and Macmillan, I.C. (1990). 'Resource cooptation via social contracting: resource acquisition strategies for new ventures', *Strategic Management Journal*, **11**, 79–92.

Tiessen, J.H. (1997). 'Individualism, collectivism and entrepreneurship: a framework for international comparative research', *Journal of Business Venturing*, **12**, 367–84.

Toledano, N., Urbano, D. and Bernadich, M. (2010). 'Networks and corporate entrepreneurship: a comparative case study on family business in Catalonia', *Journal of Organizational Change Management*, **23**(4), 396–412.

Wellman, B. (1999). *Networks in the Global Village*, Boulder, CO: Westview Press.

Wilken, P.H. (1979). *Entrepreneurship: A Comparative and Historical Study*, Norwood, NJ: Ablex Publishing.

Witt, P. (2004). 'Entrepreneurs' networks and the success of start-ups', *Entrepreneurship & Regional Development*, **16**(5), 391–412.

Zali, M.R., Bastian, B.L. and Qureshi, S. (2013). 'Promoting innovation in the MENA region: the role of social norms and individual factors in entrepreneurial networks', *International Journal of Business and Globalisation*, **11**(4), 413–26.

Zali, M.R., Schott, T., Kordnaeij, A. and Najafian, M. (2012). 'Entrepreneurs' networks affecting innovation: firms in Iran and Denmark', *African Journal of Business Management*, **6**(17), 5737–43.

11. *Ubuntu* in family businesses: a case in the Democratic Republic of the Congo

Albert B.R. Lwango

> There is a word [in South Africa] – *Ubuntu* – a word that captures Mandela's greatest gift: his recognition that we are all bound together in ways that are invisible to the eye; that there is a oneness to humanity; that we achieve ourselves by sharing ourselves with others, and caring for those around us.
>
> President Obama at Memorial Service for Nelson Mandela (2013)

> [However,] *Ubuntu* does not mean that people should not enrich themselves. The question therefore is: are you going to do so in order to enable the community around you to improve?
>
> Nelson Mandela (2006)

INTRODUCTION

Africa has an abundance of entrepreneurs who possess the ability to identify business opportunities and exploit them through their strong social capital; as a consequence the fraction of Africans who are self-employed and run their own firms is much larger than in developed countries (Fafchamps, 2004; Kshetri, 2011). However, African entrepreneurs have simultaneously implicit obligations to help their extended families (Robson and Obeng, 2008; Khavul et al., 2009).

Gupta et al. (2010) noted for this purpose that *ubuntu* is the popular principle of indigenous African business that means 'humanity to others'. In other words, people are what they are because of what all people are; the core elements of *ubuntu* are openness, sharing and welcome (Boon, 1996; Mbigi, 1997; Gupta et al., 2010). Hence *ubuntu* generates not only specific opportunities but also constraints on businesses. Smith (2009, p. 1240) noted for instance that in Africa 'a cousin can ask for a job, money, or other resources and expect to get them'.

Thus, given the importance of the emergence and succession phases in family businesses (Pistrui et al., 2006; Cadieux, 2007), and specifically in Africa, where many family businesses are emerging but very few manage to reach the succession phase, we believe that a good understanding of both the positive and negative impacts of *ubuntu* is useful for those engaging in family businesses in Africa (families and family business managers) as well as for those providing advice to them (scholars and professional advisors).

So, what are the various effects of *ubuntu* during the key stages of emergence and succession in family businesses in Africa? How do successors manage to maintain a balance between family constraints and business opportunities? We hereby aim to extend studies on the embeddedness perspective of family businesses (Steier et al., 2009), and especially the research on the integration of family businesses within social structures in Africa (Khavul et al., 2009).

This chapter has therefore two objectives. First, we propose to explore the role played by *ubuntu* – that is, 'humanity to others' (Gupta et al., 2010) – in family businesses in the Democratic Republic of the Congo (DRC). We propose to show the extent to which relying on *ubuntu* is not only useful for the emergence of family businesses, but also how it generates obligations that often complicate the succession phase. Second, we propose to explain how some talented successors succeed, against all odds, to reconcile family requirements and business opportunities in Africa.

The remainder of this chapter is organized as follows. First, we connect the social capital theory to *ubuntu* in order to explain the interaction between the family and the business (Arregle et al., 2007) and specifically the context in which family businesses are created in Africa as well as constraints they have to face, particularly at the succession stage. Second, we present the methodology of the research design and explain how qualitative data were collected and analysed. Third, we present results on the opportunities and constraints during the key stages and the role played by successors, in order to ensure a better alignment between the past and the future of family businesses (Miller et al., 2003). Finally, we conclude with a discussion, containing implications for managers and perspectives for future research.

1. SOCIAL CAPITAL AND *UBUNTU* IN FAMILY BUSINESSES IN THE DEMOCRATIC REPUBLIC OF THE CONGO

Social capital refers to advantages and opportunities that people can derive from their membership of a specific community (Bourdieu, 1980).

Accordingly, Arregle et al. (2007) proposed to extend Litz's definition (1995) of family business by emphasizing the possession of strong family social capital by such businesses. They subsequently indicated that (p. 87) 'a business firm may be considered a family business to the extent that its ownership and management are concentrated within a family unit, to the extent its members strive to achieve and/or maintain intra-organizational family-based relatedness, *and to the extent to which the family unit has strong family social capital*' (italics in the original).

In fact, while economic capital exists in the physical assets of production, and human capital is within the competences of individuals, social capital itself resides in the structure of relations between actors (Coleman, 1988; Lemieux, 2001). Specifically in dynamic emerging economies such as Africa, a strong social capital compensates for the lack of economic capital, products, qualified labour and institutional infrastructures (Acquaah, 2011; Miller et al., 2009).

Thus, although African entrepreneurs are relatively less equipped in economic and human capital, their strong social capital provides them with a valuable and alternative resource for identification, evaluation and exploitation of business opportunities. Furthermore, unlike the case for a corresponding definition of the family in North America or Western Europe, in Africa a broader set of individuals is included under the family rubric (Robson and Obeng, 2008; Smith, 2009; Khavul et al., 2009). As a consequence, in Africa the strong social capital of family businesses arises from a larger family community.

We therefore mean, by '*ubuntu* in family businesses', those various aspects of strong social capital that come from and go beyond the nuclear family. They are rooted in a kind of clan solidarity from rural areas and based on a productive and agricultural organization. *Ubuntu* is extended to family businesses in Africa since a broader set of individuals is often called to coordinate production and consumption for the welfare of its members, even in urban areas.

Camilleri (2007) gives us a clear illustration of how *ubuntu* operates in family businesses by noting that in Africa it is difficult for a 'rich' person to escape from his 'social obligations', especially if he has received from his family a part of the capital to start the business, or if family members were very involved from the outset of the business. He indicates, for instance, that family recruitment is an imperative of family solidarity, allowing the 'economic exploitation of family hired' and providing cheap labour; however, family members are not easy to dismiss.

Moreover, as in the DRC customs and family legislation provide adherence to *ubuntu* and reciprocity *vis-à-vis* the rich person of the extended family (Congolese Family Code of 1987), we expect that entrepreneurs – taken as the rich people of their extended family – should be regularly called on to ensure the well-being of their community. We also expect that the same case should apply to the successors in family businesses, because they are regarded as managers of a large community heritage. However, the idea of reciprocity exists in that the members who receive support (capital, employment or revenue) must express their gratitude to the rich member or to the extended family as a whole (Mbikayi, 1997). Then, *ubuntu* is governed by the law of solidarity, which obliges all members to indulge in mutual assistance, not only for subsistence, making the clan a body of a collective economy, but also in all other circumstances of daily life. Mulago (1973) concluded that a clan is a basic unit of social, historical, economic and even religious identification.

We therefore expect that, in DRC, *ubuntu* and related mutual obligations should be strengthened as a result of the economic crisis, depriving founders of institutional funding for the creation of businesses on the one hand and depriving extended family members of their livelihood on the other hand. As a consequence, family businesses in DRC should be marked by entrepreneurial dynamics driven by people from the same community, especially when they are away from their rural area of origin and have simultaneously to meet their daily needs. Following this, we expect that founders as well as successors in family businesses often benefit from *ubuntu* to mobilize family capital and human resources, and reciprocally they frequently face strong constraints from *ubuntu*, in order to respond to extended-family requirements. We then expect that *ubuntu* in family businesses brings valuable opportunities for their emergence as well as it generates many constraints over time, and the latter would weigh more heavily on succession.

2. THE RESEARCH METHODOLOGY

As indicated above, in order to capture opportunities and constraints during the key stages, we will focus on the effect of *ubuntu* associated not only with businesses' emergence but also with its challenges, specifically during succession. By emergence we mean both start-up capital (finance) and family early participation in the form of employment (human resources) (Pistrui et al., 2006); and by succession we mean intra-family leadership succession, as do most family business researchers (De Massis et al., 2012).

However, compared to Khavul et al. (2009), who provided insights into informal and rural family businesses in Africa, we focus on similar businesses operating in both the formal sector and urban areas. Operating in the formal sector means that these businesses are not only registered, licensed and liable to pay taxes, but their final products, production processes and distribution channels are also legal (Khavul et al., 2009).

For the above reasons, we opted for an in-depth analysis of a limited number of cases (Yin, 1994), and we selected three Bantu businesses operating in Bukavu – a major urban center in eastern DRC.

The selected businesses include a family business of the first generation under the control of its founder (FBG1) and two of the second generation. It should be noted that, for the two last indicated businesses, we consider that the first company is still engaged in the succession process (FBG2), but the second has finalized succession – as it has been more than ten years since the accession of the second generation to ownership and management (FBG2′).

Five interviews were conducted in two stages: in July 2006 (FBG2′ and FBG1) and in February 2007 (FBG1, FBG2′ and FBG2) – at seven months' interval. The concern of having both overlapping data analysis with data collection (Eisenhardt, 1989) and obtaining comparable information guided the choice of firms, interlocutors, questions and the sequencing of interviews (see Table 11.1). The three family businesses selected were all created by Bantu entrepreneurs after Congolese independence (1960). The respondents were the creators' children, eldest sons and senior managers, except in FBG1, where we interviewed the daughter of the creator. In FBG1, indeed, the father and founder is the senior manager, and his elder son, the brother of our interlocutor, is still at school and has not yet joined the family business.

The sequence of interviews went through a back-and-forth process between these companies for a comparison across cases at the same time of collection, and internal-case analysis (Eisenhardt, 1989) by repeating similar questions at two different times in order to gain familiarity with data collections and to validate the previous results. At Time I (July 06), FBG2′ is the test case for the interview in FBG1, while at Time II (February 07), FBG1 is the pilot case for the interview in FBG2 and at the same Time II (February 07), FBG1 and FBG2′ cases are the drivers for the FBG2 interview. FBG2 is indeed one additional case, because even if it shares some features with other cases, it differs significantly in one or more points (Hlady Rispal, 2002). Compared to FBG2′, the distinction relates to recent succession and the relatively large presence of family members and, compared to FBG1, it relates to withdrawal of the founder. This tactic allows the observation of similarities and differences between cases (Eisenhardt, 1989).

Thus, considering that FBG2′ has really passed from the first generation, this company was chosen as the starting point for interviews. In fact,

Table 11.1 Sequences and objectives of interviews and profiles of interlocutors

	FBG1	FBG2	FBG2′
Time I July 2006	2nd interview Contact person less open Cross-case comparison: checked against FBG2′ data from the first series of questions obtained FBG2′ 2nd series of questions, collection of new data, PILOT CASE of FBG2′		1st interview Contact very open 1st series of questions, new data collection, PILOT CASE of FBG1
Time II February 2007	4th interview Interlocutor rather open Comparison Intra-case verification Data FBG1 PILOT CASE of FBG2 Verification of data obtained in July FBG2′	5th interview Contact fairly open Checked against data from July 06 and February 07 Results in FBG1 and FBG2′	3rd interview Contact very open Cross-case comparison, checked against Data from the second series of questions obtained FBG1 Intra-case comparison, audit data from FBG2′ PILOT CASE of FBG1 and FBG2
Profile of the interlocutor	Degree in Management	Secondary school diploma	Master in Management

FBG2′ provides a summary view on the generational change. In addition, as it was a pilot case, we benefited from a strong opening from our interlocutor in FBG2′. He did not hesitate to deliver information that to others would have been confidential. The atmosphere was also useful for an in-depth interview. Unlike the other three interviews in the offices of the interlocutors, the two interviews for FBG2′ were carried out in the family house and during days of rest (Saturday and Sunday). This advantage must however be balanced because other interviews at the workplace offered us the advantage of immersing ourselves in the actual experience of these managers (interruptions, phone calls, direct contacts of our interlocutors with some partners during the interviews and so on have enriched the data collected).

To optimize interviews, we chose to avoid any question about figures. It is known that such questions are taboo in Africa (for example, managers were afraid to disclose their business volume, such as the level of sales or the number of employees, for fear of obligations surrounding taxes or union membership). We focused our questions on the relationship between business and family according to family solidarity and related to challenges of creation and succession. For the same reasons of optimization, the interviews were conducted in French and Swahili, the two languages commonly spoken in the region. With our interlocutors' agreement, the interviews were fully recorded on a recording device and following the guidelines of our protocols. We played back and transcribed interviews. This initial work was the opportunity to conduct a preliminary analysis. It gradually allowed us to define the new protocol for the next interview and to get an idea of the links between extended-family solidarity and entrepreneurship (see Table 11.1 for more information on the organization of interviews and profiles of the interlocutors). It should be noted, finally, that extracts of interviews in this study are in our English translation, and we systematically specify the firm code and the date of interview at the end of each extract. After these details on the research methodology, in the following we present the results of our study.

3. RESULTS

As noted above, results focus on the opportunities and constraints during the two key stages of family businesses, that is, the emergence and succession phases. Ultimately, we present the role played by successors to balance between extended-family obligations and business opportunities.

3.1 Opportunities and Constraints during the Emergence of Family Businesses

One of the big challenges to starting a business in Africa is related to funds. In all the three selected businesses for this study, founders received real or perceived support from their fathers to engage in small trade. In FBG2′, the father sold a cow and gave his son a portion of the money from the sale.

In FBG2, the founder would have received from his father a few Zaïres (the currency of the time) and therefore he began selling peanuts. And, as the founder father of FBG1 was a trader, he believed that his son had inherited his skill in trade. Also, in the three cases, the founders had a level of study limited to basic essentials. They were forced to abandon long and costly studies that would have had an uncertain outcome. This is evident in the following statements when we asked about the profile of the founders of the company in the three businesses:

> They went only to primary school and that's all. What do you think! All these old guys who have money today, they did not go to school. (FBG2, February 07)

> he [talking about his father] was studying at St. Therese. Then, when the studies [hesitation], when he reached a level where he felt he could stop, just able to read and write, since it was the case at that time, then he went into this business. (FBG2′, July 06)

> Just when he graduated [ended secondary school], so he has not found ways to continue to university, then he began to work. That's how he began. (FBG1, February 07)

In this way, relatives, and particularly the brothers of the founders – in this patriarchal society – experienced the same financial difficulty in furthering their studies, and were also recruited by the family business:

> when he saw his younger brothers were perhaps not able to finish their studies, while they had also initiated work together; that's how they started to work. (FBG1, February 07)

> as he finished his studies [secondary school], the family, clearly, was not able to send him to university, that's how old [the founder] was hired to start working with him. (FBG2′, July 06)

In the three businesses, the founders worked with their spouses, before being joined by younger brothers when the volume of activities increased. The brothers are privileged emissaries for foreign missions, for example to buy goods abroad. But the founders were attached only to family members that were useful for the business in the early stages. Family members are less demanding in terms of remuneration. Many of them still live under the roof of the founder of the business. This founder is in a sense their foster father, who supports the different needs of his children.

In the opinions of our interlocutors, there is a link between the provision of family resources, both human (brothers of the founder) and funding (from the father of the founder), and certain benefits that should be recognized for the benefit of family members. This is obvious from the following statements:

> somehow, they [the founder brothers] have also greatly helped because it's the family business. They started with the old [the founder] in Kinshasa, Kikwit. . . . It is clear that the grandfather helped him. And that's why somehow I also told myself that they, it's true it was his personal effort, but somehow, there was still a small departure from the family, that's why we cannot completely rule out family members being eligible for certain benefits derived from the family business. (FBG2′, July 06)

By contrast, if financial resources to start the business are not clearly from the family, such obligations to assist founder brothers still exist, but less intensely:

> If money was from the grandfather, then there could be a lot of problems; meaning 'You, you eat, you do not give anything to your little brothers.' [Here, our interlocutor presupposes the possible discourse of family members to the business founder if he did not share the wealth] But I think he does give because he always tries to give them something. (FBG1, February 2007)

Overall, from the three cases the founders mobilize financial and mostly human resources of the family for the creation and early development of the business. This is also the case in hard times:

> the one great advantage here, in this difficult time, usually they [family members] are people who can be counted upon. For example, an example during the war, when everyone was fleeing, workers fled because everyone had to save his life, but someone in the family can say it is our business, I remain [for protection of family assets, to prevent looting]. (FBG2′, February 2007)

In return, family business should contribute to the welfare of family members. Family business is therefore a symbol of family cohesion. The founder of the business also assumes the role of father-figure towards his relatives who are in business. These results are in line with family entrepreneurship as a totem, that is, a symbol of family cohesion, and where the founders play the role as a father ('baba') to maintain or strengthen those under their hierarchy. The results are also consistent with our expectation related to funding, because the funds to start businesses come primarily from the family. Moreover, in the early stages of development, the family supplies human resources on favourable terms (costs: family members 'are people who can be counted upon' . . . they say 'no that's our history I cannot let go'). The results are also in line with the advantages of family human resources and obligations of reciprocity, according to *ubuntu*. As noted by Kanoo (1997), family business provides welfare support (housing, living and educational expenses) for family members, and then they are expected to be loyal to the business.

3.2 Opportunities and Constraints in the Succession Phase of Family Businesses

In all three cases selected, unlike their parents who deliberately decided to go into business, the founders' children planned their future elsewhere:

> I never thought I could work in a family business anytime. (FBG2′, February 07)

> in my mind, I have never been prepared to work there. And now suddenly he [founder] said 'You have to work there', so it was not easy for me. Then it took pressure, [the founder said to his son, our interlocutor:] 'Now you drop me, when I need your help, you must help me' and after pressure from mom and from the little brother T, I had to return home here in Bukavu [to work in the family business]. (FBG2′, February 07)

> I went to the ISDR [High School of Rural Development of Bukavu], I did the first year, after that I was sure that I had to continue my studies. He [his father] said to me 'No, I see that you should stay close to me. We must work together.' I then said 'No.' . . . Yes, I told him that I prefer to continue studying . . . Oh, oh, oh, oh! I said 'Never.' He said besides, 'You must get married.' Ah what else! With this resistance, that's how he called other people, friends . . . I was 27, not, 26 years old. So we talked, he convinced my friends, those with whom I was close. He convinced other elders who pounced on me. Friends convinced me and told me stuff like, I have to. I dropped the studies. Then we started working with him. (FBG2, February 07)

> You know, I do not know what drove dad. As for me, here, what interested me was medicine [studies], but you see him and his ideas 'No just do this and this economy . . . You will help me . . . in Europe if the dad is a doctor, he also wants his child to become a doctor.' He said 'You're not even awake!' But when you get used to listening to this, eventually it does start to interest you. (FBG1, February 07)

In the three cases, it was by persuasion that fathers managed to integrate their children into business. This integration remains a recent phenomenon compared to the earlier trend (before the 1980s), which consisted of ensuring that children study, in the hope that they will get more chances to access the bourgeois class in large private companies or public administration, instead of just accessing the family business. Parents agree that the future of children can be ensured and substantial revenue can be derived for them from the management of the family patrimony. Thus they seek to generate in their children an interest in management. The family business also allows them to be close to each other. Founders inspire in the children the need to address both the enterprise and the family. In this logic, the company is regarded as an organization created and animated to meet the needs of the family. Thus, in several cases, the first child to integrate the business is the eldest. Also, if the elder may be exempted from taking care of the business, it is not conceivable for him not to take on his father's responsibility when his father dies. For example, in both second-generation companies that we studied, the successors have actually inherited many constraints as heads of families.

> I'm still in the patterns of old, knowing that my father died and as the eldest I continue, I am the head of the family . . . as I said in fact the old man died; [but] the old remained alive [through me], so I basically continue the role as the old did before. So on one side as a father, then as a father, of course I pay the school fees of the children, I would give advice because the old had been very insistent on it, in his will he had been very insistent on this, he said [with passion]: 'You are the father, you're their dad. To children you give them food, medical care and especially advice.' So I am first and foremost a father, I advise. Then each child, and indeed even little brothers still call me Daddy, 'baba jambo!' [hello father!], that's how even my mother calls me, even when she can even call me big brother, 'baba', that's how she calls me and that's how lucky I am . . . until now I am still the father of the family as the old wanted, and I try practically to meet the needs of all my kids as he would. This was his wish. (FBG2′, July 2006)

> and you [often speaking of himself in the second person] can never leave the family, because it is assumed that they found you capable of leading this family. Because this family needs someone to manage it, so it does not become like a family without a guide. That's it . . . including relations of the past, your own relationships and it's all the family. So if we have found someone who does not even cover 50% of these relationships, it is a failure. Because then you'll cut your family relationships maintained by the old before. And if you cut this, then you stay isolated as a family. When you stay alone without external relations, it sucks, because when there is a mess [problem], people will learn only when you are already looking for some sore point [injured], you have then already committed some damage or other. But I think it's the family initially the most important. The company also comes after, but they go together. If you manage the business as required, you also manage the family well. If you manage the family poorly, the company will not move forward. If you manage the company poorly, the family cannot progress. (FBG2, February 2007)

Thus it appears, according to the selected cases, that the successor inherits not only the management of the company but also the constraints of an extended family. The constraints also mean very delicate management of family staff, particularly those who have worked for a long time with the founder, as indicated in the following:

> as he works there since the age of 18, he may be now after 32 years (of service), myself I was a kid when I saw him there . . . he is strict, but really he is not the right man there, that's true. Once I already threw him out, but I felt the pressure from family saying that he will die. But it's true since he does not know; he does not know anything outside [interruption]. And that's just the drama and somewhere I have always condemned the old because here he did not create other openings that allow him, once he leaves the institution [family business] to do something else. And I always regretted it. (FBG2′, July 2006)

Table 11.2 summarizes opportunities and constraints during the key stages of emergence and succession in family businesses, focusing on human resources management and finance.

While, at the emergence stage, founders often address particularly the needs of their younger brothers under their roof, at the succession stage, businesses face multiple pressures from the extended family. These pressures are grounded in the Congolese family code (1987) which, according to *ubuntu*, mandates help and assistance within the family, the duty of fair distribution of income and family assets, the imposition of child support and parental authority that must be exercised by any person considered as socially and economically able to support members of the community. Over time, such constraints become urgent due to rural exodus and the need to provide means of survival for family members far from their rural area of origin. Moreover, over time, even uncles (brothers of founders involved in family businesses) become less productive but their needs increase because they have also established their nuclear families and no longer live under the roof of founders. Clearly, opportunities related to *ubuntu* at the emergence phase give rise to constraints on succession. This requires successors to address the needs of both businesses and families.

3.3 The Role Played by Successors to Balance Family Constraints and Business Opportunities

Faced with the dilemma, successors try to find positions for extended-family members and particularly for their uncles where abuses will be reduced and it is hoped that they can again be productive:

> So I thought until I was able to put him at the reception [hotel], but I'm thinking about his starting point, filing work, in Kalemie where I am preparing activities for the maize crop in August. (FBG2′, July 2006)

Table 11.2 Human resources management and finance

	Emergence stage	Succession stage
Opportunities (+)	Human resources: • Early integration of wives and later by young brothers of founders, they live under the roof of founders, who play the role of father Finance: • Funding (or experience) for the fathers of founders to start a very small business • Early integration of wives and young brothers of founders when businesses grow; they are less demanding in terms of remuneration	Human resources: • Wives continue to play an effective role but outside the formal structures • Integration of cousins, specifically those who are competent • In difficult times (when there is a war or a threat of looting), cousins in businesses protect family assets
Constraints (−)	Human resources: • Low level of education (primary and exceptionally secondary school) of founders (and their brothers in businesses) • Providing job opportunities to young brothers of founders Finance: • Parental authority of founders, support and respect for his clan members (specifically for younger brothers under the roof)	Human resources: • Keeping in the business those uncles (brothers of founders) who served for a long time, even if they are no longer competent Finance: • Participation in vocational training of cousins • Providing resources to aunts and uncles to meet their needs (medical care, food and clothing, and ceremonies for births, weddings and funerals)

> I have rejected him and I pointed him to the work site. And by then as there are still construction sites for the family . . . I have found for him an occupation in our construction sites, where he will do no damage. I cannot entrust him with an amount of $10,000. He then became an employee. So far it's like that, it's been at least four or five years we work with him like that. (FBG2, February 2007)

To avoid many potential conflicts, the successor also supports family members who want to set up their own small businesses. For this, the potential recipient has to prove that he has acquired a stake. This constitutes the ideal, but reality is often quite different. In cases of abuse, the founders easily took action against some of their brothers; however, successors have more difficulty in applying sanctions against their uncles and brothers.

> The old man had already said he cannot give him anything. The old man died while he was busy trying to negotiate again to be helped. Then for us, we were still obliged to give him another amount of US$10,000. So $6,500 in cash and we bought her a van to move around [in transportation] so he could not cash in on that money. Today, 'shuuii' [stating that all this slips away like the wind], zero, zero. So, it's an annoying element that exists here now. (FBG2, February 2007)

> Well, with the old, it was clear. [If] you had stolen, you had stolen, the law is the law, it was the prison and justice. It was like that . . . If the old man would be alive then maybe he would bring him to justice because he has hijacked. But me, being here, I say peace has a price. And when you ask to other old men [wise men], they tell you that it is useless to go to justice, and then you must close your eyes. This is the great tragedy that we have, and that's why I have to find, as I said, a legal form where there are shareholders and each one can only expect his rights up to the end of the year as profits, before, during the year, there is nothing. I want to move towards this option. (FBG2′, July 2006)

However, even if the nomination to head the company increases the power of the successors, they find it difficult to sanction abuse of their uncles. They also face enormous difficulties in responding to requests and pressures from family members. Unlike their fathers, they struggle to assert their authority as heads of an extended household. Such difficulties appear in the following cases:

> We have already seen so much. It means like you [often speaking of himself in the second person], you have just been invested, but just after investiture [family ceremony often chaired by the elders and the wise, whose purpose is to make the young successor (the eldest son) the new 'father' of the family on the death of his father] it's over, everyone goes about his job, and this becomes very light and unimportant. For me, with the experience I have today if I had previously seen someone who was living like me today, or like F [another successor of a family business], I should have refused the nomination . . . You see a guy like me; you start as heir to manage dads in their fifties. Those who should have to think at least more than you, but they are the ones who start to think less than you. This is not interesting. (FBG2, February 2007)[1]

The successors are forced to meet the demands of their extended families to preserve the peace. Otherwise, antagonistic groups are created, with claims of dividing family assets, and the risk of abandoning the family business. To meet the needs of an extended family, the successors try to invent other formulas to avoid heavy pressure from the extended family. For example, they include cousins as employees in the company, hoping that these cousins will then use their salaries to take care of their immediate families. Successors also participate in training these cousins, hoping also that they will acquire useful skills for the family business or obtain jobs that will allow them to take care of their nuclear and other members of extended families. In this respect, our interlocutors indicated that managers try to diversify contributions for family members:

> I also recently started to pay his computer training and also in management, I am dealing with it quickly so he can come lend a hand. He is the son of our uncle; the youngest brother of our father, his son must be aged 23 now, almost 23, yes 23 years. So that's our concern . . . It is our desire to integrate them. We hope to have capable people who are able to work. Let us say to our uncle, we want to integrate this child [his child]. Why? Because he has, how to say it, during the lifetime of the old man, he had only to eat [which means he did not work]. (FBG2, February 2007)

> Thus, having already educated the children, and helping their children to grow, I tell myself that it's already a way of getting rid of this responsibility, since I have already prepared the child to bear the burden of his family. That's how I'm currently thinking. And this will help because once the business will have changed in time, and since I will be able to stop playing this role of big brother [father] here, it will become a private company. And of course it will also be required that they continue to live on through their children whom I had also helped to train by paying school fees, so that's how we try to reconcile matters. It is not complicated for me to reconcile the two. It's only the question of putting into place structures and respect. (FBG2′, July 2006)

Successors also express the wish to transform the structures of companies. The objective is to ensure, in future, separate management of the company and of the family. Thus their oldest sons could continue to play the role of head of the family, according to custom. But there is no question that those children will become the head of the company. The opposition is such that failure would be certain. The legitimacy of these grandchildren of the founders would be challenged by the children and brothers of the founders. Thus our expectation indicating that the successor inherits family obligations must be upheld. In contrast, the power of the successor is not always reinforced with the investiture. Compared to the founder, the successor has less legitimacy. His power over the family business faces the claims of his own brothers and sisters and other members of the founder's extended family. This could endanger the future of the family business.

These above results are consistent with Fafchamps's (2004) observation on entrepreneurship in Madagascar, where, instead of the importance of family relationships at the start-up for family capital[2] and experiences, such relationships do not seem to be determinants of business success. In fact, forced redistribution often affects decisions on spending and saving, discouraging investment (Di Falco and Bulte, 2011). However, within family businesses, the founder and successor take on a special meaning in the context of an economic crisis and under family law, which insists on Bantu clan solidarity. This illustrates the 'family-first family business', that is, the business that exists solely to serve the interests of the family (Poza, 2007; Bewayo, 2009), and for instance in order to ensure the cohesion and survival of clan members as recommended by *ubuntu*.

CONCLUSION

Clan solidarity is the central feature of *ubuntu* in family businesses in DRC. *Ubuntu* has its roots in the tradition that promotes a broader conception of family and support bonds between members. The Congolese government relies on this tradition to consecrate an even more compelling aspect of clan solidarity (the Congolese family code of 1987), encouraging family members to surround a rich person of the clan in order to survive. Indeed, in DRC, family businesses of autochthones emerged after Independence in 1960, and since then it has suffered strong pressure from the national economic crisis and a lack of institutional funds to promote private entrepreneurship. It is in this context that family businesses appear as a symbol of cohesion to ensure the survival of clan members specifically in urban centres. In fact, removed from their rural home and on the basis of *ubuntu*, family businesses allow urban populations to cope with the crisis of the modern economy.

In two of our selected cases, the financial resources to start the business came from the founders' fathers. In the third business, even if the original capital to start the first-generation company did not come from the founder's father, the latter still considers that he has tacitly transmitted his experience to the founder. However, in all three cases, founders worked successively with their spouses before being joined by their brothers. Whatever the shape of the original family contribution, this strengthens obligations to respond to family needs: employment, income transfers from the business to the family and so on. During the start-up phase, the founder ensures management of the family and also plays the role of father to his brothers. Indeed, the younger brothers often live under his roof. With the growth of the company, the founder brought into the company other unemployed members of his clan, to whom he continues to play the role of father. Being a father is a sign of prestige in the community, and allows the founder to ensure the loyalty of members working in the company. As a father, he continues to exercise his role as patriarch of the clan, and the members of his extended family continue to benefit directly or indirectly from the means of subsistence from the business. No one should ever betray his father or compromise the family business, which is a symbol of cohesion. As Di Falco and Bulte (2011) noted, in sub-Saharan Africa the extended family (kinship) is a collective institution regulating access to resources and services. Similarly, Bewayo (2009, p. 176) claimed of African entrepreneurs that they tend to highlight 'economic survival', 'making a living' and 'providing for family' as reasons for going into business. However, entrepreneurs in family businesses in DRC are simultaneously seeking ways to avoid the constant pressure from the extended family without abandoning the clan members.

Our results suggest that transmission of the simultaneous role of father in both business and family succeeds only when the founder has transferred power directly to his child. Yet the company's survival may be compromised when the grandson of the creator is placed directly at the head of the company by his father. Successors are under great pressure from family members, to the point that they consider separating the family and the business, for the survival of the company. It is therefore not intended to preserve a model of transmission of authority at the head of the business and of the family simultaneously.

In addition, the results show that the larger the company, that is, when it reaches a certain size, the more it undergoes enormous pressure from family members. Therefore, although clan solidarity is an important factor for both creation of family businesses and survival through periods of crisis, such solidarity is less important, and perhaps a hindrance, to business growth. Thus, as stated by Khavul et al. (2009), who found that the strong family ties provided by an extended family or kinship structure can inhibit – rather than enhance – entrepreneurial action in rural and informal family businesses, we found that even in urban businesses, similar ties can inhibit growth. In addition, even for businesses operating in the formal sector, our results indicated that the law provides no real protection against the risk of expropriation by family members, and the involvement of clan members tends to endanger the survival of the company for generations.

From a managerial perspective, we recommend to founders and successors in family businesses to gradually reduce the family influence in the business. However, as the economic crisis persists, and as long as the family members have no other alternatives for survival, founders or successors must concurrently assume 'corporate social responsibility'. In that sense, as we found in the selected cases, among other things, managers of family businesses must participate in the training of their nephews or cousins. The objective is to ensure more skills among family members and/or to be sure that those nephews or cousins will take care of a number of extended-family members or at least their very close family members (fathers, mothers and children). In short, without a social security system and an adequate mechanism for institutional financing, extended families must organize themselves around entrepreneurship to launch activities that come to support members. The founder of the family business and his successor cannot shirk this social responsibility without incurring social sanctions.

Indeed, life is sacred for the Bantu people; for example, if a family member close to the entrepreneur dies of hunger while there is food in the company warehouses, in the eyes of the community this entrepreneur is like a 'muloji', 'mfwisi', 'ndoki', which means a sorcerer, the opposite of someone who strengthens vital force. Such an entrepreneur runs the risk of ostracism if he arranges a marriage ceremony for his own child. Nobody will listen to him when he speaks during family counselling (palaver). And when he becomes an old man, few people, if any, will take care of him. And meanwhile, there will even be people who owe him money but cannot pay – and the community will find all this normal. Ultimately, family entrepreneurship is called on to assume social responsibility without compromising its growth or survival through generations. Therefore the challenge of a Bantu entrepreneur is to find a balance between family needs and business prosperity and longevity.

In an academic perspective, we recommend scholars to expand ways of thinking by taking into account both spatial and temporal factors to better understand family businesses in the African and particularly in the Bantu context of DRC. As noted by Bewayo (2009, p. 176), 'the African entrepreneur tends to be much more of a "necessity" entrepreneur than an "opportunity" entrepreneur'. We found that this characteristic of the African entrepreneur has emerged in the wake of the generalized economic crisis and as a consequence of clan solidarity. It is therefore useful to explore the extent to which some entrepreneurs can become more 'opportunity' entrepreneurs, having previously participated in training or job seeking of their clan members outside the family business. Specifically, this corresponds to exploring how successors – after answering even partially to their obligations of clan solidarity – could have more opportunities to continuously grow their businesses, that is, how they could achieve discretion to create future courses of action (Mitchell et al., 2009; Steier et al., 2009), instead of suffering from family pressures that could lead to the disappearance of family businesses.

This preliminary study is subject to some limitations. First, our analysis is based on only three family businesses. Our conclusions would benefit from a larger and more diversified sample of family entrepreneurships in Africa. Such a sample may lead to heterogeneity among Bantu entrepreneurship because there may be variations between different Bantu contexts, for example according to the abundance or scarcity of natural resources. Second, addressing the problems of succession, this study has not analysed challenges facing successors in the case of polygamy. Yet we know how polygamy undermines the future of many family businesses in Africa. Especially after the sudden death of the founder, several family businesses simply disappear as a result of disputes over the distribution of the estate, which are very intense in the case of polygamy. Likewise, this study did not explicitly take into account the gender gap in both succession and growth of family businesses. However, Aterido and Hallward-Driemeier (2011) found that, in sub-Saharan Africa, sons rather than daughters benefit from having a father who was an entrepreneur and so were able to join the family enterprise. Similarly, Khavul et al. (2009) indicated that the opportunities that entrepreneurship provides for males and females may be very different, while Smith (2009) noted that East African family firms with male entrepreneurs appear to follow the concept of entrepreneurship used by Stevenson and Jarillo (1990) because they seem to look for opportunities regardless of resources; by contrast, the women appear to follow the tenets of the resource-based view by Barney (2001) because they tend to find new uses for existing resources.

In the light of these previous studies, extending this study on entrepreneurial dynamics to wider Bantu contexts and to more challenges, such as polygamy, resources endowment or lack thereof, and gender differences, will be useful to provide a better understanding of the opportunities and constraints of family businesses in sub-Saharan Africa, and specifically in several Bantu family networks.

NOTES

1. The meaning here is that it is not interesting to manage the uncles to whom successors owe respect; in the meantime these uncles behave like children in order to have support from family businesses.
2. As noted by Gough et al. (2003), in resource-deficient sub-Saharan Africa, the same physical assets such as cooking utensils or sewing machines are used for both household and business needs (Gupta and Levenburg, 2010, p. 158). This can also be seen at a wedding ceremony in the entrepreneur's family, where his Mercedes car and company truck are used respectively to convey the young couple and the extended-family members from the village. It is also the case that, when there is a death in the family, the human resources and physical assets of the business are often mobilized in the ceremony.

REFERENCES

Acquaah, M. (2011). 'Business strategy and competitive advantage in family businesses in Ghana: the role of social networking relationships', *Journal of Developmental Entrepreneurship*, **16**(1): 103–26.

Arregle, J.-L., M.A. Hitt, D.G. Sirmon and P. Very (2007). 'The development of organizational social capital: attributes of family firms', *Journal of Management Studies*, **44**(1): 73–95.

Aterido, R. and M. Hallward-Driemeier (2011). 'Whose business is it anyway?', *Small Business Economics*, **37**(4): 443–64.

Barney, J.B. (2001). 'Is the resource-based "view" a useful perspective for strategic management research? Yes', *Academy of Management Review*, **26**: 41–56.

Bewayo, E.D. (2009). 'Family business in Africa: a comparison with the US–Western model', *Journal of Global Business Issues*, **3**(1): 171–81.

Boon, M. (1996). *The African Way: The Power of Interactive Leadership*, Johannesburg: Zebra Press.

Bourdieu, P. (1980). 'Le Capital social: Notes provisoires', *Actes de la recherche en sciences sociales*, no. 31.

Cadieux, L. (2007). 'Succession in small and medium-sized family businesses: toward a typology of predecessor roles during and after instatement of the successor', *Family Business Review*, **20**(2): 95–109.

Camilleri, J.L. (2007). *La micro entreprise rurale en Afrique: de la survie à la croissance. Le cas rwandais*, Paris: L'Harmattan.

Coleman, J. (1988). 'Social capital in the creation of human capital', *American Journal of Sociology*, **94**: S95–S120.

Congolese Family Code 1987.

De Massis, A., P. Sharma, J.H. Chua and J.J. Chrisman (eds) (2012). *Family Business Studies: An Annotated Bibliography*, Cheltenham, UK and Northampton, MA, USA: Edward Elgar Publishing.

Di Falco, S. and E. Bulte (2011). 'A dark side of social capital? Kinship, consumption, and savings', *Journal of Development Studies*, **47**(8): 1128–51.

Eisenhardt, K.M. (1989). 'Building theories from case study research', *The Academy of Management Review*, **14**(4): 532–50.

Fafchamps, M. (2004). *Markets Institutions in Sub-Saharan Africa. Theory and Evidence*, Cambridge, MA: Massachusetts Institute of Technology.

Gough, K.V., A.G. Tipple and M. Napier (2003). 'Making a living in African cities: the role of home-based enterprises in Accra and Pretoria', *International Planning Studies*, **8**(4): 253–77.

Gupta, V. and N. Levenburg (2010). 'A thematic analysis of cultural variations in family businesses: the CASE Project', *Family Business Review*, **23**(2): 155–69.

Gupta, V., N. Levenburg, L. Moore, J. Motwani and T.V. Schwarz (2010). 'Family business in sub-Saharan Africa versus the Middle East', *Journal of African Business*, **11**: 146–62.

Hlady Rispal, M. (2002). *La méthode des cas: application à la recherche en gestion*, Bruxelles: De Boeck Université.

Kanoo, K.M. (1997). *The House of Kanoo: A Century of an Arabian Family Business*, London: The London Centre of Arab Studies.

Khavul, S., G.D. Bruton and E. Wood (2009). 'Informal family business in Africa', *Entrepreneurship: Theory & Practice*, **33**(6): 1219–38.

Kshetri, N. (2011). 'Institutional and economic foundations of entrepreneurship in Africa: an overview', *Journal of Developmental Entrepreneurship*, **16**(1): 9–35.

Lemieux, V. (2001). 'Social capital in situation of co-operation and conflict', *ISUMA*, **2**(1), http://www.isuma.net/v02n01/index_e.shtml.

Litz, R.A. (1995). 'The family business: toward definitional clarity', *Family Business Review*, **8**(2): 71–81.

Mbigi, L. (1997). *Ubuntu: The African Dream in Management*, South Africa: Randburg, Knowledge Resources.

Mbikayi, Kalongo (1997). *Code civil et commercial congolais*, Kinshasa: Centre de Recherches et de Diffusion Juridiques.

Miller, D., L. Steier and I. Le Breton-Miller (2003). 'Lost in time: intergenerational succession, change and failure in family business', *Journal of Business Venturing*, **18**(4): 513–51.

Miller, D., J. Lee, S. Chang and I. Le Breton-Miller (2009). 'Filling the institutional void: the social behavior and performance of family vs non-family technology firms in emerging markets', *Journal of International Business Studies*, **1**: 1–16.

Mitchell, J., T.A. Hart, S. Valcea, S. and D.M. Townsend (2009). 'Becoming the boss: discretion and postsuccession success in family firms', *Entrepreneurship: Theory & Practice*, **33**(6): 1201–18.

Mulago, V. (1973). *La religion traditionnelle des Bantus et leur vision du monde*, Kinshasa: Presses universitaires du Zaïre.

Pistrui, D., W.V. Huang, H.P. Welsch and Z. Jing (2006). 'Family and cultural forces: shaping entrepreneurship and SME development in China', in P.Z. Poutziouris, K.X. Smyrnios and S.B. Klein (eds), *Handbook of Research on Family Business*, Cheltenham, UK and Northampton, MA, USA: Edward Elgar Publishing, pp. 460–87.

Poza, E. (2007). *Family Business*, Mason, OH: Thomson Publishing.

Robson, P.A. and B.A. Obeng (2008). 'The barriers to growth in Ghana', *Small Business Economics*, **30**(4): 385–403.

Smith, G.D. (2009). 'East Africa: extended families with many rights', *Entrepreneurship: Theory & Practice*, **33**(6): 1239–44.

Steier, L.P., J.H. Chua and J.J. Chrisman (2009). 'Embeddedness perspectives of economic action within family firms', *Entrepreneurship: Theory & Practice*, **33**(6): 1157–67.

Stevenson, H.H. and J.C. Jarillo (1990). 'A paradigm of entrepreneurship: entrepreneurial management', *Strategic Management Journal*, **11**: 17–27.

Yin, R.K. (1994). *Case Study Research: Design and Methods*, 2nd edn, Thousand Oaks, CA: Sage Publications.

PART IV

Debates and Perspectives: Theoretical Challenges

12. Entrepreneurial mingling secrets: investigating the performance impact of network structure for control-based entrepreneurship using agent-based simulation

Willem Jansen, René Mauer and Malte Brettel

1. INTRODUCTION

The creation and utilization of social networks are of key importance for entrepreneurs (Jack, 2010; Slotte-Kock and Coviello, 2010). As a means of organization, social networks allow entrepreneurs to gain access to a wide variety of tangible and intangible resources provided by other parties (Hoang and Antoncic, 2003). A large body of research has determined the benefits of an appropriate network structure, effective governance mechanisms, and access to content through social networks. A central position (Brajkovich, 1994) and sufficiently large network (Aldrich and Reese, 1993) are structural characteristics that increase venture performance because they increase the accessibility of resources held by other parties. Researchers have argued for the theoretical importance of both strong and weak relationships, or 'ties' (Granovetter, 1973), and have obtained largely supportive findings through empirical research (Aldrich et al., 1987; Hite, 2005; Jack, 2005; Rowley et al., 2000). A more general theory uses the occurrence of 'structural holes' (Burt, 1992) to explain the beneficial impact of network structures by determining their efficiency and effectiveness. With respect to governance, systems that rely on social mechanisms, such as trust (Larson and Starr, 1993) and reputation, have proven more effective than contractual systems (Jones et al., 1997).

Despite these significant recent advances in research on entrepreneurial social networks, the understanding of the individual entrepreneurial networking process and its effects on the organization of the network itself remains limited. The majority of research focuses on high-level input–output effects, leaving the underlying processes opaque. Available process descriptions typically focus on the network in general and discuss phases of network development in broad terms (Slotte-Kock and Coviello, 2010). In addition, recent studies have criticized the fact that the initial starting position was not considered (Witt, 2004) as well as the lack of research on network development over time (Jack et al., 2008). Moreover, key theoretical contributions (Burt, 1992; Granovetter, 1973) assume an entrepreneurial behaviour that uses predictive planning, causal logic and the classical exploration–exploitation scheme (Holland, 1975). Despite the widespread assumption of the universality of this prediction-based approach, a growing body of studies reveals that expert serial entrepreneurs prefer an alternative control-based entrepreneurship approach. In this study, we use effectuation (Sarasvathy, 2001) as an exemplary prototype.

Effectuation is a non-predictive logic that strives to control future market development by shaping it. With respect to network creation and utilization, effectuation relies on co-creation and collaboration to jointly create a new market (Dew et al., 2008; Sarasvathy and Dew, 2005a). Initial studies indicate a positive effect of these practices – including the collaborative networking approach – on venture performance (Read et al., 2009). In light of these discoveries, in this study we re-evaluate findings regarding entrepreneurial network structure and deepen the understanding of the interaction dynamics of entrepreneurs using control-based logic and their networks as well as their impact on venture performance. We examine network structure and venture performance using agent-based simulations based on three research questions: (1) How does the network position of an entrepreneur using control-based decision logics impact venture performance over time? (2) How does the network shape of an entrepreneur using control-based decision logics impact venture performance over time? (3) How do entrepreneurs using control-based decision logics reorganize their social networks over time?

2. LITERATURE REVIEW: THE PERFORMANCE IMPACT OF THE SOCIAL NETWORK

In this chapter, we provide an introduction to effectuation theory as a representative of control-based entrepreneurial decision logic. We subsequently present an in-depth review of the effectuation process literature to derive a formal model for the subsequent simulation experiments. We conclude this chapter with a presentation of current theories and empirical results regarding the performance impact of network structure, that is, network position and shape. We expose inconsistencies with control-based entrepreneurship logic and propose possible explanations, methods of unification and alternative theories.

2.1 Effectuation as an Entrepreneurial Expert Decision Logic

Effectuation was introduced as a decision logic as a result of case studies on new venture creation under Knightian uncertainty (Knight, 1921) with expert serial entrepreneurs (Sarasvathy, 2001). These experts approached the creation of new ventures in a manner fundamentally different from traditional approaches, which employ prediction to best position a venture in an emerging market.

Contrary to the traditional prediction-based approach called causation, effectuation is a control-based logic (Wiltbank and Dew, 2006) that aspires to shape future market developments rather than forecast them. Effectuation relies on four principles (Sarasvathy, 2001). First, effectuation focuses on the use of readily available means, contrasting the causation approach to first set a goal and subsequently acquire all required means. Second, effectuation proposes project selection based on maintaining an affordable potential loss rather than maximizing the expected return. Third, effectuation proposes to embrace contingency as an improvement opportunity rather than treating it as a deviation that requires mitigation. Finally, effectuation proposes viewing other market participants as potential partners rather than competitors. In fact, effectuators organize a network of partnerships through the negotiation of pre-commitments and the exchange of new ideas to drive the finalization of an artefact (Sarasvathy and Dew, 2005a), typically a product, service, project or venture.

Introduced by Sarasvathy (Sarasvathy, 2001), effectuation has developed into an important area of entrepreneurship research (Venkataraman et al., 2012). Despite significant advances, effectuation is still considered to be in a nascent state (Perry et al., 2012). Originally derived from thought experiments, effectuation has expanded into a comprehensive decision logic including a process model (Sarasvathy and Dew, 2005a). Subsequent refinements (Dew et al., 2008; Dew et al., 2010) led to the inclusion of effectual transformation mechanisms (Dew et al., 2010). Effectuation was introduced to adjacent research streams, for example trust (Goel and Karri, 2006; Karri and Goel, 2008; Sarasvathy and Dew, 2008a). A particularly fruitful debate regarding similarities and differences of Austrian economics and effectuation helped to delineate the concepts of non-predictive control and creativity (Chiles et al., 2007; Chiles et al., 2008; Sarasvathy and Dew, 2008b). Scale development has been initiated (Brettel et al., 2012; Chandler et al., 2011), and quantitative studies revealed increased venture performance for business angels (Wiltbank et al., 2009) and new ventures in general (Read et al., 2009).

The principles of effectuation were derived from scenarios with high uncertainty. More precisely, Sarasvathy et al. (2008) identified three distinct preconditions: Knightian uncertainty, Marchian goal ambiguity and isotropy. Although these conditions typically occur 'naturally' in studies regarding new ventures, simulation studies such as this one must place particular emphasis on these preconditions to produce valid results.

2.2 Effectual Use of Social Networks – A Review of Known Processes and Behaviours

Entrepreneurs using effectual logic focus on available means: 'who I am', 'what I know' and 'whom I know' (Sarasvathy and Dew, 2005a). Consequently, social networks ('whom I know') are essential in acquiring 'new means' and 'new goals' (Sarasvathy and Dew, 2005a). Although interaction with other market participants is regarded as 'the very essence of the effectual process' (Dew et al., 2008, p. 50), research on intersubjective interaction remains sparse (Sarasvathy and Venkataraman, 2011). The following is an overview of known effectual processes and behaviours. We created an integrated effectual process map based on available studies.

As illustrated in Figure 12.1, social networks are relevant to the effectuation process in four ways. First, effectuators approach contacts in their

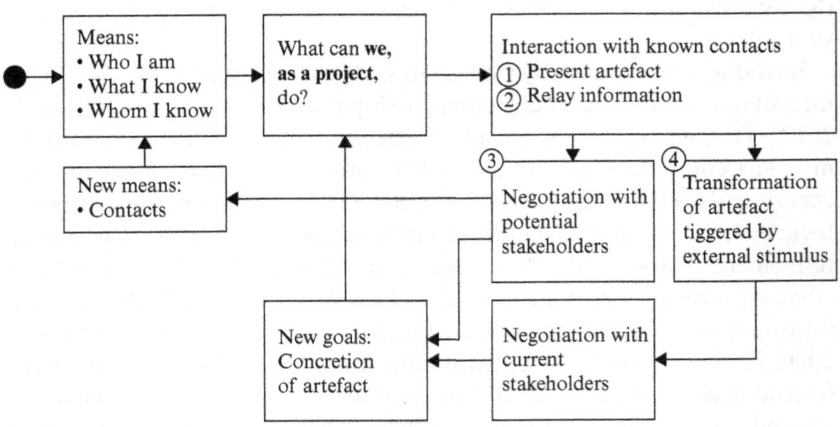

Source: Based on Dew et al. (2008); Sarasvathy and Dew (2005a).

Figure 12.1 Algorithmic interpretation of the effectuation process

social network to negotiate pre-commitments (Sarasvathy, 2001). This typically implies the prior disclosure of the artefact on which an approaching effectuator is working. Second, effectuators use social networks as a mechanism to gather and relay information. Although this behaviour is not exclusive to effectuators, it exposes network participants to new ideas, which is an important principle of effectuation (Sarasvathy, 2001). Third, effectuators engage in the actual negotiation of pre-commitments and organization of joint projects (Sarasvathy and Dew, 2005a). Finally, effectuators use transformation mechanisms to develop the artefact on which they are working (Dew et al., 2010; Sarasvathy et al., 2008). Although not every transformation necessitates social networks, we focus on transformations that are initiated by external stimuli. In contrast to negotiations, transformations lead to concretion of the artefact without the acquisition of new means.

2.2.1 Presentation of artefacts

Effectuation relies on interactions with other market participants to create a market opportunity (Sarasvathy, 2001). Effectuation uses the negotiation of pre-commitments to mitigate the risk of mistaking an uninterested party for a potential customer (Dew and Sarasvathy, 2007). The negotiation of such pre-commitment is initiated by approaching a known contact ('whom I know') and presenting the current state of the artefact (Dew et al., 2008). The literature treats this first step as a prelude to negotiations (Dew et al., 2008; Sarasvathy and Dew, 2005a). Assuming that effectual entrepreneurs will approach only a part of their known contacts, we argue for including the persistence with which effectual entrepreneurs approach known contacts in a formal model of effectuaiton. It is an individual decision or personality trait reflected in their means base ('who I am') (Sarasvathy, 2001, p. 253).

2.2.2 Relay of information

The relay of information is a central aspect of social networks (Wasserman and Faust, 1994). Although it is not exclusive to entrepreneurs using effectual logic, the dissemination of information through networks plays a crucial role for them. The incidental reception of new information regarding other market participants is an important source of contingency that effectuation teaches us to embrace (Sarasvathy, 2001). Thus the relay of such information is an important by-product of effectual networking. Although the existence and positive impact of information exchange have been studied extensively (Hoang and Antoncic, 2003), the exact process steps used by entrepreneurs employing effectual logic have yet to be determined (Sarasvathy and Venkataraman, 2011).

2.2.3 Negotiation of pre-commitments

The negotiation of pre-commitments is the key use of social networks for entrepreneurs employing effectual logic (Sarasvathy and Dew, 2005a). The results of a negotiation are two-fold: 'new means' and 'new goals' (Sarasvathy and Dew, 2005a, p. 543). 'New means' refers to the surplus of both tangible and intangible resources that the other party has committed to the development of the opportunity, whereas 'new goals' refers to the further concretion of the artefact under development. As the market is still emerging, these negotiations focus 'on the characteristics of the project . . . rather than the type and quantity of returns' (Dew et al., 2008, p. 50). In this manner, the resource base and level of concreteness grow iteratively over time, a fact that is referred to as 'two concurrent dynamic cycles' (Sarasvathy and Dew, 2005a, p. 1). Moreover, the exchange of pre-commitments is more than a one-time negotiation: participants organize a joint project and are part of it until they 'declare the effectual transformation complete' (ibid., p. 549). This high level of stakeholder involvement is conceptually different from the 'classical' transactional use of social networks. Stakeholders are continuously involved in the development of a market opportunity rather than 'just' providing resources in exchange for funds or equity.

'Effectuation assumes docility as a fundamental behavioral construct applicable to all stakeholders' (Dew et al., 2008, p. 50). Introduced by Simon (1990), docility describes 'the tendency to depend on suggestions, recommendations, persuasion, and information obtained through social channels as a major basis for choice' (Simon, 1993, p. 156). Not to be interpreted as 'passivity or meekness' (Simon, 1997), docility is an important characteristic and must be included in a formal representation of effectual negotiation.

2.2.4 Transformation of artefacts

In 2008, Sarasvathy et al. presented alternative mechanisms that effectual entrepreneurs use to further develop artefacts without the negotiation of pre-commitments. Although these transformation mechanisms lead to 'new goals' in the sense of artefact concretion, they do not contribute 'new means' because no new stakeholders are gathered.

Based on their case studies, Dew et al. (2010) list nine different transformation types applied by entrepreneurs using effectual logic. Because the present study focuses on the effect of network position and shape, we focus on transformation types that involve the use of social networks. These types (e.g. 'deletion and supplementation', 'composition and decomposition', 'free associating') can be triggered by external stimuli provided by social networks. Moreover, we argue that the application of transformation mechanisms – if triggered by external stimuli – is subject to personal docility: similar to negotiations, effectuators change their artefact based on externally provided information. Then, a similar chain of considerations in which docility plays an important role is set in motion. The only notable difference is that no new stakeholders and resources are gathered in the process.

2.3 Performance Impact of the Position and Shape of Entrepreneurial Social Networks

Hoang and Antoncic (2003) list three research areas regarding the impact of entrepreneurial networks: content, governance and structure. Focusing on structure as the best-researched category, we now review and discuss findings regarding two key qualities that characterize the social network of entrepreneurs: position (size, centrality) and shape (structural holes).

2.3.1 Performance impact of network position

The position within a network is usually defined by the measures of centrality or size. Researchers have identified a variety of benefits stemming from centrality and size, all of which have a common theme: the network enables access to resources outside the direct reach of the entrepreneur. The size of an entrepreneur's network increases the quantity (Adler and Kwon, 2002; Batjargal, 2003) and variety (Greve and Salaff, 2003; Greve, 1995) of accessible resources and improves the likelihood of their successful acquisition (Semrau and Werner, 2013). In this context, 'resources' include both tangible resources, such as funding (Vanacker et al., 2011; Zimmer and Aldrich, 1987) and human resources (Freeman, 1999), and intangible resources, such as emotional support (Brüderl and Preisendörfer, 1998), information to recognize opportunities (Birley, 1985), and access to production capacity and distribution channels (Brown and Butler, 1995). Using all accessible resources, the depicted prediction-based entrepreneur will gather knowledge of customer preferences and exploit a new idea in such a way that the demands of a predefined target group are optimally satisfied.

Control-based entrepreneurship, however, proposes a different approach to networking. Controlling the shape of a market requires influencing market participants and including them to foster joint action. Despite the difference in approach, the impact of network position in control-based entrepreneurship has not been discussed in the literature. Aside from the generally positive performance impact (Read et al., 2009), to our knowledge, control-based social networking has not been discussed at all. At best, we can assume that increased centrality, resulting in a larger means base, improves the performance of control-based entrepreneurship by enabling access to more potential partners. Thus the stark differences of the control- and prediction-based approaches warrant closer investigation of the performance impact of network position.

2.3.2 Performance impact of network shape

Hoang and Antoncic (2003) identify 'bridging weak ties' and 'structural holes' as key theoretical constructs with regard to network shape. 'Bridging weak ties' (Granovetter, 1973) refers to the finding that acquaintances loosely related to an actor are more likely to provide non-redundant information. Granovetter's conclusions have been extended by Burt (1992) and subsumed under his 'structural holes' paradigm. Not unlike the idea of an 'electron hole' in solid-state physics (Weller, 1967), a structural hole describes the absence of a tie between two actors. According to Burt (1992), entrepreneurs profit from a network rich in structural holes. Hoang and Antoncic (2003) list multiple studies (Baum et al., 2000; Krackhardt, 1995; Zaheer and McEvily, 1999) that empirically support Burt's theory. Burt proposes that entrepreneurs should actively manage their social network to be as efficient (non-redundant) and effective (focusing on contacts with an abundance of structural holes) as possible. He proposes a strategy enabling entrepreneurs to actively benefit from an effective and efficient network called *tertius gaudens*. Originally introduced by Simmel (1896), *tertius gaudens* refers to a party who benefits from a conflict between two other parties. Burt argues that entrepreneurs should reorganize their network toward non-redundant contacts to engage in information arbitrage and benefit from competition for information. Because the exploited parties are not aware of each other, the entrepreneur is not constrained by the risk of disclosure through direct communication. However, the depicted entrepreneurs behave significantly differently from control-based expert serial entrepreneurs. Moreover, Burt's strategy relies on prediction-based planning and assumes an environment of relative certainty.

In (2005), Obstfeld proposed a behavioural model that opposed Burt's *tertius gaudens* approach: the *tertius iungens*. Revisiting Simmel's work on triads (Simmel and Wolf, 1950) – the effects of constellations of three actors – Obstfeld's *tertius iungens* represents an approach that focuses on actively filling social holes to foster collaboration and the emergence of innovative projects. His approach ultimately reduces the efficiency of networks and increasingly constrains an entrepreneur by reducing his or her degree of freedom in negotiations. Building on Burt's findings that the *tertius gaudens* strategy fosters 'good ideas' but ultimately negatively affects their implementation (Burt, 2004), Obstfeld argues that the benefits of collaborative innovation and the decreased mobilization efforts might outweigh the benefits of Burt's *tertius gaudens* strategy.

Given the emphasis of both effectuation and the *tertius iungens* approach on collaboration, control-based entrepreneurship strategies, such as effectuation, appear conceptually closer to *tertius iungens* than *tertius gaudens* (Sarasvathy and Dew, 2005b). However, effectuation is classified as an approach suitable for radically innovative ideas (Sarasvathy, 2001) and could thus benefit from a network shaped in favour of a *tertius gaudens* entrepreneur. In effect, control-based strategies have not yet been associated with either strategy. Moreover, it is unclear how a network shaped in (dis)favour of a *tertius gaudens* entrepreneur affects control-based strategies.

3. COMPUTER SIMULATIONS AS A METHOD

This study uses agent-based computer simulations to examine the impact of network position and shape. As a 'third way of doing science' (Axelrod, 1997), computer simulations can create unique insights, particularly for theories in a nascent state (Davis et al., 2007), such as the control-based effectuation logic (Perry et al., 2012). In addition to their flexibility, computer simulations allow for data collection at a level of detail and accuracy unparalleled by empirical research (McKelvey, 2004). This is an important aspect, particularly for social network studies, because 'about half of what people report about their own interactions is incorrect in one way or another' (Wasserman and Faust, 1994, p. 57). Once implemented, computer simulations allow for 'virtual experiments' (Davis et al., 2007) to study available theory under varying conditions with minor effort. This approach enables the development of a deeper understanding of theory, particularly because it can be tested under boundary conditions – areas typically associated with sparse data in empirical studies.

Although computer simulations are rarely used in entrepreneurship research, 'several influential research efforts have used simulation as their primary method' (Harrison et al., 2007). March (1991) investigates the relation between exploration and exploitation in organizational learning using a form of agent-based simulation. Ganco and Agarwal (2009) use computer simulations to study the performance impact of environmental turbulence and firm characteristics for various industries. Davis et al. (2009) used computer simulation to investigate the interplay between firm structure and environmental complexity.

Using the step-based approach of Davis et al. (2007), we develop a formal model of effectuation emphasizing the use of social networks based on expert interviews and the literature review presented in Section 2. We implemented the model using the simulation framework Repast Simphony

(North et al., 2007) and the JUNG library (O'Madadhain et al., 2005) to calculate network measures. This set-up enables automatized data collection for individual agents at each time step.

4. A FORMAL MODEL OF EFFECTUAL SOCIAL NETWORKING

Modelling effectual social networking requires a formal representation of all relevant actors, objects and processes of effectual networking. This includes effectuators and their artefacts as well as end customers, representing the environment. Effectuators and end customers form a social network that allows effectuators to approach both end customers and other effectuators. According to the literature (Dew and Sarasvathy, 2007), effectuators cooperate only with stakeholders who are willing to make pre-commitments. We paid special attention to the implementation of uncertainty because this is a major prerequisite for effectuation (Sarasvathy et al., 2008).

In brief, the simulations are performed as follows: starting at time step one, all effectual agents begin presenting their artefacts to known contacts. The approached agents probabilistically relay the received artefact to known contacts. Moreover, they engage in negotiations with the approaching effectual agent. If an agreement is reached, both agents agree on a joint artefact and continue their search for additional stakeholders together. If no agreement is reached, the engaged party can decide to transform its artefact based on the information gained from the presented artefact. Over time, the artefacts are refined, and the simulation converges to a setting of multiple stable projects. The simulation is stopped after 40 steps, which is a sufficient amount of time to reach a stable state.

4.1 Objects and Actors

4.1.1 Artefact

The term artefact refers to a product, service, project or goal being finalized by an effectuator (Sarasvathy, 2001). Following the product description of arbitrary merchandise, for example a mobile phone, we formalized an artefact as a list of (feature: variant) combinations. For example, a mobile phone could be described as follows: {(colour: red), (weight: 100 g), (connectivity: 3G), (battery capacity: 2000 mAh)}. Mathematically, we formalize an artefact A as a set of (feature, variant) tuples of variable length, as presented in Equation (12.1). Each feature can appear only once in an artefact, and the number of variants per feature and the total number of features are limited, discrete and strictly positive.

$$A = \{(f_a, v_a), (f_b, v_b), \ldots \mid \forall i\, f_i \in \{1..f_{max}\}, \forall j\, v_j \in \{1...v_{max}\}, \forall a, b\; a \neq b \rightarrow f_a \neq f_b\}$$

$$f_{max} \in \mathrm{N}^+, v_{max} \in \mathrm{N}^+ \tag{12.1}$$

Moreover, with Equations (12.2) and (12.3), we define ways to mathematically access artefacts. In Equation (12.2), we define $v(f, A)$ as the variant of feature f in artefact A, if available. The variant '0' is reserved for 'unknown feature'. In our example, the variant of the 'colour' feature of our mobile phone is 'red', and the variant of the feature 'sound system' is '0' because it was not yet defined.

$$v(f, A) = \begin{cases} 0, \neg\exists f\,(f, v) \in A \\ v, \;\; \exists f\,(f, v) \in A \end{cases} \tag{12.2}$$

The set $F(A)$ in Equation (12.3) represents the set of all known features in A. In the mobile phone example, this would be the set {colour, weight, connectivity, battery capacity}.

$$F(A) = \{f_i \mid \forall v\,(f_i, v) \in A\} \tag{12.3}$$

4.1.2 Effectual agent

We model effectuators as agents pursuing the task of artefact finalization using their social network. Every effectual agent has an artefact, which is partially pre-populated with randomly drawn (feature: variant) combinations during the initialization of the simulation. Although the literature states that effectual agents can 'declare the effectual transformation complete and begin competing in alternative markets' (Sarasvathy and Dew, 2005a, p. 549), we focus on a single cycle of effectual artefact finalization. Moreover, we assume that each stakeholder enters with sufficient resources to drive transformations and negotiations. Therefore we do not explicitly model resources and potential constraints.

4.1.3 End customer

End customers represent the market demand in our current model. Formalized as agents, they fulfil the role of representing the conscious and sub-conscious market demand. The effectuation literature often notes the important role of end customers in examples, such as the customer-investors of U-Haul who helped to both shape and grow a one-man, one-truck company into America's leading provider of moving and storage resources (Sarasvathy, 2001). More recent examples are the users of crowdfunding platforms, for example kickstarter. These customers represent the market demand to entrepreneurs who ask for their funding.

Thus we formalize end customers as 'passive' agents with two distinct properties: they can initiate the negotiation of pre-commitments on approach and represent the market demand in these negotiations. End-customer agents represent the conscious market demand by an artefact that is used in negotiations. The sub-conscious demands are captured in a fitness landscape that enables end-customer agents to assess the utility of a complete artefact.

We formalized the utility of an artefact using a well-known utility function known as the 'fitness landscape' (Levinthal, 1997). The fitness landscape is a simple mathematical model that calculates a single fitness value for any given artefact, which represents the utility of an artefact for the market. Higher fitness values represent a higher market utility, that is, a more desirable product for the market.

Similar to effectual agents, all end-customer agents have an artefact representing their conscious demands. During the initialization, the artefact is partially pre-populated with (feature: variant) combinations. Although the features are drawn randomly, the respective variant for an end-customer agent is drawn to probabilistically represent the market utility. For instance, if the artefact represents a mobile phone, the utility of a high-capacity battery is considerably higher than the utility of a low-capacity battery. Therefore the 'high' variant is more likely to be assigned to the 'battery capacity' feature of an artefact than the 'low' variant.

4.1.4 Fitness landscape

We formalized the representation of market utility as an 'NK-fitness landscape', a well-known approach in management research employing simulation studies (Ganco and Agarwal, 2009; Gavetti and Levinthal, 2000; Levinthal, 1997). In accordance with effectuation theory, we implemented the simplest version of an NK-fitness landscape (K = 0), which regards products as 'near decomposable', as required by theory (Sarasvathy, 2003).

The total utility $U(A)$ of an artefact A in our fitness landscape is defined as the sum of the utility of its (feature: variant) combinations:

$$U(A) = \sum_{(f_i, v_i) \in F(A)} u((f_i, v_i)) + \sum_{f_i \notin F(A)} u((f_i, 0))$$

$$\forall f_i \in \{1 \ldots f_{\max}\}, v_i \in \{0 \ldots v_{\max}\} \quad u((f_i, v_i)) \in [0,1], \textit{randomly} \quad (12.4)$$

As indicated in Equation (12.4), we randomly initialize our utility function $u((f_i, v_i))$ for all possible (feature: variant) combinations. Moreover, we assign a value to features absent from an artefact. The fitness of an artefact representing the aforementioned mobile phone, for example, is calculated by awarding points to known features, for example 'colour', with high scores for 'yellow' and low scores for 'black'. Moreover, we assign points for missing features, for example 'surround sound system', which may be useless in business phones – and therefore score points by absence – but could be considered desirable for younger consumers. All points are then summed up to calculate the total utility value $U(A)$ of an artefact.

4.1.5 Social network

We initialize the network among effectual agents as well as between effectual and end-customer agents as an undirected free-scale network according to the generation procedures introduced by Barabási and Albert (1999). Numerous studies have shown that free-scale networks best capture the structure of real-world networks (Aiello et al., 2001; Barabási and Albert, 1999; Broder et al., 2000; Jeong et al., 2001; Newman, 2000). Scale-free networks assume that the likelihood p of having k known contacts exhibits a negative exponential distribution ($p \sim k^{-\alpha}$).

The generation process of Barabási and Albert allows for a simple creation in two steps. First, the algorithm creates a network of effectual agents. Second, the algorithm attaches end-customer agents to the network. Initially, our algorithm creates a network of effectuators by cycling through all effectuators and creating exactly one tie originating from this effectual agent i. The target effectual agent j of the tie is probabilistically chosen, as indicated in Equation (12.5):

$$p(j) \sim \beta + Degree(j)^{\alpha},\ \alpha = 1, \beta = 0.1, i \neq j \qquad (12.5)$$

The function $Degree(j)$ refers to the number of contacts known by agent j. Second, all end-customer agents are attached to the previously created network in the same manner.

4.2 Simulation Mechanics

4.2.1 Behaviours of effectual agents

Effectual agents can exhibit four behaviours to interact with their environment: approaching a known contact to present the current state of their artefacts; relaying information about received artefacts to known contacts; negotiating strategic alliances by exchanging pre-commitments; and inheriting the ideas of other effectual agents' artefacts through transformation.

These behaviours are controlled by the effectual agents' persistence and docility. Both parameters are formalized as a variable representing low persistence and docility as 0.0 and high persistence and docility as 1.0.

4.2.2 Approaching known contacts

Effectual agents can approach known contacts to present the current state of their artefacts. We formalized this behaviour as transferring copies of their artefact. For each contact, the effectual agent executes this behaviour probabilistically using the persistence parameter as the execution probability. The effectual agent can approach all known contacts – except for its stakeholders – once per turn. This behaviour is executed at the beginning of the simulation and every time its artefact changes. The recipient processes the proposed artefact in the next time step.

4.2.3 Relaying received artefacts to known contacts

Effectual agents can relay information about other agents' artefacts. We formalized this behaviour as probabilistically transferring copies of incoming artefacts to all known contacts except for stakeholders. This behaviour is triggered by every incoming artefact and is probabilistically executed using the persistence parameter as the execution probability. Again, the recipient processes the relayed artefact in the next time step. To avoid multiple receptions of the same artefact, a list of previous recipients is transferred along with the artefact to decline the reception if it has been received previously.

4.2.4 Negotiation of pre-commitments

'Even the literature that is directly focused on negotiations has mostly neglected new venture creation processes' (Sarasvathy and Venkataraman, 2011, p. 126). Despite the absence of a concrete algorithm, the literature (Sarasvathy and Dew, 2005a) implies multiple requirements for such an algorithm: (a) allow negotiation between two or more parties; (b) ensure that a position supported by a majority of participants is more likely to prevail; (c) support individual acceptance or refusal of negotiation results to ensure both self-selection into a project as well as the consideration of pre-commitments; and (d) negotiations are triggered by the approach of an effectual agent, as described in the 'effectual cycle' (Dew et al., 2008).

As illustrated in Figure 12.2, we formalized the negotiation process as a simple, three-staged probabilistic negotiation. The behaviour is triggered on reception of an artefact. First, the algorithm determines all relevant stakeholders, that is, project partners of the sending and receiving agents. The algorithm then gathers information on the artefacts of all involved

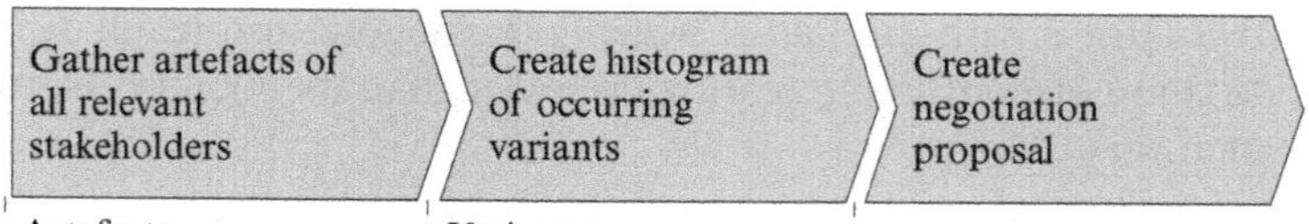

	Artefacts				Variants		
Feature	A_1	A_2	A_3	A_4	v_1	v_2	Porposal
1	1	1	1	1	4	0	1
2	2	2	1	1	2	2	1
5	2	2	1	1	2	2	2
8	2	2	2	1	1	3	2
9	–	–	–	1	1	0	1

Figure 12.2 Visualization of negotiation algorithm

agents. Second, the algorithm creates a combined list of occurring features and traverses it to create histograms of the frequency of the stakeholders' preferred variants. Third, the algorithm creates a proposed negotiation result that includes all known features. The variant of each feature is determined probabilistically using the histograms as a (non-normalized) discrete probability mass function. For instance, if one stakeholder prefers the 'colour' to be 'red' and nine prefer it to be 'blue', the colour will be blue with a likelihood of 90 per cent. Finally, the algorithm proposes the negotiation result to each stakeholder to receive feedback. A negotiation result is accepted only if all stakeholders agree on the adoption. In the event of an adoption, the algorithm replaces the artefact of each stakeholder with the negotiation result and creates new network ties between all project partners.

After a negotiation result is created, each agent individually compares it to the state of its own artefact and decides whether to adopt it. As '[e]ffectuation assumes docility as a fundamental behavioural construct' (Dew et al., 2008, p. 498), we propose a docility-based formalization of the acceptance process for effectual agents following a simple rule: a negotiation result that is more similar to the effectual agent's own artefact will require less docility to be adopted.

We formalized this rule as a calculation of the share of conflicting features in relation to the total number of features held by the artefact of the deciding effectual agent. A conflicting feature is a different variant of the same property, for example a 'red shell' instead of a 'blue shell'. We assume that as the share of conflicted-over known features for an effectuator increases, an effectuator must be more docile to accept these changes. Therefore, in our formal representation, an effectuator e with artefact A accepts the negotiation result R if the relative share of conflicting features is lower than its docility, as indicated in Equation (12.6).

$$\frac{|\{v(f_i,A) \neq v(f_i,R) \mid f_i \in F(A)\}|}{|F(A)|} \leq docility_e \qquad (12.6)$$

4.2.5 Inheriting features trough transformation

As presented in the literature review, we formalize artefact transformation as a single abstract behaviour formalized as follows: the process is triggered by an unsuccessful negotiation. The approached agent now compiles a list of features that are exclusive to the proposed artefact. Then it randomly chooses one of these features. Third, it includes the chosen (feature: variant) combination probabilistically in its artefact, using its docility as the execution probability. Lastly, the effectual agent initiates a negotiation for adoption with its stakeholders.

This formalization implies the assumption that a certain amount of docility is required to transform an artefact based on external information. Moreover, it assumes that the adoption of a previously unknown feature is significantly more likely than the change of a known feature, which represents both the agent's preferences and those of its stakeholders.

4.2.6 End-customer agents' access to the fitness landscape

During the negotiation, end customers can access the fitness landscape representing the market demand once. When confronted with the decision to adopt a negotiation proposal, end-customer agents can access the fitness landscape to determine the total utility value of its artefact and the negotiation result. An end customer only accepts negotiation proposals with improved utility. The access restriction is essential to maintain the uncertainty state of the effectual environment. Knightian uncertainty is maintained because the number of design alternatives and their respective success probabilities cannot be determined by any agent. Goal ambiguity is maintained because end customers can only voice their conscious demands in negotiations, but cannot determine the optimal variant of any feature. Finally, isotropy is maintained because the market demand for variants of known features cannot be estimated beyond the individual demand of the end customers. In conclusion, end-customer agents cannot search the fitness landscape to discover its optimum product.

4.2.7 Measures of network position

We focus on two widely recognized measures of centrality for social networks: degree centrality and betweenness centrality (Wasserman and Faust, 1994). Although both measures capture centrality, they emphasize slightly different aspects of this concept.

'Degree centrality' measures the number of known contacts of an agent. Therefore it also represents the size of the agent's personal network. For better comparability, degree centrality is typically normalized by the total number of agents within a network.

'Betweenness centrality' captures the centrality of an actor by measuring its relevance for the information flow between any two other agents in the network. An agent is regarded as important for the information flow if it is part of the shortest route or 'geodesic' between two agents. The measure is therefore defined as the number of appearances an agent makes on the geodesics of all pairs of other agents.

4.2.8 Measures of network shape

Burt (1992) defines two key measures for the shape of an actor's network: efficiency and constraint.

'Efficiency' is the degree to which the ties of an agent are non-redundant. Thus, in a highly efficient network, an agent is acquainted with contacts that do not know each other but are well connected themselves. In a network with low efficiency, all known contacts only provide access to agents that can also be reached through other ties, rendering the network largely redundant. Burt argues that entrepreneurs benefit from a highly efficient network. The exact measure is given in the literature (Burt, 1992, p. 53).

'Constraint' is a measure that captures the extent to which acquainted contacts impede the exploitation of structural holes. Whereas efficiency measures the extent to which direct ties are redundant, constraint measures the degree to which contacts are acquainted. Burt proposes that the acquaintance between known contacts – the absence of a structural hole between them – impedes the application of arbitrage and competition for information. Therefore a low constraint level indicates an abundance of structural holes, resulting in many opportunities for arbitrage and competition for information or resources.

Burt defines C_i as the measure of constraint for actor i, as indicated in Equation (12.7). The term p_{ij} represents the relative share of energy and time actor i invested in the relationship with j. For simplicity, we assume that actors divide their energy among their known contacts equally.

$$C_i = \sum_{i \neq j} \left(p_{ij} + \sum_{q \neq i \neq j} p_{iq} p_{qj} \right)^2 \tag{12.7}$$

As indicated in Figure 12.3, the constraint is lowest for a star-shaped network around an actor and highest for a complete network. Moreover, the constraint measure depends strongly on the inverse of known

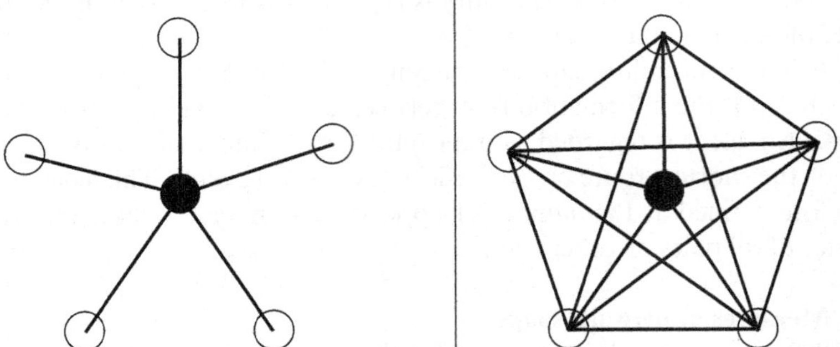

$$p_{ij} = \frac{1}{Degree\ (i)}$$

$$p_{qj} = 0$$

$$\begin{aligned} C_i &= \sum_{i \neq j} \left(p_{ij} + \sum_{q \neq i \neq j} p_{iq} p_{qj} \right)^2 \\ &= \sum_{i \neq j} \left(\frac{1}{Degree(i)} + \sum_{q \neq i \neq j} p_{iq} \cdot 0 \right)^2 \\ &= \sum_{i \neq j} \frac{1}{(Degree(i))^2} \\ &= Degree(i) \cdot \frac{1}{(Degree(i))^2} \\ &= \frac{1}{Degree(i)} \end{aligned}$$

$$p_{ij} = p_{qj} = \frac{1}{Degree\ (i)}$$

$$\begin{aligned} C_i &= \sum_{i \neq j} \left(p_{ij} + \sum_{q \neq i \neq j} p_{iq} p_{qj} \right)^2 \\ &= \sum_{i \neq j} \left(\frac{1}{Degree(i)} + \sum_{q \neq i \neq j} \frac{1}{(Degree(i))^2} \right)^2 \\ &= \sum_{i \neq j} \left(\frac{1}{Degree(i)} + \frac{Degree(i) - 1}{(Degree(i))^2} \right)^2 \\ &= \sum_{i \neq j} \left(\frac{2}{Degree(i)} - \frac{1}{(Degree(i))^2} \right)^2 \\ &< \sum_{i \neq j} \left(\frac{2}{Degree(i)} \right)^2 \\ &= Degree(i) \cdot \frac{4}{(Degree(i))^2} \\ &= \frac{4}{Degree(i)} \end{aligned}$$

Figure 12.3 Maximum and minimum value of Burt's constraint measure

contacts. As our subsequent analysis compares actors with largely differing numbers of contacts, we normalized Burt's constraint measure by multiplying it by actor degree. This normalization results in a continuous value range between 1 (star-shaped network) and 4 (complete network).

4.2.9 Measurement of performance: demand satisfaction

The investigation on performance requires the definition of a performance measure. We define performance analogously to traditional performance measures (Narver et al., 2004; Vorhies and Morgan, 2005) as the similarity of supply and demand and refer to it as demand satisfaction. The more similar an effectual agent's artefact is to those of an end-customer agent, the higher the score. The demand satisfaction $DS(i)$ of an agent i is calculated as a sum over all individual comparisons of an effectual agent's artefact with all end customer agents' artefacts, as indicated in Equation (12.8). The individual comparison score $ds(A_i, A_j)$ is calculated as the share of met conscious demands of end customer j by effectuator i.

$$DS(i) = \sum_{j \neq i} ds(A_i, A_j)$$

$$ds(A_i, A_j) = \frac{|\{v(f, A_i) = v(f, A_j) \mid f \in F(A_j)\}|}{|F(A_j)|} \tag{12.8}$$

5. RESULTS

To investigate the development of social networks of entrepreneurs using control-based logic over time as well as the performance effects of centrality and structural holes, we conducted a series of simulation experiments. We simulated an environment consisting of 40 end-customer agents and 20 effectual agents. All agents received a randomly created artefact consisting of 5 (feature: variant) combinations drawn from 10 available features and 2 respective variants. The fitness landscape and network were randomly initialized for each run. We used values of 0.6 for persistence and 0.2 for docility. To gain a sufficiently large data set, we repeated the simulation 1200 times. Each run consisted of 40 turns, which was sufficient to reach a stable state. In each turn, all aforementioned measures regarding performance, centrality and structural holes were computed for all agents. In total, we collected 1.44 GB of data that we subsequently analysed to investigate our research questions.

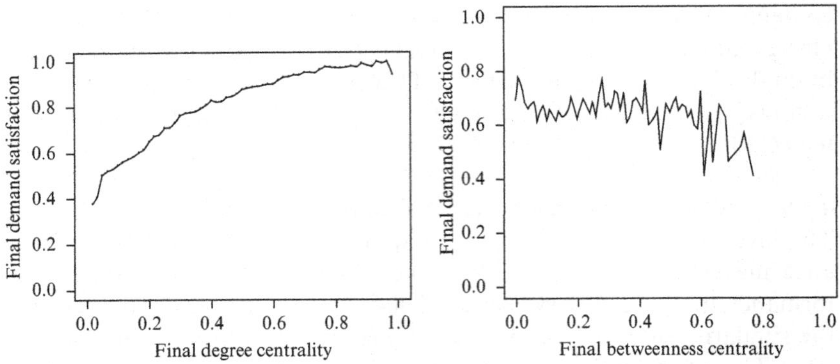

(a) Final demand satisfaction and degree centrality

(b) Final demand satisfaction and betweenness centrality

Figure 12.4 Level of final demand satisfaction over final degree and betweenness centrality

5.1 Performance Impact of Network Position

We conducted two analyses to clarify the impact of network position on performance. First, we correlated demand satisfaction, degree and betweenness centrality at the end of the simulation in a stable state. Second, we compared the initial degree and betweenness centrality to the final value of demand satisfaction for each effectuator.

For the first analysis, we extracted the final values of degree and betweenness centrality, demand satisfaction from the data. In Figures 12.4(a) and 12.4(b), we display the average level of demand satisfaction per level of centrality. To account for the continuous nature of betweenness centrality, we grouped the values into 20 possible levels of betweenness centrality.

The results clearly indicate a connection of degree centrality with demand satisfaction. Starting with an average demand satisfaction of 0.4 for a degree centrality of 0.0, demand satisfaction increases considerably up to 0.8 at level 0.4. Then the speed of growth decreases. Demand satisfaction increases to 1.0 for a degree centrality of 1.0. The correlation of betweenness centrality and demand satisfaction reveals a decrease of demand satisfaction with increasing betweenness centrality. Whereas low betweenness centrality is associated with a median demand satisfaction of 0.7–0.8, increasing betweenness centrality to 0.8 reduces demand satisfaction to 0.4–0.5. Moreover, the relationship between betweenness centrality and demand satisfaction is significantly more distorted than the aforementioned relationships.

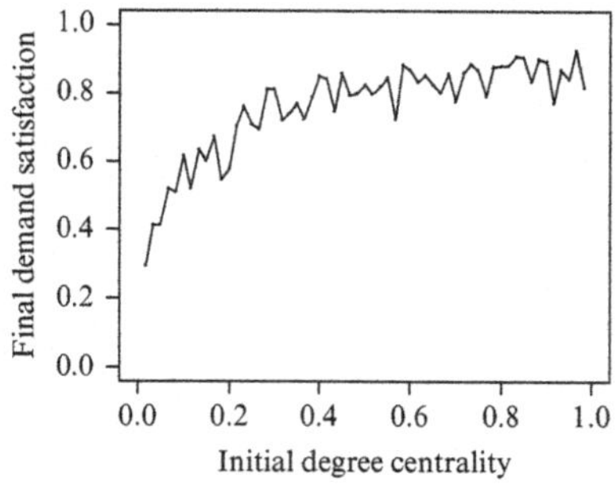

(a) Impact of initial degree centrality

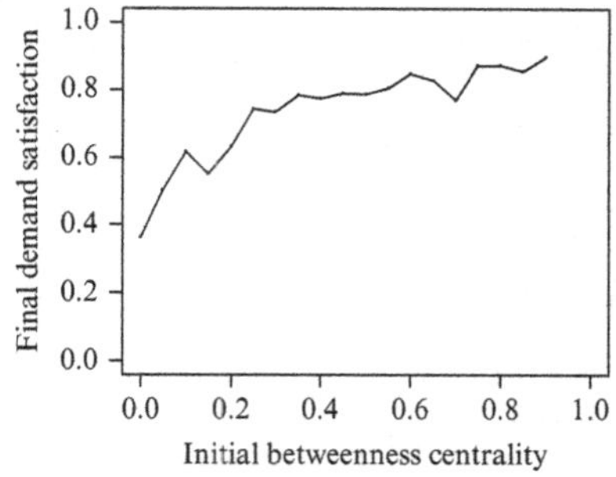

(b) Impact of initial betweenness centrality

Figure 12.5 Level of final demand satisfaction over initial degree and betweenness centrality

Our second analysis concerned the impact of initial network configuration and final demand satisfaction. Thus we analysed the impact of initial degree and betweenness centrality on the resulting demand satisfaction at a stable simulation state, which was always reached in turn 40. To ensure the availability of data over the entire range of initial centrality, we focused on a single agent, which was initialized with a given number of known contacts covering the complete range from 1 to 59.

As presented in Figures 12.5(a) and 12.5(b), both initial degree and betweenness centrality have an impact on final demand satisfaction. Furthermore, in both cases, demand satisfaction increases strongly, with centrality from 0.0 to 0.3–0.4 up to 0.7–0.8, after which demand satisfaction grows only marginally with increasing initial centrality to approximately 0.9 for both centrality measures.

5.2 Performance Impact of Network Shape

Our second series of analyses targeted the performance implications of structural holes as defined by Burt (1992). Thus we investigated the effects of constraint and network efficiency. For the analysis of efficiency and demand satisfaction, we grouped the continuous values into 20 levels of efficiency and 60 levels of normalized constraint to obtain meaningful results. As shown in Figure 12.6(a), demand satisfaction decreases with efficiency from approximately 0.9 for minimal efficiency values to 0.3 for maximally efficient networks. As shown in Figure 12.6(b), demand satisfaction increases gradually with normalized constraint from approximately 0.4 for low normalized constraint (1.0) to approximately 0.5 for a normalized constraint level of 2.5. Then, demand satisfaction

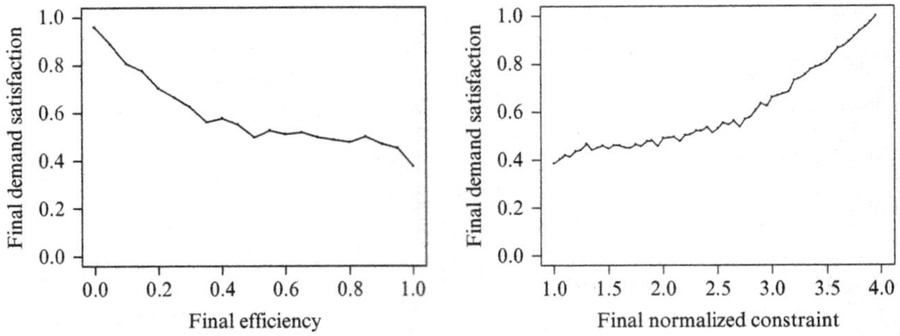

(a) Final demand satisfaction and efficiency

(b) Final demand staisfaction and normalized constraint

Figure 12.6 Level of final demand satisfaction over final efficiency and normalized constraint

increases considerably to 1.0 for the highest possible level of normalized constraint (4.0).

5.3 Development of Social Networks over Time

Our third series of analyses targeted the development of the previously presented measures over time. To better understand the dynamics of the development of effectual social networks, we tracked the development of degree, and betweenness centrality as well as efficiency and constraint for each time step of each simulation run. Figures 12.7 and 12.8 capture the average values of the aforementioned measures per time step.

As reflected in Figures 12.7(a) and 12.7(b), over time, the average degree centrality increases from an initial value of approximately 0.05 to 0.35 at

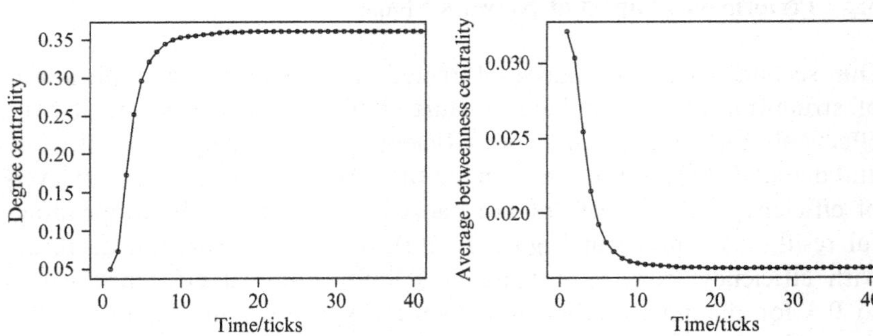

(a) Degree centrality over time

(b) Betweenness centrality over time

Figure 12.7 Development of degree and betweenness centrality over time

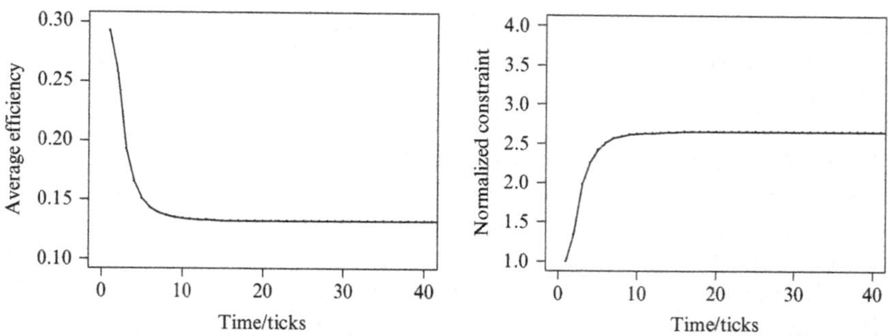

(a) Average efficiency over time

(b) Normalized constraint over time

Figure 12.8 Development of efficiency and normalized constraint over time

time step 18. The average betweenness centrality decreases from an initial value of 0.03 to 0.015 at time step 18. All values are constant after this time, indicating the stabilization of the simulation.

Figures 12.8(a) and 12.8(b) indicate that, over time, average efficiency decreases from its initial value of approximately 0.3 to 0.15 at time step 18. The average normalized constraint increases from an initial level of 1.0 to 2.5–3.0 at time step 18.

6. DISCUSSION AND IMPLICATIONS

Although the creation and utilization of social networks are critical for entrepreneurs, the underlying theory regarding entrepreneurial social networks is still underdeveloped. Moreover, 'classical' networking strategies are at odds with control-based entrepreneurship approaches such as effectuation. Focusing on the impact of network structure, we used an agent-based computer simulation of effectuation to understand how entrepreneurs using control-based logics benefit from network position and shape. Moreover, we analysed how these entrepreneurs reorganize their social networks to enhance performance.

6.1 Performance Impact of Network Position

Our simulation experiments regarding network position reveal a significant performance impact of the network position in general and the initial position in particular. Moreover, the analysis of development over time reveals that control-based entrepreneurship actively improves the network position over time. However, these developments are captured to varying degrees by established centrality measures. Although degree centrality is positively correlated with demand satisfaction, betweenness centrality is negatively correlated with performance.

6.1.1 Performance implications of final network position

Our simulation experiments indicate a strong correlation between degree centrality and demand satisfaction at the end of the simulation, which is implicitly predicted by effectuation theory: instead of predicting the market demand, entrepreneurs using control-based logic shape their market by actively including stakeholders in the creation of their artefacts. In turn, these joint artefacts meet the demand of the stakeholders, that is, project members. Consequently, the increasing size of the stakeholder group drives both demand satisfaction and degree centrality.

Degree centrality can be easily measured empirically and has been shown earlier to have a positive impact on entrepreneurial venture performance. However, the underlying reasons were different: for 'classical' entrepreneurship, high degree centrality increases the likelihood to acquire resources, such as market information or capital. For control-based entrepreneurship, on the other hand, degree centrality is a proxy for successful control of the demand landscape. The difference in underlying reasons can best be captured with betweenness centrality, a measure that cannot easily be obtained empirically because a nearly complete disclosure of the network is necessary. Betweenness centrality captures the extent to which an actor serves as an 'information hub' within a network. The role of the information hub is positively associated with performance in general entrepreneurship theory. Granovetter (1973) refers to the 'strength of weak ties', Burt's 'tertius gaudens' strategy relies on being an information hub, and several studies underline the importance of access to diverse information (Baum et al., 2000; Burt, 2004; Krackhardt, 1995; Zaheer and McEvily, 1999). Thus high betweenness centrality should result in high venture performance. However, our simulation clearly reveals that the opposite is true for control-based entrepreneurship: successful entrepreneurs using control-based logic reorganize their network through the inclusion of actors and thereby 'short-circuit' the path that is necessary for information flow between unacquainted project members. In this manner, actors increase their degree centrality while reducing their betweenness centrality. This explanation is supported by the development of degree and betweenness centralities over time. Successful entrepreneurs using control-based logic manage to reorganize their networks by increasing degree centrality and reducing betweenness centrality through their partnering approach.

6.1.2 Performance impact of initial network position

An important topic raised by practitioners is the initial impact of network position on future venture performance. Thus we analysed the impact of initial degree and betweenness centrality on the final level of demand satisfaction. Although the general positive relationship between degree centrality and demand satisfaction holds, there is an important difference: our simulation reveals that, beyond a certain threshold, additional centrality adds only infinitesimal levels of demand satisfaction for the agent. This result implies that a certain number of contacts is required to optimally apply control-based networking methods, but beyond a certain level, the initial 'connectedness' of an entrepreneur using control-based logic does not significantly contribute to performance.

Of particular interest is the counter-intuitive relationship between initial betweenness centrality and future performance, that is, demand satisfaction. Although negatively correlated for stable environments, initial betweenness centrality is positively correlated with final demand satisfaction in our simulation. In conjunction with the development of betweenness centrality over time, this paradox can be explained by the fact that an initially high betweenness centrality constitutes a potential opportunity to acquire a diverse set of stakeholders. Entrepreneurs using control-based logic can only increase demand satisfaction if they manage to successfully realize this potential through collaboration and subsequent introduction, that is, the creation of a direct network path. This behaviour, in turn, reduces betweenness centrality.

6.2 Performance Impact of Network Shape

In addition to the effects of network position, theory regarding the performance impact of network shape for control-based entrepreneurship logics, such as effectuation, is still underdeveloped. As discussed in the literature review, Burt (1992) and Obstfeld (2005) have proposed strategies for entrepreneurs to benefit from certain network shapes. Based on Simmel's concept of *tertius gaudens* (Simmel and Wolf, 1950), Burt developed an entrepreneurship approach that effectively employs networks rich in structural holes by actively keeping network contacts separate and benefits from brokering between these contacts. As we saw earlier, in 2005, Obstfeld proposed an opposing strategy called *tertius iungens*, which focuses on connecting actors in a social network. We contribute to these streams of research by affiliating control-based entrepreneurial logics, such as effectuation, with the *tertius iungens* strategy and by providing a performance analysis in a highly uncertain environment.

6.2.1 Performance impact of efficiency

The negative correlation between final demand satisfaction and efficiency indicates that highly efficient networks are not suitable for control-based entrepreneurship logics, such as effectuation. Moreover, control-based entrepreneurship logic actively reduces efficiency by introducing unacquainted new stakeholders. In effect, a network with low efficiency indicates that a control-based entrepreneur succeeded in gathering stakeholders and in shaping market demand in his or her favour.

These findings initially seem contradictory to Burt's approach to entrepreneurial networking that deems efficient networks favourable for entrepreneurs. However, a closer analysis of Burt's implicit assumptions reveals the reasons for these unexpected results. Burt's *tertius gaudens* strategy proposes to identify good ideas stemming from known contacts and to combine them in innovative ways (Burt, 2004). However, this approach implies that (1) the environment allows for the identification of good ideas and that (2) a transactional relationship with network contacts is sufficient. These conditions are unfulfilled in environments suitable for control-based entrepreneurship: effectuation, for example, assumes an entrepreneurial design space dominated by Knightian uncertainty, Marchian goal ambiguity and isotropy. It is thus impossible to assess the quality of an idea in this environment. Moreover, control-based entrepreneurship requires full commitment and continuous involvement of each stakeholder; thus a transactional relationship is insufficient. Therefore control-based entrepreneurs simply cannot employ the advantages of an efficient network.

6.2.2 Performance impact of normalized constraint and structural holes

In our simulation, normalized constraint exhibits a positive relationship with demand satisfaction. Moreover, our longitudinal analysis reveals that entrepreneurs using control-based logic actively reorganize their network to increase normalized constraint. Again, these results seem to contradict Burt's structural holes theory, which proposes a negative impact of highly constrained networks. Once more, the juxtaposition of the *tertius gaudens* strategy and effectuation as an example of control-based entrepreneurship reveals the cause: transactional relationships with stakeholders as well as the application of arbitrage and brokering are not part of the effectual toolbox. Thus effectuation has no means of profiting from structural holes. Entrepreneurs using control-based logic rather actively include new potential stakeholders to reduce the number of structural holes around them. Although entrepreneurs using control-based logic thereby constrain themselves, they also constrain their partners and bind them to their projects.

This is also reflected in the literature: Sarasvathy and Dew, for example, oppose the compatibility of the *tertius gaudens* strategy and effectuation (Sarasvathy and Dew, 2005a, 2005b). Given the necessity for co-creation and joint action, control-based entrepreneurship logics, such as effectuation, are conceptually closer to Obstfeld's *tertius iungens* (Obstfeld, 2005).

In addition to the inability to profit from structural holes, control-based entrepreneurship logics even suffer from them: in his analysis of constraint and good ideas, Burt (2004) reveals that networks with low constraint enable entrepreneurs to generate superior ideas yet fall short of implementing them. As noted by Obstfeld (2005), action toward implementation is taken by entrepreneurs with rather constrained networks. Thus an 'action-based' (Brettel et al., 2012) approach such as effectuation requires constrained networks to be successful.

In effect, both efficiency and normalized constraint reveal that control-based entrepreneurship is a successful implementation of the *tertius iungens* strategy that actively reorganizes networks to jointly shape market demand. While Burt's proposed strategy may be incompatible with control-based entrepreneurship logics, the proposed measures can successfully be applied to identify suitable network shapes for both approaches.

6.3 Limitations and Avenues for Further Research

Our study has several limitations that signal avenues for further research, which can be grouped into three categories: development of effectuation theory; empirical validation; and enhancement of our effectuation model.

Our formalization of effectuation contributes to a more precise definition of the effectual process and the entities involved. However, the current literature does not sufficiently examine the network-related aspects of effectuation. Further development of effectual networking theory requires additional case studies regarding the details of the networking process. Such studies should focus on negotiation yet include the termination of projects and the exclusion of stakeholders, as well as a more detailed understanding of resource acquisition, distribution and application.

Empirical validation of our theoretical propositions is required to either support our findings or challenge and thereby improve our formal model. Moreover, a validation of the practical applicability of our normalized constraint measure could validate our findings and contribute to theory development.

Finally, our formal model provides a multitude of improvement opportunities. First, the inclusion of resources would enable access to a vast field of research opportunities. Second, the inclusion of competing strategies would foster the investigation on conditions for normative superiority. This way, entrepreneurs could make an informed choice regarding their (networking) strategy.

REFERENCES

Adler, P. and Kwon, S. (2002). 'Social capital: prospects for a new concept', *Academy of Management Review*, **27**(1): 17–40.

Aiello, W., Chung, F. and Lu, L. (2001). 'A random graph model for power law graphs', *Experimental Mathematics*, **10**(1): 53–66.

Aldrich, H.E. and Reese, P. (1993). 'Does networking pay off? A panel study of entrepreneurs in the research triangle', *Frontiers of Entrepreneurship Research* (Proceedings of the Thirteenth Annual Babson College Entrepreneurship Research Conference), Wellesley, MA: Babson College, pp. 325–39.

Aldrich, H.E., Rosen, B. and Woodward, W. (1987). 'The impact of social networks on business foundings and profit: a longitudinal study', *Frontiers of Entrepreneurship Research* (Proceedings of the Seventh Annual Babson College Entrepreneurship Research Conference), Wellesley, MA: Babson College, pp. 154–68.

Axelrod, R. (1997). *The Complexity of Cooperation: Agent-Based Models of Competition and Collaboration*, Princeton, NJ: Princeton University Press.

Barabási, A.-L. and Albert, R. (1999). 'Emergence of scaling in random networks', *Science*, **286**(October): 509–12.

Batjargal, B. (2003). 'Social capital and entrepreneurial performance in Russia: a longitudinal study', *Organization Studies*, **24**(4): 535–56.

Baum, J.A.C., Calabrese, T. and Silverman, B.S. (2000). 'Don't go it alone: alliance network composition and startups' performance in Canadian biotechnology', *Strategic Management Journal*, **21**(3): 267–94.

Birley, S. (1985). 'The role of networks in the entrepreneurial process', *Journal of Business Venturing*, **1**(1): 107–17.

Brajkovich, L. (1994). 'Sources of social structure in a start-up organization: work networks, work activities, and job status', *Social Networks*, **16**(3): 191–212.

Brettel, M., Mauer, R., Engelen, A. and Küpper, D. (2012). 'Corporate effectuation: entrepreneurial action and its impact on R&D project performance', *Journal of Business Venturing*, **27**(2): 167–84.

Broder, A., Kumar, R., Maghoul, F., Raghavan, P., Rajagopalan, S., Stata, R. et al. (2000). 'Graph structure in the Web', *Computer Networks*, (1–6): 309–20.

Brown, B. and Butler, J.E. (1995). 'Competitors as allies: a study of entrepreneurial networks in the U.S. wine industry', *Journal of Small Business Management*, **33**(3): 57–66.

Brüderl, J. and Preisendörfer, P. (1998). 'Network support and the success of newly founded business', *Small Business Economics*, **10**(3): 213–25.

Burt, R.S. (1992). *Structural Holes: The Social Structure of Competition*, Boston, MA: Harvard University Press.

Burt, R.S. (2004). 'Structural holes and good ideas', *American Journal of Sociology*, **110**(2): 349–99.

Chandler, G.N., DeTienne, D.R., McKelvie, A. and Mumford, T.V. (2011).

'Causation and effectuation processes: a validation study', *Journal of Business Venturing*, **26**(3): 375–90.

Chiles, T.H., Bluedorn, A.C. and Gupta, V.K. (2007). 'Beyond creative destruction and entrepreneurial discovery: a radical Austrian approach to entrepreneurship', *Organization Studies*, **28**(4): 467–93.

Chiles, T.H., Gupta, V.K. and Bluedorn, A.C. (2008). 'On Lachmannian and effectual entrepreneurship: a rejoinder to Sarasvathy and Dew (2008)', *Organization Studies*, **29**(2): 247–53.

Davis, J.P., Eisenhardt, K.M. and Bingham, C.B. (2007). 'Developing theory through simulation methods', *Academy of Management Review*, **32**(2): 480–99.

Davis, J.P., Eisenhardt, K.M. and Bingham, C.B. (2009). 'Optimal structure, market dynamism, and the strategy of simple rules', *Administrative Science Quarterly*, **54**(3): 413–52.

Dew, N. and Sarasvathy, S.D. (2007). 'Innovations, stakeholders & entrepreneurship', *Journal of Business Ethics*, **74**(3): 267–83.

Dew, N., Read, S., Sarasvathy, S.D. and Wiltbank, R. (2008). 'Outlines of a behavioral theory of the entrepreneurial firm', *Journal of Economic Behavior & Organization*, **66**(1): 37–59.

Dew, N., Read, S., Sarasvathy, S.D. and Wiltbank, R. (2010). 'On the entrepreneurial genesis of new markets: effectual transformations versus causal search and selection', *Journal of Evolutionary Economics*, **21**(2): 231–53.

Freeman, J. (1999). 'Venture capital as an economy of time', in S.M. Gabbay and R.T.A.J. Leenders (eds), *Corporate Social Capital and Liability*, New York: Springer, pp. 460–82.

Ganco, M. and Agarwal, R. (2009). 'Performance differentials between diversifying entrants and entrepreneurial start-ups: a complexity approach', *Academy of Management Review*, **34**(2): 228–52.

Gavetti, D. and Levinthal, D.A. (2000). 'Looking forward and looking backward: cognitive and experiential search', *Administrative Science Quarterly*, **45**(1): 113–37.

Goel, S. and Karri, R. (2006). 'Entrepreneurs, effectual logic, and over-trust', *Entrepreneurship Theory and Practice*, (218): 477–94.

Granovetter, M.S. (1973). 'The strength of weak ties', *American Journal of Sociology*, **78**(6): 1360–80.

Greve, A. (1995). 'Networks and entrepreneurship – an analysis of social relations, occupational background, and use of contacts during the establishment process', *Scandinavian Journal of Management*, **11**(1): 1–24.

Greve, A. and Salaff, J. (2003). 'Social networks and entrepreneurship', *Entrepreneurship Theory and Practice*, **28**(1): 1–22.

Harrison, R.J., Carroll, G.R. and Carley, K.M. (2007). 'Simulation modeling in organizational and management research', *Academy of Management Review*, **32**(4): 1229–45.

Hite, J. (2005). 'Evolutionary processes and paths of relationally embedded network ties in emerging entrepreneurial firms', *Entrepreneurship Theory and Practice*, **29**(1): 113–44.

Hoang, H. and Antoncic, B. (2003). 'Network-based research in entrepreneurship: a critical review', *Journal of Business Venturing*, **18**: 165–87.

Holland, J.H. (1975). *Adaption in Natural and Artificial Systems*, Ann Arbor, MI: The University of Michigan Press.

Jack, S. (2005). 'The role, use and activation of strong and weak network ties: a qualitative analysis', *Journal of Management Studies*, **42**(6): 1233–59.
Jack, S. (2010). 'Approaches to studying networks: implications and outcomes', *Journal of Business Venturing*, **25**(1): 120–37.
Jack, S., Dodd, S.D. and Anderson, A.R. (2008). 'Change and the development of entrepreneurial networks over time: a processual perspective', *Entrepreneurship & Regional Development*, **20**(2): 125–59.
Jeong, H., Mason, S.P., Barabási, A.L. and Oltvai, Z.N. (2001). 'Lethality and centrality in protein networks', *Nature*, **411**(6833): 41–2.
Jones, C., Hesterly, W.S. and Borgatti, S.P. (1997). 'A general theory of network governance: exchange conditions and social mechanisms', *Academy of Management Review*, **22**(4): 911–45.
Karri, R. and Goel, S. (2008). 'Effectuation and over-trust: response to Sarasvathy and Dew', *Entrepreneurship Theory and Practice*, **32**(4), 739–49.
Knight, F.H. (1921). *Risk, Uncertainty and Profit*, Boston, MA: Houghton Mifflin Company.
Krackhardt, D. (1995). 'Entrepreneurial opportunities in an entrepreneurial firm: a structural approach', *Entrepreneurship Theory and Practice*, **19**(3): 53–69.
Larson, A. and Starr, J. (1993). 'A network model of organization formation', *Entrepreneurship Theory and Practice*, **17**(2): 5–15.
Levinthal, D.A. (1997). 'Adaptation on rugged landscapes', *Management Science*, **43**: 934–50.
March, J.G. (1991). 'Exploration and exploitation in organizational learning', *Organization Science*, **2**(1): 71–87.
McKelvey, B. (2004). 'Toward a complexity science of entrepreneurship', *Journal of Business Venturing*, **19**(3): 313–41.
Narver, J.C., Slater, S.F. and MacLachlan, D.L.(2004). 'Responsive and proactive market orientation and new-product success', *Journal of Product Innovation Management*, **21**(5): 334–47.
Newman, M.E.J. (2000). 'The structure of scientific collaboration networks', *Proceedings of the National Academy of Sciences of the United States of America*, **98**(2): 404–9.
North, M.J., Howe, T.R., Collier, N.T. and Vos, J.R. (2007). 'A declarative model assembly infrastructure for verification and validation', in S. Takahashi, D. Sallach and J. Rouchier (eds), *Advancing Social Simulation The First World Congress*, (1): 129–40.
O'Madadhain, J., Fisher, D., Smyth, P., White, S. and Boey, Y. (2005). 'Analysis and visualization of network data using JUNG', *Journal of Statistical Software*, **10**(2): 1–35.
Obstfeld, D. (2005). 'Social networks, the *tertius iungens* orientation, and involvement in innovation', *Administrative Science Quarterly*, **50**(1): 100–130.
Perry, J.T., Chandler, G.N. and Markova, G. (2012). 'Entrepreneurial effectuation: a review and suggestions for future research', *Entrepreneurship Theory and Practice*, **36**(4): 837–61.
Read, S., Song, M. and Smit, W. (2009). 'A meta-analytic review of effectuation and venture performance', *Journal of Business Venturing*, **24**(6): 573–87.
Rowley, T., Behrens, D. and Krackhardt, D. (2000). 'Redundant governance structures: an analysis of structural and relational embeddedness in the steel and semiconductor industries', *Strategic Management Journal*, **21**(3): 369–86.

Sarasvathy, S.D. (2001). 'Causation and effectuation: toward a theoretical shift from economic inevitability to entrepreneurial contingency', *Academy of Management Review*, **26**(2): 243–63.

Sarasvathy, S.D. (2003). 'Entrepreneurship as a science of the artificial', *Journal of Economic Psychology*, **24**(2): 203–20.

Sarasvathy, S.D. and Dew, N. (2005a). 'New market creation through transformation', *Journal of Evolutionary Economics*, **15**(5): 533–65.

Sarasvathy, S.D. and Dew, N. (2005b). 'Entrepreneurial logics for a technology of foolishness', *Scandinavian Journal of Management*, 21(4): 385–406.

Sarasvathy, S.D. and Dew, N. (2008a). 'Effectuation and over-trust: debating Goel and Karri', *Entrepreneurship Theory and Practice*, **32**(4): 727–37.

Sarasvathy, S.D. and Dew, N. (2008b). 'Is effectuation Lachmannian? A response to Chiles, Bluedorn, and Gupta (2007)', *Organization Studies*, **29**(2): 239–45.

Sarasvathy, S.D., Dew, N., Read, S. and Wiltbank, R. (2008). 'Designing organizations that design environments: lessons from entrepreneurial expertise', *Organization Studies*, **29**(3): 331–50.

Sarasvathy, S.D. and Venkataraman, S. (2011). 'Entrepreneurship as method: open questions for an entrepreneurial future', *Entrepreneurship Theory and Practice*, **35**(1): 113–35.

Semrau, T. and Werner, A. (2013). 'How exactly do network relationships pay off? The effects of network size and relationship quality on access to start-up resources', *Entrepreneurship Theory and Practice*, **38**(3): 501–25.

Simmel, G. (1896). 'Superiority and subordination as subject-matter of sociology. II', *American Journal of Sociology*, 392–415.

Simmel, G. and Wolf, K. (1950). *The Sociology of Georg Simmel*, Glencoe, IL: Free Press.

Simon, H.A. (1990). 'A mechanism for social selection and successful altruism', *Science*, **250**(4988): 1665–8.

Simon, H.A. (1993). 'Strategy and organizational evolution', *Strategic Management Journal*, **14**(2): 131–42.

Simon, H.A. (1997). *An Empirically Based Microeconomics*, Cambridge: Cambridge University Press.

Slotte-Kock, S. and Coviello, N. (2010). 'Entrepreneurship research on network processes: a review and ways forward', *Entrepreneurship Theory and Practice*, **34**(1): 31–57.

Vanacker, T., Manigart, S., Meuleman, M. and Sels, L. (2011). 'A longitudinal study on the relationship between financial bootstrapping and new venture growth', *Entrepreneurship & Regional Development*, **23**(9–10): 681–705.

Venkataraman, S., Sarasvathy, S.D., Dew, N. and Forster, W.R. (2012). 'Reflections on the 2010 AMR Decade Award: whither the promise? Moving forward with entrepreneurship as a science of the artificial', *Academy of Management Review*, **37**(1): 21–33.

Vorhies, D.W. and Morgan, N.A. (2005). 'Benchmarking marketing capabilities for sustainable competitive advantage', *Journal of Marketing*, **69**(1): 80–94.

Wasserman, S. and Faust, K. (1994). *Social Network Analysis: Methods and Applications*, Cambridge: Cambridge University Press.

Weller, P.F. (1967). 'An analogy for elementary band theory concepts in solids', *Journal of Chemical Education*, **44**(7): 391.

Wiltbank, R. and Dew, N. (2006). 'What to do next? The case for non-predictive strategy', *Strategic Management Journal*, **27**(10): 981–98.

Wiltbank, R., Read, S., Dew, N. and Sarasvathy, S.D. (2009). 'Prediction and control under uncertainty: outcomes in angel investing', *Journal of Business Venturing*, **24**(2): 116–33.
Witt, P. (2004). 'Entrepreneurs' networks and the success of start-ups', *Entrepreneurship & Regional Development*, **16**(5): 391–412.
Zaheer, A. and McEvily, B. (1999). 'Bridging ties: a source of firm heterogeneity in competitive capabilities', *Strategic Management Journal*, **20**(12): 1133–56.
Zimmer, C. and Aldrich, H.E. (1987). 'Resource mobilization through ethnic networks: kinship and friendship ties of shopkeepers in England', *Sociological Perspectives*, **30**(4): 422–45.

13. Actor-network theory and the entrepreneurial process*

Wadid Lamine, Alain Fayolle and Hela Chebbi

The success of emerging innovative firms is of profound importance. This success depends, of course, on support structures and programmes (Fayolle, 2004), but also on the ways in which nascent entrepreneurs interact with their environment. Although globalization and the global economic market have been discussed a great deal, innovations and knowledge are often produced locally by networks of actors situated in a given territory (Heraud and Levy, 2005; Littunen, 2000; Pecqueur, 1997; Rallet and Torre, 2005). Although many studies have sought to better identify the role and the importance of social networks in entrepreneurship (Hoang and Antoncic, 2003; Davidsson and Honig, 2003; Dubini and Aldrich, 1991; Witt, 2004; Hite, 2005; Jack, 2010; Martinez and Aldrich, 2011), the knowledge available today is still insufficient for understanding the complexity of this phenomenon in its entirety (Slotte-Kock and Coviello, 2010).

The purpose of the present study is, first, to improve our understanding of the creation process of innovative firms, with a particular focus on the specific characteristics of the survival/development phase (Bruyat and Julien, 2001; Fayolle, 2007); and, second, to contribute to the literature on entrepreneur networks by examining the dynamics of how ties are created and change over time (Jack et al., 2010). While this topic has generated considerable interest among scholars (e.g. Hoang and Antoncic, 2003; Stervinou and Legrand, 2008; Slotte-Kock and Coviello, 2010; Chabaud and Ngijol, 2010), we were surprised to find that few empirical studies have investigated the role of non-human objects in the dynamics of entrepreneurial networks, especially since the process of business creation is intrinsically a mixture of human and non-human elements (Bruyat, 1993; Jones et al., 2010).

Our empirical study observed the creation of an innovative company over a two-year period. This enabled us to better understand the conditions and the dynamics of how an entrepreneurial network is formed and crystallizes during the survival/development phase of the entrepreneurial process (Bruyat, 1993; Fayolle, 2007). This study, therefore, makes several contributions to the literature on social networks and the entrepreneurial process. First, this longitudinal, qualitative analysis enabled us to better understand the dynamics of the creation and development of entrepreneurial networks (Hite, 2005; Jack, 2010; Slotte-Kock and Coviello, 2010). Second, drawing on actor-network theory (Callon, 1986a), we contribute to entrepreneurship theory by investigating the role of non-human elements during the initial phases of the entrepreneurial process. This case study revealed that material objects were omnipresent throughout the process of business creation. More specifically, we focused on the role of technical artefacts in the process of network building and the increase in the nascent entrepreneur's social capital (Davidsson, 2006). Third, the unit of analysis examined here differs from that used in most previous studies. Instead of focusing on the entrepreneur as the unit of analysis, we privileged changes in the entrepreneurial network itself (Jack et al., 2010). The latter, in turn, was used as a means of improving our understanding of the dynamics of the survival/development phase.

In the following sections, we explain the theoretical interest of this research problem, the theoretical framework used, the methodology, an analysis of the dynamics of the socio-technical network and then provide a discussion of the results. The conclusion then presents the study's contributions, its limitations, and future avenues for research.

THE STATE OF THE RESEARCH AND RESEARCH QUESTIONS

The impact of an entrepreneur's social network (SN) on entrepreneurial performance (Van Gelderen, 2012) has been widely studied (Chabaud and Ngijol, 2005). Indeed, examining an entrepreneur's SN improves our knowledge of entrepreneurship by highlighting the role of collective action in new value creation (Fayolle, 2007) and the mobilization of necessary resources (Hite, 2005). The network exposes the individual/value creation pair to new ideas and new visions of the world. Moreover, the network provides a frame of reference that both offers protection and contributes to the survival and development of the new company (Davidsson and Honig, 2003).

The majority of research on entrepreneurs' networks has been quantitative, with the authors focusing mainly on the network's structure (Sarason et al., 2006). These studies certainly confirm the usefulness of quantitative research methods (Birley, 1985), yet they deal very little with the dynamic aspect of networks (Jack, 2010; Neergaard et al., 2005; Slotte-Kock and

Coviello, 2010). These studies primarily provide information on the impact of network type (social versus business) on entrepreneurial performance (Lechner et al., 2006; Watson, 2007), and on the resources mobilized through the network (Birley, 1985; Aldrich and Zimmer, 1986; Carsrud and Johnson, 1989; Shaw, 2006). In addition, some of these studies provide rich descriptions of the complementarity between strong and weak links and the way they change over time (Steier and Greenwood, 2000; Elfring and Hulsink, 2003; Lechner and Dowling, 2003; Jack et al., 2004). They also inform us about reciprocity in relationships between actors, and therefore about the nature of networks, whether they be 'calculative' or 'instrumental' (Jack et al., 2010). Although this approach tells us something about the process by which ties are formed and change, this kind of microanalysis of connections tells us little about network configurations and their development over time (Jack et al., 2010).

Moreover, in practice, if we want to study the entrepreneurial process, in which the aspect of time is central (Bruyat and Julien, 2001), quantitative approaches are less fertile and qualitative methods are better suited to addressing more subtle questions (Jack et al., 2010). On this line of thinking, Jack et al. (2004) have argued for the need to move beyond the dichotomies of strong versus weak links, microanalysis versus macroanalysis, and calculative versus instrumental networks. To do so, we should adopt approaches that are more comprehensive and take into account change over time, so that the dynamic aspect of the entrepreneurial process can be better understood. Recently, Slotte-Kock and Coviello (2010) argued that future studies should adopt a more dynamic approach to entrepreneurs' social networks in order to enrich our understanding of the subject. They proposed addressing the following questions: when and how an entrepreneur's social relations are created, transform and grow over time. They argue that such a perspective can overcome the opposition between the structure of the social network and the process of building ties. They add that empirical studies allowing us to trace the development of an entrepreneur's network over time are very rare in the field of entrepreneurship: 'the entrepreneurship literature has only just begun to investigate how relationships are developed and transformed' (p. 48).

Following Jack (2010) and Slotte-Kock and Coviello (2010), we believe that studying the dynamics of an entrepreneur's social network during the entrepreneurial process and, in particular, studying the interactions of different social actants, enables us to capture and use information about the creation, development, transformation and dissolution of ties. In addition, such a study should inform us about the mechanisms of interactions at different stages of the business creation process (Borgatti and Foster, 2003). Thus our first research question was:

How does the configuration of an entrepreneurial network change over time?

Furthermore, when social ties are constructed, non-human factors are present and influence the relationships among the actants in the entrepreneurial network (Jones et al., 2010). These factors play a fundamental role of mediation (Nicolini, 2010; Carlile, 2002; Spee and Jarzabkowski, 2009) and occupy a central place among network members (Jones et al., 2010; Korsgaard, 2011). In fact, throughout the business creation process, entrepreneurial activities are objectified as technical artefacts such as prototypes, documents, videos and machinery (Orlikowski and Scott, 2008). Yet few scholars have investigated the role of these technical objects in business creation. We found this surprising, especially since some recent conceptual studies have confirmed that entrepreneurial performance is determined by interactions of human and non-human elements (Jones et al., 2010; Nicolini, 2010). Hence our second research question:

What role do non-human elements play in the dynamics of building an entrepreneurial network?

Finally, the majority of work on SNs in entrepreneurship, which essentially focuses on the complexity of the business creation process in general, may not be entirely applicable to the specificities of creating high-tech businesses. Bruyat (1993) and Shane and Cable (2002), among others, consider that the main characteristics of venture creation and, in particular, innovative companies are: uncertainty, information asymmetry, lack of legitimacy, and the minimal performance essential for an entrepreneurial venture to survive over time.[1]

It is for these reasons that, in this study, we first adopted a dynamic approach to entrepreneurial networks and second, we viewed entrepreneurial networks as socio-technical networks (STN), composed of a mixture of human actors and non-human elements.

ACTOR-NETWORK THEORY AND CREATING INNOVATIVE ENTERPRISES

The creation of an innovative business follows a complex process (Lichtenstein et al., 2007). To account for a more complete description of this process, actor-network theory (ANT) (Akrich et al., 2006) is useful (Steyaert, 2007). It is an interesting alternative because it provides a way of thinking that allows for a dynamic and thus more complete description of a complex and changing entrepreneurial context (Korsgaard, 2011). It can do so because researchers, when examining changes in the business creation project, translate the entrepreneurial process into a narrative trajectory using a detailed analysis of an ensemble of documents, stories, discourses and artefacts, while focusing on the association/dissolution movements of human and non-human actants (Cazal, 2007; Nicolini, 2010).

Akrich et al. (1988, 2006) have shown that successful innovation depends on the success of an unprecedented association between multiple and various actors. From this association, mobilization and cooperation of all actants, an STN will emerge as well as a dynamic of production, whose corollaries are process efficiency and project success. In order to reach the stage where a stable network is built, these researchers defined an approach inspired by Garfinkel's ethnomethodology (1967), which is based on a sequence of steps called a chain of translation that can be defined in four main stages:

1. *Problematization* This is a system of associations between entities. It defines the identity of that association and the problems that stand between the entities and each of their interests. Problematization consists of formulating problems and proposing solutions (Harrisson and Laberge, 2002). This begins by defining a provisional, minimal project that includes each entity's interests.
2. *Interessement* This is the set of actions through which an entity seeks to engage and stabilize the other actors that have been defined in the problematization. A successful interessement confirms the problematization's validity. If, on the contrary, the interessement is unsuccessful, the problematization is refuted.
3. *Enrolment* This refers to the mechanism by which a role is defined and assigned to an actor. If he/she accepts it, it is a successful interessement.
4. *Mobilization* The progressive gathering together of actors who reach the critical mass that makes a proposal, project or innovation credible and compelling. According to Law (1985), this mobilization, beyond the system of alliances that it constitutes, has a physical reality. This mobilization materializes through an entire series of actions.

Applying ANT to studying the process of innovative business creation appears particularly relevant. It provides us with a methodological tool that enables us to study the dynamics of an entrepreneurial system, while giving the same degree of importance to both dimensions that make up the system: the material dimension represented by the project; and the social dimension represented by the individual. According to the generalized symmetry principle of ANT, all distinctions between facts of society and nature must be avoided (Latour et al., 1991). The close connections between human and non-human, and the individual and her/his project, mean they should be treated on the same terms and granted the same degree of importance. Moreover, using ANT to study this type of entrepreneurial process means studying the dynamics of the mobilization of a network of actants (human and non-human) that crystallizes as the process progresses.

Furthermore, given the specificities involved in creating an innovative business, anti-programmes (Callon, 1986, a)[2] may arise in four different ways: the entrepreneur's lack of credibility; information asymmetry between two or more entities; uncertainty; or simply because of divergent interests. Examining these controversies should result in strengthening the robustness of innovative entrepreneurial projects being prepared and thus be of interest to stakeholders, those people with resources that the project needs or will need. This ultimately means creating an agreement between the various actors in the form of a network that contributes the needed energy to the project.

Therefore ANT provides us with a way of thinking and a methodological tool (the chain of translation) that enables us to trace the development of the entrepreneurial system (Bruyat and Julien, 2001) by taking into account the characteristics of an innovative project. Within this system, the individual is merely an entrepreneur in the making and the project is merely an object being designed (Fayolle, 2007). It may become a stable and balanced business, just as it could collapse at any moment in the process.

As we have pointed out above, this study uses ANT to examine the dynamics of forming an STN as part of an innovative business creation project. In the next section, we present the context and the methodology and then describe the results.

RESEARCH CONTEXT AND METHODOLOGY

In order to increase knowledge on the dynamics of entrepreneurial systems, following Jack et al. (2010), we chose to analyse a single case study (Eisenhardt, 1989; Eisenhardt and Graebner, 2007). This case study offers a powerful example (Siggelkow, 2007), rich in information thanks to the researchers' immersion in the context examined.

In the present study, for two years we observed the process of constructing a network of actors when creating an innovative business in the field of nanotechnology in space. This project, called SuperNova, was supported by a French public business incubator. The project was identified and chosen on 15 January 2008 at a meeting with all the business managers of the incubator.

As part of this research, we opted for triangulation in data collection (Eisenhardt, 1989; Yin, 1989) based on participant observations (Journé, 2005) conducted starting in March 2008, analysis of complementary documents, and semi-structured interviews. These last were carried out every four months. The frequency of these meetings was defined with the entrepreneur, taking into consideration our expectations and objectives, the entrepreneur's availability, and the estimated timing of the progress of venture creation. The first interview took place on 14 March 2008 at the incubator. Other interviews were held on 6 October 2008, 19 January 2009, 15 May 2009 and 28 September 2009 in the entrepreneur's research laboratory at INSA in Lyon, France. The final two interviews were conducted on 31 January 2010 and 30 April 2010 in the company's new premises. This company, founded on 5 October 2009, was set up within an incubator in the Lyon, France area, dedicated to high-tech businesses.

A total of nine semi-structured interviews was carried out. The first two, with the business consultant who was advising the entrepreneur, helped introduce us to the entrepreneur's field of expertise (engineering). The six interviews with the entrepreneur were rich in information about the project's history and its development over time. Particular emphasis was placed on network building and the role of technical artefacts. In this context, it should be noted that a confidentiality agreement was signed requiring that the transcripts of the recorded interviews be re-read by the entrepreneur, which was justified by the need to protect his innovation.

In addition to the interviews, we attended meetings and visited the research laboratory in order to understand the situational logic of the different contexts within which the project was created. At the same time, we contacted other actors who were part of the entrepreneur's network. Our presence in the research laboratory gave us the opportunity to observe and handle the material artefacts, to examine the different versions of prototypes, to watch the recordings of all the experiments, and to analyse the drawings and plans with the entrepreneur. Complementary information, including videos, images, business plans, and application to the national OSEO grant competition were exchanged by email. The collected data were discussed by telephone, either to check their accuracy, or to follow the progress of certain project-related items such as meetings with key actors in the network, the results of competitions or feasibility tests of prototypes. Furthermore, three group interviews were conducted. The first was with the main actors of the entrepreneur's network. It took place in the incubator in the presence of the entrepreneur and the business adviser. The second occurred with the entrepreneur and his two associates, and the third interview was with the same people but, in addition, there was a fourth actor in charge of the project's IT development. These group interviews gave us external perspectives and opinions on the project and its creator. All the data collected were subjected to a thematic content analysis following ANT methodology. Using NVivo8 software as a data analysis tool provided structure and order to the data, and facilitated extracting the main ideas (Hampton et al., 2011).

Before we present the results of this research, it should be noted that this methodological choice was both risky and innovative. It was risky in the sense that there were no guarantees as to the outcome. This methodological choice was original, however, in that there was a close connection between the researchers and the case study. Such an alliance has the potential to be seen as 'treason' (Callon, 1986a) in the event of failure. Table 13.1 summarizes the main elements of the methodological approach used in this study.

Table 13.1 Summary of the methodological approach

	Research methodology			
Approach	Longitudinal and exploratory (four-month interval between interviews on average)			
Context	The SuperNova project: creating an innovative enterprise in the field of nanotechnology in space as a result of research carried out by the entrepreneur as a student. The project was supported in a public business incubator of the Rhône Alpes Region in France, Créalys.			
Data collection	2 interviews with the business adviser helping the entrepreneur	6 interviews with the entrepreneur	Participatory observation (since March 2008)	Additional documents
Date	15/01/08 and 18/02/08	14/03/08–06/10/08 19/01/09–15/05/09 28/09/09–31/01/10 30/04/10		
Duration	3h	20h		
Type of information collected	Introduction to the entrepreneur's field of expertise (engineering). First presentation of the individual and project.	History of the project. Evolution of the project. Building the network. Controversies.	Visit to the research laboratory. Participation in assessment meetings within the incubator.	Business plan. Application for the OSEO competition. Videos of the experiments. Different versions of prototypes.
Analysis	Thematic content analysis using NVivo8 software 19 free nodes identified in advance A double coding, 95% reliable according to Cohen's Kappa 254 codes obtained in total			

TRANSLATION OF THE SUPERNOVA PROJECT

The content analysis gave us access to a mass of data that was organized as well as rich in information, all of which we utilized for the socio-technical description of the project. This description was prepared in accordance with the principle of generalized symmetry (Latour et al., 1991) and following the chain of translation approach advocated by the theory (Callon, 1986a). This description revealed the history of the project, its development over time, the dynamics of constructing a network of actors, and the current state of the enterprise.

Table 13.2 situates these different phases in the process of building a network in time, and provides information about their duration. The transition from one phase to another was carefully studied with the entrepreneur.

The following section explains the main characteristics of this dynamic in greater detail.

Towards a Problematization of the Initial Entrepreneurial Context

SB was a young entrepreneur of 23 years, and an engineering student at INSA in Lyon about to graduate with a mechanical engineering degree. He decided to start a business to take advantage of the results from one of his student projects (Phase 1). His business would offer companies a service validating electronic components in a simulated space flight in the extreme conditions of space (Statement 1). This validation service would be sold through two products developed by the entrepreneur: a 'deployer' and a nano-satellite that would be integrated into a rocket and sold to customers. SB partnered with ST, an IT engineering student (Phase 2) who joined SB a few weeks before the start of the study. Putting this business idea into practice, however, required a number of essential actants such as an IT partner, an electronics partner, an incubator, a research laboratory, a milling-machine-lathe operator, the French National Space Centre (CNES), an agency for promoting research–business partnerships (INSAVALOR), and a launch service agency.

However, most of these entities refused to cooperate because of several problems related either to the project or to the entrepreneur himself (Phase 3). For example, among these difficulties were: the technical problems of nano-satellites, which were yet not ready for commercialization; the project's ambition, which was too great for a 23-year-old entrepreneur; the perception that the space field is for large firms and agencies; the unfavourable policies of the country; the student's inexperience, which increased uncertainty about the success of the project; the lack of financial

Table 13.2 The various phases of building the entrepreneurial network

Phase	1	2	3	4	5	6	7	8	9
Number of actors	2	3	4	11	19	30	34	51	70
Human	1	2	3	7	15	24	25	39	58
Non-human	1	1	1	4	4	6	9	12	12
Date	Intention to work in the space field determined at age 18	30/06/07	14/03/08	06/10/08	19/01/09	15/05/09	28/09/09	31/01/10	30/04/10
Duration	5 years	About 12 months	2–3 months	4 months	4 months	4 months	4 months	4 months	End observation of the network development

and material resources; the power inequality between the young entrepreneur and large institutions; problems concerning the export of dual-use goods; and the lack of legal status for the company.

> (Int1)[3] The space field is perceived by people as unattainable . . . When there are young people like us who want to enter the field with the skills and resources that we have, people look down on us and don't take us seriously. In our society, space is often seen as a sector reserved for large firms or agencies (NASA, ESA, EADS) . . . and this prejudice poses a real problem . . . These barriers require us to spend enormous amounts of time and energy convincing people that what we do is based on real technological and business opportunities.

> (Int2) Another reason that we could be criticized is the risk in our business, due to the uncertainty of our project, which is starting out in an untapped area. People we contacted told us: 'But we would run a huge risk with your project!'[4]

Creation of the Entrepreneurial Network: Interessement, Enrolment and Mobilization

The interessement of actants

To deal with all these difficulties and to be able to engage the interest of the people needed to start his business, SB changed the goal of his project three times. For example, to deal with technical problems that prevented some actors from joining the project, he changed from nano-satellite development to pico-satellite development (from Phase 4 to Phase 5).

> (Int3) Initially, I planned to work on the femto-satellites that weigh less than 100 grams. I thought that was something feasible and innovative conceptually. But in my opinion, this product must wait because the market isn't yet ready for it. In addition, in terms of mastering the technology, it would be difficult to place very high power in such a small product. So we must first focus on innovating with pico-satellites, I mean, we'll try to work on our platform system to make more space available for customers' payloads.

Then, to interest customers who were confused by the complexity of his offer, he changed the project from selling a satellite and a 'deployer' to a more general offer of spatial certification. This change simplified the procedure for the customer by limiting the number of client interfaces to only one person and resulted in a change to the business model (from Phase 7 to Phase 8). SB did the same for those people who thought that the project was too risky and uncertain. In Phases 5, 6, 7 and 9, he created a series of prototypes with the help of two metallurgists (Versions 1–4), which provided technological proof of concept for the project. Similarly, to work around the lack of legal status for the company that would allow him to export, during Phase 8, SB created a business association with two other people, which allowed him to have a business registration number. Finally, to interest the launch service providers who refused to collaborate early in the project, he used the competitive market to his advantage during Phase 6 by negotiating with three international launching stations simultaneously. This negotiation strategy also enabled him to interest other national and European actors, including the French Ministry of Research, the Ministry of Defence, the Regional Council of the Rhône Alpes and the European Business Network. Here, the incubator played the role of catalyser in bringing these institutions closer to the venture and in building relationships with them. This negotiation strategy bore fruit and ended with the signing of a partnership agreement with the Indian Space Station (Phase 9). Among other things, this partnership enabled the entrepreneur to receive one of his first orders from an Indian research centre.

Enrolling and mobilizing actors

Having identified a large number of actors and gaining their interest, SB managed to enrol a relatively large number of them. In fact, the number of entities interested in the project and who agreed to contribute increased from two in Phase 2 to about 70 six months after the launch of the business. In the project's development trajectory, we observed a shift in the pace and the intensity of rallying new actors (see the change from Phase 7 to Phase 9). This was due to proving the technical feasibility of the project by the successful flight test of the last two 'deployer' prototypes. This successful interessement was obtained through numerous arrangements, negotiations, adjustments and adaptations. For example, between Phases 7 and 8, SB successfully negotiated with teachers to provide an entire class of students approaching the end of their engineering studies. The aim was to work on developing the various satellite components while maintaining a certain technological lead in the market. He was able to mobilize three groups of three students each to study and implement various aspects of the project.

> (Int4) There are several student final-year projects working on both the prototype and the satellites. We took on four work placement students that we don't pay, it's an arrangement we negotiated with teachers. We don't pay them, but they help us. Why? Because the subject is fascinating and teachers are interested in these kinds of projects that motivate students. They are students at the end of their general engineering studies . . . four are working on the business plan and our future third product, ground stations. Then a ninth intern will be joining us, working on the artificial intelligence that we'll integrate into the satellite and finally, there is a tenth intern who is at an IUT [Technical Institute], who is working with me on the deployer.

These university actors contributed to the technical development of the project. They succeeded, under the entrepreneur's leadership, in creating a working prototype with guaranteed repeatability of results. This allowed the entrepreneur to obtain a patent on the deployer and consequently gain legitimacy (Tornikoski and Newbert, 2007) and credibility (Shane and Cable, 2002) in the eyes of major institutional players.

> (Int5) What we've noticed in the past two months, when we released the 'deployer', which already works and is in an advanced stage with a patent pending, people see us differently. So we see a change in attitude at all levels. It's amazing! There has been no change in the project, but with just a little video that shows a mechanism that works, they look at you differently!

It should also be noted that the entrepreneur was able to exploit certain contingencies that led him to make new connections with people he met by chance in the course of his business activities. These contacts were interested in his initial idea and mobilized in the process of building his project. To give an example, at one point in the project's development, SB had a heat problem with the 'deployer'. While talking with his partner about this problem in a train, an interested passenger joined the conversation and solved the heat problem. In fact, this person was one of the French specialists in the field with whom SB has still kept on good terms and to whom he regularly turns when he needs electronics expertise. Nevertheless, some of the interessement actions were not as successful. For example, the entrepreneur was unsuccessful in enrolling an electronics engineer specialized in space, because he did not manage to distract that person's interest from another competing project, which was working for EADS, where the perceived risk was much lower.

The Chain of Translation of the SuperNova Project

From the above developments, we can see that engineer SB was able to crystallize an entire, stable, socio-technical network around his project (Provan and Kenis, 2007), whose core consisted of the entrepreneurial team and the project. The results of our study confirm that a company in the process of being created is always the provisional result of ongoing actions that are embodied in temporary form as a statement, object, text or report. This is a project in continuous design (Fayolle, 2007). The initial concept, as it was presented by the entrepreneur during our first interview, underwent a series of transformations and shifts. The initial concept stated in the research laboratory was transported in an iterative way from the world of speech (statements) to the world of paper (reports, articles, presentations, patents), then the world of instruments (prototypes, algorithms, videos) and finally to the world of discourse (statements again).

In this case, the fact that the entrepreneurial project circulated (Latour et al., 1991) in different registers from one world to the next enables a contextualized and contingent reading of business creation (Steyaert, 2007). Such a reading enables us to avoid dichotomies between the register of discourse and the register of instruments; between the registers of scientific statements and business statements; and between technology and marketing registers. This circulating inscription occurred through the different versions of the prototype that proved its technological feasibility. Furthermore, circulating inscription demonstrates the capacity of the business plan and the various reports to prove the profitability and sustainability of the venture, and the capacity of videos to communicate the various technology demos and the project's future prospects. These non-human objects are situated on the border between worlds that at first glance seem separate, which ultimately enables them to serve as connection points linking actors who were initially in separate worlds. Thus circulating inscription confirms the importance of non-human, including written, elements in the business creation process. It thereby avoids discontinuity between statements, prototypes, business plans and videos taken alone, and ensures a continuous, rather than fragmented, reading of entrepreneurial networks that evolves over time. This meant a translation that, at every step, moved the entrepreneur towards the desired final script of his project. Figure 13.1 shows the development over time of the chain of translation of the SuperNova project.

PRIMARY RESULTS AND DISCUSSION

In answering our two research questions, this case study confirms the importance of entrepreneurial networks during the pre-creation phase

Statement 1 ⟶ PPT Presentation 1 ⟶ Business Model 1 ⟶ Prototype version 1 ⟶
PPT Presentation 2 ⟶ Business Model 2 ⟶ Statement 2 ⟶ Market study ⟶
Prototype version 2 ⟶ Incubation Agreement ⟶ University Partnership Agreement ⟶
Business Plan version 1 ⟶ Prototype version 3 ⟶ Demonstration video 1 ⟶ Patent ⟶
Demonstration video 2 ⟶ Application to OSEO ⟶ Statement 3 ⟶ Prototype version 4 ⟶
Business Model 3 ⟶ Business Plan version 2 ⟶ Company Statutes

Figure 13.1 Translation chain of the SuperNova Project

of the entrepreneurial process (Neergaard et al., 2005; Jack et al., 2008). However, the results also revealed differences from most previous work on entrepreneurs' social networks. These earlier studies offer us a wealth of information on network structure and especially the complementarity between strong and weak ties (Steier and Greenwood, 2000; Elfring and Hulsink, 2003; Lechner and Dowling, 2003; Jack et al., 2003) and the kinds of the resources mobilized through networks that effect entrepreneurial performance (Birley, 1985; Aldrich and Zimmer, 1986; Carsrud and Johnson, 1989; Shaw, 2006; Lechner et al., 2006; Lechner and Leyronas, 2007; Watson, 2007). Yet there are two gaps in these studies that are relevant here. The first is that these studies tell us very little about the dynamics of building links and the changing configuration of the nascent entrepreneur's network over time (Jack, 2010; Slotte-Kock and Coviello, 2010). The second is that, despite the importance of non-human elements in interactions of social actants (Jones et al., 2010; Nicolini, 2010), the question of their role in the entrepreneurial process has rarely been studied, even less so in relation to the specificities of the survival–development phase of creating an innovative business.

The results of our longitudinal study shed light on the dynamics of building a nascent entrepreneur's socio-technical network. In essence, the translation of the entrepreneurial trajectory in this case enabled us to overcome the human/non-human dichotomy in studying entrepreneurial networks and to continuously observe the emergence of new entities that are constantly weaving ties that bind them together. These ties contribute to the emergence of hybrid configurations (Callon, 1992, p. 61). We identified the three main configurations of the entrepreneurial network (Figure 13.2). Each is characterized by the problems, the different actors, and the registers of discourse to which they belong. To do so, we based our investigation on the following aspects: the specifics of the SuperNova project; the four characteristics of any innovative entrepreneurial process (Bruyat, 1993) (minimal performance, ambiguity, uncertainty and information asymmetry); and the chain of translation (Callon, 1986a).

1. The Scientifically Oriented Configuration

The first configuration involved the first four phases of construction of the network. These phases were, in particular, characterized by several actors who refused to join the SuperNova project, and this refusal was based solely on SB's student status. This shows that the first kinds of problems encountered by the entrepreneur were mainly related to 'lack of legitimacy'. Indeed, this accentuated the difference in perception between actors; hence the 'information asymmetry'. In addition to these problems,

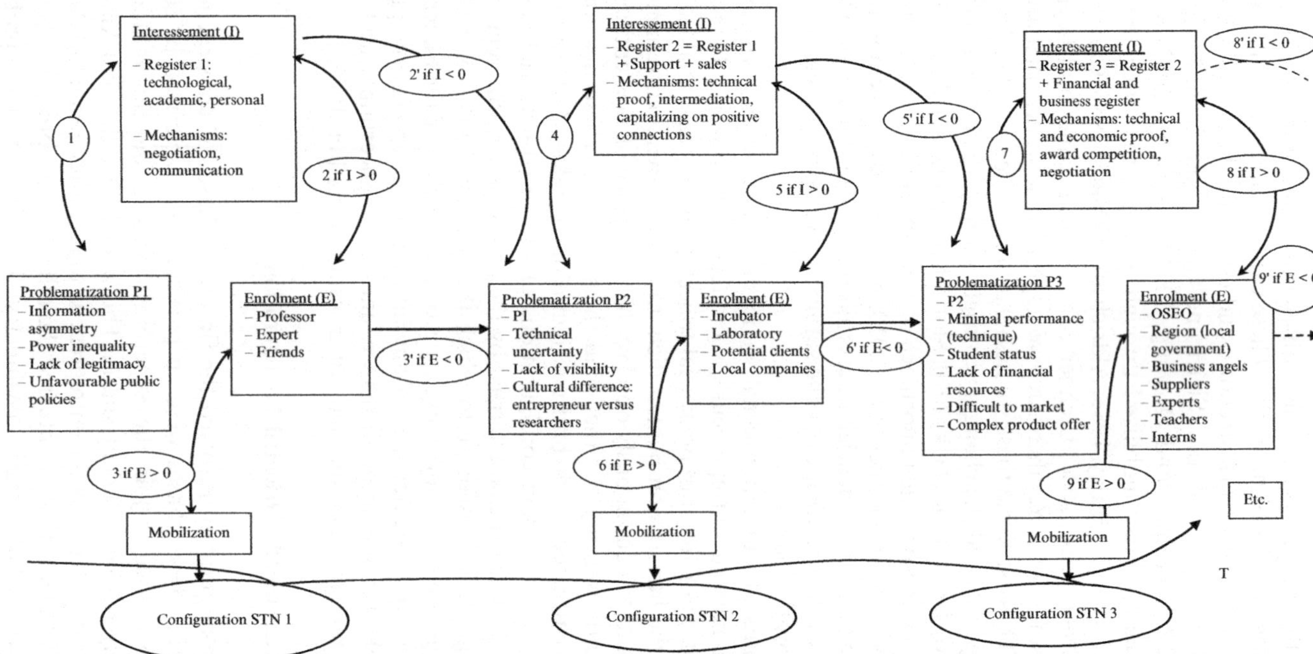

Figure 13.2 Reading SuperNova's entrepreneurial trajectory through ANT

there was power inequality (between launch service agencies and SB, for example) and the unfavourable public policies for starting this type of project. To overcome these controversies, entrepreneur SB tried to interest several actors in his project. To do this, three registers of discourse were essential: those of technology, the university, and the entrepreneur's personal knowledge. In the case of SuperNova, SB changed the technical characteristics of his product to attract as many people as possible who could contribute added value in accomplishing the project. He negotiated prices and took advantage of attending international conferences to talk with people about his project. All these elements enabled him to overcome preconceived ideas that this sector was reserved exclusively for large enterprises. Certain experts, teachers and friends finally joined the project, demonstrating enrolment and mobilization according to the translation chain (Akrich et al., 2006). Despite the entrepreneur's efforts during this first phase, some actors needed for the project continued to refuse to collaborate. Hence the second configuration of the STN.

2. The Support-oriented Configuration

As part of the second stage (Phases 5 and 6), we observed that the nature of the problems faced by SB changed, necessitating the use of new arguments to convince new actors and thus take advantage of their resources. In addition to the difficulties mentioned above, uncertainty and lack of visibility greatly influenced the behaviour of potential partners. Returning to Bruyat's theories (1993), we consider that the factors connected to the individual/project unit were the real source of uncertainty, rather than the external environment of the project. Specifically here, this meant technical aspects involved in manufacturing the product prototype. In this situation, negotiations turned out to be essential for convincing others. Proof of concept was also used to convince partners. This interessement, based on several actants, then led to the mobilization of new partners, such as local businesses and incubators. Their mobilization allowed SuperNova's entrepreneur to expand his network and, above all, to take advantage of certain financial resources and experts in the field.

3. The Business-oriented Configuration

Despite the changes over time in SB's network, we found that some key players were still missing for the proper development of the project, such as business angels, financial actors and other businesses. According to the chain of translation, the last could not be enrolled despite the variety of registers used. Hence the formation of the third configuration, which includes Phases 7, 8 and 9. In this context, other problems emerged, such as the complexity of and the technical delays in the product, the lack of financial resources, and the student status of the project's entrepreneur. All these factors made it difficult to sell the validation service. This can be interpreted in the light of 'minimal performance'. Indeed, in just a few months, the SuperNova project was not able to achieve minimum performance in the characteristics of the product, which resulted in a delay in terms of competitive advantage (Hannan et al., 1996). In this kind of situation, the registers cited in the previous steps needed to be complemented by financial aspects. Negotiations and technical and economic proof, such as new prototypes or versions of the business plan, were needed to interest new people and convince them to join the project. Once a role was assigned to them, these people fed into the network and were occasionally mobilized. Finally, a new version of the socio-technical network was developed.

Table 13.3 summarizes the different configurations of the STN, their descriptions, the technical artefacts present in each, and their roles.

Regarding the role of technical artefacts, the answer to our second question shows that the circulating inscription (Latour et al., 1991) of these non-human artefacts (see Figure 13.1 and Table 13.3) articulates the entrepreneurial network, which we qualify here as a socio-technical network due to its mixed nature. These artefacts act as a bridge between different communities (Carlile, 2002; Spee and Jarzabkowski, 2009). Although the human actor (entrepreneur) is at the origin of the object, each network element plays an active role in the entrepreneurial process. Specifically, our research identified four key roles of non-human elements in the entrepreneurial process.

1. *Representation* In this case, the chain of translation illustrates the intermediary role that technical artefacts can play when they stand as spokespersons (Callon, 1986a) for the individual/project unit (Bruyat, 1993). Technical artefacts play a dual role of representation when they reflect an entrepreneur's intentions, aspirations and abilities to complete his/her project. Moreover, non-human elements can make projections about the future of the entrepreneurial process, because the technical artefact itself is usually an ephemeral object and a promise of the desired outcome. By taking on this role of representation, technical artefacts thereby become a means for communication that reduces the gap between the representations perceived and the information asymmetry (Bruyat, 1993) that may exist between entrepreneurs and those they interact with. However, the artefact may also betray the entrepreneur with a bad, involuntary, or uncontrolled representation (Callon, 1986a; Nicolini, 2010).

Table 13.3 Evolution of the nascent entrepreneur's STN

Configurations	Description	Artefact	Role of the artefacts
Configuration 1 Scientific	Scientific-oriented configuration. Entrepreneurial context marked primarily by a lack of legitimacy and information asymmetry	Statement 1 Business Model 1 Power Point Presentation 1	Reduce information asymmetry Mobilize commitment of the first contacts at the university and the incubator Translate the entrepreneur's intentions
Configuration 2 Support	Support-oriented configuration. Entrepreneurial context marked primarily by uncertainty and lack of visibility	Statement 2 Business Model 1 Power Point Presentation 2 Prototype (2 versions) Market Study Business Plan 1 Incubator Agreement University Partnership	Demonstrate the technological development of the project Evidence of the entrepreneur's ability to achieve his goals Prove the new value of this offer Access to the university's resources Access to the resources and services of the incubator Entrepreneur's self-confidence Speed up the pace of completing activities
Configuration 3 Business	Business-oriented configuration. Entrepreneurial context marked primarily by minimal performance and a lack of financial and human resources	Prototype (Version 3) Video Patent Video 2 Business Model 2 Create company with associates OSEO Application Statement 3 Prototype Version 4 Business Plan 2 Company Statutes	Legitimacy Reducing uncertainty Self-confidence Reducing information asymmetry Access to financial resources Proof of achieving required minimum OSEO Award: financial resources Proof of the project's viability and feasibility Learning Strengthening connections

2. *Translation* The materialization of an intention, an idea or a programme in the form of a technical object does not always happen without transformation. The entrepreneur runs the risk of shifting from one register to another unintentionally. The resulting object does something other than what was intended originally. This is what we mean here by translation.
3. *Organization* The reading of the entrepreneurial trajectory shows that the project followed a progressive development through multiple versions of prototypes, business plans, presentations and videos (Figure 13.1). Given the experimental nature of the entrepreneurial process, the emergence of different versions of these artefacts (from the statement through to achievement) followed an iterative path of trial and error (Bingham and Davis, 2012), each time mobilizing different resources, skills and actors. We observed that, in moving from one version to another, the entrepreneur developed new knowledge and new entrepreneurial skills that would then be mobilized in future versions. This learning, which is cognitive, technical and managerial at the same time (Bingham and Davis, 2012), resulted in changes to the business model, perfecting the prototypes, and business plan improvements. This learning in action was transformed into the organizing force of the entrepreneur's network, which in turn strengthened the overall coherence of the entrepreneurial system (Bruyat and Julien, 2001; Fayolle, 2007).
4. *Acceleration* Our results showed the catalysing effect of the technical artefact on the STN configuration's rate of creation and development, and thus the speed of the project's accomplishment as a whole. Moreover, this can be explained by the role that the prototype, video or document played regarding: (1) the legitimacy that the entrepreneur acquired by concretising statements made into a functional and powerful object; (2) the gap in perceived representations, by reducing the information asymmetry that existed between the entrepreneur and the actors he was trying to interest; and (3) uncertainty, by showing proof of concept feasibility or the validity of the business model. From the moment the entrepreneur developed an artefact, this caused an increase in the number of ties created. This increase had an impact on the quantity and quality of resources and skills mobilized through the intermediary of these new ties.

In addition, our results also show the importance of proof of concept (Cazal, 2007) in the process of creating an entrepreneur's STN, and the entrepreneurial process in general. Indeed, doubts about the entrepreneur's ability to make his ideas a reality were only eliminated (or lowered) once he had proven the technical and/or commercial feasibility of the venture. This proof (or truth) put an end to the controversies (Callon, 1986b) around the individual/project unit and gave way to confidence (Stervinou and Legrand, 2008) and to legitimacy (Hite, 2005). This proof then either unblocked a situation so that new ties could be formed, or increased the intensity of an existing relationship.

CONCLUSION

The results of this study enrich our understanding of the dynamics of building a nascent entrepreneur's network. This research is one of the few empirical studies to have examined entrepreneurial networks in both their social and material dimensions. The results confirm that a nascent entrepreneur's STN moves through at least three configurations: scientific, support and business. These configurations shown in Figure 13.2 prove the usefulness of ANT for understanding the dynamics of creating an entrepreneurial network. Drawing on ANT enabled us to examine the STN of the nascent entrepreneur differently. In addition, this theory informed us about the dynamics of forming connections, the problems encountered, the registers mobilized, and the resources that facilitate access. This research has also highlighted the importance of the role of technical artefacts. In particular, four key roles were identified in this case study: representation, translation, organization and acceleration. In terms of methodology, this research is one of the few studies that have focused on the dynamics of building a nascent entrepreneur's network in a longitudinal way and in real time. It provides a methodological protocol combining parts of the chain of translation with the specifics of creating an innovative firm. Through this qualitative study, we have also confirmed the relevance of using a single case study as suggested by Eisenhardt and Graebner (2007), in particular when studying the dynamics of building entrepreneur networks (Jack, 2010).

On the managerial level, our results may help nascent entrepreneurs to better manage the creation process by optimizing the building of their networks and better mobilizing artefacts such as prototypes, presentations and business plans, which are likely to increase their legitimacy (Hite, 2005). For incubators, this study may improve the effectiveness and efficiency of their support methods. To this end, managers and business advisers should promote and diversify networking. They can foster the abilities of the entrepreneurs they work with to gain access to privileged networks (Chabaud and Ngijol, 2010), and to do so in line with the project's progress. In addition, business advisers should also make entrepreneurs aware of the way in which they should mobilize and present technical artefacts in interactions with their contacts.

Certainly, this exploratory study has limitations as to the degree of generalization of its results. First, the technological and highly specialized nature of the project may influence the network dynamics and the importance of the technical artefact's mediation role (Jones et al., 2010). Second, the personal characteristics of the entrepreneur and, in particular, his social skills (Baron and Markman, 2003) may have influenced his ability to interest, enrol and mobilize actors in his network. Furthermore, this research has focused on a particular phase of the entrepreneurial process, that of survival–development (Bruyat, 1993). None the less, we believe that extending this study into the later phases of the process, particularly the growth phase, would contribute to a better understanding of the changes over time in the configuration of an entrepreneur's STN. Finally, more in-depth studies on the experience of nascent entrepreneurs from other, less innovative business sectors should be done. Such future research should verify whether non-human elements play an important role in, and in the pace of, creating configurations of entrepreneur networks. Finally, we observed that, throughout the process, the nascent entrepreneur was faced with multiple problems and obstacles to creating his business. Thus, what is the role played by entrepreneurs' perseverance and their abilities to overcome such problems (Van Gelderen, 2012)? In conclusion, the present study opens up new avenues of research for analysing further the role of non-human objects in entrepreneurial network formation and in the field of entrepreneurship more generally.

NOTES

* A more comprehensive version of this chapter was published in the journal *International Management* (*Mi*), **19**(1), 2014, 158–76), with the authorization of the editor-in-chief of *Mi*.

1. For more information on the specificities of the business creation process, see Christian Bruyat's doctoral thesis (1993).
2. ANT considers as an 'anti-programme' a human or non-human entity that is able to disrupt the project, but which may also turn out to be indifferent or positive if the project manages to modify the opposition by rallying them.
3. Interview number 1.
4. The original interviews in French have been translated by the translator.

REFERENCES

Akrich, M., Callon, M. and Latour, B. (1988), 'A quoi tient le succès des innovations? Premier épisode: l'art de l'intéressement', *Gérer et comprendre*, **11**, 15–29.

Akrich, M., Callon, M. and Latour, B. (2006), *Sociologie de la traduction*, Textes fondateurs, Paris: Presses des Mines de Paris.
Aldrich, H. and Zimmer, C. (1986), 'Entrepreneurship through social networks', in D.L. Sexton and R.W. Smilor (eds), *The Art and Science of Entrepreneurship*, Cambridge, MA: Ballinger, pp. 3–23.
Baron, R.A. and Markman, G.D. (2003), 'Beyond social capital: the role of entrepreneurs' social competence in their financial success', *Journal of Business Venturing*, **18**, 41–60.
Bingham, B.C. and Davis, J.P. (2012), 'Learning sequences: their existence, effect, and evolution', *Academy of Management Journal*, **55**(3), 611–41.
Birley, S. (1985), 'The role of networks in the entrepreneurial process', *Journal of Business Venturing*, **1**, 107–17.
Borgatti, S.P. and Foster, P.C. (2003), 'The network paradigm in organizational research: a review and typology', *Journal of Management*, **29**(6), 991–1013.
Bruyat, C. (1993), 'Création d'entreprise: contributions épistémologiques et modélisation', thesis for a doctorate in Management Sciences, Grenoble.
Bruyat, C. and Julien, P.A. (2001), 'Defining the field of research in entrepreneurship', *Journal of Business Venturing*, **16**(2), 165–80.
Callon, M. (1992), 'Variété et irréversibilité dans les réseaux de conception et d'adoption des techniques', in D. Foray and C. Freeman (eds), *La technologie et la richesse des nations*, Paris: Economica, pp. 275–324.
Callon, M. (1986a), 'Éléments pour une sociologie de la traduction', *L'Année sociologique*, **36**, 169–210.
Callon, M. (1986b), 'The sociology of an actor-network: the case of the electric vehicle', in M. Callon, J. Law and A. Rip (eds), *Mapping the Dynamics of Science and Technology: Sociology of Science in the Real World*, London: Macmillan, pp. 19–34.
Callon, M. (2006), 'Pour une sociologie des controverses techniques', in M. Akrich, M. Callon and B. Latour (eds), *Sociologie de la traduction. Textes fondateurs*, Paris: Presses des Mines de Paris, pp. 135–57.
Callon, M. and Latour, B. (1991), *La science telle qu'elle se fait*, Paris: La Découverte.
Carsrud, A.L. and Johnson, R.W. (1989), 'Entrepreneurship: a social psychological perspective', *Entrepreneurship and Regional Development*, **1**, 21–31.
Carlile, P.R. (2002), 'A pragmatic view of knowledge and boundaries: boundary objects in new product development', *Organization Science*, **13**(4), 442–55.
Cazal, D. (2007), 'Théorie de l'acteur-réseau et GRH: traductions et modèles', XVIIIe Congrès de l'Association Francophone de Gestion des Ressources Humaines, Fribourg, September.
Chabaud, D. and Ngijol, J. (2005), 'La contribution de la théorie des réseaux sociaux à la reconnaissance des opportunités', *Revue internationale PME*, **18**(1), 29–46.
Chabaud, D. and Ngijol, J. (2010), 'Quels réseaux sociaux dans la formation de l'opportunité d'affaires?', *Revue Française de Gestion*, **36**(206), 129–47.
Davidsson, P. (2006), 'Nascent entrepreneurship: empirical studies and developments', *Foundations and Trends in Entrepreneurship*, **2**(1), 1–76.
Davidsson, P. and Honig, B. (2003), 'The role of human and social capital among nascent entrepreneurs', *Journal of Business Venturing*, **18**(3), 301–31.
Dubini, P. and Aldrich, H. (1991), 'Personal and extended networks are central to the entrepreneurial process', *Journal of Business Venturing*, **6**, 305–13.

Eisenhardt, K. (1989), 'Building theories from case study research', *Academy of Management Review*, **14**(4), 532, 550.

Eisenhardt, K. and Graebner, M.E. (2007), 'Theory building from cases: opportunities and challenges', *Academy of Management Journal*, **50**, 28–32.

Elfring, T. and Hulsink, W. (2003), 'Networks in entrepreneurship: the case of high-technology firms', *Small Business Economics*, **21**(4), 409–22.

Fayolle, A. (2004), 'Compréhension mutuelle entre les créateurs d'entreprise et les accompagnateurs: une recherche exploratoire sur des différences de perception', *Management International*, **8**(2), 1–14.

Fayolle, A. (2007), *Entrepreneurship and New Value Creation: The Dynamic of the Entrepreneurial Process*, Cambridge: Cambridge University Press.

Garfinkel, H. (1967), *Studies in Ethnomethodology*, Bristol: Polity Press.

Granovetter, M. (1973), 'The strength of weak ties', *American Journal of Sociology*, **78**(6), 1360–80.

Hampton, A., McGowan, P. and Cooper, S. (2011), 'Developing quality in female high-technology entrepreneurs' networks', *International Journal of Entrepreneurial Behaviour & Research*, **17**(6), 588–608.

Hannan, M., Burton, D. and Baron, D. (1996), 'Inertia and change in the early years: employment relations in young, high technology firms', *Industrial and Corporate Change*, **5**(2), 503–36.

Harrisson, D. and Laberge, M. (2002), 'Innovation, identities and resistance: the social construction of an innovation network', *Journal of Management Studies*, **39**(4), 497–521.

Heraud, J.A. and Levy, R. (2005), 'University–industry relationships and regional innovation systems', in P. Llerena and M. Matt (eds), *Innovation Policy in a Knowledge-based Economy*, Berlin and Heidelberg: Springer, pp. 193–219.

Hite, J.M. (2005), 'Evolutionary processes and paths of relationally embedded network ties in emerging entrepreneurial firms', *Entrepreneurship Theory and Practice*, **30**, 113–44.

Hoang, H. and Antoncic, B. (2003), 'Network-based research in entrepreneurship. A critical review', *Journal of Business Venturing*, **18**(2), 165–87.

Jack, S. (2010), 'Approaches to studying networks: implications and outcomes', *Journal of Business Venturing*, **25**, 120–37.

Jack, S.L., Drakopolou Dodd, S. and Anderson, A.R. (2004), 'The strength of strong ties and the entrepreneurial process', *International Journal of Entrepreneurship and Innovation*, **5**(2), 107–20.

Jack, S.L., Anderson, A.R. and Drakopolou Dodd, S. (2008), 'Change and the development of entrepreneurial networks over time: a processual perspective', *Entrepreneurship and Regional Development*, **20**(2), 125–59.

Jack, S., Moult, S., Anderson, A. and Dodd, S. (2010), 'An entrepreneurial network evolving: patterns of change', *International Small Business Journal*, **28**(4), 315–37.

Jones, O., Macpherson, A. and Thorpe, R. (2010), 'Learning in owner-managed small firms: mediating artefacts and strategic space', *Entrepreneurship and Regional Development*, **22**(7), 649–73.

Journé, B. (2005), 'Etudier le management de l'imprévu: méthode dynamique d'observation *in situ*', *Finance, Contrôle, Stratégie*, **8**(4), 63–91.

Korsgaard, S.T. (2011), 'Entrepreneurship as translation: understanding entrepreneurial opportunities through Actor-Network Theory', *Entrepreneurship and Regional Development*, **23**(7–8), 661–80.

Latour, B., Mauguin, P. and Teil, G. (1991), 'Une méthode nouvelle de suivi socio-technique des innovations: le graphe socio-technique', in Vinck Dominique (ed.), *Gestion de la recherche. Nouveaux problèmes, nouveaux outils*, Paris: Armand Colin, pp. 419–77.

Law, J. (1986), 'On power and its tactics: a view from the sociology of science', *The Sociological Review*, **34**(1), 1–39.

Lechner, C. and Dowling, M. (2003), 'Firm networks: external relationships as sources for the growth and competitiveness of entrepreneurial firms', *Entrepreneurship and Regional Development*, **15**, 1–26.

Lechner, C. and Leyronas, C. (2007), 'Network-centrality versus network-position in regional networks: what matters most? A study of a French high-tech cluster', *International Journal of Technoentrepreneurship*, **1**, 78–91.

Lechner, C., Dowling, M. and Welpe, I. (2006), 'Firm networks and firm development: the role of the relational mix', *Journal of Business Venturing*, **21**(4), 514–40.

Lichtenstein, B.B., Carter, N.M., Dooley, K.J. and Gartner, W.B. (2007), 'Complexity dynamics of nascent entrepreneurship', *Journal of Business Venturing*, **22**, 236–61.

Littunen, H. (2000), 'Networks and local environmental characteristics in the survival of new firms', *Small Business Economics*, **15**, 59–71.

Martinez, M. and Aldrich, H. (2011), 'Networking strategies for entrepreneurs: balancing cohesion and diversity', *International Journal of Entrepreneurial Behaviour & Research*, **17**, 7–38.

Neergaard, H., Shaw, E. and Carter, S. (2005), 'The impact of gender, social capital and networks on business ownership: a research agenda', *International Journal of Entrepreneurial Behaviour and Research*, **11**(5), 338–57.

Nicolini, D. (2010), 'Medical innovation as a process of translation: a case from the field of telemedicine', *British Journal of Management*, **21**(4), 1011–26.

Orlikowski, W.J. and Scott, S.V. (2008), 'Sociomateriality: challenging the separation of technology, work and organization', *The Academy of Management Annals*, **2**(1), 433–74.

Pecqueur, B. (1997), 'Processus cognitifs et construction des territoires économiques', in B. Guilhon, P. Huard, M. Orillard and J.B. Zimmermann (eds), *Économie de la connaissance et des organisations*, Paris: L'Harmattan, pp. 154–76.

Provan, K.G. and Kenis, P. (2007), 'Modes of network governance: structure, management and effectiveness', *Journal of Public Administration Research and Theory*, **18**, 229–52.

Rallet, A. and Torre, A. (2005), 'Proximity and localization', *Regional Studies*, **39**(1), 47–59.

Sarason, Y., Dean, T., Jesse, F. and Dillard, J.F. (2006), 'Entrepreneurship as the nexus of individual and opportunity: a structuration view', *Journal of Business Venturing*, **21**, 286–305.

Shane, S. and Cable, D. (2002), 'Network ties, reputation, and the financing of new ventures', *Management Science*, **48**(3), 364–81.

Shaw, E. (2006), 'Small firm networking: an insight into contents and motivating factors', *International Small Business Journal*, **24**(1), 5–29.

Slotte-Kock, S. and Coviello, N. (2010), 'Entrepreneurship research on network processes: a review and ways forward', *Entrepreneurship Theory & Practice*, **24**, 31–57.

Siggelkow, N. (2007), 'Persuasion with case studies', *Academy of Management Journal*, **50**, 20–24.

Spee, A.P. and Jarzabkowski, P.A. (2009), 'Strategy tools as boundary objects', *Organization Studies*, **7**(2), 223–32.

Steier, L. and Greenwood, R. (2000), 'Entrepreneurship and the evolution of angel financial networks', *Organization Studies*, **21**(1), 163–93.

Stervinou, S. and Legrand, C. (2008), 'Etapes clés du développement d'un réseau d'entreprises: proposition d'une grille d'analyse', *Management International*, **13**, 61–74.

Steyaert, C. (2007), 'Entrepreneuring as a conceptual attractor? A review of process theories in 20 years of entrepreneurship studies', *Entrepreneurship and Regional Development*, **19**(2), 453–77.

Tornikoski, E.T. and Newbert, S.L. (2007), 'Exploring the determinants of organizational emergence: a legitimacy perspective', *Journal of Business Venturing*, **22**(2), 311–35.

Van Gelderen, M.W. (2012), 'Perseverance strategies of enterprising individuals', *International Journal of Entrepreneurial Behaviour and Research*, **18**(6), 630–48.

Watson, J. (2007), 'Modeling the relationship between networking and firm performance', *Journal of Business Venturing*, **22**, 852–74.

Witt, P. (2004), 'Entrepreneurs' networks and the success of start-ups', *Entrepreneurship and Regional Development*, **16**, 391–412.

Yin, R.K. (1994), *Case Study Research: Design and Methods*, Thousand Oaks, CA: Sage.

Index

actor-network theory 335–56
artefacts as non-human actants 336, 338, 339, 352–4
acceleration 354
methodological treatment 340, 349
organization 354
representation 352
role of 353
translation/transformation 354
chain of translation 339
case study (circulating inscription) 343, 347–8
creation of entrepreneurial network 345–8
enrolment and mobilization 339, 346–7
interessement 339, 345–6
phases 344
creation of innovative business 338–40
problemization/interessement/enrolment/mobilization 339
extant research 336–7
network creation phases 344
socio-technical networks (STN) 338, 339, 343, 353
study
aims and contributions 335–6
research questions 338
context and methodology 340–42
overview 20–21, 355–6
results: configurations 348–55
business-oriented 351–5
case study's entrepreneurial trajectory 350
scientifically oriented 349–51, 353
support-oriented 351, 353
see also control-based entrepreneurship; dynamic perspectives

advantage seeking 217, 224–5
advertising 94–5, 149
advisor networks, *see* family firms; social network structures of nascent entrepreneurs; women entrepreneurs
Africa 279–97
artefacts, viewed through
actor-network theory 336, 338, 339, 352–4
control-based entrepreneurship 307, 308–9, 312–18

bifocal view 113–14, 124
business network perspective, *see* formal networks; repositioning of startups
business opportunities formation, *see* opportunities formation

chain of translation 339, 343–8
clusters 222–9, 270–74
collective strategies, formal network study 189–210
actors' relationships 191–5
content of case study 203–4, 206–8
cooperation versus coordination 190, 193–5
competition and 201
dyadic coordination and resources 191–3, 206–7
intensity and polymorphic nature 201–5
map of case study 200
satisfaction 205
extant literature 191–5
resource based view (RBV) 207–8, 209
study
aims 189–90

analysis 199–206
case study 196–7
methodology and design 197–9
organizational structure element 191, 208–9
overview 13–14, 209–10
competitiveness, *see* firm competitiveness
connectedness 221, 225–6
context, *see* family firms; firm competitiveness; social network structures of nascent entrepreneurs; *ubuntu* in family businesses
control-based entrepreneurship 303–29
agent-based computer simulations 311–12
artefact 312–13, 316
fitness landscape 314–15
effectual agent 313
end customer 313–14
mechanics 315–21
agent behaviours 315–16
artefact transformation 318
end customer access to fitness landscape 318
initial position impact 327
negotiation process 316–18
network shape measures 319–21, 327
social network 315
artefacts 307, 308–9, 312–18
effectuation 304–6
as entrepreneurial expert decision logic 305–6
four principles of 305
as non-predictive logic 304
use (known processes and behaviours) 306–8
artefact transformation 308–9
pre-commitment negotiation 308
pre-commitment/state of artefact 307
relay of information 307
literature review 304–11
performance impact of position 309–10
performance impact of shape 310–11
overview 18–20
research limitations and future avenues 329–30
research results and implications 321–5
development of measures over time 324–5
performance impact of constraint and structural holes 328–9
performance impact of efficiency 328
performance impact of position 322–3, 325–6
final position 326
initial position 327
performance impact of shape 323–4, 327
see also actor-network theory
coordination versus cooperation 13–14, 190, 193–5
competition and 201
dyadic coordination and resources 206–7
organizational consequences 208–9
cultural values 266

Democratic Republic of Congo 279–97
dynamic perspectives 30–31, 337
network imprinting 116, 123
see also actor-network theory; dynamic social network study (Netherlands)
dynamic social network study (Netherlands) 49–73
extant studies (instrumental and dynamic views) 51–7
dynamic view 53–7
instrumental view 51–3
location/'everydayness' 49–50
social capital benefits 52–3
overview 6–7, 70–72
resources 52, 54
study
aims 50–51
analytical strategy 62
delineation (name-generating questions) 58–60
dependent variables 60–61
independent variables 61

limitations and future options 72–3
overview 70–72
results on network changes 62–70
change in network size and composition 77–8
network size and composition 76
variables 60–61
see also dynamic perspectives

early-stage entrepreneurs 11, 165–6, 168, 170–75
economic development 136, 157, 230
economic gain 81, 97–8
economic typologies 271–5
effectuation, *see* control-based entrepreneurship
efficiency economy driven countries 271–5
ego-centred network 117, 241
embeddedness 115, 218, 222–4
entrepreneurial economy 157–8
entrepreneurial networks 50, 242
process stages/phases 34–5, 54, 56
entrepreneurial process, *see* actor-network theory
European Union 222–3
evolution of social network studies, *see* Dutch entrepreneurs' venture creation; opportunities formation; small businesses in USA; repositioning of start-ups
exchange flows 192
expectation 146–7, 168–71, 174–5, 205
dynamic of 115
translated into demand 133
external actors/relationships 34, 223–4

F-PEC scale 237–40
factor economy driven countries 271–5
family firms 236–59
definitions (dichotomy to F-PEC scale) 237–40
members outwith ('Family Jugglers') 240, 244, 255, 256, 257–8
research findings 248–58
overview 257–9
qualitative 253–7
continuing support 255–6
'Family In'/'Family Out' 253
hazards 257
overview of sample 254
start-up phase 253, 255
support from members outwith 256–7
quantitative (nature of ties) 248–53
research methodology 244–8
qualitative study 246–8
quantitative study 245–6
supporting independent enterprise 241–4
see also social network structures of nascent entrepreneurs; *ubuntu* in family businesses
firm competitiveness 217–30
advantage seeking 217
entrepreneurial firm 217–18
evolutionary phases 54, 56
interfirm relationships and firm liabilities 220–22
knowledge spillover and connectedness 225–6
overview 15–16
performance/effectiveness 51
differentials 223, 224–8
levels of effect 219
private benefits 227, 229–30
socioeconomic embeddedness 218
spatial dimension of networks 222–4
structural holes 224
firm performance, *see* firm competitiveness
formal networks
case studies, *see* collective strategies; Oxfordshire; women entrepreneurs
definition 159
literature on 9–11
France, study in collectives 196–210

Global Entrepreneurship Monitor (GEM) project 264, 266–7
Grampian region study 246–59

information relay 307
innovation 265, 335, 338–40, 341
innovation economy driven countries 271–5
instrumental view 51–3

integrative model 3–4
inter-organizational analysis, *see* collective strategies
interfirm networks research 220–22, 224

knowledge spillover 225–6

literature, relating to
  control-based entrepreneurship (effectuation) 304–11
  cooperation versus collaboration 193–5
  dynamic and instrumental social networks 51–7
  formal business networks 9–11
  major studies 2–4, 29–35, 32–3
  management and organizational theory 220
  network theory 30–31, 158–65, 220–24, 229, 264–6, 336–7
  resource dependence theory 31, 34
longitudinal approach 50, 55, 86–90

management and organizational theory 220
management of social network 81–2, 102–7
MENA (Middle East and North Africa) region study 263, 266–73

Netherlands, *see* dynamic social network study
network imprinting 116, 123
network literature, *see* literature
network paradigm 151
Northern Ireland study 165–75
Norway start-up study 117–24

occupationally based professional (OBP) networks 129–31, 139, 141, 151
opportunities formation 79–108
  process phases 80–81
  social network management and 81–5, 102–7
  structural holes and 224
  study
    limitations and future options 107–8
    methodology and case studies 86–90
    overview 7–8
    results 90–98
      comparative studies on weak ties 101–2
      demonstrating potential economic gain 97–8
      entrepreneurial discovery and evaluation 90–93, 99–100
      rolling-out of services proposal 96–7, 100–101
      skill in resource acquisition 93–6, 100
    see also opportunity identification
opportunity and constraints in Africa 285–8
opportunity identification 34, 36, 263–4, 265, 269, 275, 281; *see also* opportunities formation
organizational structures 191, 208–9
organizing stage 35, 36
Oxfordshire, formal network case study 129–52
  formal networks 129
    types of activity 131
  logic of services 133–5, 146–7
  network logics (activity types) 130–33, 140–46
    place, density and size 132–3
  networks as resource 135–6, 147–51
  place 129–6, 148, 151–2
  study
    framework 129–30
    logic of services (expectations) 146–7
    methodology 138–40
    network logics
      area characteristics 140–41
      types, size and chronology of networks 141–6
    networks as resource (outcomes)
      material advantages 149–50
      sectoral differences 149
    OC2 Arc 137–8, 140
    overview 11–12, 151–2

Panel Study of Entrepreneurial Dynamics (PSED) 38–9

performance impacts of position and shape of networks 309–11, 322–9
place 129–6, 148, 151–2
prediction-based approach 304, 305, 309–10
private benefits 227, 229–30
problemization, chain of translation approach 339, 343, 345, 347, 349–52
public funding 145

qualitative and quantitative methods 336–7
  applied to family firms 245–8

reciprocation 12, 161–3, 173, 176–9, 281–2
regional differentials 136, 157–8, 224–8
repositioning of start-ups 113–25
  business network reference 114–15
  network imprinting reference 116
  study
    cases, history and problems 118–20
      actions taken 120–22
    overview 8, 124–5
    research analysis 123–4
    research method 117–18
resource acquisition 85
  collective strategies framework 207–8
  differing phases 54
  entrepreneurial skill in 93–6, 100, 220
    weak ties and 36, 101
  literature overview 30–31
  logic of services 133–5
  social capital in DRC businesses 280–82
  types of resource 50, 52–3, 71
resource-based view (RBV) 52, 133–5, 207–8
resource dependence theory (RDT) 31, 34, 43
resource types 52
Revel cabinet-makers 196–210
rolling-out of services 96–7, 100–101

Science Oxford 138
size 135, 140, 141, 224, 309
small businesses in USA
  extant literature 30–34
    resource dependence theory (RDT) 31, 34, 43
    social network and entrepreneurship 30–34
      entrepreneurial process stages 34–5
  study
    aims 29–30, 42
    discussion of findings 42–4
    future research 42
    measurement instrument 38–9
      ties and venture creation stages 39
    non-response bias 40
    sample and data collection 37–9
    ties, strength of 40, 42–3
    using resource dependence theory 43
    using social network composition 35–7
      analysis of 40–42
small world phenomenon 220–21
social capital, *see* resource acquisition
social exchange theory 161, 162–3, 168, 173, 178–9
social network literature, *see* literature
social network structures of nascent entrepreneurs 263–76
  advisory network composition and impacts
    international 269
    market 269
    MENA region 267
    opportunity and resource gains 263
    private 268
    professional 269
    workplace 268–9
  extant literature 264–6
  study
    aims and data collection 263–4
    conclusions on economic typology 275–6
    methods and analysis 270–75
      cluster analysis, operating phase 273–4

cluster analysis, start-up phase 271–3
see also family firms
social network theory (SNT) 80, 160–61
social skills 81–2, 93–6, 102–7
socio-technical networks (STN) 338, 339, 343, 353
stability and growth 35, 36, 339
start-ups
in business networks 115
family support 253–4
MENA region, *see* social network structures of nascent entrepreneurs
opportunities and constraints in Africa 285–8
repositioning, *see* repositioning of start-ups
strategic management research 223
structural holes 224, 327–9
tertius gaudens and *tertius iungens* 310–11, 326
succession 282–3, 288–97
SuperNova project 340–41, 343–55
Survey on the Social Networks of Entrepreneurs 57–8
Sweden, start-up study 117–24

tertius gaudens and *tertius iungens* 310–11, 326, 327–9
ties
dyadic 190, 191–3, 206–7
dynamics, *see* actor-network theory
first client 97–8
gendered view 173
homophily/homogeneity 222, 256
loss of, *see* repositioning of start-ups
strong family 241–4, 248–53, 295
theories 35–7, 39, 40–44, 81–2, 134, 101–2, 221
time 337
longitudinal approach 50, 55
measurements of social network development 324–5
network imprinting 116, 123
transformation of artefacts 308–9, 318, 354
trust 146–7, 241, 243, 265

ubuntu in family businesses 279–97
case selection and data collection 282–5
research aims 280
and limitations 296–7
research overview (clan solidarity) 294–7
results 285–94
funding, education constraints, cohesion during emergence 285–8
human resources and finance 291
paternal persuasion, family duty during succession 288–90
successors' role 290–94
social capital defined by *ubuntu* 280–82
see also family firms
United States of America, *see* small businesses in USA
United Kingdom of Great Britain
family firms (Grampian region) 241–2, 246–59
women entrepreneurs (Northern Ireland) 165–75

value 130, 208
venture creation 305
actor-network theory and 338–40
literature review 30–35
small business, *see* dynamic social network study (Netherlands); small businesses in USA
stages
opportunity identification 34, 36, 263, 265, 269, 275, 281
organizing 35, 36
stability and growth 35, 36, 339

women entrepreneurs, formal network study 157–81
entrepreneurial economy 157–8
extant literature
androcentrism 165
different units of analysis 159
social network to social exchange theory 160–64
static, cross-sectional approach 160

overview 12–13, 179–81
research design and process
164–8
context 165–6
data analysis 168, 169
data collection 166–7
participant selection 166
regional development policy
context 157–8
research results 168–75
benefits perceived to accrue 174–5
motivations and expectations
168–71
networking behaviour 171–4